D1565754

Assassination at St. Helena

Assassination

at St. Helena

The Poisoning of Napoleon Bonaparte

Sten Forshufvud
and Ben Weider, C.M.

With foreword by David G. Chandler

Edited by H. T. Mitchell

MITCHELL PRESS
VANCOUVER, CANADA

Canadian Cataloguing in Publication Data

Forshufvud, Sten.
    Assassination at St. Helena

    Bibliography: p.
    Includes index.
    ISBN 0-88836-028-2

1. Napoléon I, Emperor of the French,
1769-1821 — Death and burial.   2. Arsenic
poisoning.   I. Weider, Ben, 1924-
II. Title.
DC212.F58   944.05′092′4   C78-002168-1

First Edition
© Copyright 1978
Sten Forshufvud and Ben Weider

Printed in Canada

Editor's Preface

ASSASSINATION AT ST. HELENA is far from being another account of the accepted history of Napoleon Bonaparte. It is substantially the detailed report of a long delayed crime investigation.

The basis of that report is here described by Ben Weider, president of the Napoleonic Society of Canada. Its substance, deeply significant to history, is presented by Dr. Sten Forshufvud of Göteborg, Sweden, discoverer of the evidence of a killing that had lain concealed beneath the surface of history for 140 years.

Contents of this volume have been arranged to give convenient access to its information. It is intended thus to serve as the definitive reference source on the Forshufvud thesis. At the same time it offers the less professional reader the interest and drama of what is essentially an absorbing story of detection and deduction.

In Part II there exists the first comprehensive review of Napoleon's career ever published in which poisoning is taken into historical account. This applies particularly in relation to three historic battles that profoundly influenced the course of world events. Part III traces the means by which the poison cup was used as a weapon in the contest for the French throne, with its climax in Napoleon's death at Longwood House on St. Helena.

The authors and editor do not regard this report as a closing of the file. Out of these revelations more facts of meaning may still come to light, worthy to be included in future editions.

Acknowledgement is made of the kindness of the eminent historian, David G. Chandler, in contributing his illuminating introduction.

H.T. MITCHELL
Editor

Contents

Foreword

DAVID CHANDLER, M.A. (Oxon.), FRHist.S, FRGS

"DEATH IS NOTHING," wrote Napoleon to General Lauriston in 1804, "but to live defeated is to die every day."[1]

There is no doubt that the emperor, whose fate it would be to live out the last six years of his life as a captive on an isolated South Atlantic island, had his fair share of near brushes with the 'grim reaper' on the battlefield. His great military career might well have been stifled at birth, for at the siege of Toulon in late 1793 he suffered all of three wounds — having his forehead gashed by a bayonet on 15 November, his chest slightly injured when a horse was killed under him one month later (16 December), and then, the very next day, receiving quite a serious injury to his left inner thigh — again from a British bayonet — during the fierce fighting on Pointe L'Eguilette overlooking the inner harbor of the great naval arsenal.

Over the following 22 years of his active military career he had a further 18 horses killed beneath him in battle. In Marengo in June 1800 he sustained a glancing blow from a spent ball on his left riding boot which tore away the leather and removed some of the skin beneath. Nine years later, at the storming of Ratisbon, he received a painful but not very serious injury to the Achilles tendon just above his left heel, and later that same campaign, on the second day of the Battle of Wagram (6 July) his left leg was again grazed by a cannon ball.

Over the years he also survived two shell bursts. A shell fell beside him in the siege-lines before Acre, but he was saved on that occasion by the prompt action of two soldiers standing close to him who unceremoniously flung their general to the ground and covered him with their bodies. All three escaped, save for being covered with sand, and Napoleon promoted his human

1

shields to officer rank on the spot. He was probably never closer to death in action than at Arcis-sur-Aube on 20 March 1814. A howitzer shell, its fuse smoldering, plunged into the earth a few feet from the emperor, who calmly rode his mount straight over the smoking missile. "The shell exploded, the horse, disembowelled, went plunging down, taking its rider with it. The emperor disappeared in the dust and smoke. But he got up without a scratch . . ."[2]

Some might consider that Napoleon bore a charmed life on the battlefield, but from first to last his own attitude to death was that of a fatalist. "All that is to happen is written down. Our hour is marked and we cannot prolong it a minute longer than fate has predestined,"[3]

In addition to the perils of active service he also survived several assassination attempts. At the *coup d'état* of *Brumaire* in November 1799 an enfuriated member of the *Conseil de Cinq-Cents* drew a dagger upon him, but was restrained by a grenadier before he could strike his blow. In September 1800 a second attempt on his life was narrowly foiled on the steps of the Paris *Opéra,* and Christmas Eve the same year saw the explosion of the "infernal machine" on his way to (again) the *Opéra.* But fortunately his vehicle had passed the critical spot before the detonation occurred, causing havoc behind him.

According to his valet Constant — whose recollections are not invariably accurate — the year 1800 also saw an attempt to eliminate the First Consul by the placing of poison in his favorite snuffbox. What is absolutely certain is that he narrowly escaped a plot to kidnap and possibly murder him in late 1803 — the notorious Cadoudal affair in which both Generals Pichegru and Moreau were implicated; and in 1809, in Austria, he was almost stabbed by the 18-year-old student fanatic, Stapps, whose knife was narrowly deflected by the watchful General Rapp when the would-be assassin was merely an arm's length from his intended victim.

Clearly Napoleon had his bitter enemies, amongst them a number of members of the exiled House of Bourbon. For a number of years Louis XVIII apparently hoped that Napoleon might restore him to the throne of his ancestors, but this illusion was shattered after the coronation on 2 December 1804. It may well be that the emperor was in greater peril than he knew over the next decade — not so much from the known perils of the battlefield or from the pistol or dagger of the straightforward assassin — but from the concealed hand of the poisoner.

Napoleon's personal health was generally sturdy and sound. His energy was both immense and sustained. To cite only two examples from the mass of evidence recorded by his contemporaries, this bursting energy was both physical and mental. On 1 May 1805 he reputedly covered over 50 kilometres on horseback during a whirlwind tour of the battlefield and environs of Marengo, exhausting four horses in the process, not to mention his accompanying staff.

Napoleon could be equally demanding — of himself and others — in the council chamber. Over the 18th and 19th September 1806 he is known to have dictated 102 letters to successive teams of perspiring secretaries almost without pause, as he prepared the final details for the launching of his devastating campaign against Prussia.

"Work is my element," Napoleon once asserted. "I was born and made for work. I have recognized the limit of my eyesight and of my legs, but never the limits of my working power."[4]

We know again from the recollections of his closest associates, that he was very moderate in his eating and drinking habits, and rarely would accept any form of medicine. And yet, at a number of very critical moments during his military career, he was abruptly afflicted by incapacitating and transitory illness. At Austerlitz he was suffering from a severe attack of conjunctivitis — but on 10 December, 1805 he could write to Josephine ". . . my eye trouble is cured." In May 1809, after the close of the unsuccessful battle of Aspern-Essling, he returned to his quarters at Kaiser-Ebersdorf, at 3 a.m. on 23 May, and sank into a depressed and totally lethargic daze for the space of fully 36 hours, during which time his staff could obtain no orders from him.

This was very untypical of him, but worse was to follow three years later. Before the battle of Borodino he was afflicted by an attack of acute dysuria and swelling of the legs, which he attributed to the dampness of his bivouac area. Next day (6 September 1812), he developed a persistent dry cough, hoarseness, difficult and irregular breathing, and an irregular pulse rate. Most accounts attribute this to a severe cold, but there may have been more to it than that. James Kemble is of the opinion that he was suffering from coinciding attacks of acute cystisis and pyelitis.[5]

Next year, after the battle of Dresden, fought amidst pouring rain, he was afflicted by severe vomiting and diarrhoea, which was at the time put down to some garlic in a mutton stew or some off-color *pâté-de-foie-gras* that he had eaten, but once again the timing and nature of the indisposition give one some cause to wonder, as toxicologists will declare the odor of garlic under certain conditions is barely distinguishable from that of arsenic.

Throughout the following month Napoleon was plunged into despondency and relative inactivity, finding it hard to make firm decisions. Then at Leipzig, on the night of 17/18 October, he was again attacked by severe stomach pains and lay doubled-up on his camp bed. "I feel bad. My mind resists but my body gives in." Was this, as Kemble asserts, duodenitis arising from a prolonged anxiety state . . . or due to something much more sinister?

The most frequently discussed indisposition occurred within the period of the climactic series of engagements that ended Napoleon's active career. It was an illness that struck on the night of 16/17 June, 1815, immediately after the battle of Ligny, when it required the ministrations of Prince Jerome, Baron Larrey and Marchand to get their imperial master over the crisis. This may have been linked to prolapsed piles associated with complete exhaustion, as some have speculated, although important evidence exists that Napoleon did not, in fact, suffer from this complaint, as his faithful valet attested. Whatever the cause of his illness that night, its effect on his power to reach decisions on the morning of the 17th proved critical. Instead of issuing effective orders for the proper pursuit of the defeated Prussians and the coordination of effort with Marshal Ney required to trap Wellington at or near Quatre Bras, the emperor spent the whole morning viewing the battlefield of Ligny, the scene of his considerable victory that previous day. This period of hesitation or at least inactivity proved of the utmost importance in determining the outcome at Waterloo and Wavre on the 18th.

On a number of very important occasions, therefore, Napoleon was very much off-form. It would be a bold man who would assert that each of these highly inconvenient lapses in the emperor's state of well-being was due to other than natural cause. The strains of high command in any war are immense, and many a general has succumbed to one form of trouble or another on the eve of, actually during, or immediately after a major engagement. It is just that Napoleon seems to have had rather more than his share of such misfortunes, given his normally excellent state of health, which persisted through his middle as well as his earlier years.

One way and another, therefore, Napoleon was no stranger to the thought and near-reality of death. The actual circumstances of his demise on St. Helena have been shrouded by doubt and surmise ever since that fateful day, 5 May 1821. Today the most generally-held belief is that he succumbed to carcinoma of the stomach[6] — the supposed cause of death of his father in 1785. But the evidence of the post-mortem reports — there were three independent accounts of the autopsy findings — is in some ways conflicting and not all medical authorities are in agreement with this finding. Some, including the French historian, Dr. Guy Godlewski, postulate a death due to hepatitis and a gastric lesion rather than a cancer. It is hard for the inexpert layman to judge the purely medical evidence and the inclination for the modern scholar to accept the most generally held view is extremely strong — until some positive evidence to the contrary is produced and carefully tested. Academic caution is at once traditional and very necessary.

The hypothesis that Napoleon did not die a natural death is no new idea. During his captivity, and immediately following his death, strong rumors circulated particularly but not exclusively in Bonapartist circles, that the emperor was being subjected to the attention of a poisoner. Some accused Sir Hudson Lowe of this villainy, but however unpopular that unpleasant but possibly misunderstood personality became, relatively few contemporaries gave such accusations much credence. It is now clear that the British government, far from trying to cause or hasten Napoleon's demise, took positive steps to guard against any such occurrence. The posting of sentries around Longwood which

Napoleon so bitterly resented — and the insistence that he should be accompanied by a British officer whenever he went riding — were measures dictated at least as much by a genuine concern for the safety of his person as by a wish to ensure that he did not attempt to escape from the island.

Those who argue that the need for such security precautions was baseless, given the presence of a Royal Naval flotilla off the island, ready to intercept any such attempt, are not on very strong ground; even at the present time, despite the resources of electronic surveillance and other scientific measures, it is very hard to devise a fool-proof system, as the deaths of the Baader-Mainhoff terrorists in the custom-built German prison in October, 1977, serves to illustrate. To shield Napoleon from possible assassination attempts, the authorities attempted to keep a tight control over all individuals arriving at and departing from the island, although they realized that only a Draconian policy of protection and supervision had much chance of shielding their distinguished prisoner from an assassin's bullet, or knife-blow. This the authors of the book freely accept as true.

However, how could they hope to guard Napoleon from an enemy placed, hidden, within his personal entourage? Forshuf-vud's thesis is that Napoleon was administered arsenic, in calculated doses, over a number of years and finally succumbed to poisoning by the hand of one of his closest associates, Charles-Tristan, Count de Montholon — the *coup de grâce* being in the form of poisoning with mercuric cyanide in a lethal dose, just prior his death.

The evidence of the hair samples from Napoleon's head is of central importance to this allegation which Sten Forshufvud and Ben Weider have set out to prove.

The arsenical content of hair samples which had been preserved by Napoleon's valets, Marchand and Noverraz, was demonstrated to be abnormally high by tests conducted in the early 1960's. When Sten Forshufvud first produced this thesis[7] it was received with strong resistance in French academic circles. The evidence was dismissed on hypothetical grounds that there were many ways other than poisoning, whether accidental or deliberate, which could account for the presence of the high content of arsenic. Doubt was also cast on the authenticity of the hair samples. But that they contained an abnormal arsenical content could not be denied following the publication of the findings of Dr. Hamilton Smith, head of the Department of Forensic Medicine at Glasgow University. He had subjected individual hairs to an irradiation examination at the Harwell Atomic Research Centre, situated near London, England, but the evidence reached was not to be conclusive as to numbers or dates of poisonings — only that arsenic had been received into the system of the subject.

For many years, the author of this Foreword shared the common view, doubting the validity of the evidence produced. A meeting with Ben Weider, whom I know and respect as a serious Napoleonic historian, in the course of a shared pilgrimage to the battlefield of Waterloo in 1975 — during which he revealed his total conviction that Napoleon had been intoxicated by arsenic and had finally succumbed to mercuric poisoning — caused me to reconsider all of the available evidence. This by 1975 included an important development — the discovery of a technique by Dr. Smith, whereby the arsenical content of a single hair could be accurately measured in a series of small segments. By this method, it had proved possible to date with considerable accuracy the timing of the various dosages of arsenic that had been introduced into Napoleon's system, and this closely fitted a pattern with the more circumstantial evidence that will here be found treated at length. Calculations of the time involved in the growth of a hair could be made and compared with the arsenic-altered characteristic of the sample under analysis. Thus a sharp picture of some accuracy could be built up for the period 1820 to 1821, when the hair was shaven from Napoleon's head.

For the evidence of the state of the hair at the time of death, reliance had to be placed on, amongst others, the sample that had come down from the emperor's valet, Abram Noverraz. The evidence of the intake of cumulatively a large amount of arsenic at different times is impressive. The indication would seem strong that Napoleon's malady at St. Helena was caused by poison deliberately administered. It is well worth noticing that many of the symptoms that Napoleon evidenced on the island belong to the syndrome of arsenical poisoning.

The attribution of the deed to Count de Montholon is a

prominent feature of this book. Inevitably, if one accepts that Napoleon died from poison, the finger of suspicion, and indeed of accusation, must point in the direction of this somewhat enigmatic figure. The progressive changes in the composition of the Longwood entourage — and the deliberately provoked quarrels and in-fighting amongst members of Napoleon's staff that led to them — would fit well with such a belief.

The sudden death of the major-domo Cipriani, on the 26th February 1818, closely followed by those of a woman and a child (both members of the Montholon household) also merits close examination as some historians have accepted it as fact that these deaths were caused by acute arsenical poisoning.

Certainly Montholon had opportunity to administer poison on numerous occasions. Equally, as a major beneficiary by Napoleon's will (as he was no doubt fully aware, having been present at the drafting and as one of the three executors appointed by its terms), Montholon did indeed stand to benefit personally by his master's death; this regardless of whether or not he was an agent of the Bourbon government, as Messrs. Weider and Forshufvud are convinced was the case.

This aspect of the Forshufvud thesis, as it was first propounded in 1961, has been particularly hard for scholars, especially French ones, to accept. Many historians, indeed, declare themselves to be wholly unconvinced, amongst them Napoleon's most recent biographer, who writes as follows:

> *"De quoi est mort Napoléon? Sten Forshufvud a imaginé un véritable roman policier fondé sur l'empoisonnement à l'arsenic et designé le coupable: Montholon."*[8]

> "Of what did Napoleon die? Sten Forshufvud has made up a veritable detective story based upon poisoning with arsenic and indicated who was to blame: Montholon."[8]

Tristan de Montholon is, indeed, an enigmatic and sinister figure. Many historians have tended to accept at its face value the bland autobiographical sketch that Montholon included in the introduction to his *"Récits de la Captivité de Napoléon à Sainte-Hélène"* (1847). According to this, he was a soldier of some experience, the recipient of five wounds during the Austrian campaign of 1809, subsequently promoted to *Général de Brigade* in 1811, and ultimately, after escorting Napoleon from near

Fontainebleau to Paris in March 1815, and thereafter serving as an Imperial aide-de-camp with *l'Armé du Nord*, attaining the rank of *Général-de-Division* on 15 June of that year.

None of these particular claims is supported by the records. Although Montholon did serve as an aide to Joubert, Championnet, Augereau, MacDonald and Berthier in turn between 1800 and 1809 — thanks in large measure to his stepfather's (the Count de Sémonville's) influence with Maret, the confidant of Napoleon — there is no record of either his wounds or his claimed promotions in the dossier held by the Ministry of War. It would indeed seem that he never advanced beyond the rank of colonel during the Napoleonic Wars. Consequently he earns no entry in Six's famous *Dictionnaire Bibliographique des Généraux et Amiraux Français de la Révolution et de l'Empire* (2 vols. Paris 1934).

He was, as he claims, sent as Minister-Plenipotentiary to the Grand Duke of Wurtzburg in early 1812, but the emperor removed him from this post in September of the same year, after the discovery of his secret and unacceptable marriage to Albine de Vassal. Similarly, Montholon's claim to have held a court post from 1809 which brought him into close contact with his master does not bear close examination. He was appointed a chamberlain to the Empress Josephine in December 1809, thanks again to his step-father's influence, but does not appear to have carried out many duties.

Following his disgrace in 1812, he spent a long spendthrift period, dissipating his father's money, before briefly holding a National Guard command on the Loire for one month from March 1814.

It is not beyond the realms of reason that such a suave but unscrupulous and unprincipled man could also have been an agent of the sinister Compte d'Artois, who was brother to Louis XVIII. The Bourbons, more than any other party, had reason to fear the possibility of a further attempt at a Napoleonic restoration as their popularity rapidly waned in France and Europe. A desire to remove, once and for all, the exile of St. Helena and the perils he represented must have been tempting.

This is not to deny that Montholon's subsequent career and activities deserve to earn him a further measure of suspicion. His sale of substantial parts of the documentation from St. Helena, in direct contravention of Napoleon's known wishes, indicates his desperate desire for ready cash in the years that preceded his eventual receipt of the 2,200,000 francs from the Emperor's bequest. Indeed, he was declared bankrupt in 1829 and had to flee to Belgium to escape his creditors. Moreover, his attitude toward Sir Hudson Lowe and to the reasons for Napoleon's death were ambivalent — he shifted his ground unexplicably on these matters over the years. If he had been liked by Dr. Henry, Montchenu and Sturmer (and to a lesser degree by Marchand) he was very much disliked by Bertrand, Gourgaud, Balmain and Dr. O'Meara and by the valet Ali (born Saint Denis) whose forthright criticisms of both Montholon and his supposed recollections form an important part of the case against him. The *Récits* are in large part — at least for the period 1815-1818 — lifted from the writings of O'Meara and Las Cases. Only a quarter of the book — the least convincing part — is devoted to the three last years of Napoleon's life, being based on Montholon's own writings.[9] By any standards Montholon appears to have been a scheming and unscrupulous man. His accusers though they are, Sten Forshufvud and Ben Weider in this work are at some pains to examine the self-justification by which a Montholon or any other agent of royalty could have pursued the King's wish against a man categorized as an outlaw and the enemy of peace in Europe.

The authors have produced a fascinating and deeply researched book. It well could lead to considerable changes being written into the history of Napoleon's last years on St. Helena. Certainly the matter of Napoleon's illnesses and death have never been more exhaustively scrutinized. The story the authors unfold and the scientific evidence they furnish at the end of the volume are more than enough to provide justification for careful thought and reconsideration.

REFERENCES CITED IN THE FOREWORD

1. *Correspondance de Napoléon Ier* Vol. X (Paris 1870) p. 69.
2. H. Camon, *La Guerre Napoléonienne – précis de campagnes,* (Paris 1925) Vol. II p. 152 (fn).
3. W. H. Hudson, *The Man Napoleon* (London 1915) p. 228.
4. E. las Cases, *Memoirs of the Empéror Napoleon* (London 1836) p. 359.
5. James Kemble, *Napoleon Immortal,* (London 1964) p. 193.
6. See Kemble, *op. cit.,* for a full discussion of this point, especially p. 278, also P. Garnière, *Sainte Hélène, Terre d'Exil* (Paris 1971).
7. Sten Forshufvud, *Napoléon – a-t-il eté empoisonné?* (Paris 1961) and in the English edition, *ibid., Who Killed Napoleon?* (London 1962).
8. Jean Tulard, *Napoléon, ou le Mythe du Saveur,* (Paris 1977) p. 453.
9. See Godlewski, chapter 6, *Les Compagnons de la Captivité* in Marcel Dunan's *Sainte Hélène, Terre d'Exil* (Paris 1971), pages 128-138 for a full examination of Montholon's character and record. Godlewski however does not mention the possibility of any link with the poisoning thesis.

Part One

Discovery and Accusation

Ben Weider

The story of Napoleon
produces on me an impression
like that produced by the
Revelations of St. John the Divine.
We all feel there must
be something more in it,
but we don't know what.

— GOETHE

1

The Forshufvud Thesis

KNOWING THE TRUTH about the life of Napoleon Bonaparte
involves knowing how he died.

It is the purpose of this book to deal, in terms of both evidence
and deduction, with that subject. Two basic premises will apply.

One relates to Dr. Sten Forshufvud's discovery, by means
of irradiation or neutron activation tests, that Napoleon was
repeatedly poisoned. Hair shaved from Napoleon's head, soon
after death, to permit the giving of souvenirs and the making of a
death mask, yielded section by section conclusive evidence of
many separate ingestions of arsenic. The poisonous chemical
element was carried through the digestive system and
bloodstream into tissue and bone and, of course, into the
structure of the hair.

The second premise is that circumstantial evidence taken
from eyewitness accounts of the life of the Emperor at St. Helena
must point to one individual attendant as culpable. That
courtier, a minor noble identified by close and long-standing
family ties with the Bourbon succession, had opportunity,
competence and credible motive to achieve secretly the removal
of any likelihood that Bonaparte might return to claim a throne
that had been recovered for the house of Bourbon by Louis
XVIII. Materially, that courtier had benefited hugely by Napoleon's death under terms of a will he helped draft.

The careful piecing together of the elements of evidence,
separately slight and open to question, into a completed mosaic
powerfully incriminating in total effect, is the substance of this
book.

Almost as gripping as is Sten Forshufvud's own first person
account of his search for the truth about Napoleon's premature

death is the series of circumstances preceding his evolving of what is now referred to as the Forshufvud thesis.

Dr. Forshufvud's principal text is the story of one of the immortals of history reduced to mortal distress in circumstances of captivity that his officially conceded rights on St. Helena failed to disguise. In such a plight the best and the worst in Napoleon would emerge in alternating periods of furious frustration and quiet resignation. The product of the author's documented research pictures Napoleon in more earthy and human terms than do most books that have dealt with his life. His moments of kindliness, generosity and courteous consideration toward those who shared his experience are surprisingly many considering the extremities of feeling to which his captive life and increasingly severe and frequent bouts of illness had reduced him.

An author less understanding than Forshufvud of what Napoleon previously had shown himself to be in terms of human qualities might have done less well. He could have failed to gather and include, from winnowing the contents of memoirs of the Emperor's contemporaries at St. Helena, small but illuminating insights that revealed more about Napoleon's inner nature than ever could come from describing Napoleon the conqueror. In war and politics of Europe and the Mediterranean rim he was a stupendous personality. In the sickroom at Longwood he was a suffering human creature baffled by loss of what he had believed in — his fortunate destiny, his abnormal energy and his unconquerable spirit. Chiefly Forshufvud would cast light on the persistent and deliberate undermining of the health of the exiled hero of France.

It was because I long had been impressed by the powerful intellect, many-sided qualities and great achievements of Napoleon and had become an avid collector of Napoleon memorabilia, that I came to know Dr. Forshufvud. I first met him in the 1960's, when he was under a certain amount of attack by a few historians and physicians in France and Scandinavia for having dared write so sensational a revisionary postscript to the established history of the Emperor Napoleon. There was no objection to it being theorized that Napoleon had been murdered. But, that the Emperor could have died by the hand of a trusted member of his suite who was a titled Frenchman rather than by foreign treachery was unexpected. And it was unacceptable to a small but influential group in Paris.

Before meeting Sten Forshufvud I had been deeply moved by his first recounting of conclusions that, if defensibly well-founded, must cause all past assumptions about Napoleon's later battles and his death in exile to be drastically changed.

Well before the Forshufvud theory had disturbed the world of historically complacent historians on the subject of Napoleon's concluding years I had developed through my own reading deep doubts about Napoleon's illnesses and death. It seemed impossible to accept the deterioration of Napoleon's physique as a health experience unrelated to the tremendous political enmities he had aroused. Considering that only the flesh-and-blood anatomy of one individual existed as a barrier to the realization of ambitions he had thwarted, would it not have been very likely that some subtle foul play, using skills that for centuries had been known to exist in the courts of Mediterranean countries, would be attempted?

While I had harbored the suspicion that a poisoning had occurred I lacked, of course, Sten Forshufvud's skilful insights as a student of medicine, nutrition, blood functions, with knowledge of chemistry and toxicology. I could not regard as natural the strange collapse of the young Emperor's health at what should have been in terms of climate, virtually a health resort. From the background of my own career's study of the human body's characteristics and capabilities, and particularly with its performance when put to the test of extraordinary emotional stress by a naturally brave and resilient nature, Napoleon's individualism and early death were out of pattern with all we know about him up to the time of his fateful defeat at Waterloo in Belgium.

For many years, in the field of health, strength development and competitive muscular exertion, I had come to have profound respect for the ability of the human body to respond at times almost supernaturally to the commands of inner motivational force. I did not need to be told that a man with Napoleon's inexhaustible energy should not, in his prime-of-life years and at decisive battle occasions, find his body failing in its former response to demands upon it. He mistrusted the faltering medical practises of his day and, in some respects, was more knowledgeable about the rules for good health than were the doctors who bled and blistered their hapless patients for everything but fractures.

His powerful intellect functioned within a slim but strong and energy-charged body. Through it he was endowed far above the human norms. Beyond that, Napoleon was one of those rare beings gifted with a computer-like quality of the mind. This acute mentality he had begun to evidence in mathematics as early as in the period of his cadetship at military school. Under the exigencies of war it came to underlie a reputation for brilliance that was inspiring to friends and dismaying to most opponents.

Before being ravaged at critically inopportune times by unaccountable illnesses, he was authentically a military genius. Too often to represent mere luck he was able to defeat forces much larger than his own through his ability to make swift calculations on the probable results from exploiting each amongst a number of choices of action open to him. In the fast-changing circumstances of battle as well as in disposition of forces prior to engagements, this was his secret item of personal weaponry.

In the years of Napoleon's most spectacular successes as a military leader personally responsible for campaigns and decisive battle strategies he acted upon conclusions with a degree of accuracy that suggested the miraculous. He was virtually a one-man strategic command base. His legendary reputation of invincibility, before he suffered poisoning, was such that its existence alone was worth many battalions to him in the field. Even under the judgment of a retrospective century and a half of study of his campaigns, military historians have accorded Napoleon the highest possible respect. He was at his zenith from 1795 to 1805. But through the written commentaries of specialists examining the records of Napoleon's later exploits, from 1805 to 1815 when his leadership judgments at times were uncertain and unwise, there run the puzzled comments upon his strange lack of acuity or his torpid if not physically distressed condition at certain critical battles. Because the strategy of action centered so much in one able mind Napoleon had long enjoyed advantage over his enemies — but his style of command was a major weakness should he be physically impaired. Until Forshufvud read the St. Helena accounts with a revealing clue to their true meaning there were no plausible explanations for the onset of puzzling changes in what had been a consistently brilliant mind in a tireless body.

So efficient a mental mechanism as Napoleon's could not exist and function under the rigors of his arduous, personally commanded campaigns had it not been harmoniously related to an equally superior physical and nervous system. While Napoleon was a general, commander of the Army of the South, then of the Grand Army of France his body responded to the almost ruthless demands upon it by his creative imagination. Following him, whole armies would do the impossible. His health survived the drive of a superhuman determination on occasions in the face of discouragements otherwise demoralizing to his followers. Inspirational leadership could infuse injured, sick, battle-worn men with some shared part of Napoleon's spirit, persistence and audacity. The physical system that could survive such demands could not fail to have been fully as worthy an instrument as the computer-like mind and the political sagacity with which it normally functioned.

Napoleon's story abounds with testimony of the truth of that supposition. In the period of his life when he served France only militarily and without serious thought of rulership, Napoleon as a brilliant young general and rising field commander was increasingly heroized in Paris. With a growing personal conviction that he was no ordinary person but a soldier of destiny, he could go on year upon year working military miracles. Even in the first phase of the era of his consulship, his health remained part of the growing legend of his immunity to normal fatigue. The belief grew — and Napoleon exploited it to good advantage — that he was of iron-like durability. It was only when he ascended a throne the Bourbons were not ready to relinquish that physical changes that reduced his effectiveness began to be seen. The coincidence challenges attention.

How could it happen that so dauntless and tireless a leader would become subject to a weakness of decision that would disqualify a junior in his first command? Specifically, why was

Napoleon physically ill and vomiting at critical stages of battles it was vital to win? Once he could lead forced marches, work on plans and correspondence far into the night while his men slept, snatch a few hours rest under his greatcoat spread on an army cot, and be ready for the next day's long march that, by design, would bring him to a battlefleld fresh and ready to engage a surprised enemy.

This man, who had anticipated by more than a century the strategies and psychological advantages that would develop in an age of motorized warfare, suddenly began to suffer some characteristic symptoms of "nervous stomach". Always, before that, when he was only General Bonaparte, the adrenalin flow must have been magnificently adequate to the demands he confidently could place on heart and nerves and muscles when necessity demanded.

Could that change relate to someone's wish that Napoleon should seem much less supernaturally heroic? Was it planned and arranged that he might appear much less the stuff of which, historically, kings and emperors were supposed to be made? Was part of the purpose to undermine his confidence in his own physical capabilities?

One knew about the menace to Napoleon's life arising from the Declaration of the Congress of Vienna by the royalist states partial to continuity of the Bourbons in power. When Napoleon was declared formally to be outside the laws of civilized society, although once legitimately Emperor, chosen popularly and anointed by the Pope, he became fair game for subversive action — even for assassination — in the interest of world peace.

Then, at St. Helena, as we learn from many eye-witness accounts, the process of his physical deterioration changed to disintegration. He was corpulent when he left Elba, exhibiting the bronze-like pallor of a confirmed arsenophagist. Some said he had grown soft in idleness, spending too much of his time in the Pompeiian-style hot baths in Elba where he lolled and soaked for hours at a time. But on tropical St. Helena he would call for hot tubs to overcome his chronic chills. He was seldom in other than ill health there and died at 52. That age was far too young for a man who had been capable of swift recovery from reverses met in the fortunes of war, and with a body once as resilient as his spirit. From observation of prisoners of war we know that there were always some whose spirits were too strong to quell and from whose numbers the successful escapers came. Napoleon was authentically of that type — a survivor of misfortunes and escaper from apparently certain defeat.

There were all these unnatural contradictions that on the face of it should not have existed. They had bothered me as I had read more and more deeply into the life of this excitingly complex soldier of fortune whose fortune at the peak of his career was so remarkably good. The erosion of his health was one mystery that should not have been so baffling. It suited his enemies all too well for the Emperor's death to pass into history as it had done with great attention to its incidence and little to its cause. Could this finely-devised instrument for living, for decision-making, for action and exertion — a kind that comes along unexplainably once in a thousand years or more — really have wilted into infirmity so prematurely, to die in bed from natural causes? As Forshufvud has wryly commented, the report of the post-mortem was partly true. It was "natural" that a man should die who had usurped and would try to regain a throne from descendants of the old regime of France.

Forshufvud's first and incomplete revelation of his discovery was in his book: "Who Killed Napoleon?" published in the early 1960's in several languages. It preceded the further development of hair analysis techniques at the University of Glasgow. Thus it could ask a question and suggest the answer. Until more research was done it could not accuse. I read it knowing it had been scoffed at in criticisms by a group of 'Napoleonids' in Paris. Some had impressive credentials in their fields. My conclusion was that their rebuttals were weak and unconvincing as measured against the evidence. They seemed content to disregard the supporting facts and treat the whole thing as amusingly far-fetched. Obviously the case required still more research and presentation. The very nature of its development gave it elements of sensationalism. Enough wild speculation and nonsense had been written by hacks along with the solid history of Napoleon that so startling a new version of the Napoleon story surely would meet suspicion. Understandably it could be thought that here was one more author cleverly theorizing to capitalize on a science-fiction trend in book-readers' tastes. Those who attacked it from any degree of prestigious background, even without qualifying their case against the Forshufvud finding, would hold an advantage, initially.

I had sought out the author to satisfy my own growing curiosity about him and the controversy he was causing. It was at a time of intense discussion within a small and at times quite emotionally involved environment with which I have long been identified in Paris — the Napoleonic Society of France. Its members had been unready for so drastic a revision of Napoleonic history as Forshufvud's theory. I asked the author for an interview.

In the man I met were blended qualities one could instinctively like. He had a direct sincerity that wore well through many hours of discussion that explored his discoveries and deductions in great depth. From him were obtainable at last believable explanations of numerous things in Napoleon's career about which the books I had read left only unanswered questions.

Until he had turned up the clues of arsenical poisoning in newly-issued volumes of notes by Marchand and Bertrand, and had become aghast at what they signified, Sten Forshufvud had merely read in depth the Napoleon literature, old and new, as I, too, had done. It was reading for historical interest that had grown into a pleasantly interesting avocation. But, as with so many who have read with any degree of intellectual curiosity about the life of this commoner who, at almost the end of the era of the great feudal monarchies of Europe, was a self-made Emperor, the greatest of them all, the more one read the more one was left unsatisfied. Why had the great career collapsed into such a complete anti-climax?

But once the suspicion of foul play had been aroused by symptoms he recognized, Dr. Forshufvud no longer read for pleasure. He became, on this subject, what he had been for the greater part of his adult life, a science researcher.

In our many long conversations and with files and scrap books of correspondence, analytical reports, notes and photostats spread before us, he told me the story of his studies. I needed to know, too, about his life. As background to what seemed a profoundly significant historical discovery there was his dedication to research in the field of blood plasma, the circulatory system, and of related tooth and bone structure nutrition. It was in furthering his early medical training, his studies of histology and his biological research that he had picked up along the way, but had never previously had cause to use, an incidental broad general knowledge of toxicology.

I liked what I saw of directness and dedication to the factual in his mental processes. I found him stubborn in defence of what he regarded as proven. It was clearly a mind wide-ranging in its interests and well disciplined by years of research. There were flashes of humor that suddenly could break through his Scandinavian reserve and characteristic rather solemn dignity.

We agreed to pursue the subject of the Forshufvud revelations together. When work had arrived at the stage where Sten Forshufvud's second and much more definitive book was in process, we finished with our Canadian editor and publisher, a research review in the first of eventually three manuscript conferences. The first, held in the Quebec Laurentians, ended with a toast . . . to Napoleon.

"I have been wondering," Sten mused, "about what might happen if in the course of time we go to our reward and Napoleon should say he wants to meet us. What do you think he might say to us about all this?"

I ventured to suggest that if Napoleon included in his remarks anything about de Montholon, what he would say might not sound well in heaven.

"Ah," my friend said in a tone of mild surprise. "You then think it could be . . . *in heaven?*"

2

The Making of an Investigator

Now a septuagenerian, Dr. Forshufvud since youth had read widely and with deep interest of the life of Napoleon Bonaparte. It had never remotely occurred to him, however, that from what began as reading for enjoyment he would contribute ultimately to the huge store of literature on the Emperor a book that must fundamentally alter the Napoleon story.

The Forshufvud career early turned to odontology. At 21 he was the youngest qualified dental surgeon in Sweden. To further his studies he went to the University of Bordeaux. There, under the encouragement of the famous histologist, Georges Dubreuil, he made several research discoveries which would long involve him in the field of laboratory research. On returning to Sweden he continued his biological studies at the Faculty of Medicine at Lund where he published and defended his thesis for the degree of M.D.

He studied at both the Bacteriological and Pathological laboratories of Sahlgren Hospital and the Biological Laboratory of the Zoological Museum in Göteborg. Later he was accorded the privilege of using research facilities at the Nobel Institute of Physics and in that city in 1948-9 was acting professor at the Faculty of Odontology.

During biological research Dr. Forshufvud made the original discovery of how blood plasma circulates in the paracapillary tissues located between the blood capillaries. He had reasoned that there must be an as yet unrecognized system of plasma transmission from the blood capillaries out into the paracapillary tissue and thence back into the bloodstream. With the aid of advanced methods of depiction he succeeded in identifying and recording for the first time these normally transparent and invisible vessels. He has published in learned journals and lectured in support of his revolutionary theory on this phase of blood circulation and function in the human system.

Dr. Forshufvud is a scientist by profession, an historian by avocation. As a scientist he was accustomed to the discoveries of science being accepted as fact when corroborated by controlled experiments that have satisfied the basic principles of laboratory testing. The injection of a political or emotional consideration into what, to him, should have been an unprejudiced pursuit of the truth to correct the judgment of history was a wholly unexpected development.

Dr. Forshufvud went on with his personal affairs. He refrained from jousting publicly with those historians, physicians and others who chose to refer to him as an "obscure dentist" — from Göteborg of all places! To his critics he was a non-professional historian who had ventured into the rarefied atmosphere of the austere French halls of historical knowledge. What he had found was both unwelcome and abrasive to some sensibilities in circles related to the study of French history.

But, as published in small editions in various languages, the Forshufvud book with its challenging title "Who Killed Napoleon?" had irrecoverably put the cat amongst the pigeons. The author had raised questions that must be answered; questions based on valid evidence.

Letters came from history readers of the Napoleonic themes in many countries. There was so distinct a ring of truth to what Forshufvud offered that certain persons dedicated to establishing the facts beyond doubt provided encouragement. The researcher found he could not abandon his study simply because of a hostile reception on the part of persons prejudiced in favor of letting the proverbial sleeping dogs lie undisturbed.

To the ranks of the Napoleonids, seemingly forever hungry for more lights and insights to reveal the complex character of one of history's most memorable men, were added a certain number of individuals who sensed in the Forshufvud disclosure the haunting elements of a daring exploit hitherto unrealized. As a mystery story it was fascinating.

Consider its content: Conspiracy in the realms of royalty, nobles and aristocrats as actors, a foremost hero of history, war and intrigues of its aftermath; the austere Duke of Wellington and events following the celebrated Battle of Waterloo, the color of the British Navy under the great Admiral Nelson; an exile banished under massive guard to an infinitely remote tropic island in the South Atlantic Ocean, the travesty of a hurriedly assembled minuscule "court" for the former master of the Tuileries and Fontainebleau and the center of all ceremony in his nation. There were, too, the elements of conflict with an anxious and arrogant governor of the island, life in the makeshift "palace" that later would be a stable; intimate insights into the mind of the man who had made whole nations tremble at his military might and be revived from defeat to enjoy the enlightened civil rules he established. This was a man for whom no task was too great to attempt, no detail too small to engage his attention as planner of the restoration of France to periods of peace, progress and reconstruction after the Revolution. All that, climaxed by awareness that a clever practitioner of the arts of the Medicis lived within the provisions of Napoleon's restricted rule over his tiny court. There pathetic attempts at gaiety were shadowed by the fact that the Emperor, still a bestower of largesse, the maker of a Will in which all his retainers could feel a hopeful interest, was suffering and dying of an unknown, apparently incurable malady called a climatic illness.

With such a manuscript an experienced editor might well reprove a novice writer of fiction. He had strained too much and so overloaded his tale with color and drama as to remove all hope of it being believable.

As if to cap the ultimate of what was bizarre in this new mystery story, springing demandingly from Marchand's and Bertrand's memoirs, there was the fact that, after a long unawareness, and at so famous an atomic research center as pioneering Harwell in England, a revealing discovery had been made as if by science magic. In several tests an atomic reactor, responding to the requests of one of the world's foremost authorities in forensic laboratory studies, had cut like a laser beam through the concealment of a certain tragic fact of history. This, after almost a century and a half had passed.

Since there no longer could be doubt that repeated poisonings of Napoleon had occurred, history would have to be adjusted to the discovery. It would have to recognize that all that had been written about Napoleon's years on St. Helena had been in the absence of a critically important fact: Behind the guard of some 5000 British military dedicated to continuous watchfulness the guarded Emperor had not been safe from assassination. It was indisputable that a secret poisoner had penetrated the defensive apparatus and had destroyed the imperial prisoner, encased in a veritable cocoon of safety measures. Moreover, the poisoner had achieved an all-but-perfect crime. Its failure lay only in the fact of final disclosure by Dr. Forshufvud's probing examination with deductions drawn from the long-cold clues.

Fate has been very deliberate in dealing with the death of a favorite who, in his lifetime, so often had been touched with great good fortune. We may speculate on the silent years while, in the unfolding of time and of the capabilities of science, the accidents of fate were preparing a man, improbably a biologist at Göteborg, to solve various scientific problems for which he became peculiarly prepared while never suspecting how his skills some day would be used.

3

History's Debt to Louis Marchand

EVERYTHING ABOUT NAPOLEON'S unnatural death was matched by the strangeness of the way it was found to have occurred.

The team that solved the mystery consisted of Louis Marchand, the long-dead first valet to Napoleon, acting as informer through the pages of a diary written during the exile years at St. Helena, and Sten Forshufvud who, alone amongst many doctors who must have read the memoirs when published in the latter 1950's, recognized the clearly depicted symptoms of poisoning and began his long search for the truth. There was help from other memoirs, such as those of Bertrand, Arnott and Count de Montholon, but the Marchand account alone would have provided what a suspicious admirer of Napoleon in Göteborg, Sweden essentially needed for his basic exercise in pure deduction.

At this point the reader knows something of Forshufvud. Who was Marchand, his collaborator?

When at the time of his first abdication in 1814 Napoleon was at Fontainebleau and due to be sent by victorious allied enemies to rule the small island kingdom of Elba, his not-so-faithful first valet, belying his name Constant, fled the situation. In his place there was provided for the Emperor a competent young man named Louis Marchand, then 23 years of age. He would remain with Napoleon at Elba, accompany him during the triumphs and despair of The Hundred Days and, in 1815, go with him to St. Helena to be a vital part of the royal household at Longwood.

Marchand was the personification of the perfect valet — attentive, discreet, literate, shrewd, observant and loyal beyond the call of his duty. He was an artist of some education and ability as his sketches from St. Helena reveal. Napoleon was

28

personally responsive to such an estimable servant, giving him his complete confidence and treating him almost as a son. In bequeathing him 400,000 francs in his famous Will, the Emperor commented: "The services he had rendered me were those of a friend."

It was not in Napoleon's power while at St. Helena to honor Marchand with the title of Count, but as such he would refer to him as a polite measure of recognition. This was known to be the case farther afield than St. Helena and when Napoleon III came to power the faithful Louis became indeed Count Marchand.

Befitting the role of first valet to an emperor, Marchand was a careful and reliable observer of the scenes and circumstances around him. History was first consciously indebted to him for the many sketches made at Longwood House, where the drama of Napoleon's long drawn-out assassination was played to its dreadful end.

It was known at St. Helena and in France that Marchand diarized events while there. This he appears to have done chiefly to record for his family's interest over the years to come what had happened during his years in exile with Napoleon. It was explicitly understood in his family that his communications were privileged and never to be exploited — for he was the Emperor's first valet and as such was in a most confidential position. Nothing in Marchand's writings ever revealed other than a deep respect for Napoleon. Thus Napoleon was made additionally unique for he belied the common adage that no man was a hero to his valet.

Commandant Henri Lachouque, who edited and prepared Marchand's memoirs for publication, wrote of Marchand: "He was the most modest, the most devoted and the most loyal amongst all the members of the imprisoned Emperor's household." More than that, he was a faithful diarist.

When the memoirs finally were published in France in 1955 they caused little stir and were not widely translated or read. After all, so many persons had long before preceded Marchand with their accounts of life at Longwood or on St. Helena. What more could be said? Further, it came to the public domain soon after translation of the almost undecipherable shorthand notes of Napoleon's grand marshal of the palace, General Gratien

Bertrand. By comparison with Bertrand's terse but sometimes spicy notes, faithful Marchand's diary prose was very tame reading indeed.

But the long unavailable memoirs must now go down in history as a veritable time bomb — timed by fate to explode after that far more history-shaking detonation at Hiroshima.

The painstaking accuracy with which Louis Marchand recounted events at Longwood House and especially those of the sickroom, just as they occurred, made almost the equivalent of a doctor's casebook of careful notes detailing the progressive decline of a terminally ill patient. For Sten Forshufvud what it contained was priceless stuff.

In his situation of distressing isolation from France, of tensions and suspicions, feuds and recriminations, jealousies and complaints within the household, Marchand diarized with simple candor and without spite. Of what he wrote nothing needed to be stripped away as dubiously useful by reason of petty prejudice or as being the expression of personal vendetta or rancor against some abrasive fellow exile. Had he written less objectively and with more bite in his comments his memoirs, when they appeared in Paris, might have commanded wider public attention.

As it was, the quiet, faithful recordings of life at Longwood by a quiet, faithful valet were received with only quiet appreciation. They were a deceptive carrying case for the aforementioned time-bomb contrived by fate to blow the cover from a careful crime — if truly crime it was — to end the menace of a brilliant and ambitious man the powers of Europe had one day converted from Emperor to an outlaw beyond the pale of legal protection.

Why did the disclosure lag so long behind the events in Napoleon's place of imprisonment? Very probably because Marchand knew his place. He was a confidential valet trusted by an emperor and what he saw and heard he well knew he should keep to himself.

Since he diarized without thought that a certain Henri Lachouque in Paris one day would give his writings to posterity after an improbably long period of sustained secrecy spanning generations of the Marchand family, it is remarkable that Louis Marchand took the time to write so informatively. That he did so might be accepted by any practising fatalist as good evidence it was from the first ordained that Marchand should render this added measure of service to his emperor. It was no small assistance to history.

But Marchand's meed of posthumously rendered service did not end there. He received as a memento of his master's affection the donation of a lock of hair shaved by Marchand's friend Noverraz, second valet at Longwood, on the day following Napoleon's death. Marchand had placed the hair in his *reliquaire* along with sketches of the funeral cortege and the place of burial. The lock of hair remained faithfully preserved through the years in the hands of Marchand's descendants, still in the original envelope identified as to what its contents represented by words in Marchand's familiar handwriting. The collection contained, too, the famous playing card on which Marchand had written down Napoleon's last testamentary dictates.

When Marchand wrote on the envelope "Les cheveux de l'Empéreur" he had qualified the memento for its historical mission of the 1960's. And neither he nor his superior, Count de Montholon, who may well have seen the contents of the envelope, could know it would one day, long after they were gone, silently tell more about the years at Longwood than the total of all the other envelopes of correspondence and all the massive dossiers of plume-written manuscripts celebrating the subject of the Emperor's fate on St. Helena.

It was from this envelope that, one day in Paris, while Commander Lachouque and Sten Forshufvud looked on, Mrs. Forshufvud would carefully extract with tweezers a strand of the Emperor's hair to be analyzed for arsenic.

From Dr. Hamilton Smith's work at the University of Glasgow's Laboratory of Forensic Medicine and with radioactivation testing at Harwell Atomic Center in England the world would first learn that during his time at St. Helena Napoleon had been poisoned. The indicated doses of arsenic were such that severe sickness and physical deterioration would result from the amount of the poisonous chemical element in his system. An historical verdict!

Through Sten Forshufvud, Louis Marchand was testifying at

the resumed post-mortem examination into the nature of Napoleon's mysteriously fatal illness.

He would tell only what he saw, accusing no one. Even if his beautifully handwritten text had been available for reading right after being committed by plume pen to paper, the damning significance of what it conveyed would have aroused little if any alarm at that time. Foul play would only be indicated after the fact of a laboratory analysis for arsenic of a wisp of silky, red-brown hair at first unidentified to the analyst as to its physical source.

Henri Lachouque, now deceased, knew that the Napoleon hair specimen retained by Marchand's descendants was absolutely genuine. In all more than 140 analyses eventually would be made, all on souvenir hairs donated in life by Napoleon or cut on the day following his death. All had the same distinctive color, combined with such silkiness that one could think that they had come from a very small child.

Lachouque's commitment to the belief that Napoleon had been poisoned was so unqualified that he wrote a congratulatory introduction to Dr. Forshufvud's book. He promised more hairs to be given to the Chief of the Police toxicology service in Paris. At first approved, the giving of a certified specimen lock from this source was suddenly cancelled when the nature of Sten Forshufvud's suspicion, based on tentative research beyond the mere fact of poisoning, was realized.

4

Death Under Medical Direction

THE SECRET METHODS of most skilled assassins of the fifteenth to eighteenth or early nineteenth century in Europe were mystifying to the uninitiated. Knowledge and care were necessary to ensure that fatal results ensued without the means being recognized and the poisoner discovered.

As a cover, it was a preferred practice to use medicines familiarly prescribed by doctors and with doctors in attendance.

Calomel, harmless under common usage, latently could release a content of deadly mercurial salts if mixed in the stomach with milk of bitter almond. In Napoleon's time the relatively inert chemical contained in bitter almond was blended with orange flower water to add a pleasant taste to the beverage known as orgeat. The sharp tang of bitter almond provided added piquancy to the palate.

With proper attention to quantities and timing a poisoner thus might function without recognition in the presence of physicians — and, indeed, with the cover and help of their ministrations — to set up a deadly chemical reaction in the stomach of the victim. This was feasible since the two mutually unfriendly substances, conceivably preceded by tartar emetic in emetic wine, would have passed, without any tell-tale evidence, through the mouth and oesophagus of the patient. They would only have highly activated, corrosive properties when internally brought together, as though in a living chemical retort.

If taken without a period of preparation, the calomel and bitter almond, reacting with released mercurial salts from the one and hydrocyanic or prussic acid from the other, could be defensively expelled by retching actions of the stomach trying to free itself of so hostile a content.

For the would-be poisoner the answer lay in first diminishing the capability of the stomach to act spontaneously in its own defense. There was available in that commonly prescribed remedy of the times, tartar or emetic wine, the solution to this problem of ensuring that the corrosive material would be retained. Deadly mercuric cyanide will rapidly be taken into the bloodstream; corrosive sublimate will badly corrode the stomach wall. A series of doses of emetic wine, therefore, would inhibit the natural expelling reaction. It would affect the mucous lining of the stomach walls, cause swelling to partially immobilize the pylorus muscle through abnormal demands upon it involved in repeated vomitings. The benign theory in using emetic wine was that induced vomiting would clear the stomach by this harsh procedure. It was a much-used medication just as calomel was a common purgative. Bitter almond was the rare and dangerous additive sometimes supplied for anything but benign ends.

An assassin, educated in the skills of his trade, would know the effect, if not the precise method involved, when enough tartar emetic was consumed to cause the stomach to retain the bitter almond preparation and the calomel. Together they would react there one upon the other.

All this destructive power of mercuric cyanides could be released within the body of the victim with the record showing that what the patient received was customary medicine the doctors themselves ordered or approved. The incidents of such treatment in the days when subtle poisoning was practised would tend to become lost in the distressing conclusion that the victim had died of the plague or an unsuspected cancer.

Thanks in particular to Louis Marchand we know that Napoleon was treated with tartar emetic, by his physician's decision, on several occasions shortly prior to receiving his abnormally large dose of the purgative calomel. We know, also, that Napoleon requested and received refreshing draughts of the orgeat that had suddenly appeared on his bedside table, and that shortly before that time an otherwise purposeless shipment of kernels of bitter almond had been received for use at Longwood. Who had ordered the bitter almond is not positively known but suspicion points clearly to one person. From Marchand we know the constituent parts and circumstances for a fatal, disguised poisoning all existed within the sickroom just prior to Napoleon's lapse into extreme passivity, then unconsciousness and death. The symptoms described were entirely consistent with a poisoning by the method here described. His death struggle began immediately after the calomel was swallowed.

In the presence of the aftermath of such deadly competence the attending physicians Antommarchi and Arnott were joined by four British medical practitioners to form an autopsy team. None of the British doctors appears to have had any background in toxicology or as pathologist or anatomist. Antommarchi, who conducted the dissection, was a relatively good physician. He did not approve the calomel prescription. Certainly his qualifications as an anatomist were beyond doubt and no observing British doctors commented adversely on his skill in dissection as relating to post-mortem requirements.

Antommarchi found the liver to be enlarged but otherwise healthy. The stomach walls plainly had suffered great damage from corrosion. At one point a perforation had existed, but the opening had been sealed off by an adhesion with the lining of the adjoining liver. The closure would reduce danger from peritonitis and explain a knife-like shooting pain that caused Napoleon to suspect he was dying of a cancer pre-disposed to attack him through a tendency inherited from his father. The poisoner could capitalize to great advantage on this misapprehension and it would prejudice historians in favor of the cancer explanation of death. But cancer theories would benefit by some visible tumor or swelling. A circular swelling existed in understandable relationship to the fact that mercuric salts usually provoke swelling of the circular pyloric muscle.

Lacking more substantive evidence to explain death the baffled doctors brought in what amounted to a waffling, indeterminate report. They could not afford to say they were mystified. The corroded state of the stomach was suggestive of a cancerous, ulcerated condition or one "leading to cancer", they said. The swollen liver, undoubtedly affected by arsenic intake over an extended period of time, was abnormal as to its enlargement, yet it would seem undamaged to the naked eye.

Antommarchi noted ulcerous corrosion of the stomach but no

tumorous growth anywhere. The dissected liver tissue indicated no cirrhotic or diseased condition. But St. Helena had a reputation for endemic hepatitis, so Antommarchi's thesis fastened blame mainly on the tendency of the Emperor to suffer from what seemed to be repeated bouts of hepatic illness. Antommarchi would sign no coroner's statement that even implied the existence of a cancer and overlooked his preferred explanation of hepatitis.

Only Count de Montholon, in a private letter to Paris and whose statement was to gain currency in the press and in public discussion, reported positively that Napoleon had died of a clearly recognized, tumorous cancer. Trustingly, history would accept the cancer theory in Montholon's correspondence as the commonest explanation of the fact that Napoleon had died at a time of life when, given his fundamentally tough constitution, he might more logically have been enjoying prime health and vigor.

5

The Post-Mortem 'Reconvened'

BY ENLISTING THE internationally respected scientist of forensic research at the University of Glasgow, Dr. Hamilton Smith, to study one phase of the mystery of Napoleon's premature death Dr. Forshufvud in effect had revived after some 140 years the handicapped and inconclusive Napoleon autopsy and post-mortem. The fact that this was done after so long a lapse of time made its task difficult in some ways but fortunately science could overcome the passage of time.

The original post-mortem report was inexact, its medical authors lacking today's knowledge and methods. Had the six British physicians and one Italian surgeon-pathologist present possessed the report of Glasgow University's Laboratory of Forensic Research they would have known Napoleon had been the victim of systematic arsenical poisoning.

What was available at the autopsy through mere visual observation of the damaged organs was entered in the record with an ambiguity that confused and misled interpreters of the findings.

Any autopsist of today, in the presence of a verdict on the *corpus delicti* such as exists in Hamilton Smith's analytical findings on Napoleon's hair, would not presume that either cancer or climate was the killer. Positive evidence of victimization by frequent poisonings in such degree of severity would lead the investigator to believe that assumption of death from natural cause must be open to the greatest of doubt. A searching examination under suspicion of foul play then would become inevitable. There would be no longer any tendency to be misled by the fact that arsenic intoxication provides certain symptoms resembling familiar and non-fatal illness. The hunt would then

37

be on for the truth. Moreover, officers of the law would be advised that circumstances warranted action. The suspicion that some person guilty of the poisoning had managed, alone or with help, to poison so frequently and systematically would preclude a verdict of "death by natural cause".

It may be imagined what consternation a positively-worded autopsy verdict of death for the Emperor following upon heavy and repeated ingestions of arsenic over extended periods of time would have caused in that spring of 1821. On St. Helena such a report would have struck with stunning force, throwing the little island society into turmoil. No one at Longwood could then escape the shadow of doubt as to possible blame for the crime. Even the Governor, his chief officer in charge of police, doctors and stores department personnel would be suspect in the eyes of a public as outraged in England and America as in France or elsewhere in the world.

In 1821, as the renewed Bourbon regime grew unpopular, the Napoleon legend already was being nostalgically remembered for its glory days. It was a dangerous time for the Bourbons — and consequently for Napoleon.

As to the small groups of attendants in Napoleon's household, a sudden discovery that evidence pointed clearly to an assassin being some previously trusted person in their midst would have empoisoned the atmosphere of a court in mourning.

So where would fall the greatest weight of evidence incriminating one of their number? Who had motive, skill, opportunity and means to accomplish not one or two but scores of instances of poisonings? Who stood to profit most by the death of this once honored and powerful man who had been reduced to living an almost larval existence inside a cocoon of presumed security? Who would be identified as the human ichneumon fly that penetrated the cocoon as a predator?

So many were by then gone, so few remained to play out the last, tragic act of the drama of the Isle of Exile. Count Las Cases and son were in Europe, Cipriani was dead, Madame de Montholon had been sent away. Brave Gourgaud had departed in grief over Napoleon's wrath with him. The earlier suspected doctors, O'Meara and Stokoe, had been banished by the British. This left only a very few to be suspect.

As if seen standing on a stage, awaiting the suspenseful denouement of a writer's mystery play, they would have been the Grand Marshal Bertrand, the chief valet Louis Marchand, Napoleon's doctor Francesco Antommarchi, his second valet Abram Noverraz, and the Count de Montholon, *le maréchal de camp,* in Napoleon's own terms "the most faithful of the faithful".

But since there was in 1821 no verdict of poisoning, much less an actual accusation, all these men would depart St. Helena under no cloud of suspicion whatsoever of having done Napoleon to death. So history was to have no enlightenment such as a penetrative questioning of each attendant by examiners for a competent court of investigation almost certainly would have yielded. Made aware of poisoning, who would have recalled suspicious actions significant of guilt? What would recollections of the baffling violent illnesses of Napoleon have signified then to those loyal to him at his micro-scale court?

We may be sure that climatic illness, chronic hepatitis from an endemic disease, or Napoleon's father's "pyloric cancer" would have been unacceptable as easy explanations of death if arsenic intoxication had been unquestionably proven. And history, of course, would have been written very differently in accordance with the discovery that the Emperor had fought some of his most critical and decisive battles in a poisoned condition.

6

For History's Judgment

Is IT UNFAIR at this time to impugn the reputation of a French aristocrat who served and was trusted by Napoleon, when neither the man accused nor any of his descendants can offer definitive rebuttal to definite allegations?

Sensitivity in some quarters on that point will be understandable. And yet, since Napoleon belongs to the ages, history in search of knowledge must be served. The light cast upon events of Napoleon's life must be as impersonal and revealing as the beam of an X-ray camera.

Those persons, too, who had voluntarily cast their lives to be henceforth part of the Napoleon story or whom Fate chose to place within the area of universal interest, unavoidably had become part of history. Regardless of their own desires or of what their descendants might prefer, they forever after would be denied the privileges of privacy. This having been destined for them, even in their own time, what ghost of history almost one hundred and sixty years later can plead for privacy much less claim to have been libelled by posterity?

Certainly not Napoleon nor any of his descendants received such immunity. Uncounted authors have ransacked history, para-history and sheer legend for something to feed the public appetite for information about him.

Does Sten Forshufvud, by reason of his pertinacity in going beyond the mere discovery of poisoning into the less precise but challenging field of pure deduction as to the identity of the poisoner, thereby go beyond the bounds of ethical authorship?

Such an accusation was implied in the criticisms of some readers in Paris — criticism that followed an early, eager intellectual response.

Dr. Forshufvud was welcomed with open arms and every assurance of co-operation when he first visited Paris with details of his discovery. In official quarters he was promised further specimens of Napoleon's hair for corroborative testing. They were found and sent to the toxicological laboratory of the Paris police. Several days later they were ordered returned. There was lively speculation about an opening of the Emperor's tomb and an opinion that this would not be difficult to arrange.

It must seem more than sheer coincidence that the whole attitude of the Parisian collaborators concerned changed to one of non-co-operation immediately it became known that this scientist from Göteborg had melded into his conclusions the opinion that in the undoubted presence of a poisoning, a trusted French noble could be identified as probably the poisoner.

Professional historians characteristically and no doubt with reason are wary at any time about the conclusions of the unqualified. They tend to assign to that category those whom they may find active in their field without either invitation or the academic sanctions that go with a prescribed apprenticeship.

Sten Forshufvud not only was an historian by avocation rather than by right of academic degrees but he further was disturbing about an accepted "fact" of history — Napoleon's presumed cancer. What he announced he had discovered, if accepted, would call for the reconsideration if not the re-writing of so much past published work on Napoleon. Beyond that, the Forshufvud writing seemed a puzzling mixture of a doctor's casebook on a medical problem and a detective's conclusions after elaborate study of a murder case. It would have been remarkable if the first reactions of typical French historians — and particularly of those who had spent years on their own published books in the field of Napoleonic history — should have been found to be enthusiastic about so startling a revision as Forshufvud's thesis.

Thus Dr. Forshufvud experienced only a partial break-through with his theory. He could live with his convictions and his conscience so far as the issue of Montholon's responsibility was concerned. Particularly this was true after he had received the results from Dr. Hamilton Smith's new and more advanced system of analyzing the arsenic readings from consecutive 1 cm segments of hair specimens. These results, he was confident, clinched his case. They could be tied in with the St. Helena diaries and memoirs describing the daily condition of the Emperor and this he proceeded to do.

If the laboratory results were sensational, Sten Forshufvud could not help it. If his reading of the circumstances at St. Helena were, as some have said, like the plot for a Hollywood film, he likewise could not help that. The drama to be found in the story of St. Helena had been injected long ago by actions of some people five or six generations past. The researcher merely proceeded from what he knew to what he logically deduced from the available record. What emerged could be expected to speak for itself. It would be for history to ponder.

Inevitably this book's published research now will cause a sharply focused shaft of light to be directed upon the intriguing but somewhat shadowy figures of the Count de Montholon and his Countess. Neither had distinction in history beyond a presumably rather peripheral relationship to the distressing accounts of Napoleon's exile years. Albine de Montholon is presumed to have added a much-needed touch of feminine charm to the bleak household at Longwood that played at being a court. Charles Tristan de Montholon's quite sleazy yet genteel image before and after St. Helena was illuminated favorably in nearly all of the many works on Napoleon's exile; this, by virtue of his attentive and solicitous attitude toward Napoleon and the Emperor's resulting appreciation. His pictured virtues there redeemed him of shortcomings of judgment or ethics prior to or after that period of service to the Emperor.

There is as yet so little of assembled account of the de Montholons' lives before, during and after St. Helena that modern historical researchers will not find it easy to examine and explain these interesting and wholly improbable intervenors — or intruders — into the final phase of Napoleon's life. Forshufvud's text recounts some intermittent returns of de Montholon to public visibility. This occurred chiefly in the publishing of the Montholon *Histoire* about events at St. Helena. In fact, it was this book, drawing dishonestly long after the events upon Las Cases' history, O'Meara's writings and other island accounts while representing itself to be a currently kept memoir that greatly aroused Sten Forshufvud's suspicions as to the real role and the character of Count de Montholon.

In any case, once it had been discovered beyond doubt that Napoleon had been the victim of poisoning, it was inevitable that the case would have to be taken by someone beyond that bald, scientific conclusion. Knowing Dr. Forshufvud, I should add that it was inevitable that he, himself, would go on to finish the job. Throughout his career he has been a researcher. His familiar function scientifically has been a form of deductive investigation. In many respects a successful criminal investigator and a good research scientist will have marked points of similarity in their procedures. Indeed, as every reader of detective stories true or fiction knows, the two are frequently teamed in action.

Napoleon was a confirmed fatalist. As Forshufvud relates, the Emperor once said his life span was foreordained and that nothing could alter the predestination by Fate as to the time of death. Being of this mind, Napoleon would have no difficulty in ascribing to a delayed functioning of his guiding fate the accident whereby it fell to Forshufvud's lot to resume the abortive post-mortem on his death. How could one explain, other than as an act of Fate, that the first man who recognized Napoleon's symptoms as indicating chronic intake of arsenic should have happened to be, as well, so inveterate and lifelong a reader of Bonaparte's histories and biographies? Napoleon heartily believed in concentrating enough competence and power at the right place and time to achieve a given objective. It was as though his sometimes fickle fate had satisfied his formula for success in this instance.

As to books published on Napoleon whose authors would have written a different account had they known the secret uncovered at Harwell Atomic Center and at Dr. Hamilton Smith's University of Glasgow laboratory of forensic medicine, they are literally numberless. An edition of the Encyclopedia Britannica published nearly half a century ago estimated the number of separate and distinct titles of books celebrating the life of Napoleon at more than 200,000. This was based on a count by a German researcher in the subject. Recently a French historian offered the opinion that 400,000 would be closer to the actuality.

Except in the case of de Montholon's own book of memoirs, none of the many titles produced dealt with de Montholon and his wife as actors having more than minor roles in the drama of St. Helena. Of course, this would be as had been wished.

To this extent, then, Forshufvud does more than add a mere footnote to history. He is in this volume saying fortrightly that history should be revised to recognize solid evidence of poisoning and that the circumstances of Napoleon's death must be re-interpreted in what amounts to a drastic revision of historical assumptions.

If as is now scientifically indicated Napoleon did not die of natural cause then he could only have died from misadventure or by deliberate intent. He desired that the truth be known.

Forshufvud's theory of poisoning seems unassailable. The evidence leaves little if any room for doubt. It is when he pursues his subject into the Longwood establishment in search of an unconfessed poisoner that his thesis becomes one of bold deduction. He now assumes historians will free their minds of preconceptions and of emotion based on political or other loyalties and will examine what is known about Charles Tristan de Montholon dispassionately.

History will not be satisfied merely to accept it as a fact that Napoleon was poisoned. Inevitably, it will re-examine all that is dependably known about the court in exile in the light of the chilling fact that a poisoner was present — that he was not a rumor but a reality. The Harwell tests will never go away.

A malign intent toward the usurper of the Bourbon throne is not illogical to assume. How certainly history will place responsibility for Napoleon's death on de Montholon, the Emperor's most trusted Longwood aide, remains for time to disclose. We have here attempted to be correct as well as convincing and to give the reader the means of studying how conclusions of the Forshufvud thesis were reached.

In a very real sense, Forshufvud was an archeologist. He worked not with the shattered bits and pieces of materials from the rubbish piles of antiquity but with words. These were words from sentences formed currently with the experiences at Longwood; writings in a language not his own by non-literary men with no thought of literary use. One suspects that Bertrand

and Marchand often wrote to relieve pent-up emotions overlain by a sense of drama and of the horrible anticlimax of their dying Emperor's life.

The dedicated young valet, Louis Marchand, had been privy to the most intimate facts of Napoleon's final five and a half years and to much that had preceded his sovereign's condemnation to exile. If he wrote compulsively and thus committed the closing episodes of Napoleon's career to history, as would have been possible for no one else to do, he obviously felt a necessity to observe the disciplines of confidentiality. His passion for privacy still was sufficiently durable, generations after his death, to ensure that his papers would not reach the public eye. Fourteen decades were to come and go before this self-assumed and transmitted pledge of secrecy was broken. The ultimate result was a release to Forshufvud of vital new knowledge. It was Marchand's last, crucial service to his emperor not less great because he himself was unaware of how he served.

The withholding of the memoirs of General Bertrand was perhaps as much a matter of a low level of initiative to publish as of any pronounced desire to draw a veil over a long period of playing reluctant witness to a cruel aftermath of greatness.

Whatever the motivations to write and to keep the product from the eyes of those insatiably curious to understand the riddle of one of the most complex personalities of all history, the fact is that from the late nineteen-fifties onward, there had become available the product of an unplanned service to history by two of Napoleon's most trusted attendants, an officer and a first valet — each a devoted friend. Neither of these authors of notes about daily happenings at St. Helena could have suspected how his writings, in the hands of a perceptive scientist, would point to the evidence of poisoning. Even less could these court attendants, unaware that a deliberate poisoning was taking place virtually before their eyes, have had any inkling of a long-distant future time when the facts they had recorded would serve the investigative mind of someone like Dr. Forshufvud.

Having proven scientifically that Napoleon had absorbed heavy but sub-lethal doses of arsenic and that his death could not have been attributed to climatic conditions at St. Helena or by such natural causes as the autopsy indicated, Dr. Forshufvud

continued his investigative studies. It may be wondered if he was
out of his area of expertise. In fact he was medically very much at
home in his newly-entered and unanticipated avenue of research.

Patience, persistence and an admirably analytical mind all
would help in the study Forshufvud began in the hunt for the
probable poisoner.

Of the very many books at his disposal only those that
recorded the testimony of eye-witnesses to the events at St.
Helena now were of value. It seemed that nearly everyone who
had been at St. Helena and who was literate had put pen to paper
on the subject or had talked to an author who quoted him
extensively. Inevitably there would be discrepancies.

Who of the witnesses was believable? What part of the
testimony related credibly to the theme as tested through the
science of toxicology? When and how often were there instances
in which the known ingestions of arsenic were operative in the
known symptoms of Napoleon's periodic severe illnesses?

Who had access to Napoleon's food and drink? Who in that
limited group had both motive and opportunity to poison?

Who in the changing and ever-reducing numbers of those
close to Napoleon at Longwood remained to the end as the
innermost of the inner circle? It could only be someone who was
always there when the distressing symptoms occurred. It could
not be other than someone who was thoroughly trusted and who,
finally, was not absent at the time of death.

Who in the court could know the arts of the poisoner? Were
the chemicals of poisoning known to be on St. Helena?
Specifically, was there on the island the reagent that, without
leaving telltale evidence in the throat of having swallowed a
deadly poison, could enter the stomach and there change a
massively heavy dosage of the relatively harmless cathartic
calomel to deadly mercuric cyanide?

Who were present at the post-mortem which Napoleon
himself had so urgently directed should be made upon his body
to determine the nature of his mysterious and uncharacteristic
physical weakness? What qualifications, what motivations did the
doctors have to serve as performers or witnesses of an autopsy?
Could that unfortunate and ungracious man the governor, Sir

Hudson Lowe, have influenced the post-mortem team — persuaded them to exonerate the British of blame for holding Napoleon on an island the French tended to believe was unsuited to human habitation? And who at St. Helena had a personal reason to attribute mysterious illnesses and deaths in the household of the deposed emperor to reasons of climate or disease peculiarly endemic to what previously had been a health recovery base for the British Navy and Merchant Marine? Could it be the poisoner?

All these and many more questions entered the medical researcher's systematic and painstaking investigation into the circumstantial evidence still available so very many years after the killing.

That there had been a killing Forshufvud did not doubt. He took it to be as demonstrable as the verdict of a common laboratory experiment into the death of any human or animal organism. He even reproduced, in three laboratory animals that had previously been ordered destroyed, the coup de grâce end that had been ordained for Napoleon. The clever poisoning system employing doctor-approved medications worked in the case of the laboratory animals. Calomel and orgeat produced unconsciousness, then death.

If Forshufvud had stopped his account of forensic research short of the actual denouement and had left his final conclusions unstated as a tantalizing question for history to ponder and debate it would have sheltered him almost wholly from serious criticism. His less complete thesis would have been more widely acceptable. But it would have been wholly uncharacteristic of the man not to finish what he had begun.

Of what purpose is research that lacks the courage to interpret its findings? Sten Forshufvud has not been lacking in that quality, as a reading of his text will prove. That he has been humanly moved by his especial insight into the dramatic events at the celebrated isle of captivity — which he visited in the course of his studies — will be obvious to the reader.

Having reduced by elimination all excepting one in the court of exile who had opportunity, motive, background and skill to effect the death of the Emperor by poisoning, Forshufvud made his accusation. It was, he said forthrightly, the Count de

Montholon. Yet in doing so he conceded to his accused the possibility that he acted at St. Helena as one who considered himself legitimately an executioner, reaching a man condemned internationally, one formally denounced as an enemy of peace and living beyond the protection of the law. Moreover, he could have had the self-image of a patriot who risked his own life to perform a dangerous service to the Bourbon cause in France; perhaps to save his country — indeed, all of Europe — from renewed wars.

How, in truth, the man who killed Napoleon saw his victim and his own secret but significant role in history never will be clear. Certainly in nothing he is known to have written or said did Montholon present himself openly for reward or blame. No co-conspirator has talked. No documents or memoirs of royalty hint at the long-kept secret or unconfessed execution.

It is interesting to speculate on whether or not the Montholon success as a secret agent of the ruling house of Bourbon recruited and directed by the King's brother, d'Artois, could have drawn, in any court on the continent of Europe of that period, a verdict of murder. The Declaration of Vienna respecting Napoleon, disturber of the peace in Europe, had never been withdrawn. Technically the deposed monarch lived and died beyond any right to receive the protection of law within the jurisdiction of the countries signatory to the Declaration.

We may imagine the overwhelming embarrassment to Britain were the post-mortem to have discovered poisoning and a police investigation resulted in an accusation that none other than Count de Montholon was responsible. The question of jurisdiction would have been confusing. Was it a legal possibility for culpability for murder to exist under law if a deposed emperor, citizen of no country, prisoner of a power holding him in behalf of an *ad hoc* alliance of enemies that had defeated, denounced and stripped him of his rights under the law, had met death at the hands of a Bourbonist servant loyal to his King? It must be remembered that Montholon still held the rank of Major General by warrant bearing the signature of that King. Certainly it would have been one of the most celebrated and controversial homicide cases of all time.

But in Forshufvud's eyes the removal of the Napoleonic

menace to the security of the Bourbon regime was a political affair. Its management would have been directed by persons at the highest level of policy control. As for the appointed executioner, he would have had little if any choice in the matter. He was royalist-born and raised and his military commission made him a soldier subject to the instruction of superiors who had selected him for a difficult and dangerous duty. Under these circumstances he need not have considered himself responsible for anything other than an execution done in the service of the King whose enemies he was bound to oppose.

Part Two

The Victim

Ben Weider

What a romance
my life has been!

— NAPOLEON

7

Man and Legend

THE HUNGER OF the world to be informed about Napoleon has been a remarkable phenomenon of history and literature. More than a century and a half after the end of the immensely dramatic events of Napoleon's life a high level of interest persists. It is as though there has always existed a universal sense of a story unfinished. The writer-philosopher Goethe once made just such an observation. In this sensitivity his remark could seem almost to have anticipated and invited the recent discoveries by Dr. Forshufvud.

As a military genius Napoleon is ranked with Alexander the Great and Julius Caesar. Unlike Alexander he was more than an aggressive and infinitely ambitious conqueror of nations. His Italian background would contribute naturally to an interest in the exploits of the greatest Roman. As with Caesar, he was a ruler always most at home in the soldier's role. But he recognized that nations conquered could only be truly possessed if they were uplifted. His policy was to offer them the civilizing and calming experience of life under a rule of law and of civil achievements. Thus as a civil administrator he was likely to reconcile rather than subjugate peoples who first had feared their defeat would lead to near extermination.

No Ghengis Khan or Charlemagne in any instinct to exploit power savagely, Napoleon Bonaparte still was pictured by his enemies as The Ogre, the ruthless scourge of Europe. But no ogre could have pacified the conquered or produced codified laws and put down civil administration corruption as did Napoleon. That he was so beloved by his troops, even in the face of disastrous defeats and losses experienced under the fortunes of war, tells clearly enough that he had humanly appealing qualities, even if these were sometimes contrived. He could strike terror and he could charm, as circumstances might require. His instinct was to build, not lay waste.

The contradictions in the characteristics of the man have made him impossible to classify in any broadly simplistic terms.

He was a tyrant with a heart. He was remorseless in war but considerate of the defeated. He was forgiving toward the treachery shown him by men he had elevated to power and wealth. He denied freedom to the press in France but he gave the people rights and protection under codified laws such as had not before existed in France. He believed in the existence of some power that ordered the universe. He ensured freedom of worship for Catholics, Protestants, Jews and Mohammedans. He fought the feudal monarchies of Europe but converted his country from republicanism to a monarchical system, at the same time removing class or caste barriers. Any able Frenchman, though of humble origin, should be able to attain highest recognition of his abilities in government, the Army, law and the learned professions or in business and industry. He enriched himself and his family from the rewards of his wars but, even in periods that called for the sacrifices of war, gave the people of France confidence in their gold-backed currency in lieu of the nearly worthless paper money that had caused the country to live in economic stagnation arising from currency and price inflation. He gave the world France's example in adopting the metric system of measurements. He could be a coarse and boorish soldier or a diplomat with a cool self-control to match the mettle of his calculating friend and enemy, the great Talleyrand. He foresaw the unity of Europe in an economic community but in his era it was an idea whose time had not yet come.

Like many another student of his life Aubry, a modern French biographer, attempted to report upon him objectively and ended with superlatives. Napoleon he has described as "the greatest personality of all time, superior to all other men of action by virtue of the range and clarity of his intelligence, his speed of decision, his answering determination, and his acute sense of reality, allied to the imagination on which great minds thrive." (O. Aubry, Napoleon [Paris 1964] p. 374)

Perhaps away from the cannonading, the adulation and the

hatreds of the struggle for power on the continent of Europe, in the remote stillness of St. Helena, a very few of all the persons who felt they had experienced opportunity to judge the inner and essential nature of Napoleon would be privileged to see the flesh and blood man beneath the actor's exterior. They were surprised and some were relieved to discover so unexpectedly humble and human a person within the awesome hero of great wars and dramatic political events. This comes through with clarity in Dr. Forshufvud's elaborately researched text.

The story of Napoleon I begins on the Island of Corsica on August 15 of the year 1769.

In 1768 when France had proceeded under the agreement of Genoa to take charge of the legally ceded Italian island with its insularly independent people, French troops were needed to quell the resisting inhabitants. Many in Corsica refused to admit the validity of the transaction of transfer completed without local consultation. They demanded the right to a constitution of their own. Their intrepid leader, Paoli, conducted a brave but futile resistance before fleeing to England.

Serving under the French commanding officer at Ajaccio was Count Louis-Charles-René de Marbeuf, a bachelor career-officer of the force of occupation. As the resistance movement weakened toward its final collapse in May of 1769 there was leisure enough for the officer cadre of the occupying contingent to take stock of the local amenities. And it would have been unthinkable that they should have failed to be fully aware of Letizia Buonaparte. She had been a bride at 14 to Carlo Buonaparte, who then was 18. Carlo, a drop-out at law, became a local member of minor regional officialdom, a fixer of petty problems and a sympathizer with Paoli's declining cause.

If Carlo Buonaparte, descended of distantly noble but latterly undistinguished Corsican stock, was not of himself particularly impressive this could not be said of his dark-eyed wife. She had the striking beauty of the Eastern Mediterranean women who had inspired the canvases of master artists through the ages. But she was married and the mother of an infant, Joseph, born in the spring of 1768. She was good to look at, a feast for the hungry eyes of young officers absent many months from Paris.

As it turned out it was Marbeuf, remaining as senior military administrator, who befriended the young Buonapartes even to the point of being billeted in their home.

When Carlo's young Letizia gave birth to a second male child, the youthful parents called him Napoleone. Nothing in the record of Carlo's life suggested he would sire such a son as this infant became; and Marbeuf would little suspect to what measures of interest his friendly association with the Buonapartes would cause him to render great service to his country as he arranged the early education of Napoleone.

Carlo Buonaparte, an indifferent provider, had reason often to be absent from Ajaccio and for extended periods of time. Marbeuf, who had gratefully taken quarters in the Buonaparte family menage, found pleasant relaxation there away from his officer duties. He played the role of an influential friend to the family and of godfather or surrogate parent to a succession of young Buonapartes.

Letizia, endowed with an unusual degree of independence, stronger of character than her husband, raised children of whom, as the famous "Madame Mère", she would be maternally proud. They would be by no stretch of definition either ordinary or orthodox in their behavior. From the first, they presumed that rules were for others. They would go their way and, with Napoleon's rise, become members of a new dynasty, a nascent royal family of Europe, imaginatively created and sustained by Napoleon the First.

Typical of their Corsican blood, the young Bonapartes, though they might quarrel amongst themselves, displayed filial and familial loyalties that would bind them durably long after they had reached adult years. They were Italianate enough to believe deeply in the sanctity and continuity of family ties.

It would be to the second of the children born to Letizia that the family would be indebted for fame and exalted positions. If there were inherently one amongst them quieter and more thoughtful than the rest, it was Napoleon, yet he was the one who would go the farthest, alter the world the most, taking the rest upward with him as any true Corsican would be expected to do. He would lead them to dizzy heights; some, such as Jerome and Louis, would not gladly go. With Napoleon the Corsican, in excess of good fortune, one shared, assisted and gave patronage. This he would do on a truly royal scale to blood relatives and to good friends so long as he had power and wealth to share.

Napoleon's first evidence of latent genius lay in a boyhood aptitude for mathematics. It was a satisfying science. One dealt in problems for which there could be no choice of answers, no bothersome debate on degrees of rightness or wrongness — only the disciplines of correctness. For a subaltern of artillery, one could have a future with a good capability in knowledge of numbers.

Marbeuf saw very early in Napoleon the material for an exceptional officer. First he would have him sent to school at Autun to learn to speak and think and dream in French, then to a military school at Brienne that graduated young men of spirit and dash — and logic. It was fit and proper for this to be done for the Corsican youth because, by grace of less than a year's time, he had been born a subject of France, not of his native Corsica. Moreover, there were registration privileges in military education available to young nobles whose families lacked affluence. Marbeuf knew his army.

Every evidence exists that Marbeuf's role as patron, an honored one in Latin society along the Mediterranean, was crucially influential in determining that Napoleon would make a proud career, given the privilege of attending an elite officer training school. Without Marbeuf the second Buonaparte might well have become a Corsican guerrilla. His latent talent might have been exhausted in skirmishes against the soldiers of France. Instead, he would become more French than the French, the leader of all the soldiers of France.

It was another of the myriad contradictions of which the story of Napoleon's life abounded that having been trained amongst the bluebloods of France at Brienne military academy, and at *L'École Militaire,* he would come to the world's attention as a brilliant young officer in a regular army turned revolutionary. Yet, on many occasions, he would have need to put down the bothersome activities of undisciplined peoples. And ultimately he would restore imperialism and constitutional monarchy in France, enjoying unexampled popularity with soldiers whom he paid with coins collected in overrun regions. In time that enthusiasm for his leadership was communicated to the civilian populace. Against the performance of the Directory and the national council his achievements would quickly build his reputation. In due course he would be elected a first consul for life, then Emperor, confirmed by popular referendum. In the Europe of his time, a continent of ancient monarchies, the army was a way to monarchical power that had been closed to commoners since antiquity. It was not closed to Napoleon.

The origins of Napoleon's extraordinary natural gifts will never be explained to the complete satisfaction of history. Marbeuf would say he had once been wildly in love with Letizia, but there is no indication that Letizia's feeling toward the count was other than that of great but restrained appreciation.

Napoleon's lifelong apprehension that he might have inherited a tendency to cancer from his father indicated well his own confidence in the legitimacy of his birth. But if Marbeuf were merely a good friend to the family, his generosity and his assistance toward the education of the children would be bound to promote speculation. There is an interesting note in the memoirs of the savant Monge. That eminent scholar, who had been with Napoleon in Egypt to found a new center for learning in the visualized Napoleonic empire of the East based on Alexandria, recalled a conversation with Napoleon aboard *La Muiron*. Conversations at sea are apt to draw out confidences. Napoleon is quoted by Monge as having said he wished he had had Marbeuf as his real rather than foster father. He would then have understood how he had become possessed of his unusual talent for military strategy.

If the ambitious Letizia was conscious of gossip it did not in the least deter her from enjoying the practical benefactions of a good and influential friend. Carlo was restlessly unsettled and often away. Fatherly Marbeuf was continuously in Ajaccio, attending to his not very arduous military and administrative duties. In fact the French officer would manage to spend the rest of his life there, much contented with his ultimate posting as military governor of the island and happy in his acceptance into the lively household of Carlo and Letizia. Could he hope often to meet, as an officer of an occupying force, a family that would make him additionally at home by surmounting the entrance way with his name done in seashells and embedded in plaster, to announce the fact that this was where he, Marbeuf, resided?

As for Letizia, she lived and died without dignifying gossip with any outright declaration and apparently without feeling any necessity on her part to speculate on how so amazing a nestling should have come from the Buonapartes' brood of thirteen children born and eight nurtured to adulthood.

Grateful for the hospitality at the hands of the Buonapartes, Marbeuf arranged a charter of nobility for Carlo. It conferred a certain distinction on the regional advocate and settler of minor affairs amongst the fig and grape growers and winemakers of the sunny island.

When Carlo died at 38 while under medical treatment at Montpellier it was Marbeuf who rose signally to the occasion with help. By means not wholly clear, he was able to obtain for Madame Bonaparte a helpful state pension.

As to her friend Marbeuf it can be said that without his intervention in the affairs of *la famille Buonaparte* Western history undoubtedly would have been much different.

There can be no doubt that it was Marbeuf, the soldier, who persuaded Carlo and Letizia that they should arrange for Napoleon to accept, as the second son in the family, the role traditionally reserved for the first born — that of career soldier. Trading places with Joseph, his eldest brother, who went into training for the priesthood, Napoleon proceeded willingly to prepare for his lifetime in military adventures. Only a few years would pass before Joseph, relieved of religious commitments, would begin to collect satisfying rewards for his compliant acceptance of second place. The compensation would include the occupancy of two thrones.

8

Fortune's Favorite

NAPOLEON COULD HAVE had no sense of neglect or under-privilege in childhood and youth. There was for him no heritage of hatred for the aristocratic or the well-to-do such as would later be seen to have warped the personalities of some of his revolutionary marshals and generals. From his upbringing and early officer training came a predisposition to move away from Jacobinistic political radicalism toward the militarily pragmatic.

Graduated from *l'Ecole Militaire* in Paris in 1785, with spelling of name changed to Bonaparte, Napoleon, until he was 19, took postgraduate training at the artillery school at Auxenne. He was technically qualified to become thereafter master of his own destiny and manager of the quick succession of opportunities fate would present to him.

He acknowledged his good fortune in having studied while at Auxenne the science of artillery combat under du Teil, brother of France's foremost authority on the strategies of fire-power mobilization and concentration. So well did he learn the theory and practice of the uses of artillery in war that his demonstrations of the power of well-drilled, highly mobile artillery came to be cited instructionally the world over. In his swift series of advancements successively as commander in chief, first consul and finally emperor, Napoleon never ceased to be essentially what he had set out to be — a gunner.

By 1793 a series of desultory duties, marked by rebellious doubts as to his future, had culminated in his abrupt and somewhat forced departure from his native Corsica as potentially a rootless officer of fortune. He was 24 years of age, a professional soldier of junior rank whose papers at the war office described him as an exemplary practitioner of artillery maneuvers — a useful reference. He was sent to Toulon where older and less able officers were trying to recapture the harbor and city which had been treacherously surrendered to British naval occupation. It was Napoleon's great chance.

His recommended plan of action to recover the base by making the harbor entrance unsafe and the basin untenable to Admiral Hood's flotilla was adopted with relief by the corp's inadequate officers, unfamiliar with the theory of laying or relieving siege. Under severe fire and with a personal courage that inspired his followers, Napoleon on his sector cleared his enemy from a strategic site close enough to the roadstead to allow fire to be laid across the mouth of the harbor. Lord Hood, recognizing the immediate danger to his entire flotilla, lost no time in leaving Toulon. It was to be Napoleon's first and only successful fighting encounter with the British Navy.

News of the recovery of the great base with the assistance of a daring junior officer brought the producer of eagerly desired good news to the attention of the senior command in Paris. Thereafter, though he would experience reverses in fortune, the stage was set for his entrance upon the scene, with all France as an audience, as if by the design of a meticulous playwright. In exile, Napoleon would tell his historian, Las Cases: "Centuries will pass before the unique combination of events which led to my career recur in the case of another."

Normally Napoleon, after graduation in 1785, would have spent 15 years before receiving his captaincy and perhaps another 10 to 15 years as a captain. But in December of 1793, after his coup at Toulon, he was made General of Brigade. Two months later, his credentials confirmed by that best of all testimonials, a conspicuous victory, he was appointed to the command of artillery, then inspector general, in France's army of Italy. Over the years France would promote him successively until he was not only in command of the Grand Army of France, First Consul, Consul for life, but finally Emperor of the French and King of Italy. Yet the British Government, calling him Lieutenant General Bonaparte, would not address him by a title of higher rank than he occupied in his middle twenties. He had been recognized as consul by the British at the Peace of Amiens.

Falsely accused of Jacobinistic plotting, Napoleon was briefly imprisoned but cleared of the charge. In 1795, when the Revolutionary army was under the direction of Paul Barras, entrusted with home defenses, the non-military Barras would recall Napoleon's conspicuous service at Toulon. He seconded his services to be next in command of the Army in Paris.

As a soldier spectator watching the first march of a mob on the Tuileries in 1792, Napoleon expressed to his friend Bourienne his wonder why artillery, charged with grapeshot, had not been used to clear the mob from the area around the palace. He would twice have occasion to exercise that inclination to grape-shot strategy in Paris. The first time was in 1795 as he put down an incipient insurrection with a few bursts to sweep away the rebels in the rue Ste-Honoré, breaking up a threatened march on the Tuileries. The action was bold, swift, ruthless and successful. Barras quickly yielded to Napoleon his own position in command of the Army of the Interior, and instructed him to restore order in the capital. His action of the 13th Vendemaire had blocked a planned Bourbonist revolutionary coup against the weak administration. The once slightly yet recognizably Jacobite Napoleon had cowed the Paris mob.

So fast ran the sequence of events in young General Bonaparte's life that only five months later, having been in command of the Army of the Interior, he was politically a figure of extreme visibility in stabilized Paris; he had married the beautiful and vivacious Creole, Josephine Beauharnais, for-merly mistress of Barras — with the latter's complaisance — and had been appointed to command the Army of Italy, with headquarters at Nice. Widow of the guillotined Viscount de Beauharnais, Josephine had survived the revolution with difficulty and was living precariously in what was the earliest small nucleus of a new and brittle salon society of members of the lately risen and distinctly gauche élite in Paris.

Josephine de Beauharnais, six years older than Napoleon, saw in this man whom her friend and protector Barras called "the little Corsican general", an end to penury and of living by her wits. For Napoleon, whose amorous affairs had been of a catch-as-catch-can sort, in the exigencies of his army life, she represented access to a social stratum in post-revolutionary Paris that could advance his interests. Beyond that, however, Napo-

leon evidently cared deeply for Josephine. She would be the one
woman in his life who could give him not merely affection but
sound advice from womanly intuition as to people and situations. Each of the pair would form other attachments during
Napoleon's numerous and at times long absences from Paris, but
they were brief and passing. Not until he divorced her to marry
the attractive but vapid young Austrian archduchess, Marie
Louise, would Napoleon fail to return to the sometimes faithless
Josephine and to heap favors of money and jewels upon her. She
would tire of life in Fontainebleau and the Tuileries and order,
to her indulgent spouse's account for payment, the purchasing
of her beloved villa, Malmaison. Napoleon, who had been
destined to remain in no house or palace for more than a few
weeks at a time — until he was consigned to the hated Longwood
House — preferred Fontainebleau's magnificence, but after his
divorce he would frequently visit Josephine at Malmaison.
Ironically, it would be at this gracious garden villa that he would
assemble his last company of supporters for flight abroad. That
would be slightly more than a year after Josephine's death but
even in the extremity of his position, Napoleon would not have
failed to recall then the faithfulness of Josephine as a friend,
unfaithful and unresponsive to his love letters as she had been
while she was his wife.

But in the early spring of 1796 Napoleon's world was bright
and promising. Before the month was out he would be at Nice,
organizing his staff and laying his plans. Josephine made a show
of accompanying him but then remained in Paris.

The industriousness of Napoleon is legendary. It was needed
in the new commander-in-chief. France's armed forces were
ill-clothed and badly provisioned for want of money. Napoleon
knew he could not count on his impoverished War Ministry for
more. The official hope was that his men would forage a good
part of their needs from local supply. Napoleon, to the delight of
director Barras, capitalized on necessity.

9

A Man for All Occasions

IN THE FOURTH year of the revolution the army of the National convention under such generals as Hoche, Menon, Dugommier, Moreau and Massena had not only secured the borders of France but had carried a crusading, republican or anti-monarchical war beyond the borders of France — in particular to the feudal states along the Rhine. The French people longed for victories that would give them peace, with secure borders. They welcomed in Napoleon a new hero, greater than all the others. In his series of brilliant and strikingly swift campaigns against the principal enemy, Austria, there were ushered in what France henceforth would remember as its days of greatest glory, accompanied by security.

After the three-day battle at Arcola against 17,000 Austrians in November, 1796 where Napoleon executed for the first time his strategy of the forced night march with surprise attack at the enemy's rear at dawn, he tasted the heady wine of popular acclaim. He became fully convinced that he was not only invincible but ordained by destiny to have a distinguished place in history. In due course his army would accept and exalt the legend. Had its young commanding general not led them to the Italian plains an ill-equipped, ill-fed, motley collection of 30,000 would-be conquerors and plunderers with the hope of heightened fortunes, saying: "Soldiers, you are hungry and all but naked; I am about to lead you into the most fruitful plains in the world. Rich provinces, great cities lie before you. There you will find honor, glory and riches."

Then began the French army's lasting love affair with the slight, gaunt young general who won where others might have lost, who exhorted excitingly like a French patriot, if in a

64

Corsican's accent. He had great awareness of what men wanted. And what Napoleon promised, he delivered. As his troops, like later legions of Caesar's campaigns, swept through minor kingdoms, states and dependencies, not only living off the country but exacting tribute in a rich flow of wealth, he fulfilled his prophecy to the soldiery and still could send money and treasure to Paris. This was new and gratifying. So young a man, he not only fought in his individual style and won but he made his campaigns profitable. His army not only paid rich dividends to the empty treasury in Paris, it began to fill palaces and museums with priceless art of the Mediterranean.

Under these circumstances France was willing then and for epochal years to come to accept Napoleon's drafts upon the young manpower of the country. His divisions must be kept at strength. War was costly in lives but under Napoleon's campaigning against countries hostile to the experimental republicanism of France, the country in money terms could afford it. Until 1812 Napoleon's casualties were usually modest compared with those of the enemy and as measured against the confidence that the country could be less fearful of invasion.

By 1796 General Bonaparte, 27 years of age, was exacting settlements measurable in a golden flow from invaded areas — including a tribute of approximately twelve million francs from the Pope. He began to engage in ad hoc diplomacy under his own initiatives. The Directory at Paris contained no figure of strength to check the young general's growing independence. In truth, it had no desire to quarrel with his success. Napoleon became more than a general. As commander of the Army in Italy he negotiated treaties, dictated terms, propitiated or punished the enemy. There, too, he began to develop his hitherto unsuspected skills in civil administration.

It was not surprising, therefore, that with every added incursion into the rich depths of Tuscany and Lombardy Napoleon should find himself in situations that rehearsed him for the role of emperor. After all, it was in physical terms a veritable empire he was conquering. Now he could visualize attaching ancient kingdoms and principalities to France.

The Directory of five at Paris, republican, Jacobinistic and agnostic, was too inefficient and uncertain to keep subserviently in order its new commander of the Army of Italy. Napoleon raised the banners of liberty and equality in Italy, yet he could parley with monarchical heads of state in practical terms and reach agreements that satisfied expediency. He could bleed the Pope of money while pragmatically conceding the right of Catholics to their religion, their cathedrals and their church properties. Napoleon did not come as another Cromwell, battering the structure and edifices of the church. His fighting proclivities apart, and as seen in non-military discussions with all levels of the church hierarchy, he was a rather pleasant if occasionally disturbingly blunt and penetrating young man.

Not all of his officers were impressed. Moreau was older and much his senior in years of service time. He resented the unprecedented rise in rank of one he considered a raw youth. The Gascon General Bernadotte was equally critical. From his first interview with Napoleon he returned to his staff and said: "I have seen yonder a man of twenty-six or twenty-seven, who wants to appear fifty, that augurs no good for the republic." Napoleon would do his best to win them, but at the end they would join the allies and fight to end his empire, Bernadotte as the Crown Prince of Sweden and ultimately King.

Before another year had passed, Napoleon had readied his conquered Italian territories for annexation and had forced Austria to sue for peace. Belgium and the left bank of the Rhine had been ceded to France. Only the consent of Britain was necessary to secure firmly these territorial extensions of post-revolutionary France.

Although England once had sinned against the institution of the anciently-accepted rights of kings by seizing, trying and beheading Charles Stuart, now she was ruled by a constitutional monarchy holding sovereignty at the pleasure of a vigorous Parliament under Pitt the younger. Her Cromwellian revolution was long past; the somewhat sympathetic ties with European royal families, including the Hapsburgs and Bourbons, were a fact of British life and politics. Under Tory leadership the British had thought less about the sublime in the French Revolution than of its well publicized excesses. Beyond that, British diplomats tended to be more sanguine of the prospect for a fruitful peace in a divided rather than a forcibly-unified continent of Europe. Should the lands below the Channel moat be melded under such a leader as the astonishingly battle-wise General Bonaparte, a policy of consent to the permanence of such a powerful hegemony of states could consolidate the new republicanism of France. Even worse it could close European markets to British commerce, except on France's terms, and put limits on the otherwise hopeful prospects to prosper from the inspiringly wide-spread British Empire.

For his part, Napoleon early knew that Britain's non-compliance and active opposition must be reckoned with. Any hopes he might have to make France the dominant power of Europe — which meant, of the world — must have the willingly given or compelled assent of the political and mercantile policy makers in London. But against Britain compulsion would be hard to enforce. Her insular position and superior naval strength sheltered her from France as they had from Philip's great Spanish Armada.

There was consideration of a frontal across-the-Channel attack on Britain. Since Napoleon's military power base then existed largely in Italy, and his navy was inadequate, that became impracticable. He must pursue another route to ultimate supremacy.

10

Via Egypt to High Office

A PEACE WITH BEATEN Austria having been effected by the Treaty of Campo Formio in October, 1797, Napoleon, consulting with Talleyrand, felt free to approach obliquely the knotty problem of England's obdurate resistance to his grand plan. He would postpone the plan of invasion across the Strait of Dover. Instead he would pursue the Alexandrian path of history in a drive to the East, taking Malta as jumping-off base, Egypt as the anchor for an empire of the Orient. Alexander had found the Egyptians easy to handle. He might hope for the same experience. From Egypt he could move to Syria and the Levant while placating, if possible, their and Russia's ancient enemy, Turkey of the Ottoman Empire. The surrounding lands secure, his engineers would proceed to carve a canal through the sands of the Suez into the Red Sea, which would become the seaway to the Indian Ocean. Then, whether by land or by sea or by both, he would have his route to India.

As Napoleon then saw it, Pitt of Britain might well be dismayed enough, by the gradually unrolling plan of strategy, and growing domestic unrest due to the cost of empire-building, to meet him accommodatingly at a bargaining table in London — a city he was determined to visit, whether by invitation or by force.

On May 19, 1798, from many rallying ports along France's Mediterranean shore, Napoleon's expedition, contingent by contingent, set sail, covered by a competent naval flotilla from Toulon. By strange mischance and good fortune for the French, Horatio Lord Nelson found the hunting bad. The contingent's unresisted seizing of Malta enroute would be noted with concern and perhaps hostility by Russia. Greece, Turkey and Britain would disapprove. But Napoleon had read history.

He knew the role of Malta for invasions, particularly in the Crusades, and he himself was planning to go on through the lands of Darius and Suliman. With the British searching flotilla mercifully elsewhere, on July 1, 1798, Napoleon's expedition landed safely and without interference west of Aboukir. Without pause, Napoleon pushed on under conditions of incredible desert heat and thirst to meet the numerically strong but militarily inferior Egyptians. Physically tortured and spiritually discouraged as they were by the seemingly impossible mission on foot through soft, scorching sand, generals and soldiers alike considered unnatural their commander's utterly indomitable determination to succeed.

Arrived at the refreshing shores of the Nile, Napoleon still pressed his campaign with great urgency. He defeated the brave but outmatched Mameluke cavalry at battles amongst the pyramids, achieving great losses to the Egyptians with remarkably light casualties. The fighting was over in three weeks.

But while Napoleon was triumphantly engaged up the Nile, Nelson's Mediterranean fleet caught the still assembled transport that had brought his army to Egypt. The battle of Aboukir Bay on August 1, 1798 saw this fleet, so essential to Napoleon's grand plan of an eastward thrust, almost decimated. This would not be the last time Nelson would frustrate Napoleon's vaulting ambition.

Establishing a worthy and respected native civilian government in quickly pacified Egypt, and discovering the ways of Mohammedanism, Napoleon continued to plan his thrust to the east. It must have been a peculiarly difficult task, in many ways. Not the least of his troubles was that he had learned from Paris reports that Josephine had formed a romantic and conspicuous relationship with a young army officer, to the entertainment of social and military circles there. Napoleon's vaunted sang-froid under any and all embarrassments was for a time shattered. He deeply loved Josephine, as his passionate letters showed, and he was proud.

It was at this time and in an unaccustomed mood of obviously reckless rage that Napoleon led an attack on Syria and laid futile siege to the stubborn fort at Acre. Once again an English fleet commander, Sir Sidney Smith, would be the pursuing naval nemesis of his elaborate enterprise. Smith intercepted and took possession of the carriers transporting artillery for the campaign. Without his heaviest weapons, Napoleon reluctantly abandoned the siege. Retreating, he encountered and brilliantly defeated a relieving army under Abdallah Pasha. Again there was a trek across desert wastes under conditions of heat and disease, with grievous loss of lives. There followed at Cairo a Turkish invasion attempt which was turned away at Aboukir at great cost to the Turks. But Napoleon, in returning to Egypt, had retreated wholly from his cherished plan of Asian conquest. It was the story of another Caesar — without the relief of a Cleopatra.

Cairo was left administratively improved by Napoleon's period of intervention in Egyptian affairs. It is remarkable that during this Egyptian interlude, emulating his historic mentor, Alexander, he established a warm relationship with the Egyptians who first had stood in awe of so famed a figure. Indeed, he related to people of the eastern Mediterranean so well that he could speak seriously of embracing Mohammedanism and devoting the rest of his life to Islamic affairs. But Nelson's and Sidney Smith's attacks on his sea forces had ended his dream of an Empire of the Orient to link with France and Italy. More realistically inclined, Napoleon passed command of his army in Egypt to Kleber. Without the formality of obtaining permission from the War Office in Paris, and at the very real risk of being captured by the British Navy, he gathered savants and civic planners who had been taken to Egypt and set sail for Frejus, in France. His welcome there and elsewhere on the route to Paris was tumultuous. His victory over the Turks at Aboukir was remembered, his defeats and disappointments forgotten.

In Napoleon's absence, affairs of the republic had lapsed into so parlous a state only a firm military leadership or, as was suggested by the royalists, a return of the Bourbons to power, could prevent national chaos. As provisional leader of France Abbé Siéyès was talking openly of his need for a military leader of force and firmness. In Napoleon, exactly the kind of man he needed had appeared in Paris, amidst great public acclaim.

Once more Napoleon's belief that he was fated to rule and restore France leaped high. To all but the Bourbons he became again the man of the hour. But for that tireless plotter, d'Artois, this was a disconcerting development. A laboriously planned coup was all but ready to release. Succeeding, it would return Louis to his throne. Now they must again wait for the republicans to fail.

There had been, indeed, public disillusionment over delayed arrival of the Revolution's promised benefits to the masses. The Jacobins, whose ranks included the remnants of the makers of the Terror, shared with the royalists a vested interest in disorganizing government and the economy.

Prices were high and there was little respect for the currency of France as paper money drove gold and silver coinage into hiding. Food and other essentials were in short supply and peasants, especially of the still heavily Catholic Vendée region of western France, were restless and hostile. Conscription for military service was taking too many of their able young men.

Siéyès and Napoleon, with the help of a still jealous and stiffly unfriendly Moreau, accomplished the political in-fighting for control of the powers of the councils of the Ancients and of the Five Hundred. There Jacobin and royalist contention underlay the struggle for the crucial margin of strength that would produce control of the republic. "I seek a sword," Siéyès had cried, before Napoleon arrived — and it was only the sword he wanted from Napoleon. But so skilful were Napoleon's maneuverings on a totally different and unfamiliar field of conflict that he and his brother, Lucien, would soon neutralize Siéyès' efforts to emerge with supreme power. The council, riven with the discord of the royalist, Jacobin and republican debate, was unwilling to listen to Napoleon.

When Napoleon's "sword" of authority was unsheathed it was supported by the strength of a force of eagerly loyal grenadiers whose drums beat out the charge as troops cleared the room of the Council of Five Hundred while brother Lucien, president of the Council, gave his blessing to action that was to become celebrated as the coup of the 18th of Brumaire. The rump of unexpelled and friendly council members authorized a provisional consulate of three. Of this group, by dominance of personality and prestige, Napoleon soon was senior member then the First Consul, functioning under a new constitution.

It was at this juncture that Bourbon agents discussed with Napoleon the possibility that he might work to effect a return of the Bourbons to power. Were he to play 'General Monk' to Louis Eighteenth's Charles II of Britain, it was promised, he could count on fine rewards and a brilliant future.

Napoleon's blunt reply was that any attempt to restore a Bourbon to kingship would cost enormous slaughter. Such a monarchy, he said, had no place in any plan for France. In plainest terms the messengers learned that Napoleon was not prepared to master-mind a Bourbon restoration. Within the period of that interview, it could be defensibly argued that Napoleon in effect laid his stepping stones to the throne — and condemned himself to death.

11

Legacies of Leadership

IN 1799, AT AGE 30, the affairs of a nation at his command to change and mold almost wholly as he personally chose, with health and energy equal to his illimitable ambition, Napoleon's successes had inspired in him a strong sense of adequacy to his self-selected tasks. His verve and sureness were contagious. At last, in a country suffering from a post-revolutionary sense of having been severed from its past, still growling and trembling from the excesses of the Terror, was a brilliant young leader come to give order and direction to the nation.

Frenchmen of his generation would hardly realize that this almost incredible military genius, who had succeeded so dramatically in war, had done much to qualify himself to play statesman. He had delved into the triumphs and mistakes of the Greek and Roman civilizations. In the days when he served his apprenticeship to the arts and science of war, he had had educational introduction to Greek and Roman history which would encourage him to read such historians and philosophers as Herodatus, Pliny, Cicero, Thucydides, Livy, Tacitus and others. Today this would be called getting historical perspective. But having qualified in the role of conqueror, in the course of his later career he quite unabashedly could picture himself as a figure of history, one of a company of past great leaders, military and civil.

Beyond any of his fellows, in training for war, he had early begun to explore the written accounts of men and governments of the great Mediterranean civilizations. Not merely the battles of Alexander and Julius Caesar interested him. Their administrative efforts he studied, too. When he moved into the Tuileries, palace of the Bourbons, he would instal a bust of

Brutus, the Roman patriot. If Caesar was an example, Brutus was a reminder that one could not ignore the human instinct to rebel against unbridled power. It would explain Napoleon's constant sensitivity to a need to consider public opinion. He would use his power to uplift France in a myriad ways the people could see and approve.

His move from the Luxembourg palace to the grandeur of the Tuileries he warranted on grounds of practicality. Luxembourg was inconvenient and cramping. For great plans and events he needed room. In the Tuileries the consul would be where the Bourbons had been — and of course, the seniors of the ancient house would not fail to observe this usurping of their place. Napoleon would see to it that he would still have democratic ways. There would not be any great public outcry against his gradual exercising of the old privileges of all the past inhabitants of the Tuileries.

Napoleon was a better student and philosopher of history than Rousseau, architect of the Revolution. He believed that deeply engrained in the French people was a love of theatre in their affairs. He abandoned the Cromwellian bleakness of the philosophy he had early heard from Robespierre's lips — he had been a protégé of the great Robespierre's brother — and while still first consul restored much of the pomp and ceremony that had dazzled Parisians for many generations as the kings played out their royal dramas while keeping deliberately in public view and hearing.

Legitimately a genius at war, in the view of credible critics, surely Napoleon must be conceded no less an acclaim for the finesse he displayed in being kingly, for those who wanted a king, and a republican chief consul and eventually a people's "revolutionary" monarch for Frenchmen who once had been willing to suffer the agonies along with the exultation of revolution rather than go on with their lot under the sceptered rule of the house of Bourbon.

In exquisitely calculated measure Napoleon blended the army's love of its 'little corporal' and his authentically Jacobin origins with his country's appreciation of the four years of peace and stability, and the citizenry's lost divertissement in state pageantry. Around Parisians, as plain as day, were fast appearing all the many physical evidences of the work of the new ruler in the Tuileries. Risen from the people of the revolution, wearing on his hat at ceremonies the tricolor cockade of France's insignia of revolt against the Bourbon dynasty, without a drop of royal blood in his body, this relative youth was responsible for an elevation of the country's material life and spirit. His works were physically taking shape and this despite occasional attempted interferences by royalists and by those die-hards amongst Jacobins who wanted Bastille Day to go on forever.

The revolution had released and Napoleon had organized and directed energies and initiatives beyond anything the people of France had thought to be latently within their race. The Bourbonists silently suffered as they watched the imitator of the panoplies they had cultivated to represent the splendor of the historic French Kingdom, personified in its King. The Jacobins raged impotently at the rise of a dictator who was taking France away from a spirit of vengefulness, arrogating to himself the functions of the Directory and the Council of State and doing it to national applause unprecedented in the history of France.

As a student of history, Napoleon knew and would say that his future depended upon new works, new achievements, a spirit of continuously bold emprise which would give the French un-ending evidence of this new and exciting era of national progress. There must not again be dullness. He gambled that this new spirit would be acceptably embodied in him, a man not of the old royalty but displaying royal manners, and functioning as one who was at home in the great edifices that were part of the heritage of the French nation.

With the cool calculation of a director of the new national theatre of France, Napoleon would dress and deport himself to be an occupant of the foremost office of France. Already he knew the power of his controlled fury with stupidity or opposi-tion to terrify those who might fail him. Equally, he knew that to his now demonstrated ability to persuade men happily to serve their country through his agency, he now must add the immense psychological advantage that fame and magnificence can give to personality and presence.

He was a world pioneer in evolving a central banking system. Even without it he had already taken charge of the chaotic currency situation and, though the country was still weighed down by the burdens of war, boldly placed France's monetary system on a gold standard. The paper assignats of the Directory, almost worthless in the hands of the receiver, disappeared. The resulting confidence generated in the common medium of exchange earned the youthful leader popular gratitude and inspired investment and enterprise. Prices became stable again. He gained a lasting psychological advantage in his relations with a public responsive to his efforts to produce secure boundaries and domestic stability.

In the turmoil of the revolution and the post-revolutionary period the rule of law in France inevitably had suffered. Napoleon introduced reforms and inspired a high degree of codification of the civil law. The result was that, in addition to the constitution adopted in 1799, a virtual bill of rights was established in terms of common sense and practicality. The well conceived advantage was that the performance of the courts of justice could be weighed against the rights of the citizenry in clearly established and published terms. The Code Napoleon was a watershed event in France's history. Other countries were to borrow freely from this measure for justice under the law.

Without dedication to religion through any denomination, Napoleon supported the principles of freedom of religion, respected the rights of the Catholic Church to its properties and the people to their places and services of worship without encouraging any retreat from the Revolution's separation of Church and State.

As an individual he was more than ordinarily dedicated to the proposition that racial discrimination was damaging not merely to the injured but to the well-being of the nation. He was at heart an internationalist in his attitude toward nationals of other countries. His ability to establish at will an almost instantaneous rapport with strangers and foreigners was an extension of humanistic tendencies that could exist in the same mind and personality with the capability to hurl scores of thousands of men into almost certain death for the glory of France and his own insatiable hunger for achievement through victories at arms.

Pursuing his tolerance of the rights of individuals within the codes and constitution of France he was always ready to remind the masses that, with monarchical power, he still upheld the motto of the Revolution: 'Liberty, Equality, Fraternity'. Consistently, he was the first monarch in Europe to ensure to Jews in France and Italy the rights — civil, property and religious — that until his time were denied them in all other countries.

Above all, he encouraged in France an aristocracy of learning while democratizing its processes. Access to education having been hugely widened, Napoleon insisted that opportunity to make use of learning for the advancement of individuals and the nation should be unrestricted and encouraged.

In his own area of exercised right to reward he commonly advanced common soldiers or non-commissioned officers to officer rank in the field in instant recognition of some act of extreme bravery or initiative. For this and his common touch he was revered in the ranks. He discouraged an elite officer class, as such, and his saying was quoted around the world that a field marshal's baton was in every young soldier's knapsack.

A high proportion of Napoleon's officers had come from rough and humble origins. Some carried a degree of crudeness and vulgarity through their lives who were men of high rank and distinction. They had won their epaulets by obedience, dash and bravery. With Napoleon's personal-command style of military operation, that kind of officer could be extremely valuable and responsible for many a victory. It was only when he placed highly valorous but low intellect marshals in positions where — as when he himself might be ill — he would need swift and changing battle judgments to be made that he would suffer from their inability to think.

The debate has been unending as to the merits and demerits of Napoleon's one-man-command-post type of army management. His results were good for so long — indeed, until he began to be the victim of illnesses now believed to have been deliberately imposed upon him — that his methods had high merit. He had men of resourcefulness in Davout, Caulaincourt, Carnot, Macdonald, Poniatowski and others. Largely unresolved is the question of whether or not under Napoleon's system such a talent as that of a Wellington could have been developed.

The significance of the suppression of snobbery in Napoleon's army while giving pride and recognition full play touched the life of France much more widely than in merely martial affairs. The emperor who had the wholesome instincts of a burgher was good for the release of talent within all strata of society. The wrong accent or the lack of a certain stripe and color of cravat has closed no doors in France from Napoleon's day down to modern times.

Popular education, which had languished, grew with a great increase in the numbers of institutions of learning established. There ensued profoundly favorable effects on the rate of literacy in France and in the ability of the average youth to make a useful contribution to the life and progress of the country. At the seats of higher learning stimulus was given to rapidly increased enrolments in the fields of advanced learning: in medicine, law, engineering and the sciences, and in officer training. Class consciousness was discouraged so that any citizen could aspire to advance, limited only by personal ability.

Architecture and the arts flourished under the encouragement of Napoleon's kingly consulship. Modern Paris still acknowledges as Napoleon's gift its right to be referred to as the world's most beautiful city. Medieval streets of jumbled structures had given way to wide boulevards. Quays and bridges changed the Seine from a traffic inconvenience to a cherished feature of the city's life.

Always conspicuously concerned with the well-being of even the lowest ranks of the army of France, Napoleon reformed a condition whereby many wounded veterans of France's campaigns were living without health, money or organized care. Les Invalides grew as a hospital and nursing home for disabled or aged war veterans. Napoleon would ask at St. Helena that his final entombment should be on banks of the Seine in Paris, where his ashes now repose.

In the intervals of peace but as well when he was in the field and heavily involved as supreme commander of France's army forces, often in close contact with the enemy, Napoleon received and dealt with a mass of correspondence and dispatched specific instructions for the conduct of civil affairs. For instance, in giving France its national center for the performing arts, the Théâtre Français, Napoleon, in the midst of the severe problems of the Russian campaign, wrote at Moscow and sent to Paris the guiding rules and regulations whereby the society administering the theatre would operate.

It was usual for this duty to engage the services of a battery of secretarial aides, headed by his friend and secretary, Bourienne. To these he dictated in turns. Often such work continued far into the night while others of his top command were snatching sleep against the next day's arduous demands. Napoleon, in his prime, as chroniclers of the time testified, seemed wholly immune to physical or mental fatigue. The vast bulk of his orders and letters, from the time he became chief executive of France and her conquered border states until he left for exile, plainly supports such testimony.

The validity of his policy of using royal trappings in a France so recently released from centuries of monarchism would have been confirmed in his own mind after both of his abdications. Driving with his entourage down the road to embark for Elba, no longer Emperor of France and King of Italy, his coach was pelted and jostled by peasants. Again, after Waterloo and his second abdication at Fontainebleau, he was bereft of nearly all support of the marshals he had made wealthy and famous and would learn that, in Paris, already the city had written him out of its calculations of who and what things were then of concern.

But early in the year 1800, at the outset of his chief consulship, Napoleon was demonstrating, to the pleased surprise of the current populace of France and to the amazement of historians ever since, a deft sureness of touch as he began dealing with the problems of a country truly on the edge of collapse of its monetary system and of its equally shaky governmental system of administering public affairs. Without war to distract him from his new interest, and with the powers of chief consul virtually whatever he wanted to assume them to be, Napoleon moved with characteristic speed and determination. He combined, with repression of press criticism, an expeditious set of reforms that saved the situation. In so doing he was a benevolent dictator long before he would become an Emperor.

Until illnesses began to sap his strength, Napoleon's career in his hey-day was a triumphant time of self-realization and of unfettered release of previously unknown administrative capacities. From 1800 until his downfall, as nearly as one man, in body and mind, could personify France, the slight, indefatigable Corsican might be called 'The State' in France. Other men have commanded authoritarian power over greater numbers of people but none other in history himself originated and administered so complex and far-ranging a set of reforms and rules for the administration of a relatively modern state as did Napoleon. His restraint, sense of justice and safeguards for an enlightened government were such that though they were framed for an authoritarian state administered as a military regime and continued under his monarchical rule, they would later serve well as the basis for conducting the affairs of a number of constitutional monarchists and republican governments, down to modern days. These principles would survive the tests of time, of war emergencies, and the needs of popularly elected and advanced societies. More than at any time before Napoleon's rise or after his going from the Tuileries and Fontainebleau, France gave international leadership and influenced the procedures of civil administration for the new era of industrialization and popular education which would usher in the modern age of science and commerce. Here the genius of Napoleon was not least of all evidenced by his exertion of power which might have been despotic and restrictive. Instead, giving France a heady sense of leading civilization across new and non-military frontiers, he developed a unique degree of national pride and confidence through a sovereign statesmanship that had far more of intrinsic merit than the bread and circuses in Rome of the age of the Caesars.

12

The Struggle for a Throne

THE PEACE OF AMIENS, signed in March 1802 between Britain and France, grew in part from Napoleon's commitment as first consul to bring peace to his nation. This good resolution was reinforced by the fact that France's ally, Denmark, had seen its fleet destroyed at Copenhagen by Lord Nelson who obviously was in a position to checkmate any physical preparations for the rather indefinite plan to invade Britain. Napoleon could plead that the British had delayed his peaceful intentions by defeating Kleber's forces in Egypt in March of 1801. With Pitt out of office and honors between the two countries about even, a brief and amiable relationship existed between France of the first consulate and Britain under the less militant Fox.

The affairs of state found Napoleon and Josephine rehearsing for later roles in which they would wear crowns and ermine robes of royalty. When the first consul and Madame Bonaparte held court it was Josephine who was well qualified to take the lead in returning to the Tuileries the graces of court life in a manner not seen since Bourbon days. Napoleon, whose manners at first were more soldierly than suave, was adopting kingly ways but with a robustness of style reminiscent of the pre-medieval warrior kings of Europe.

British plenipotentiaries and political leaders, visiting the capital of a customarily enemy country, were impressed by the changing face of post-revolutionary Paris. With most their chief interest was in meeting the now celebrated soldier, Bonaparte, elevated to the position of a peacetime head of state. It apparently was impossible that an exchange of visits could be arranged between George III and Napoleon. The monarch would be met not by his equal in regality but by a citizen soldier who, though adopting some of the ceremonial styles of monarchy, was the head of a *republican* state.

It is possible that the situation in which Napoleon was less than a king or a prince-regent in courtly precedence but more powerful than any wearer of a crown in all Europe may have caused him to think of a time when he might have vaulted all the obstacles and be a fully accredited king, dressed in the purple robes honored since antiquity as the garb of royal rulers.

In any case, as part of the retreat from the revolution, Napoleon extended a welcome to many royal emigrants to return to France. He invited those who had remained to renew their contributions toward French society. The era was both helpful and disconcerting to the Bourbonists. They no longer could point to Napoleon as the arch-enemy of royalists. However, they could more conveniently conduct their own unending efforts to regain at least part of their former lands, mansions and inherited privileges. Specifically excluded, however, were all who had been members of the Bourbon royal household.

Napoleon, the rough soldier who had never lacked for boldness, was submitting to becoming gradually more polished and sophisticated. He was reassured by public acclaim, pleased to be at peace with the Church of Rome through his arranged Concordat, and to have a growing personal identification with titled people of the Old Regime.

The rising sense of social occasion and his actor's awareness of his need to develop a presence to accompany his already legendary fame would have erased Napoleon's remaining vestiges of the Jacobinism he first embraced as an ambitious young soldier. A more acute sensitiveness to the effects upon the Bourbons of being excluded from his amnesty provisions, might have served him well then and later. It was one of the myriad contradictions of the Napoleon career and character that he feared in a generalized way the Bourbon revenge but he was not fearful of their friends. On the contrary, he attempted cultivation of their confidence in him, perhaps with a hope, even then, that he might stand, in every essential respect and by every outward sign, fully level with those of old royal lineage in France. From that point there could be no knowing where an almost absurdly favoring Fate might permit him to continue his ascent.

Not all the revolutionary generals could make the transition to the old order of court ceremonials. They could not forget that two million Frenchmen had died in the revolution to abolish Bourbonism. They saw the old trappings of the imperial court returning to use. Moreau, one of the most reserved and unresponsive to the new order amongst Napoleon's generals, was one day invited by Berthier to breakfast at the Tuileries, later to attend the levee of the chief consul, thereafter go on to Notre Dame for the *Te Deum* at which Louis XVI's former archbishop would preside, then to have lunch at the Tuileries. Moreau was confident enough of his military essentiality to Napoleon to reply gruffly: "I accept the last part of your invitation."

In 1802 Napoleon had furthered his upward course when he became president of the Cisalpine republic. With this honor went almost total personal power to order the course of affairs in the conquered areas east of the Alps. Such authority may in itself have suggested that the first consul should be consul for life. The senate approving the proposal, in May of that year Napoleon's peaceful overthrow of the basic tenet of republicanism was completed. It was logical that he should next be given the right to name his successor. In the absence of an heir, this right, too, was accorded him. It was a gradual rise toward kingship.

The course of peace with England was frequently placed under the strain of statements made in the land of free speech and freedom to publish. In London newspapers and in Parliament protests arose at the accumulating rights for Napoleon to exercise the prerogatives of great individual power while launching France on an era of empire building. The ancient sovereignty of Switzerland was removed through an invasion of an army of 40,000 under General Ney. Britain reacted with alarm to this evidence that Napoleon's France was on the move again and that strategically-located Switzerland had become in effect a province of France.

Through the treaty of Amiens France had gained new rights of commerce in various seaports. But in the ensuing peace the secret provisions of earlier treaties came to light. When to this annoyance was added the charge that privileged representatives of France had been using freedom of travel in Britain to map some leading seaports, the strain on relations became extreme.

At this juncture Napoleon attempted to repair the breach with the Bourbons and the royalists. On the condition that Louis XVIII, then resident in Poland, would sign a deed of renunciation of all claim by the Bourbons on the throne of France, Louis could live in Italy and Bourbon princes would be given independent Italian dominions. Louis haughtily, courteously and yet insultingly replied through an intermediary in Warsaw. "I do not confound Monsieur Bonaparte," he said, "with those who have preceded him. I esteem his bravery and military genius . . . But he is mistaken if he supposes that my rights can ever be made the subject of bargaining and compromise." The rejection is said to have infuriated Napoleon chiefly becaue Louis chose to recognize him only as *Monsieur* Bonaparte. He angrily denied that he had empowered the intermediary to make such an offer. But Bourbon princes of the time testified that the approach had been made and repulsed. For their part the Bourbons undoubtedly were as much affronted by the suggestion of demotion to rule insignificant principalities as Napoleon had been shocked to be addressed as mere "Mister" Bonaparte.

Under the strain of re-arming in both their countries, Napoleon confronted and denounced the British ambassador, Lord Whitworth, at a levee in Paris, the vehement accusations of British breachings of the treaty occupying two hours of intemperate language that embarrassed Talleyrand and the court. On May 18, 1803 Great Britain, again under Pitt, declared war on France. Britain seized French ships and cargoes. Napoleon ordered the arresting of some 10,000 British travellers, many of high positions, in France.

Soon it was as though no period of relative friendship had intervened. Napoleon was threatening an invasion of Britain. Generations in Britain would hear the story of the watch of soldiers and volunteers, with King George III among them, on the southerly coasts of England, and of the patrolling ships of the Royal Navy. In the winter of 1803 France's many ports were so closely blockaded that no flotillas could escape to rendezvous at sea and give protection to a planned landing of armies under Soult, Ney, Davout and Victor — interfering with Napoleon's cherished wish to tour London as a conqueror.

Depending in some degree on the inclination of their sympathies, historians of the nineteenth century have disagreed on the circumstances and interpretation of the Cadoudal and Pichegru resistance to Napoleon's new imperialism. The Bonapartist version is that Moreau and Pichegru, whose sphere of command was with the army on the Rhine, had long harbored a sense of resentment against the preference given by Napoleon to the marshals who had risen with him in the army of Italy and on the Austrian front. Pichegru was found to have corresponded with Bourbonist factions. Other accounts describe the rift as due to dissatisfaction of such former revolutionary and republican generals as Carnot, Moreau and Pichegru with the return of a form of government closely resembling monarchical power.

To the charge that he was aping Bourbonism and bending French affairs in the direction of a revived imperialism, Napoleon responded with his Legion of Honor. It would democratize the granting of honors, recognizing exemplary service to France, from whatever direction, civil as well as military, it might come. Ever after, Napoleon would wear the symbol of the Legion on his Chasseurs of the Guards uniform, and France would cherish its honored recognition of meritorious duty in the nation's interest.

Pichegru was banished for his Bourbonist sympathies and affiliations and Moreau was accused of being the focus of republican plans to depose Napoleon. Upon Pichegru's secret return from England to Paris, allegedly with British assistance, and in furtherance of Bourbonist plans of the Duke of Artois, the charge was made that Georges Cadoudal and other Chouan leaders had conferred with him to plot against Napoleon. It was announced that security police had discovered a new plot against the life of Napoleon. Cadoudal fled but Moreau, declared to have conferred with Cadoudal and Pichegru, was arrested. He admitted to attending meetings but denied that he was part of a conspiracy to produce a coup in which 150 men would assemble in the uniforms of the consular guard at Malmaison and seize Napoleon.

Moreau's popularity in France was such that his trial for treason resulted only in his banishment to America for two years. Cadoudal and eighteen associates were tried and executed.

Out of this presumed conspiracy to overthrow and possibly kill Napoleon there came the retaliatory illegal seizing of the Duke of Enghein at Baden, near French territory. Charged with having conspired with the Bourbons and with England to overthrow the Bonaparte administration, he was given summary trial and executed. Murat, Talleyrand, Caulaincourt and Savary expedited the judgment of death under a verdict which enemies of Napoleon declared had been pre-determined by the chief consul. Napoleon ever after contended that while the trial did not conform with the provisions of the law, it was conducted in the atmosphere and emergency of a treasonous conspiracy and that when the circumstances were considered the verdict of guilty was justifiable. Enghien was depicted as having planned to lead a force against Salsburg under a plan worked out by the confessed rebels, Cadoudal, and Pichegru.

Throughout the feudal states of Europe and in England the death of the Duke of Enghien was called murder, and opinion was newly inflamed against France. Both Pichegru and the British captain accused of having landed him in France died under circumstances in prison that struck dissidents with fear. The incident reinforced the enmity of the Bourbon adherents and so angered neighboring countries, with whom France was still at peace, that talk of war revived.

On April 30, 1804, scarcely a month from the incident of d'Enghien's execution, it was proposed in the tribunate that in recognition of the eminence to which France had risen, the new tranquillity in the land, a restoration of the finances of the country and the introduction of just codes of law the chief consul should be confirmed in office for life. It was added that supreme power should be hereditary in the person and family of Napoleon. From there it was but a short step to agreeing that Napoleon's new title should be Emperor of the French and King of Italy.

In a public plebiscite on the return to an outright monarchy, three millions voted affirmatively, not more than three thousand against.

The revisionary change, creating a royal house of Bonaparte in which Napoleon's family members would be the new royalty, was given effect in the coronation of Napoleon and Josephine at

Notre Dame on December 2, 1804. For that occasion Pope Pius VII, acquiescing to what amounted to a command religious performance, officiated up to the point of the actual placing of the crowns. At that point, Napoleon took his crown firmly in his own hands and placed it on his head. He repeated the startling gesture of independence in the crowning of the Empress Josephine.

In one brief act the soldier who, but for the grace of a single year, would have been foreign born, who was a commoner and once a Jacobite member of a revolutionary army, made a compromising gesture toward the Church, embraced the concept of hereditary monarchy, defied convention, and gave the common people of France and the world-at-large the clear evidence that he was his own man. He wore the crown, not because it had been bestowed upon him by chance of birth and heredity, or by gift, but by the works of his own hands — hands that would not allow others to finish the ceremony.

The boldness of that ceremonial gesture is without parallel in history. It was the supreme paradox of Napoleon's life that, reaching for the symbol of the most orthodox of all forms of rulership, he should introduce wilfully so unorthodox a departure from one of the most ancient of the royal rituals of Christendom. How studied and premeditated it was is open to speculation. Certainly it occasioned pain to the devoutly religious, tending as it did to demean the office of the church's Vicar of Christ. In France the royalists said — but only in whispers — that the usurper of the throne was insufferable and must go. And the republicans, wanting no return to the chaos from which France had so lately emerged, smiled and turned more tolerant toward the new Napoleon.

As the year 1805 opened, Napoleon would be conscious of two further achievements essential to his ultimate satisfaction. He must free himself from the disapproval and the military threat of England, a country he reluctantly respected and admired — and he must have descendants to perpetuate the fulfilment of his ambitions. At 36 he could foresee his place in history. But he must still deal vigorously with the obdurate enemy above the English Channel. That he had succeeded so well in improving the affairs of France would seem to legitimize an ambition to do as much for all Europe.

One reads the record in vain for indication that at this point in his career Napoleon felt seriously insecure from two significant circumstances. He had no navy to challenge the sea supremacy of Britain; and he had committed the unforgivable in rejecting the role of military caretaker of the Bourbons' throne. He had dared to occupy that throne himself, probably to the future total exclusion of the former ruling family. Yet these were the two forces that would lead to ultimate defeat, exile and death.

Genius though he was, militarily and administratively, Napoleon seems to have been remarkably insensible to the predictable outrage and enmity of the Bourbons. And the reaction of the hereditary dynasts of the house of Bourbon would have been one of growing fear. Hatred spawns in such a favorable bed of mental anguish. As the Bourbons would see it, the Corsican soldier-adventurer, assuming their throne, not only had conquered externally on a scale they could not have equalled but had won the affection of the people as the Bourbons seemed destined never to do. And worst of all, he had summarily tried and killed a Bourbon prince of Conde, *le duc d'Enghien*. If he could do that how much less safe were Bourbons like Louis the Eighteenth and his brother, d'Artois!

How could Napoleon Bonaparte who, from his Corsican origins should have been a cautious, sceptical man, have been so naively trusting in the face of a constant royalist conspiracy well known to him to exist?

In abandoning even the posture of attempting an invasion of England and shifting his attention to Austria, Napoleon set in motion two naval procedures, one French and one British. He freed for wider service against France the Royal Navy's ships of the English Channel fleet under Nelson. Coincidentally, he created a need for his Atlantic fleet, commanded by Admiral Villeneuve, to move into the Mediterranean to secure sea transport of army personnel and materiel through bases along the Mediterranean shore. The operation was hazardous for the combined French and Spanish fleets since Britain's strongest and most aggressive arm in war would inevitably close with the allied fleet as it maneuvered for passage through the Straits of Gibraltar. The secure Gibraltar station commanded that gateway to the Mediterranean. For France severe and unaffordable losses to her fleet would be risked, but once through the Straits the ships could be deployed along a friendly shore.

Napoleon's orders to Villeneuve were to sail from Cadiz, avoiding the enemy if possible but to engage them fully if in any situation of challenge they were not inferior to the enemy in strength. The terms were consistent with Napoleon's familiar style in many an army dispatch, but the sea was not his element.

Villeneuve left Cadiz on October 19, 1805 with 18 ships flying the tricolors of France and 15 the flag of Spain. Nelson, who was perhaps as brilliant a master of strategy at sea as Napoleon on land, divided his fleet of 27 ships into two columns. He then proceeded to perform the sea maneuver of splitting the enemy force to cut off, outnumber and destroy one major segment of the fleet. It was a tactic remarkably similar to the Napoleonic formula for a successful land action.

The battle off Trafalgar Bay on October 21 lost Napoleon 60 per cent of his fleet. From that point forward his campaigns of necessity were confined to massive land actions. The forces allied against him could count on the advantage that went with ability to blockade ports of Napoleon's empire, old or recently acquired. As regards trade and transport it was a severe handicap to the development of Napoleon's economic policy of continental solidarity against Britain, perennially the stumbling block to peace on his terms. Psychologically, this helped Britain bolster the future alliances from 1805 until 1815, a period when British ships and British money often were all that kept the forces of France's enemies in the field.

Deprived though he was of seapower, Napoleon exercised with great skill and dramatic effect his advantage of operating from a strong, central land base. He was favored, too, by his almost constant practice of seizing the initiative, by his swift land movements of men and materiel of war and the intangible strength of the high average level of morale he was able to instill in officers and soldiers alike. Men who fought for Napoleon had a way of becoming 'larger than life', more heroic than they had known themselves to be. This was the immeasurable advantage that seemed to generations of military historians to warrant their conclusion, after all of Napoleon's mistakes had been tallied, that he was unexampled as a military commander of armies in either large or small scale operations.

Later than in his own time, under the drier judgment of other wars and peacetimes, it would tend to be written that Napoleon had begun to falter as his military fronts greatly extended and his personal-command-post strategy in war became incapable of containing all the events of action within his personal comprehension and control. If this is generally conceded to be a sound appreciation of what was happening in Europe as his eastern front extended to the Baltic and Russia, we must now, as well, take into reckoning the fact that a new circumstance had developed. The man at the one-man-command post, upon whom so much depended, was personally faltering from sudden illnesses. They were such as never before had come to partly paralyze his decision-making judgments.

It will be naive and unrealistic henceforth not to appreciate that increasingly he fought against injuries being done him physically by an unseen and unsuspected enemy. The damage inflicted was and remains incalculable in any scale at our disposal, but it was real. We must contemplate the fact that science today tells us positively that Napoleon was poisoned with arsenic at a time which could and no doubt did include the days of the Battle of Waterloo. He had very similar symptoms at Borodino, Dresden and Leipzig. Borodino began his downfall, Leipzig opened a period that led to his first abdication and Waterloo destroyed his great military career.

War has no way of conceding a truce to a commander of armies on the basis that he has become ill. Military historians attempt total impartiality of judgment. They would remark the illnesses of Napoleon as incidental to accounts that in great detail review the rights and wrongs of decisions made in the heat of battle in the later Napoleonic wars. The Forshufvud discovery must impel some significant reassessments to be made, bearing in mind the very strong likelihood that Napoleon commanded — or failed to command — the details of some major battles while his system struggled to cope with arsenic. Against this poison his stomach rebelled and his bloodstream carried to his normally hyper-acute mind in the noise, smoke, blood and confusion of battle a chemical that could not fail to reduce its efficiency.

It may be impossible to define from what particular time forward Napoleon experienced the symptoms of poisoning, but a reason to consider him the source and embodiment of all their frustrated hopes to reign and rule again in France was certainly given to the members and supporters of the house of Bourbon when Napoleon first revealed his intention to occupy their idle throne.

13

A Man for Power and Glory

WE HAVE LOOKED in brief outline but still with enough detailed observation of the career of Napoleon Bonaparte up to the founding of the First Empire to allow us to see a man ruthlessly committed to doing good things for his country as he perceived the definition of his country's good to be. We have seen a thrustful man, on his way to being the central figure of the civilized world of his time.

Knowing him at this formative phase of his career, while still developing his ultimate dream of world dominion for France, will help us to appreciate the adjustment he was suddenly compelled to make when he was received as a respected captive and taken to the infinitely smaller field of places, men and events as emperor ruling the Island of Elba.

Later we shall see him at St. Helena, reduced as though viewed through the reversed end of a telescope. It will be hard to recognize in him then the youthful courageous soldier and bold planner who would consider it his fate-ordained duty to change the world just as he would change a great city.

With his accession to the throne of continental Europe this strangely talented soldier of frequently contradictory reactions and behavior had been constant in one thing, at least — his frankly eager and unconcealed pursuit of power. In this he could draw on a resource of physical and nervous energy of astonishing vigor. His personal force welled up from a rugged constitution in support of an inquisitive, receptive, unfettered and coolly analytical mind.

Essentially, when he became no longer the chief consul but Napoleon I, Emperor in place of Louis XVIII, he had set in motion a chain of events that would bring him to his cruel death.

Yet in the interval he would transfix the world with both the glory and the menace of his actions.

Following his coronation Napoleon seemed almost mystically endowed. He would go on to his most brilliant of armed achievements in the victory over Austria and Russia at Austerlitz in 1805, wiping out the third coalition of enemies. He lost the friendship of Prussia and of Bourbon Spain and once more courted British co-operation — but still in vain. He fought the Battle of Jena in 1806, defeating the Prussian army wholly and from Berlin directed a campaign calculated to blockade the continent against Britain. That nation of merchants and man-ufacturers, exploiting advantages of its industrial revolution, had committed its vigorous economy to exports and its Royal Navy to keeping open the trade routes and ports of commerce around the world. For Britain there could be no return to insular self-sufficiency. Now she must export to live. Napoleon threatened her with trade disaster.

After the battle of Friedland in 1807 continental Europe seemed in France's care. A period of warm friendship between former enemies France and Russia grew out of the personal accommodation of Napoleon and the young Tsar Alexander, as they worked out a treaty of peace on a conference raft in the river at Tilsit. In their memorable meeting it was agreed that Europe would be shaped to their design and that France should feel free to include Turkey in her orbit and move to weaken Britain's hold in India and Asia. Russia would support the continental system of trade. The embargo against Britain was expanding.

Once more Napoleon did violence to the security of the house of Bourbon. He had replaced the King of Naples with his brother Joseph. Now he forced Charles IV of Spain to yield to Joseph his more important throne at Madrid. Marshal Murat, who had married Napoleon's sister Catherine, became the appointed King of Naples. But in Spain Bourbon sympathizers produced continuing revolt and in 1808 the faltering rule of the incompetent Joseph was shaken by a military defeat at Baylen.

Britain had sensed that Spain was France's most vulnerable front. Thus Arthur Wellesley's army was set ashore in friendly Portugal in August, 1808 to begin the long and arduous

Peninsular campaign. It would grow and sap France's strength, with losses rising to 50,000 men a year; and it would consume some of her most prestigious military commanders. Here, in fact, was the beginning of the Bourbons' revenge. The legend of French invincibility, so valuable to Napoleon, was slipping.

While Austria re-armed and Napoleon and Tsar Alexander jousted, within their accord, over Russian sensitivity to prospective French influence in Turkey, elsewhere in Europe, with Britain's encouragement, insurrectionists took heart to oppose French rule. The great empire had begun to weigh heavily on victorious France. The insatiable needs of the army diverted the nation's manpower. Yet the famed and costly battle of Wagram (1809) was gloriously won against Austria and by 1810 France's dominion over European territory stretched from Spain to Turkey and from Belgium to the Baltic. Napoleon freely appointed kings, princes and dukes to serve the new Napoleonic empire. In deeds as well as in form and title he acted a part appropriate to the world's most powerful emperor.

Though Britain and the Spanish Bourbons were leeching French strength and in turn suffering in the process, by 1811 Napoleon's image had grown more Caesar-like than ever. He bestrode Europe, commanding it with the rapidity of his military actions, though his favorite campaign designs were becoming familiar to his enemies and more resistible. He was subject to recurring illness. His battles cost him more to win. Yet as emperor he was now a man to walk with the greatest of hereditary kings and princes. He had initiated boldly a new monarchy that now could not be denied its claim to legitimacy — except by Britain and the Bourbons.

At the unsettling age of 40, in 1809, Napoleon was conscious of his place in history having been inerasibly written. But time was passing and his lack of an heir posed the prospect that he might leave no one of direct descent to continue his new house of Bonaparte. Josephine would mischievously tell friends the situation was through no fault of hers; but assuredly she had reached an age when a pregnancy was unlikely. The reports reflecting on his virility had reached and nettled Napoleon, who broke the news to a swooning empress that he must have a younger wife.

Even before the divorce, Napoleon had discussed with Alexander the possibility of an arranged marriage with the Tsar's sister. When he learned that the empress-mother would not agree the Franco-Russian cordiality generated at the momentous meeting in Tilsit was affected. The thought that his first male heir might unite the kingdoms of France and Russia was exciting enough to be abandoned with reluctance and with a troubled sensing that ties with the young and amiable Tsar were not as strong and enduring as he and the "little father" of Russia had publicly avowed them to be.

The marriage with Josephine was dissolved, with approval of Napoleon's council, by declaring null the ceremonies that had united them. Bearing in mind her dalliances while he was in Egypt, Napoleon found it not impossible to do his duty to France and put Josephine aside. His empress would continue to be addressed as Empress and was given a pension of 2,000,000 francs to which Napoleon added another million from his privy purse.

The disaster of Wagram having befallen Austria after the catastrophic defeat at Austerlitz, the emperor Francis of Austria would be in a mood after the signing of the Treaty of Schoenbrunn to ensure peace between his country and France. Gen. Berthier brought him the diplomatic message from Paris that the Emperor Napoleon, once more marriageable, would look favorably on a union with the house of Hapsburg. The twenty-three-year-old archduchess Marie-Louise was the medium in mind. The Corsican upstart was not acceptable to the Empress at St. Petersburg, but to Francis of Austria he could seem more bearable as a prestigious son-in-law than as an apparently unbeatable enemy. It was a deal.

When Marie-Louise, conducted in state to Paris, had for the first time laid eyes upon the formidable yet gallant suitor in palatial surroundings her reactions toward the still youthful-looking Emperor were seemingly as favorable as were his toward the pretty if somewhat vapid girl who would replace Josephine at Fontainebleau. She is said to have exclaimed: "Your Majesty's pictures have not done you justice."

Marie-Louise was young and nubile and Napoleon's appraising eye would inform him that she should meet his requirements fully — quite as well as such a union would serve France's interests. A marriage would lower the risk of further war with Austria. The fair archduchess would be a pleasant partner in the worthy plan to give the world another Napoleon.

The marriage ceremony was celebrated in the Catholic faith of the Hapsburgs and of Napoleon's mother in April 1810. A year later, to Napoleon's inexpressible satisfaction, an infant son was in the waiting cradle and soon he had been christened — 'Napoleon', of course — in a great ceremonial service.

The natal year 1811 was one, therefore, of great felicity for Napoleon and for France. The country had observed with mixed feelings the costly wars in which the Emperor won new glories to raise both the country's pride and its operating cost of government. There was an ever-rising sense of France having firmly established herself in the civilized world as the bringer of new dispensations to peoples east of the Rhine. Of course the chilling accompaniment was the constant drain on youth and treasure of the country. Yet Napoleon's persuasive argument was undeniable: Wars to safeguard the borders of France and the revolutionary advancement of French interest against intolerant kings should be fought on foreign soil. This had been the national purpose since 1792. If France now longed for a cessation of war, she must agree that Napoleon kept the conflicts from creating havoc within France — and the heady victories supported the fervent hope of peaceful years to come.

All the world loves a royal infant.

Napoleon's talent in stage-managing the increasingly regal exercises of state had exhilarated the spirits of the populace of France. First he was the hero who had brought peace to France, then the savior of the core purpose of the revolution. This had been to give the people liberty from oppressive royalty of the Bourbons and from the extreme ecclesiasticism and the state-secured privileges of the Roman church.

Now, like many another happily calculating monarch, Napoleon could act in public the appealing role of loving father . . . and the father image caught the emotional sensibilities of a would-be republican people who had feared they were to be cheated of what they had been promised and sacrificed so much to buy — liberty, land ownership, rights under the law. They rejoiced in stories about the beautiful male child — *"l'Aiglon"* was a term of endearment and it recognized the proud father. Almost from the start he had been called *l'Aigle.*

Napoleon's *affaire de coeur* with the masses of the people of France had elements of inconsistency. But then, so much in all that there was about the man and his life was filled with contradictions.

He was cherished as emperor of a nation that had gone through a veritable hell to be republican. Most of those who were hostile to Emperor Napoleon were royalists, many of them working underground for the return of the Bourbons. Napoleon had come to believe that the people were more opposed to the Bourbons than to monarchy. He affronted some with his trappings of royalty. And yet the love of royal ceremony and great occasion was deeply ingrained in the French by monarchs who had lived like kings and dressed like peacocks. In modern times, they had showmanship and much of what it covered was shoddy and ineffectual of benefit to the rank and file of citizens.

Napoleon created and lived his own almost instant legend. He came from nowhere that was visible, was the story-teller's poor soldier without a fortune but with adventure in his heart and a great actor's mystique in evoking emotional response to his terse and challenging oratory.

Deeper than that true but somewhat superficial estimation of Napoleon's preferment to become a hereditary ruler was a more potently significant fact. Napoleon was of the burgher class. He was the previously unimaginable, ultimate burgher who could stand in royal ermine robes, wearing a jewelled crown.

He thought like a sensible man of the people, struggled upward, succeeded where the great majority would fail; he believed in hard work, self-discipline, abstemious habits of eating and drinking; and when he went to war he could still march and ride and fight like the junior officer he once had been. He came under cannon fire and had horses shot from under him. He studied the field of coming battles so closely, and at night, that a scouting party might easily bring him down or capture him. He bore a charmed life. Men died around him but he was never grievously wounded and never captured.

Few men to this day can understand the extraordinary mind of Napoleon, but the people of France undoubtedly felt they knew him. He was a monarch because he wanted to be a king — even an Emperor of kings and princes. But he was the king of the common people, still the "little corporal" of the soldiers of the Old Guard, and he was brave and victorious. To crown all his qualifications to appeal to the hearts of the people of France he had now the heir he wanted and that many had gone to church and prayed would be his.

Regardless of the fact that France was at war in Spain and her shaky alliance with Russia was weakening, 1811 was not a bad year for the people of Napoleon's country. Unsuspected except by a very few, of whom the mercurial Talleyrand undoubtedly was one, this was the last of the "good vintage" years for France and for la Grande Armée de France. The cold winds of 1812 were waiting to blow from the steppes of Russia.

Napoleon was politically sensitive enough to know that Tsar Alexander was learning wariness and that he suspected the peace with Austria was cemented by a marriage. Alexander could fear it might have been arranged to permit a France allied with Poland and Lithuania, to come uncomfortably and permanently into a position of next-door-neighbor to Russia. Napoleon already was calculating the logistics of a possible period of two-front warfare against England in Spain and Russia in Europe — two of the most powerful forces on earth.

14

To Moscow and Defeat

NAPOLEON'S APPROACH TO the bitter experience of his career's first major reverse was by a route that had for him no road signs of warning.

What he would later call the Spanish ulcer of Wellington's dogged campaign in Spain signified the implacable enmity of Britain. Unable either to defeat or establish a basis of bargaining with Britain for a practical working accord, Napoleon strengthened his hold on the northerly coast of the continent. Annexing Holland, where his brother, King Louis, had yielded to Dutch influence and had been summarily removed, he went on to absorb, as well, the Hanseatic strip of seacoast to the border of friendly Denmark. The German states watched helplessly. Sweden was less co-operative. That country had resented and resisted the demands of powerful France that she forego the advantages of British commerce and promote the Napoleonic continental system. When King Gustavus-Adolphus was declared insane and deposed, the Swedish royal family's line was excluded from providing succession, interests in Sweden curried the favor of the most powerful ruler in Europe to regain the lost Pomeranian provinces and Finland. They welcomed Marshal Bernadotte, the Prince of Ponte Corvo, as Sweden's crown prince and commander of her armies.

Napoleon at St. Helena later said that gratitude to Bernadotte for having married Mademoiselle Clery, an early sharer of a romantic interlude in his life, had motivated him in conceding to Sweden so competent a marshal as Bernadotte. Historians accept it as fact that when Napoleon attempted to exact from him a commitment never to take up arms against France, thus committing Sweden not to resist his new and vast hegemony of

Europe, Bernadotte refused. He was still the independent officer who had resented Napoleon's rise and predicted ill of it. He had refused to support Napoleon at the critical 18th Brumaire. Far from being friendly or neutral toward his benefactor, the Napoleonic military prince would be an unhelpful witness to France's misfortunes in the Moscow campaign and eventually the Emperor's arch-enemy.

One of the apparent great benefits to France of the peace with Austria had come when the Emperor Francis approved French troop movements through Austria. Granted in peacetime, the concession immediately worsened relations between Tsar Alexander and Napoleon, confirming as it did to the Tsar his fear that Napoleon, having married Marie-Louise, the next thing would be "to drive us back into our forests."

Russia, in 1811, was suffering increasingly from restrictions on her trade produced by the continental system and was undermining France's plan by partial removal of the agreed embargoes. She met protests from Paris with evasions. Napoleon, who considered Tsar Alexander still the somewhat effete young man of Tilsit, moved troops into the Baltic area and especially into the Grand Duchy of Warsaw. The build-up of French and Austrian troops near the Polish border of Russia and throughout northern Germany and the fear that Napoleon would espouse the cause of Polish and Lithuanian independence were a source of uneasiness. Alexander cited in defense of his trade policy the action of Napoleon in permitting some imports at high tariffs to licensed trading firms.

Encouraging the grand seignor of Constantinople briefly to take the field against Russia, increasing pressures on Sweden and Russia to oppose England's attempts to reach European markets, and holding Prussia in restraint only by the scale of hostile forces that surrounded her, Napoleon in the winter of 1811-12, built his Grand Army of Russia. By spring it had an estimated strength of 850,000. Beyond that he had control of large enough forces in his empire and zones of influence to command a total of almost 1,200,000 men. Of these he could put some 800,000 in the field. Allowing 150,000 to oppose Wellington in Spain, he had 650,000 to use against Russia, if necessary, in support of his embargo against British commerce in European ports.

Defeated and sullen, Prussia was forced to promise 20,000 men to Napoleon; Austria would provide 30,000, by treaty — and neither country could certify that officers and men of these forces, accustomed to meeting the French as enemies, would put their hearts into any struggle against Russia under Napoleon's command. The compelled alliances were too new to be dependable in 1812.

There was available to Napoleon a brave and eager ally in Poland. She had lost independence and provinces to Austria and Russia and eagerly looked to France as her deliverer. But to hold the advantages won in making peace with Austria Napoleon had agreed to recognize Austria's right to retain Galicia. Napoleon said he wished the Poles well in their aspirations to be independent; but to ensure that there would be only one enemy in a war with Russia he regretfully sacrificed a fully dedicated alliance with the Poles, whose territory he would have to cross.

As the prospect of war and invasion from the west increased early in 1812 Tsar Alexander was less dismayed than Napoleon's strategies anticipated. On the basis that the enemy of his enemy was a friend, he moved toward the willing British and negotiated for peace with Britain's ally, Turkey. He must be able to count on concentration of his armies against only one enemy — especially, against one as formidable as Napoleon's France. He studied Napoleon's wars. He had learned much from his own experience in war in Poland when he had been forced to the treaty table at Tilsit. Even more, he observed that when Austria and Prussia had accepted Napoleon's challenges to great pitched battles, as at Austerlitz, Wagram and Jena, they had been vulnerable to the superior performance of so masterful a tactician as Napoleon. They had accommodatingly chosen to fight his kind of campaign. The British under Wellington, on the other hand, had avoided decisive encounters, fought and retreated through scorched country to extend their enemies' lines of communication. If he sent an army westward to release Prussia from vassalage to France, he might gain a powerful ally but the cost would be high and Napoleon's expectations would be served. It would be better to trade distance in deliberately wasted lands and play for time. Eventually an even stronger ally than Prussia could come to his aid — midwinter of northeast Europe.

Talleyrand and Fouché warned Napoleon against becoming involved in a campaign in eastern Europe. To Fouché he said: "My destiny is not yet accomplished. The picture exists as yet only in outline. There must be one code, one court of appeal, and one coinage for all Europe. The states of Europe must be melted into one nation, and Paris will be its capital."

Far less optimistically minded than Napoleon, Talleyrand and Fouché saw the hazards that faced the confident Napoleon. Russia could easily field 400,000 regular troops and 50,000 Cossacks, all loyal to one country, and with shorter and internal lines of communication. France would fight far from home and with an army almost half composed of soldiers of the armies of countries France had subdued. It is possible that it was at this juncture the rejected Talleyrand and Fouché lost their dedication to Napoleon and became potentially recruitable by the royalists and the d'Artois Bourbon conspiracy.

When Alexander's minister in Paris protested the build-up of massive armies near Russia's borders, Napoleon replied that he was not accustomed to regulate the distribution of his forces by the suggestions of a foreign power. The Russian minister picked up his passport and left Paris.

But the Tsar was not overlooked in the invitation list when the new king of kings invited the crowned heads of the countries of Europe east of the Rhine and attached to the Empire of the house of Bonaparte to attend a gala gathering of the heads of friendly nations at Dresden. The messenger with Alexander's invitation was denied admission to deliver it.

For this brilliant occasion Marie-Louise was brought from Paris to share the near realization of her husband's cherished dream of a united Europe. In such an empire Napoleon, succeeded by their son, Napoleon the Second, would symbolize the supremacy of France. Only Russia's intransigence — considered a passing event in history — remained to be dealt with, as Napoleon counted the mounting strength of his many divisions. As events would prove, the celebration in fact marked the point where the far-flung Bonaparte Empire began its descent from the high and all-too-sharp peak of its power and glory.

The game plan of 1812 was indicated by the uniforms provided for the expedition eastward. They were as brilliant as if for a ceremonial parade and of light materials suitable only for summer. The Emperor was so confident of success that he made scant provision to protect his troops against the rigors of a winter on the Russian front. He was moving against Russia at the head of 470,000 men while Russia had in the field some 260,000. Nothing he had encountered in his military career warned him that he could not count on a relatively quick series of battles from which he would arrive victoriously at a peace conference in Moscow or St. Petersburg, dictating terms to his former friend, Alexander. At worst, he would have captured comfortable cities for winter quarters, reformed and strengthened his forces to complete the mopping up operations in the spring of 1813. He had let contracts in Poland, Saxony and elsewhere for supply to augment what he could expect to forage in pacified areas of occupied Russia. In the performance of these contracts the Emperor would be badly served.

The most valued of all his marshals were with him, confident from their many hard but successful adventures at arms. All that they had done in company with their royal commander-in-chief had been an exciting preparation for this climactic campaign. Every marshal, every general would win new honors, a more commanding place in military annals of France if not in world history. They had become wealthy and lived in luxury. A few regretted leaving their comfortable stations in life. But all had responded again to the summons of their brilliant founder of the new Napoleonic empire. It was to be a war against Tsar Alexander of the largest, most populous country of Europe, the last rival power that could be reached by land forces. After Russia there would be only England left to consider. When war started in June the massive expedition began to move eastward.

Wilna and Smolensk gave the first indication of what was to come. They lay in the path of the Grand Army and hopefully would make new staging centers for the advancing armies. But when entered both were found empty and desolate. Smolensk was stripped of food and supplies and of any useful population. The enemy under Barclay de Tolly had chosen to yield them, but only as useless shells. The enemy fought minor battles of orderly retreat, always elusively small in numbers involved and always accompanied by swift-moving swarms of Cossacks that suddenly scourged the flanks of Napoleon's three main advancing sections and as swiftly dispersed.

The great army, with its artillery denied effectiveness enroute but essential to any final determination of the issue, lumbered eastward on a broad front, eager for action. Ney, King Joachim (Murat), Davout, Maret, Prince Poniatowski, Berthier, Prince Eugene, Oudinot, all were fighting a new kind of war, still confident in the generalship of Napoleon.

Never had Europe seen such a procession of wagons of supply, so many men, women and children of the "irregulars" or camp-followers who moved with the army, servicing it with parasitic intent and dependent on it, ready to winnow newly-covered ground for food or booty. Napoleon considered he had been provident enough in the amount of supplies transported to meet the needs of so great a force. But as the army felt its way eastward, always organized to fight on the plains so suitable for campaigns of motion, and as the towns and villages and farms yielded nothing and the populations of townspeople and peasants moved away with the retreating Russian army, the quartermasters' reports on supply grew worrisome. The army was a thousand miles from the border of France.

What gradually became clear was that there might be no great battle short of a fight for Moscow, itself. In July came news that Alexander had signed treaties with Britain, Sweden and Spain. In August the news of his peace with Turkey became official. From the Turkish front a force of 50,000 moved north to join the main army and northern forces were released and consolidated in the path of Napoleon's advance. Alexander had succeeded in confining the war to one front.

Just as important to the outcome was the recruitment and arming of Russian peasants displaced from occupied areas and the rapid swelling of reserve and new armies in the rear. Priests of the Russian church declared it a holy war in which none should remain to serve the invader in any way.

On August 16 there had been prospect of a major battle at Smolensk but after attacking a concentration of the enemy and being thrice repulsed Napoleon moved again in force to discover that opposition had ceased. He was drawn forward deeper into enemy territory. When Kutusoff replaced Barclay de Tolly it was rumored the retreating would stop and the great, decisive battle would not be long in coming.

It was on September 5, between Borodino and Moskowa on the main road to Moscow, that the Grand Army at last came upon the enemy, about 120,000 strong, positioned on high ground, beyond a deep ravine with a wood on their right and solidly supported by artillery. The forces were well matched.

Here was fought a battle from which historians and military leaders more than a century and a quarter later might have been prepared for such an epic as the defense of Stalingrad against Germany. Peasants, whose only military identification was a cross sewn to their smocks, fought with fanatical bravery. As they fell in droves others rushed in to take their places. Of one division of 30,000 men only 8,000 remained at the end of a day of fighting under the fire of eight artillery pieces — but the ground was not taken until the late afternoon when the Russians fell back to new positions.

Napoleon had opened the fighting at Borodino on the 7th at four o'clock in the morning. At the end of twelve hours of unremitting attacks, repulses, rallies and attacks — the severest battle in Napoleon's career — he ceased action with each army in the position occupied when it had begun. Losses and capture of artillery had been about equal in each case and the toll of casualties of that one day between 75,000 and 100,000 killed and wounded was the range of the estimate of losses.

On the 8th Kutusoff retreated in good order and was not pursued. Napoleon's force was returned to strength by arrival of two fresh divisions from Smolensk. Eager to continue the fight away from such a position of enemy advantage as had helped deprive him of a decision at Borodino, Napoleon pressed forward but without another major engagement. On the 14th his soldiers marched over the slope of the Hill of Salvation and with exultation beheld the Gothic spires and oriental cupolos, palace towers and battlements of the great structures of ancient Moscow. There was no sign of any army of defense.

Napoleon reined his horse and gazed on the unfamiliar scene. "Behold at last that celebrated city!" he exclaimed. Then he added, "It was time." Better than his generals Napoleon undoubtedly knew the unexpected hazard that had developed in this great adventure. His mathematical mind would have computed in specific terms a problem in logistics which would suggest disaster if the Russians' strategy of fighting retreat were accompanied to the end by the policy of treating the land they abandoned as cruelly as if it had been an enemy's ground, not their own. It was strange that no delegation of burghers came to meet him and offer continuance of city life.

Murat had ridden in the van of the army to the gates of Moscow and returned to report that commander Milarodovitch of the rear guard had met him with an offer and an ultimatum. He would surrender Moscow peacefully providing he was given two hours for his army to withdraw. Otherwise, he would order the city to be burned. Napoleon, contrary to his customary policy, accepted the terms and soon was within the city, followed by the army and the horde of irregulars.

Moscow was all but deserted. Prison doors had been unlocked to release criminals who joined with the almost disorganized ranks of the French army of occupation to loot stores, palaces and churches. At first there was rejoicing in the prospect for billeting in so immense and empty a city. But at midnight came the first alarm of fire. In the four days that followed, from many acts of arson, a consuming conflagration saw Moscow's great buildings, including the Kremlin, of centuries of tsars, standing in a sea of surrounding flames. Only about a quarter of the city escaped the ravaging fire.

Of all Napoleon's varied experiences, he had seen nothing like this self-immolation of a great capital. It was an act he could not understand; he knew Parisians would be incapable of so terrible a sacrifice of the city they deeply loved. The Kremlin palace and citadel on its rise stood above the destruction. There Napoleon took quarters and reported in triumphant terms to his people at home the occupation of the enemy's capital. His letters did not include his frequently repeated words as he gazed out over the blackened scene in Moscow: "This bodes great misfortune." At the same time, he wrote to the Tsar a blandly-styled proposal of negotiations for peace. Alexander's answer came puzzlingly in the form of total silence. He would persist in it — on the advice of Kutusoff through whom Napoleon was forced to entrust communication with the Tsar. The wily Russian commander delayed communications far into sunny October while Napoleon lingered in uncertainty, awaiting hopefully a favorable answer from Alexander while his 95,000 men became steadily outnumbered by the growing force under Kutusoff. Indeed, the Russian force in total, by the attritions of engagements and illnesses that beset the French, overtook and passed Napoleon's remaining army strength.

The uncharacteristic indecision by Napoleon at this time has been remarked by historians, as it was certainly unhappily observed by his marshals. Beginning at Borodino, his marshals had become aware that Napoleon was different. Some historians have speculated on the degree to which ill-health may have deprived him of a positive victory at the costly battle on the 7th of September.

David Chandler, in his closely detailed commentary on Borodino in *The Campaigns of Napoleon* (P. 796), observed regarding Napoleon's condition on the night of September 5/6: "Unfortunately, he was far from enjoying the best of health; he was suffering from a heavy cold and an old bladder complaint had recurred. These facts were to have an important bearing on his conduct of affairs over the following days." Noting an error in the emplacing of guns at too great a distance from their target on September 6th, preliminary to the battle of the following day, Chandler observed ". . . such an error would not have slipped past Napoleon's eagle eye in the days of his prime. Indeed, his ill-health seems to have taken heavy toll of his efficiency on this occasion."

So much significance did Chandler attach to the factor of Napoleon's indisposition at that time that he reported concerning the events of the 7th: "Indeed, Napoleon was not showing himself to the best advantage on this battlefield. His staff were shocked to find him listless and apathetic, and he made no attempt throughout the day to go forward and see for himself. Instead, he mooned around in his Schivardino command post, listening to reports and ceaselessly demanding the rechecking of the news he received. Ill-health and a growing weariness were taking their toll with a vengeance."

The accounts of eye-witnesses on Napoleon's condition immediately before the battle of Borodino, next year at Dresden — affecting the outcome of the Battle of Leipzig — and finally before Waterloo are remarkably similar. It is only recently that we have become aware that Napoleon, long before his death, received periodical ingestions of arsenic. We may conclude that he had been disabled seriously by a steadily recurring ailment whose symptoms resembled those of arsenical poisoning. We cannot dismiss as out-of-the-question a serious possibility that arsenical intoxication was a secret weapon employed against him in partially disabling doses at Borodino.

If Borodino and the Moscow campaign in general marked the beginning of the end of the long success story of Napoleon's many battles, it is conceivable that the tasteless, odorless chemical powder was part of the beginning of an end that was as exalting for the Bourbons as it was disastrous for Napoleon.

The long retreat from Moscow, which began only when it was finally clear that Alexander was a person of more mettle than Napoleon judged, is so dramatic and famed an event of history that its terrible details may be touched only in outline from this point until Napoleon had returned to Paris on the 18th of December. First Murat then Prince Eugene had command of the retreat. Incredibly stoical and courageous Ney, who had been made the Prince of Moskowa for his feats of brave generalship at Borodino, repeatedly survived the impossible in many rear-guard actions. He inspired in his men the will to survive.

The sufferings and slaughter of the French of the regular army and the irregulars in trying to cross the half frozen Beresina over two inadequate bridges or over the ice has seldom been equalled in the annals of hardship in war. Typhus and dysentery, starvation and death by exposure to the freezing temperatures of November and December, the ceaseless harassment of the Cossacks combined to reduce the once disciplined corps, excepting the Imperial Guard, into something approaching a veritable rabble. Ney would emerge literally the last man out of Russia. The force Napoleon had led was reduced by March 6, 1813 to merely 93,000 men. Of these only 25,000, struggling westward, had belonged to the main army group.

Amazingly, Napoleon's indomitable spirit was not destroyed. He would not allow himself to concede defeat on the scale that all those around him could see. On reaching Smorgoni he announced in a bulletin on December 5 that from there he must return to Paris to deal with an attempted coup and to "watch Austria and Prussia". Significantly as to the unmentioned pressures developing within his civil establishment he wrote: "I have more weight on my throne that at headquarters." But he would raise another army, he said, and return to fight in the spring. What he could manage to surmount was the memory of the carnage he had seen, the knowledge that Austria and Prussia were deserting him, and the fact that the legend of his invincibility had been destroyed. He could in his own mind admit to the fact of defeat but he would not use the word. He must and did continue to believe that he could rebuild his shattered army, fight again and win. In Paris, he would talk of his victory at Borodino, his unchallenged entrance into Moscow — never once of the near total loss of a proud army.

15

From Leipzig to Abdication and Elba

RECOVERED MILITARILY FROM the shock of the virtually total loss of the great army taken to Russia in 1812, Napoleon in April of 1813 was in the field west of the Rhine with 200,000 men. He fought at Lautzen and Bautzen indecisive but costly battles in May and counted in his losses the grievous death of his best friend and grand marshal of the palace, Duroc. To General Bertrand he paid the high compliment of appointing him to replace Duroc. In so doing he substituted one totally dedicated man for another. The new grand marshal would rarely be absent during the next 8 years of complete devotion to the Emperor. Bertrand's St. Helena notes would constitute one of the two keys that made possible the unlocking in this age of the mystery of his master's death.

The truce signed June 1, 1813 was negotiated with the help of Austria. Britain refused to attend the peace conference at Prague and war was resumed in August with each side revealing, in the enlargement of its numbers, that it had used the armistice to strengthen positions.

His army ringed by enemies at Dresden, Napoleon's strategies were worthy of his reputation for audacity and skill. It was his last outright victory, filled with episodes of fast-shifting actions that bore the stamp of typical Napoleonic planning overlain by spur-of-the-moment revisions and with personal involvement. Said an account of the times: "St Cyr already began to despair when the imperial guard made their appearance, crossing the bridge from the eastern side of the Elbe, and in the midst of them, Napoleon. A German author wrote: 'It was then that, for the first time, I beheld his face. He came on with the eye of a tyrant, the voice of a lion, urging his breathless, eager soldiers.' "

Napoleon's former senior generals, Moreau and Bernadotte, were commanders for the enemy, Moreau having suffered accusation, brief imprisonment and deportation to America for allegedly treasonous conspiracy. He was recruited by the Tsar to help the 'Army of the Nations' drive Napoleon back to France and, if possible, from the military and political stage in Europe. Bernadotte commanded the Army of Brandenbrug. At Dresden their former commander gave them a refresher course in tactics from the opposite side of the battle lines.

But on the night after his brilliant disorganization of the enemy near the capital of Saxony, Napoleon fell ill. It was presumed that a meal of mutton, seasoned with garlic, had deranged his stomach. We may suspect he had been poisoned. But however ill the meal had made the Emperor his fortune was better than that of Moreau. In the haze of an August morning Napoleon had observed what appeared to be a furtive reconnaissance group in a copse at some distance and ordered a cannonade to be laid. The indications suggested that some person of importance had been wounded. In the evening a peasant brought a greyhound to Napoleon, saying it had been owned by a great man who had been killed. On a plate on the collar was engraved the name of its owner: Moreau.

For three weeks Napoleon lingered at Dresden in unaccustomed idleness and apparent indecision. His symptoms were consistent with arsenical poisoning. By then his enemy had brought great strength against him in the region around Leipzig.

In the great Battle at Leipzig, Napoleon with some 170,000 men led by marshals including Marmont, Macdonald and Ney, was opposed by some 300,000 in the three armies of Russia, Prussia and Austria. (General Bertrand was in command of a corps there.) The Dresden illness had delayed Napoleon in mounting the attack on Leipzig. The enemy, given precious time to increase the strength of their numbers and to unite forces, used the time effectually.

Unable to make headway despite a mighty artillery bombardment and costly charges, Napoleon ordered withdrawal. It was in that affair's conclusion that Prince Poniatowski of Poland, one of the most tragic and truly gallant figures of the Napoleonic wars, was killed. He saw not only the Leipzig engagement tide turn against the French but watched with sadness the obvious end of the Polish dream to link the future of Poland with France and recover national independence. Strategy had earlier dictated to Napoleon that, at Poland's cost, he give preference to a period of peace with Russia, yet the Prince never wavered in his loyalty to the Emperor. His 5000 troops at Leipzig had shrunk to 2000 when he was commanded to stay and cover the retreat over the one remaining escape bridge. This his small force did with great courage and vigor against overwhelming odds. The evacuation was amazingly successful, thanks to the prince's dogged obedience to the man he worshipped as a friend to Poland. Before his rear-guard could follow the last of the army across the bridge it was blown up prematurely, trapping many officers and soldiers in the path of the enemy. The wounded prince drew his sabre and to the officers, who had the opportunity to surrender, said: "Gentlemen, it is better to fall with honor." The responding officers, joined by a few cuirassiers, rode headlong into the advancing columns. Poniatowski slashed his way through their lines and plunged his horse into the river. He abandoned the animal in the stream, reached the opposite bank and catching a riderless re-mount reached a second river, lined with riflemen. Again he rode his horse into the river under fire, winning the far shore, but as he spurred his mount up a sharp declivity it reared and fell backward pinning him under water until he had drowned. The prince's last words to Napoleon had been: *"All of us are ready to die for your majesty."*

Part of the great enigma of Napoleon's quality of personality was his rare ability to arouse in officers and common soldiers, beyond any norms of military experience, a selfless dedication to him. It could move men to fight like lions and count loyal sacrifice in combat to please the Emperor a fair exchange for life itself.

Consider Ney who, in a rear-guard action in the retreat from Moscow, found himself with his small band on a field of recent battle strewn with corpses. He was in a hopelessly exposed position when Cossacks appeared in great numbers along the rim of a ravine in which he was proceeding. A Russian officer summoned Ney to lay down his arms. "A marshal of France never surrenders," he replied. Rallying his men, he charged up the hill against the enemy. Beaten back with severe losses he rushed again and again, standing off the greatly superior forces, then took his party through the enemy's lines at night and escaped. Having performed his mission in the rear, he rejoined the main force. Napoleon shouted with joy at seeing the man he had given up as lost. He then and always after referred to Ney as "the bravest of the brave."

Out of this kind of almost insane loyalty history's wealth of stories of the heights to which Napoleon could inspire otherwise unexceptional men to great acts of valor have swelled the numberless legends of the Emperor's legions.

Bernadotte of Sweden, whom Napoleon placed in line for the throne of Sweden, long since had turned against the Emperor. The crown prince had never fully conceded devotion to the Emperor even when Napoleon was showering him with money and privileges. When Sweden, without an heir to follow its aged king, asked Napoleon for a warrior prince, he sent able Marshal Bernadotte. He hoped thereby to ensure friendship between the countries in resistance to Russia. When Sweden eventually was forced to choose between Russia and France, her king and ministers discreetly favored placating Russia. Bernadotte then broke with Napoleon to lead armies against him. It was another painful demonstration of the very many Napoleon had been given that loyalty could not be bought.

Within a few weeks of the disastrous events of Leipzig there began one of history's most rapid dismantlings of a great empire. So fragile was the bond that held together countries that had not united voluntarily under the aegis of imperial France, that the mere awareness that Napoleon had suffered a second major reverse was enough to start the processes of dismemberment. There followed a rapid reversal of Napoleon's assembling of the pieces of a Napoleonic-ordered society east of the Rhine. Had Napoleon's grand plan been reinforced by the passing of time, with people of the newly-added states gradually grown accustomed to the philosophy and the various practical advantages of unity, Napoleon's benevolent intentions for a lasting Federation of Europe might have built up constituencies of population in each country determined to preserve his enforced new era.

Those close to Napoleon in his October and November march that now retraced painfully his ebulliently confident expedition in the spring to punish Russian and Swedish deviations from his continental economic trade plan, commented on his remarkable emotional control. When it was apparent that his "army of children" had been hopelessly weakened by the severity of its casualties that he could not police the farthest boundaries he had established, Napoleon displayed great calmness and philosophical acceptance of what he was at that point powerless to change. His composure and confidence seemed unnatural, given the scale of his losses and the visible damage to his prestige. Repeatedly he salvaged morale and organization from what threatened to change his beaten army to a rabble of desperate and undisciplined men. As long as he was in the center, those who surrounded him reflected his resolution and his purposeful drive toward safer zones in areas of grudging hospitality. He joined his men and reverted from relative aloofness of an emperor in command of armies to a field officer directing retreat, as any of scores of generals under his command might have done. It was another of the many instances when Napoleon did not merely create army life but lived it, in intimate touch with danger. He knew fatigues from illnesses that had sapped his vitality in the past two campaigns, but drove himself in the manner of Julius Caesar who descended from his chariot to walk, rub his shoulders, resist attacks and share rations with his battle-worn legionnaires.

The retreat from Moscow had been a dreadful experience. Napoleon then ended his participation when he left to hasten back and deal with a reported attempted coup in Paris. The retreat from Leipzig was an equally poignant experience. He could see all he had built at great cost of lives and treasure fading as if a euphoric dream had been excitingly experienced and as suddenly had dissolved. Yet life on the homeward march would not be as disappointing as his shock in discovering the deterioration of his position on the home front.

For those in Paris whose responsibilities were to keep the domestic affairs of France moving under the powers Napoleon had centralized there, the breaking away of Holland, Hanover, Hesse and Westphalia and the obvious total dissolution of the leagues of Rhenish and Hanseatic states was devastatingly disheartening. Their discouragement did not lack for cultivation by the royalists. King Joseph, faithful to his brother in the civil establishment in Paris, was no substitute for the calmly confident Napoleon who characteristically worked best under stress.

Many historians have seen the battle at Leipzig as matching in significance the dire events of the Moscow campaign of 1812. It went far to destroy the psychological advantage of Napoleon's presumed near invincibility. From that point until his first abdication the weight of numbers of his main adversaries Prussia, Russia and Sweden with Austria added at mid-year, all financed in large part by drafts of money from London, was more than the brilliance of Napoleon's tactics and the dogged courage of his marshals and men could resist. Britain discouraged any cessation of the struggle with threats to cease money payments.

Encouraged by their successes and the magnitude of the forces that had been mobilized, trained and equipped in 1813 to take the field under Tsar Alexander, the allies had brushed aside Napoleon's proposals for peace. He had offered to release Illyria, Spain, Holland and the Hanseatic states. To the Tsar, Blücher, Metternich and Bernadotte nothing less than a return to old boundaries and Napoleon's complete defeat and unconditional surrender now would be acceptable.

The allies mobilized more men and resolved to carry the war into France. Napoleon gathered a new army of 100,000 to resist.

As the enemy forces, 300,000 strong, poured over the frontier of France the powerful fortresses of French strength — an equivalent to the Maginot Line on the French frontier 125 years later — would be bypassed and their competent 150,000 troops immobilized, with many captured. Without laying siege to these fortresses, the converging allied armies isolated them and fought their way into the valleys of the Meuse, Loire and Seine to reach the gates of Paris.

The bitter closing struggle so filled the Seine with floating corpses of men and horses that its waters became unusable. Napoleon's official newspaper, *Le Moniteur,* withheld news of the growingly desperate military situation but the Seine silently reported its own discouraging news.

Against this tide of misfortune a characteristically undaunted Napoleon resisted with individual actions that military historians admire. He counted on Marmont and Mortier, with 50,000 men, to defend Paris. Soult had been rushed to the Spanish front to bolster resistance to the Duke of Wellington's triumphant push beyond the Pyrenees into France.

Returning to hearten uneasy Paris, Napoleon quarreled with ministers, legislators and several senior military advisors who believed France should ask allied terms before Paris was laid in ruins. All Napoleon's passionate urgings to continue were heard by senators without sign of revived spirit.

Crying, "I am the State — the only representative of the people!" he dismissed the legislative senate. He released King Ferdinand, hoping thereby to promote a rising of Spanish Catholics to undermine the position of Wellington's British, Portuguese and Spanish forces. The Pope, too, would be freed from Fontainebleau and a Concordat was reached to reconcile positions of Church and State in France.

Unseen behind France's military fronts in the Rhenish territories and in Spain, where all the news was continuously dispiriting to the War Office, lay the invisible third front of royalist intrigue and subversion. The resourceful Talleyrand early saw Napoleon's problems in stark realism. Shielding his hand from view, as later events would show, he actively assisted the underground forces of d'Artois. That arch conspirator had another powerful ally in Francis of Austria. Tsar Alexander would finally concede the logic of a Bourbon restoration.

Napoleon returned to the war front, planning to mobilize his outnumbered effectuals to come behind the advancing allies in actions that could release his Rhenish fortress garrisons for active contact with the enemy supply lines — a typically bold Napoleonic maneuver of obvious merit.

But in the midst of this tactic came the news that the fast-moving allies were at the edge of Montmartre. It compelled Napoleon to return.

Now again, at Paris as at Leipzig, greatly superior numbers of allies drove in on the defending forces. Out of touch with Napoleon, Marshal Marmont asked and was given time to remove his army from the beloved city, so saving it from destruction. He agreed to fall back on Fontainebleau with forces that on the way met Napoleon. The agitated Emperor refused to believe that Paris was in the enemy's hands. He went on to learn that the fickle in a city whose every feature bore his mark of constructive modernization and improvement, were ripping down Napoleonic monuments and replacing tri-color cockades with white. It was his first deep draft of the bitter wine of public inconstancy and ingratitude. His reaction was one of utter rage. Marmont and Macdonald he accused of treason and cowardice. But the futility of further fighting was impressed on him by other marshals.

Alexander's reassuring speeches and pleasing personality, which Paris had observed with relief after it had braced to feel the whip of the avenging old Prussian Blücher, first stunned the city with disbelief then sent it into wild scenes of welcoming rapture. The years of war might be over; Paris had been spared.

Subtly, Talleyrand identified the Bourbons with the atmosphere of national relief. The city gave a confused welcome to a vast and colorful army of soldiers dressed in a great variety of gaudy uniforms. The spectacle so filled the streets of Paris with bizarre interest and excitement that it seemed Napoleon was being remembered by Parisians only as one whose symbols should be speedily removed. Almost at once they would be replaced with the white cockades and the fleur-de-lis and portraits of King Louis.

Alexander could afford to be engagingly friendly with all whom he met in Paris and his considerable charm caused him to be lionized. He took his time about directing a force toward Fontainebleau where Napoleon had learned from his leading marshals that they would not support him further. They urged his abdication. He finally consented.

It was Alexander who declared that Napoleon, who once had been his friend, should retain the title of Emperor. He should rule some such island as Elba, the island to be under his administration and he to have a court, a security force and a navy all in scale to his miniature domain.

In the two weeks that Napoleon remained at Fontainebleau after his abdication on April 4, 1814, he saw the return of the

Bourbons to power. A provisional government under Talleyrand had prepared the way for Louis by declaring Napoleon deposed. A document which Talleyrand had ordered printed was posted weeks before the king had been reinstated bearing the printed affix: "Michaud, printer to the king."

Marmont would always be regarded by Napoleon as the leader of the military defectors, he having disobeyed the Emperor's orders to defend the city and recruit the help of citizens of Paris against any invaders. But soon after other marshals including Ney, Macdonald, and ultimately Soult would declare their loyalty to the provisional government or to the king.

To accompany him to Elba and serve as a token army, Napoleon was allowed to select 600 members of his Old Guard. Tears flowed in the emotional farewell as he bade his corps of guards good-bye, embracing the eagle of one of his standards, then pressing it to his lips. Not even remotely would it enter the minds of the arrangement-makers that Napoleon, who could not hold his empire with the loss of one and a quarter millions of army personnel expended in the wars from 1812 to 1814, would recover his army, using only this six hundred plus another five hundred, as he denounced the terms of his exile and set foot again on French soil.

Napoleon had attempted to stipulate that his Empress and his son should live with him on Elba. His wish was ignored and he would learn that the Emperor Francis had arranged for his daughter and grandchild to return under Austrian escort to Vienna. He would not see either of them again. His child would be renamed Francis Charles Joseph and would be raised an Austrian. As the Duke of Reichstadt, he would be isolated from French influence. Learning of his father's life or use of the French language would be denied him. The Hapsburgs had no plans for him ever to occupy the Bourbon throne.

As for the royalists, one potential Bonaparte pretender to the throne would represent trouble enough. There should be no thought of permitting Marie-Louise to accompany her husband and produce more young Bonapartes.

Marie-Louise would write impassioned letters to her husband at Elba for several months. But with time their tone grew casual and they ceased. Some maker of Austrian policy, presumed to be

Metternich, had assigned to the morally weak young woman a chamberlain, Neipperberg, described as more than ordinarily prepossessing. Her marriage was never annulled but in fact it had ended that summer through alienation of affection.

Later, when Napoleon returned to the Tuileries and l'Elysée, Marie-Louise would declare her complete disinterest in recognizing her marriage or resuming her former role. She had become virtually a prisoner of her family and of her infatuation with Neipperberg. It was the ultimate in offensiveness and humiliation to Napoleon that he should learn that his wife had offspring from her new attachment.

The royal family in Vienna could sacrifice a helpless member in the interest of power politics. She could be misused again for revenge. Yet, in his famous Will, written at St. Helena, Napoleon strangely would say — or be guided to say — that his Empress from the household of the Hapsburgs had always been a good wife to him. Dying, he expressed toward her the tenderest of sentiments.

At Malmaison Napoleon's first Empress was mortally distressed by the collapse of her former husband's magnificent empire into disloyal confusion, with his very life in danger. Josephine may have been drawn closer to Napoleon then in sympathy and understanding than at any time in their years of brittle married relationship. Two months after Napoleon had left for Elba she had sickened and died, her final thoughts much concerned with his safety.

16

The Hundred Days

THERE IS NO DOUBT that Napoleon on Elba was well informed by agents on the state of things in France under Louis XVIII and d'Artois. The Bourbon restoration's honeymoon with the people of France was not fated to last. In spite of attempts by the allies to help the grossly stout and partly infirm Louis enjoy the goodwill of the citizenry, his reputation for learning nothing while in exile was soon justified. The bent of the King and d'Artois was toward a reign in the ways of the Bourbon tradition.

To republicans who had hoped a constitutional monarchy would embrace provision for a rising level of rule by democratic decision the signs of a return to the old monarchistic system were so repugnant that by comparison the Bonapartist regime could seem essentially populist.

The mood of France was changing. Peasants in the interior of France, where Cossacks had scorched the earth and pillaged, the people were injured beyond tolerance. The 150,000 war veterans who had been released by the allies and returned to their homes were living on half pensions, resentful of what had happened to France in their absence. Paris in the hands of men in enemy uniforms was galling. They remembered nostalgically Napoleon and his victories, not the errors and reverses they had suffered.

Under the constitutional monarchy royalists who had lost lands in the Revolution and whose property still could be returned to them were recovering old estates to the alarm of small landholders who had gained much from land distribution. Fear grew that the benefits of the Revolution for agrarian peoples would be stripped from them. Many tenures and many titles and privileges conferred in the years since 1792 seemed in danger of being lost by a royal declaration that Louis' reign had never been legally interrupted. The implication was that no legal government had existed in his absence. The confusion thus bred was impossible to rationalize.

There had been relief when the war had ended and Napoleon was no longer calling up the kind of conscripts he had swiftly moulded into fine fighting forces in the war in Saxony. But now, as Napoleon would have been clearly informed, there was public dissatisfaction with the peace as the new year of 1815 began for unhappy France.

It is remarkable that on an island where many royalist eyes had been set to observe whatever actions could seem to threaten the resumed reign of Louis XVIII that alarms were not raised about visible preparations by Napoleon to leave the island.

The Emperor's decision to depart had not been made overnight as the precision of arrangements testified.

Napoleon was by terms of his abdication to receive 6,000,000 francs a year. Josephine and other members of his family were to divide pensions totalling 2,500 francs. Separate funds would provide for the costs of governing the island. When Napoleon became aware that none of these payments had been made, he considered his abdication promises no longer bound him. He could return to France without having breached the terms of his surrender of the roles of Emperor of France and King of Italy.

His unauthorized departure was typical of the Napoleon style. His sister Pauline gave a ball on the night of February 26, with all the officers of Elba's army invited. At about midnight the surprised soldiers were mustered by drummed message and commands to board the brig *Inconstant* and six small sailing craft which had been provisioned for an expedition.

The craft separated and sailed without attracting attention of any patrolling naval ships. On March 1, within a few hours of one another, they discharged their passengers — most of them fiercely loyal members of Napoleon's Old Guard — for assembly as a marching party. The starting place was near Cannes, the destination Paris.

So began the famous Hundred Days. They would end Napoleon's career in a burst of frenetic activity. The effort briefly revitalized unhappy France and sent the Bourbon king and his followers into exile or discreet retirement. The upper stratum of French society, whose members found easy the adaptation to Bourbonist monarchy, observed neutrally what amounted to an army coup, since it was in the army that "the usurper" had his power base.

The return from Elba was an act of monumental effrontery to the monarch after only ten months on the treasured throne. The inconceivable had happened. The principals in the struggle were far too emotionally exercised to realize that the significance of the prize was changing as the century progressed. To them it still symbolized a privilege and prestige valid in all the historic terms of highest politics. Napoleon would speak of the throne itself as no more than a little wood and some pieces of velvet — and yet wager his life for it.

There was no resistance to their landing nor were there demonstrations of joy in the first five days of marching, with all except Napoleon on foot. A hundred Polish lancers were among them, carrying their saddles on their backs against the time when horses could be found.

When the advance guard of forty grenadiers came face to face with a battalion sent to arrest the march, Napoleon dismounted and advanced alone. There was silence as he closed the distance. Some paces behind him were a hundred of the Guard with muskets reversed. Halting, he threw open his surtout to show the star of the Legion of Honor and cried: "If there is a soldier amongst you who wants to kill his general — his Emperor — let him do it now. Here I am!"

The instant reaction remains a dramatic scene from history written about and depicted on stage and screen whenever the Napoleon story has been presented.

"Vive l'Empéreur!" was everywhere the cry as soldiers cheered and broke ranks to surround the grey-clad, stocky figure. Not a firing piece had been loaded in the battalion ordered to challenge him. All swung toward Grenoble, on the way meeting the Seventh Regiment under Colonel La Bédoyère, an officer of noble birth recently promoted by warrant of Louis XVIII. The scene was repeated and La Bédoyère ordered a drum opened, disclosing a large collection of tricolor cockades for distribution.

The commandant of the garrison at Grenoble could persuade no soldier to fire and when the locked city gate was ceremoniously opened by Napoleon with a lightly charged howitzer and his party entered, he was dragged from his horse and carried on uniformed shoulders toward the nearest inn amidst shouts of delirious joy.

With that spontaneous welcome by the army — only its general dissenting — the authorities in Grenoble next day paid homage to the returned Emperor. Now Napoleon had 7000 soldiers. He pushed on to Lyons, the second-largest city of France. There d'Artois was waiting with Marshal Macdonald to deny the column entry to the city. The two were left standing while the soldiery, recognizing Napoleon, broke ranks to surround and welcome him.

Marshal Ney had confidently promised Louis that he would capture and cage Napoleon and bring him to the King. He, too, was quickly converted to resuming his familiar position as a loyal Bonapartist. Just a year before, at Fontainebleau, he had denied Napoleon, refusing to serve him further. As he did with generosity in the case of many other senior officers who had gone over to the royalists and regretted it, Napoleon welcomed him back so warmly that, to his later regret, he would entrust much of the management of the battle at Waterloo to him.

At the Tuileries and Fontainebleau the welcome given Napoleon would be described by him in exile as the hours of highest happiness and satisfaction of his life. It had taken him only twenty days to change his standing dramatically from a deposed monarch landed with a small battalion of "invaders" on a beach on the Gulf of Juan. He was again Emperor, already presuming to rule by published decrees. His rivals, the Bourbon King and his brother had fled as they saw the writing on the wall spelling out the slogan "Vive l'Empéreur!"

Napoleon foresaw the return of his wife and son. When they did not come he conspired to liberate them from their different form of captivity in Vienna but the plan was discovered and foiled. He foresaw, too, and promised faithfully that he would bring only peace to France, with liberty and equality as promised by the Revolution. What he could not foresee was that within three months he would be in Paris at l'Elysée, without the privilege of staying there; that Paris would be in the hands of foreign enemies and that soon he would be a man without a country.

On his next abdication, he would not even have an island. Instead, an island of infinite remoteness would have him, entrapped on a windy plateau, ringed around by volcanic peaks. In that remote place he would remember that his enemies had tried and executed his "bravest of the brave", Marshal Ney, for the crime of having returned to his service. He might envy him the swift dispatch.

Meanwhile, in late March of 1815, his faith restored in his destiny to bring France glory, he would have learned of the Congress of Vienna's meeting where he had been condemned as an outlaw, the enemy of the peace of Europe. It is probable that the formal declaration signed by representatives of all the countries he had once defeated in the years when fortune constantly favored him caused him little worry. He was served again by Carnot who had mobilized for him the armaments and ordnances of war and in the next three months would arrange for new miracles of supply.

He had experienced sickness while at Elba but now he had what was for him the best of all tonics — complete preoccupation with planning for war. True, in this he was doing what he and his agents had told the people of France he would not do again — but the choice had not been his. More than calling him a man who lived outside the law — a strange declaration when he had become again veritably the law in France — the Congress of Nations at Vienna had announced a gigantic crusade against him. The great alliance would put a million men in the field to remove him from power. All its declarations would speak of war against Napoleon, not against France. Talleyrand, in joining the Congress, had ensured this distinction henceforth would always be made. If they were to be believed, the issue would be a million men against one man.   '

Taking stock, Napoleon could see that Spain was no longer a diversion to split his enemies' strength. Tsar Alexander, Blücher, Bernadotte, Schwartzenburg and Wellington of the Peninsula fighting, all would come against him. But had not the old magic of Fate favored him brilliantly in these past months?

Who else was there who could come back from exile to a great throne in just three weeks?

If the old monarchies had outlawed him he had outlawed the Bourbons. He had officially declared their sovereignty invalidated by the fact that they had not, while in possession of the Crown, adhered to the commitments they had made to the people of France upon their return.

War being inevitable, the armament plants worked day and night, armies of men and women made uniforms, others produced muskets and ammunition. Cavalry horses were bought and the roads reverberated to their hoofbeats as they were rough-trained and brought to marshalling points. April passed, then May and it was early June. Without conscription Napoleon and Carnot had done the impossible: There were 375,000 men in barracks and camps in the restored and re-invigorated Grand Army of France! Let the enemy come — Napoleon was himself, again!

They would come at France through channel ports of Holland, Belgium and Denmark; at many crossings of the Rhine and through diverse routes from Austria. Prussian, British, Hanoverian and Dutch armies would spearhead the attacks. Later but not long later there would be Cossacks, Silesians, reluctant Poles and Swedes under Bernadotte. Blücher was old and fighting, surely, his last war. Wellington had done damage to France on the Peninsula but this was Napoleon's own fighting country, where he had been trained in artillery drills.

No battle in history has been more analyzed and criticized than that of Waterloo. It need not be fought in detail here.

Through the more penetrating accounts of it runs the common theme that for some reason, from his first hours in the area of the coming great battle, when he was vigorous and buoyant, optimistically telling his men that there were 90 chances out of a hundred that they would carry the day, an unusual torpor and indecisiveness set in. Armies of that period carried no physicians to take the pulses, temperatures and blood pressures of the commanders as being perhaps significant to medical history. The exact nature of Napoleon's condition is variously described as being "off form" to staggeringly ill.

There is little doubt that, with so many eye witnesses having remarked it, Napoleon could have seemed indolent and unclear in his mental processes and instructions to generals. He delayed in decision making, uncharacteristically failed to follow up a brilliant stroke in breaking the lines of Blücher's army with his smashing blow at Ligny. By normal practice Napoleon would have sent cavalry and cuirassiers after the fleeing Prussians and rendered them far less capable of rallying to come with strength to Wellington's aid. No part of his strategy was more important than for Grouchy to pursue, contact and keep Blücher's forces from joining with the British. Yet Napoleon's instructions to Grouchy were far less clear than they should have been; and the lack of Grouchy's weight at Waterloo while he wandered out of contact with his real task assignment is believed by many to have cost the French the victory they came so close to achieving at that fateful occasion.

Some have depicted Napoleon as having been seen to be physically ill, having difficulty in bladder relief, suffering extreme lassitude between bursts of energy when he would mount his horse and ride to study the field. Every description of the battle by historians who have studied it in depth attests that it was not pursued by Napoleon as were battles he fought when he snatched victory from far less promising situations than he had faced at Waterloo.

Writers of history have been aware of the determination of the Bourbons to reclaim their throne from Napoleon, but not of their method. Only now can they appreciate the fact that more than the resistance of patriotism and old enmities thwarted Napoleon's historic plans for a world order of his bold devising. His illnesses at crucial battles were either overlooked or only casually commented upon in all historical account from his own time until now. Some historians, noting his new and growing inability to concentrate and his periods of lassitude, referred to the condition as indolence and lack of initiative. Those observers may be excused if events at St. Helena are remembered. At that time the beaten genius of war was perhaps the most closely guarded prisoner of history. Yet step by step he was approaching death through the same agency as had accomplished his military downfall. His every move and symptom had become the subject of careful medical observation; his symptoms were crying out for recognition as those of poisoning; yet it was solemnly decided that he had died of natural causes.

Since Napoleon felt no sense of dependence on doctors to guard his health, his physical condition in war is nowhere precisely documented — not even to the extent of the rudimentary medical knowledge of that period.

Historians are seldom by training qualified to cast a physican's appraising eye at a military commander's only sketchily indicated physical condition. The chroniclers' intense preoccupation with man and material management in battle would, in any case, provide medical men with few symptoms to go on were they to become curious about the possible relationship of the physical health condition of a given general to the conduct of his part of a particular engagement or campaign. Wounds were understandable. But for a general to be performing below par because he did not feel well was outside of history's scope of vision.

We are not at all venturesome today if we proceed on the surmise that the poison plot was actively operative at Ligny and on the night and early morning before Waterloo and that the fatal lack of Marshal Grouchy's 35,000 men, sent to meet and divert Blücher from reinforcing Wellington, was only part of the effect of the clarity of thought that Napoleon's marshals then found puzzlingly missing in their supreme commander.

In a way untypical of Napoleon's resourceful style of warfare, his marshals at Waterloo were ordered or allowed again and again, without support, to batter their superb cavalry and cuirassiers against the deadly barrages and bayonets of the unyielding British squares. When it was too late, the Emperor would throw in his beloved 40,000-strong Imperial Guard and see it demolished. It was then that Wellington could dismount, raise his sword and cry, "Up and at 'em, boys!" in a routing rush that swept away resistance. Only minutes earlier he had been patching an all but broken front.

But surely this illness had been the Dresden and Leipzig experiences all over again. There was the sudden sickness — perhaps from food poisoning — the irresolution, the inactivity while the enemy shifted position and his numbers increased to dominant proportions; the painful strictures, sweating and chills and watering eyes when it was utterly vital to be clear-headed and instantly responsive to sudden opportunity or necessity with a staccato volleying of orders. Yet he must now do as he had always done — move, ride and give orders, simulating his former effectual command of battle detail.

Military historians have dwelt on this illness of the Emperor's and his uncharacteristic indecision amounting to torpor before the Battle of Waterloo. In varying degrees they have been inclined to imply that he had been out-generalled by Wellington and Blücher. He had won his great reputation for prevailing over larger forces by highly flexible maneuvers in which he divided and defeated his enemies segment by segment through the element of surprise and with tactics of stunning swiftness. Such action, to succeed, depended on a single general command of singular decisiveness. Napoleon's military genius existed in a rare mixture of intuition and calculated comprehension. He thought for his marshals. But all of this, to work, depended on endless energy effectually expended and a high degree of mental health at all times.

Preceding the great engagement on June 18, fought most intensely in a narrow salient south of Mont St. Jean, was a day of fighting at Quatre Bras and Ligny.

Napoleon, as Wellington remarked at the time, had given Blücher "a damn good licking" at Ligny. His actions then were a denial of his tenets of conflict; pursue, destroy the enemy's power and will to continue. Napoleon knew that Blücher's object was to unite with Wellington's force and block the thrust of the French toward Brussels.

Had Napoleon, instead of assuming the Battle of Ligny had caused such disorganization to Blücher's army that he would need three days to recover effectiveness, pressed on to make the routing of Blücher's exposed columns complete, Wellington might have had far less chance in the crucial last hour of the Battle of Waterloo. The indifference to opportunity puzzled not only the Emperor's marshals but generations of historians.

Still more unexplainable was Napoleon's failure to direct or even clearly to instruct Grouchy in his diversionary role of ensuring that Blücher would not unite with Wellington. Military historians have never agreed on the degree of Grouchy's culpability in denial of victory to the French. Some have charged that he was deliberately disloyal to Napoleon or had no heart for a battle he might avoid on the plea of unclear instruction. What can not be doubted is that Napoleon's liaison with so critical an element of his battle strategy as awareness of the disposition hour by hour of Grouchy's corps was wholly inadequate to the occasion.

On June 18, in densely packed Brussels, the rumor swept the city that the Duke had been defeated, his army in disorganized retreat. And Paris was still rejoicing over the exaggerated accounts of victories at Ligny, Quatre Bras and Wavre. Soon the situation was reversed: Napoleon, as best he could after losses of more than 55,000 men against the allies' 50,000, with a tired, dispirited escort of guards, was reorganizing his scattered forces to resist the expected allied advance toward Paris.

In Paris Talleyrand ordered Fouché, head of Police, to keep in touch with Napoleon. It would free him to play a game of favoritism to the royalists in anticipation of the arrival of the allies en masse to lay siege to Paris. Talleyrand was perhaps the only man in Paris who had a well-defined purpose. He was going to help the planned Bourbon restoration.

Wellington's first need was rest and, without washing the grime of gunpowder smoke from his face or undressing, he threw himself on a bed and slept. How close Napoleon came to carrying the day none would know better than Wellington and in his first rush of relief and candid confession of the narrowness of the victory he had won he next day wrote revealing lines to his brother, William Wellesley-Pole:

> You'll see the account of our Desperate Battle and victory over Boney!!
> It was the most desperate business I ever was in; I never took so much trouble about any Battle; & never was so near being beat.
> Our loss is immense particularly in that best of all instruments British Infantry. I never saw the Infantry behave so well.

Later it would be said that the issue was never really in doubt, but the supreme commander of the allied effort, elated and sad by turns, mourning the loss of many friends, would be under no illusions about the mighty pounding his resolute squares had taken as the French cavalry and cuirassiers mounted charge after charge against their ranks. The issue was seriously in doubt for Wellington until Blücher came on the scene just as the dreadful losses of cavalry before the British position were bringing Napoleon, Soult and Ney to the realization that the almost-won battle could turn into a ghastly defeat.

In any list of the decisive and history-affecting battles of the world that at Waterloo inevitably stands at or near the top. Inherent in its high element of drama has been the extreme narrowness of the space between victory and defeat for Wellington and Napoleon — so little seemed to intervene between glory and disaster for each.

When even the Imperial Guard had been routed, the battle was over.

Napoleon's friends were dumfounded by the news, his enemies on the home front harried him with weapons he could not oppose. He was soon under pressure of his marshals as well as members of the Council to abdicate. He tried to renounce the throne in favor of his son, the young King of Rome. But that was not to be. If Paris was to be saved — and with it possibly their own skins — his former senior supporters now knew that again as in 1814 nothing less than an unconditional abdication by the Emperor would satisfy the allies. The armies were converging on Napoleon's beautiful city — the place he had designed especially for massed marches of triumph.

Napoleon, still shaken by the defeat he had thought was impossible and almost undoubtedly suffering the after-effects of another arsenical poisoning, would blame his failure on a mistake in placing Ney in command. Ney was a magnificently brave batterer but that was the nature of his generalship in the field. In Grouchy, likewise, he had chosen badly. He had left Davout in Paris and had better marshals than Grouchy in inferior roles. Moreover, what he had needed there was his brother-in-law, Murat, instead of his determined but unwise brother, Lucien. We can not know, better than Napoleon could hope to do, that even with the wrong generals he might have won. He had been victorious with greater odds against him in previous battles. But he could not overcome Wellington — and, above all, arsenic trioxide, too.

As for Wellesley, the Iron Duke, the deep satisfaction of having at last met and bested the great Napoleon would have been destroyed had he learned that he had beaten a poisoned man.

17

Prelude to Exile

AT MALMAISON NAPOLEON lived the hours of his Gethsemane. He knew that all doors in Europe were closed or closing to him. In the place of his fiercely faithful Old Guard he was "protected" by troops of the National Guard under the hostile General Beker. He was tantalized by awareness that in the disorganization after Waterloo the allies had fallen temporarily into a vulnerable separation of their armies. It would be in the tradition of his brilliant wresting of victory from apparent defeat for him to appear again on the field with fresh forces that had not been committed to the struggle in Belgium. He could maul one, then the other of his two main enemies in the field.

But he had abdicated. Ney and most other marshals had turned against him. No one would take seriously his urgently-pressed offer to fight as a mere general of the army. He well knew that with every passing day the allies' forces, already superior in numbers, would swell to overwhelming proportions and surround Paris.

Under orders of Talleyrand, Fouché, representing the civilian police strength of the nation, was dominant now. While the soldiers guarding Napoleon were clearly performing the functions of captors, Fouché dissembled kindness and concern in the interest of his future relations with this resilient man. He urged him to take advantage of two frigates at Rochefort to transport him and his suite to friendly America. Lacking an alternative, this would be the Emperor's intention. He might not have thought that when Fouché assured him he had asked for him from Lord Wellington safe conduct to America that his request had automatically served as an alert to the British. Fouché would know they would advise commanders of naval units to intercept escape.

132

"Wherever wood can float there I will find the British flag," Napoleon once had said of the vigilant British Navy. In this instance he would not be wrong.

But in the meantime, while lodged at Malmaison, he must suffer a deeper mortification of the spirit than was his lot at Fontainebleau at the time of his first abdication. Whereas he had then remained the Emperor Napoleon, with a sovereign domain, now he was deposed, outlawed and struggling to avoid the danger to life of outright condemnation in France. Scarcely less grim would be the demeaning position of a man who no longer had a country — and no invitation to join another.

Once, at 24, he had been imprisoned to answer a charge of suspected disloyalty to the Revolution. But then he had no throne to lose, no pageantry to forego, no Empress and kingly son to part from. Most of all, then, he had stayed confident of what lay ahead; now he was losing command of an army, leadership of a nation, and his great dream of world domination. Hardest of all to bear would be the separation from his child of five, the treasured vessel of Bonaparte and Hapsburg royal blood.

All his elaborate construction of an Empire that placed France in debt to the Bonapartes for an interlude of glorious if costly supremacy in Europe had fallen into disarray.

The affair at Waterloo, the dreadful events of June 18 when, between noon and early evening, his life's work had been shattered along with the body and spirit of that special pride, the famous Imperial Guard, was nightmarish. From it, for all the time there remained for him, there could be no relieved awakening.

He would have preferred that the last days in France should be at Fontainebleau and the Tuileries. But Malmaison was where he had been told to go — and that only as a stopping place enroute to exile. The royal villa was still Josephine's though Josephine had been dead since a year ago. He had come to visit Josephine at times after the marriage annulment until Marie-Louise had strongly objected, and he had let the friendship go. The two million francs he had given her as a post-marriage dowry along with the many other gifts showered upon her had lifted her well above the hazards of return to penury. But he had discovered and confirmed the fact that his love for Josephine was not extinguishable. And like so much else he had cherished and now had given up, she too was of his brilliant past. It was ironical that his last days and hours in the vicinity of Paris should be with something close to the living presence of the woman he had loved and put aside in pursuit of a self-directed destiny. He had said it was a divorcement to secure the future of France by ensuring a dynastic succession of Bonapartes from Napoleon the second onward. But it had been for ambition, too. Except that a son had been born of his wedding to Josephine's successor — a son whose right to the throne he had tried desperately and unsuccessfully to make a condition of abdication — all of his strategies in Empire building had come to nothing. The borders of his beloved France had been crossed on all fronts and the enemy would enter Paris peacefully.

Napoleon's determination to face his ordeal rather than take the cowardly way of suicide in those dark days at Malmaison tends to belie the belief of some that he had tried to take his own life at the time of his first abdication. In 1814 his experience had been grievous, but Alexander had shown him respect. In this new downfall all had gone and he well might fear death by execution. The Declaration of the Congress of Vienna placing him outside the law could condemn him still.

Almost unnerved by lingering illness and by the pressures of his disaster Napoleon still managed the organizing habits of his lifetime. He had long ago placed monies providently in the hands of dependable relatives. To bankers in Paris, Berne and London he had recently transferred savings. On this he might draw in the indefinite future. Now, he ordered the gathering at Malmaison of the personal and portable wealth that lay readily at hand. There was no interference by Fouché or others with that operation. Coinage, plate, jewellery, snuff boxes, miniature paintings, small artifacts of gold were packed in travelling boxes. With these he could continue to reward services of a personal kind as he had done in the past. Later his British captors would tally it all but for the present it was the ready-at-hand residue of a short lifetime of material providence and of commissionings to artists and artisans of France and Italy. Amongst them were many made famous by the Emperor's patronage. Mounted guards attended as Napoleon's yellow caleche drove rapidly through the green countryside on the dusty road to Aix with the Emperor and his treasured possessions.

It was when his party, divided as to route, reached and reassembled at Aix that Napoleon learned from the sympathetic mayor of the blockade of British naval craft at western seaports including Boulogne and Rochefort.

Blücher's army was driving toward Paris and Blücher would be disposed, if he could, to conduct an execution and talk about it later. By Talleyrand's manipulation the royalists were in control in Paris. The Bourbons then would vividly remember that Napoleon had ordered the execution of their Duke of Enghien. Napoleon's Austrian relatives by marriage had possession of his wife and son who were to live in Vienna.

HMS *Bellerophon* was posted alertly ready to pounce on any escaping craft, large or small. Napoleon, accompanied by Savary and Bertrand, presented himself formally to the courteous but sharp-of-mind Captain Maitland who quickly disabused him of any thought that the Royal Navy would co-operate with an escape by ship to America or the West Indies. He consented, however, to the Emperor's aide, Gourgaud, going to England to deliver the message asking the government for its help in allowing safe conduct to America. The answer reiterated Wellington's first reply to that proposal. There was, then, the other possibility. From aboard the *Bellerophon,* to which had come Napoleon and the principal members of his party for prospective exile, Napoleon sent this historic message to the prince regent of England:

Rochefort, July the 13th, 1815

Royal Highness,
A victim of the factions which divide my country, and to the hostility of the greatest powers of Europe, I have terminated my political career and come, like Themistocles, to seat myself on the hearth of the British people. I put myself under the protection of their laws, which I claim from your royal highness, as the most powerful, the most constant and the most generous of my enemies.

NAPOLEON

Fate had it that there was in power in Britain the Conservative Government of Lord Liverpool. It was an administration less likely to sympathize with the man who had cost Britain so many anxious hours of channel watching from fear of invasion, so many casualties, so much in trade and treasure than would be the case if the appeal to generosity were made to a government of Liberals.

Napoleon had had his agents in Britain. He was not unaware of the love-hate relationship of his name and personality amongst the rank and file of British people, military and civilian. Essential propaganda of war apart, the British, he knew, valued no victory at arms over other than a worthy enemy. It was something planted deep and rather oddly within the British character — something carried over from the age of knighthood and the cavaliers, but perhaps understood better by Nelson's officers than by those of the Duke of Wellington. If, as Wellington was to say, the issue at Waterloo had been decided on the playing fields of England, it followed that the winners of a contest could give without reserve the traditional "three hearty British cheers" for the defeated force.

Lord Liverpool was counselled by Wellington, who knew St. Helena Station well from visits between periods of service in India. They would guide the prince regent on the tricky question posed by Napleon's diplomatic surrender to Maitland on the *Bellerophon.*

In surrendering and asking asylum Napoleon placed Britain's policy-makers in a quandary. Even though the echoes of the cannonading only recently had died away, there were many in Britain, some highly placed, who reluctantly admired the self-made emperor. But this was the disturber of the peace in Europe. Wellington long had wished to test his generalship against Napoleon's. He knew the rare warmth of affection that existed in the Army of France for Napoleon and that his own cold, punctilious style of command denied him more than respect and confidence. Somehow, Napoleon aroused far deeper emotions in his followers. But for all his innate austerity of manner Wellington was human enough to respect and feel a sense of responsibility for a superbly effectual fellow craftsman in the skills and psychologies of warfare.

In Belgium, Wellington had been brushed by the chill spectre of an overwhelming defeat. The highest testimony of respect he could pay to the man who had cost Britain so much for so many years was to favor a policy of keeping him alive but in as remote and safe a place of confinement as could be arranged.

Napoleon could not be expected to appreciate the compliment. When the *Bellerophon* had carried him with quiet satisfaction to Plymouth, small craft set out from there, from Portsmouth and Torbay filled with sailors on leave and civilians all hopeful of getting a glimpse of the captured 'ogre'. Curiously, they found themselves somehow moved to cheer when the sallow-faced man with the almost hypnotic eyes looked down upon them from the ship's rail or the castle. So much enthusiastic cheering went on that an order went out from naval command that demonstrations of this kind must cease. The order carried its own message, surprising to those who wondered what the mystique was that lay behind an enemy's personal magnetism applying without seeming effort to ingratiate himself. Some in Parliament thought that if Napoleon could meet the Prince Regent he would charm him just as he had once won Tsar Alexander. Napoleon counted unrealistically on a body of opinion developing in his favor in Britain. Friends were there amongst the people of Britain — surprisingly many — but they were without political power and not organized or led to act.

The Emperor was kept on the ship rather than being allowed ashore for hospitable civilities only partly in order to avoid unwelcome fraternization. A perhaps hopeless move was afoot in London to obtain from the court a writ of habeas corpus whereby Napoleon could enjoy justice in the accustomed British style. No civil writ could be served on the admiral aboard the *Bellerophon* for release of a dangerous person detained for security reasons of the first magnitude.

Napoleon's most earnest plea was that he be treated in England just as other deposed leaders of states had been courteously welcomed to life in exile. Britain, calling him General Bonaparte, refused to recognize him as royalty. This was a petty technicality, inasmuch as none would know better than the British that only an emperor could have mobilized the armaments and men to seize and hold almost the whole of Europe's land mass as their "General" Napoleon had done.

Wellington thought St. Helena would far better satisfy the demands of the situation than would a country mansion in Britain. He remembered it as having a good climate. It would do admirably, provided a careful watch was kept against rescue attempts by Napoleon's friends.

The famous adversaries of Waterloo would spend the remaining years of their lives under circumstances of greatest contrast.

Wellington, born in the same year as Napoleon, would live to be 83. He continued for a time as commander-in-chief of the army, then, as a statesman, rose to the eminence of prime minister. He was buried under the dome of St. Pauls in London, honored by a nation that would rank him in its histories with such heroes as Drake, Marlborough and Nelson.

For Napoleon, whose position in the two decades preceding the great battle in Belgium had been infinitely the more exalted of the two commanders, the years until his death at 52 reflected, unknown to himself and to the world, a silent, hidden contest — one that could only end when all menace of the house of Bonaparte to the house of Bourbon had ceased to exist.

Long after the agonies of Napoleon's dying, the years would redress some of the wrongs done him. His name today is conceded its place amongst the ten most influential men of history. No Bourbon and no other person of his era has ranked so high.

All of this was hidden from foreknowledge when, on July 31, against his dignified remonstrances, accompanied by outbursts of passionate protests and weeping by the countesses Bertrand and Montholon, it was made clear to Napoleon that he must accept exile. On the seventh of August he was conveyed with his party aboard Sir George Cockburn's *Northumberland,* with St. Helena the destination.

Part Three

The Tragedy at Longwood

Sten Forshufvud

The godlike Ulysses is not dead upon the earth;
He lingers still a living captive within the breadth of ocean,
In some unapproachable Island, where savage men detain him.

— HOMER'S *The Odyssey*, book 1 v. 195

Prologue

IN DEFEAT THE AURA of greatness surrounding an heroic figure inevitably fades. Thus exposed to bolder, more critical examination by the curious, the subject may no longer be held in former awe or veneration.

Standing on the deck of H.M.S. *Bellerophon*, gazing down upon the bustle of small surrounding craft in the British naval port of Plymouth, Napoleon Bonaparte was still, like any great army leader of history, an actor conscious of being on stage. But now his stage had shrunk!

This was the enemy's ship, for two weeks now anchored off a previously unreachable shore. By agreement of the courts and parliaments of his foes in Western Europe, he was at the pleasure of those who could decide if he would live or die. If he should live, they would command the details of his exile. He, the conqueror of nations, the maker of laws, architect of cities and states, a supreme ruler anointed Emperor by the Pope, must not appear dismayed or humbled. He must remain self-possessed, with dignity intact. Composure under stress was always part of his cultivated style, an element of his legend.

Two months had passed since the epic events at Waterloo. The battle had ended the hundred fateful days since his tentative landing, then triumphal return to Paris from Elba. He had commanded once more a revitalized army of France. But then on the battle days, as on so many other critical occasions, he had suffered a sickness for which there was no accounting. It had made him staggeringly ill and indecisive, yet he had somehow to command the events of the battle. The plan, the strategies of action, the morale of his army all revolved around his hour-by-hour leadership.

His superb cavalry had nearly shattered the stubborn lines of his allied enemies into confusion. If only the German, Blücher, had been a little later on the scene, if only Grouchy had not delayed or lost contact with the plan, but had savaged the German columns as planned, to divert Blücher, the day still would have produced another victory for France. How different then would be his present position! Glory in Paris instead of defeat. Above all, if he had not again suffered that accursed return of sickness, of overwhelming lassitude on the crucial days of battle . . .

Well, it was over and done with. Yet there was this much hope: that the unpredictable English would be chivalrous in victory. He came with his small retinue into whatever kind of exile his fate and enemies might arrange for him. He had asked asylum as a royal refugee; the right to a residence somewhere in England. He had the means to sustain himself, for he had not been stripped of his money or of all his personal treasures. Exiled in England, at least he would be near France, ready if opportunity arose. When would the British make up their minds?

Of most of his accompanying compatriots, equally looking into an inscrutable future, little could be said. They had come together in a helter skelter way. Young Louis Marchand, his devoted valet, would follow him unquestioningly into any sacrifice. He had good reason to trust Marchand. Two of his generals, Bertrand and Gourgaud, would be staunch and faithful as ever. Bertrand's young wife had chosen to accompany her husband. She was a woman of character and intelligence.

And then, rather surprisingly, there were the count Charles Tristan de Montholon and his Countess. Once he had punished this young man for marrying a faithless and divorced woman. Now de Montholon had come forward, quite unpredictably, with his mate at his side, declaring they would follow him to the ends of the earth, if necessary. Such loyalty, relating to no past record of personal dedication, was unexpected. Well, at least the Countess might add some sparkle to his established residence, wherever that might be. As for the others, Bertrand and Gourgaud had served him faithfully in war. He could count on them. Only time would tell what his lost luck had put at his disposal for comfort and support.

18

Toward Other Stars

NORTHUMBERLAND'S SAILS were set to a moderate westerly wind and she had settled to her pace on the long Atlantic swells, her destination lonely St. Helena.

Meditating and melancholy, Napoleon looked back to the receding shores of England. For a time, at least, he must give up the cherished dream of becoming an honored exile in a country upon whose graciousness in victory he had placed inordinate hope. He had gambled on generosity; but what better could he have done?

To the east and south lay the familiar continent of Europe — his continent. As to every country there he could feel a degree of personal possessiveness. Certainly he carried in his memory vivid vignettes implanted in peace and war touching almost every capital excepting London. So many places and people; the leading actors and the common people of so many lands. The images of great days, desperately exciting days, surged into his mind. Life in these countries would go on without him. Would he be forgotten? Would he ever return? He must believe in his own legend. He was a man of destiny, a man apart. He knew nothing of how he would return, but he *must* believe he would. His task in exile would be to wait, as at Elba, to study his chances and to be ready once again to turn defeat into victory.

Only fifty days ago he had been the emperor of a French-led hegemony of Western Europe. Now defeated, he was being transported to St. Helena. So infinitely far removed, it would be a severity of banishment he had not expected. Perhaps if he had listened to some of his friends in the new United States of America and had tried escape . . . But he chose to gamble on honorable terms of asylum as a rejected head of state. Instead this trap of his enemies' making had snapped shut on him. Captive . . . exiled to nowhere.

Napoleon had once observed that wherever his grand strategy had turned, there he had been fated to find the British Navy — obstructor of his plans, filcher of his all-but-won victories, and destroyer of his destiny. So it had come to this, that he was physically in the hand of that self-same shadower of his actions.

Clearly, the officers on board had been well instructed concerning him. They were stiffly polite; but they had been commanded to recognize him only as a lieutenant-general. Yet he was, or so recently had been, His Imperial Majesty, the Emperor of France and King of Italy, anointed by the Pope in God's name to preside over the late fate of France and the nations he had brought to heel.

Lieutenant-General Bonaparte! As far back as his first entrance on the stage of Europe he had been General Bonaparte. This, surely, was a calculated insult. He had been Commander of the Army of France, first consul, consul for life, then Emperor. He glowered over the sea and sought the pose of calmness that was, equally with a flashing temper, his legendary characteristic. Let them call him what they would. He could still display the qualities of emperor. He could, for a time, play Gulliver amongst the Lilliputians.

A few paces from the defeated monarch stood a small group, conspicuous in the brilliance of their uniforms. These were to be Napoleon's principal attendants at St. Helena, his friends and associates and supporters during five and a half exile years that ended in his death at 52.

Not then but much later in the light of modern investigation, it could be known that one member of the party had a mission of a supremely sinister kind. It called for certain qualities in extraordinary measure. He must be an actor of consummate skill to avoid discovery. He must have loyalty to purpose in the face of the unusually engaging personality of his intended victim. These were essential attributes along with dedication enough to accept danger, skill in execution, nerves of steel and a high degree of self-discipline and alertness. Few in France could have known of the man's assignment. No agent of counter espionage in Paris or elsewhere had alerted London's Whitehall to any threat to their undertaking to be guardians of "the scourge of Europe". The British were resolved to place such a watch upon the person of the man who had skipped from Elba that neither he nor any earthly power could manage his unapproved return from the ultimate in isolation.

The composition of Napoleon's retinue on the *Northumberland* and, indeed, life aboard the ship may be reviewed in some depth and leisure. Time will hang heavy enough on our hands, for this will be a long and often tiresome journey to come below the stars of the Southern Hemisphere and toward the unknowable fate the French attendants would share with their awesomely famous countryman. Any of the Emperor's previous remoteness will be hard to retain in the confined spaces henceforth allocated to him as 'Lieutenant-General' Bonaparte. Oddly demoted as to rank, he was to be a general with a difference.

First there had to be officers of higher rank around Napoleon for his way of life to be lived in some sort of simulated continuity. There would be a grand marshal of the palace, a major-general, a *maréchal de camp*, a chamberlain dressed in uniform of a French naval officer, and a page. Could another lieutenant-general of history boast as much? There were, as well, two quite young and attractive ladies of the court. They stood there, hatted and heavily coated against wind that otherwise would have tossed elaborate coiffures and whipped their dress skirts to the confusion of the honest British tars.

For a lieutenant-general such an attendance should be grand, indeed — enough to turn his head. But to Napoleon, whose mind was still of its adopted imperial cast, this was a disparagingly small court. It might even represent calculated ridicule.

There were some incongruities about the scene, perhaps more apparent to the English ratings than to more senior personnel and passengers of the *Northumberland*. The attendants with their gaudy uniforms stood in a knot as though they had come on stage, not quite knowing their parts, and without direction. Theirs now would be unrehearsed roles. Obviously they related to that other figure a little distance off — Napoleon himself. The Emperor was anything but a sculptor's classic model suggesting noble power. The hat conformed with the pictured image of Napoleon. The greatcoat, the green tunic, the white breeches were appropriate to a military figure. But what about those patent leather buckled shoes, sized for a woman, those white stockings over calves bulging with fat, the squat stature of the man who tilted back a little to counterbalance a frankly protrusive stomach?

Could this truly be the giant of Europe, the man whose exploits of valor and passion under fire at Toulon even the junior ranks of *Northumberland's* officers would likely have known; for was he not once the youth who had forced the great Admiral Lord Hood to up-anchor and take off with the royal flotilla from Toulon Harbor? Was this obese little man once the stripling general who stood shoulder to shoulder with his artillerymen, pumping iron from the point of land his brigade had wrested bloodily from the British only scant hours and minutes earlier? How could the footfalls of such small, delicate shoes have shaken the world?

But the British officers, having studied their history courses at naval college, no doubt knew familiarly the stories of ancient conquerors. What if they could have seen this figure in other garments? Replace those ridiculous breeches and shoes with toga and sandals. Ah, then you might well imagine him a Roman emperor — an Augustus, a Trajan, even a Julius Caesar. For that squarish, too-large-for-the-body face and head, housing the brilliant mentality of a true genius in the sciences of war and the arts of government, often had cowed and demanded the immediate respect of those who were at first inclined to see only his unimpressive stature.

The curious gaze of crew members of *Northumberland* was directed that day on the figure of one who would be for centuries almost the patron saint of all men endowed with great ambition but not with the gift of a proportionate physical presence. At their distance they could not feel the mesmeric power of his piercing, grey-blue eyes.

As for the young military officers near Napoleon, they would be impressive enough in any company.

The finest uniform on deck was that of Grand Marshal of the Palace. The French, always gifted with a way for clothes of distinction, had excelled themselves in Napoleon's time with the ceremonial and dress costumes suitable for a grand marshal.

The risen-from-the-ranks wearer was Henri Gratien Bertrand; and he had been with Napoleon ever since the days when the Emperor had been commander-in-chief of the Army of France in Italy. His army rank was that of full general.

It was well enough that his military plumage should elevate him above all the rest, for he was the closest military aide to the monarch, had sustained him when his great army had been all but wiped out east of the Rhine states and again at Waterloo. He had known the frustrations of life when the Emperor in his first abdication had been given the Island of Elba to rule — as Emperor of Elba — not Emperor of France.

To Bertrand, head of the little company of attendants, Napoleon would be Emperor until death. He had experienced the incredible unbloodied march after landing near Cannes from Elba, the recovered throne, the exultation of a nation that arose once again to his almost magical power to conjure up visions of all of Europe united under French suzerainty. He had not quit the Emperor after the calamitous events of the mighty battle at Waterloo. This was the utterly loyal officer whose commitment to his leader was so complete that one day, with a great unanimity, it would be agreed in France that his body, through centuries, should rest beside that of the man whose side he had never left at any time of crisis during life.

Bertrand was also a count. But in Napoleon's mind the title, which was one of his own manufacturing and bestowing, would not equate with one like Montholon's. That young man, irregular though he might be, could trace his aristocracy back to the old regime in France. Napoleon had made it clear he expected to enter history as the first of a dynasty and to be succeeded by his son, l'Aiglon' — later called by the Austrians the Duke of Reichstadt. Yet he had always stood more than a little in awe of certified and sanctified royalty. Not in all his career had he laid rough hands upon anyone who had been anointed to rule and on whose head there was an hereditary crown.

This deference shown by a self-made monarch for those descended of royalty and the aristocracy, and whom he clearly envied all the while he held them in his power, was an attitude of the Emperor that may have played into the hands of Count de Montholon. He had received acceptance so unquestioningly into the very small company of persons who would share the Emperor's company in exile.

In such company de Montholon was called general rather than *maréchal de camp.*

Gourgaud was another who had been awarded a baronetcy empty of any foregoing historic significance. He became a *baron de l'Empire.*

The chamberlain of the court would be the wearer of the uniform of a captain of the French fleet, Emmanuel Dieudonné Las Cases. He was short in stature but every inch a true and royal count. He had emigrated from France during the Revolution and in England had published under the name "Lesage" an imposing historical and geographical atlas. It gained him a considerable reputation as an historian. More than that, it had made him financially independent of royal favors.

Through some event experienced during his exile, Las Cases had come to be unfriendly toward the House of Bourbon. Some writers have been unkind enough to suggest that while he may have helped Napoleon somewhat during the painful first expatriate years, the count's motives in joining him came from a lively sense of self-interest. As an historian he would be well aware of Napoleon's existing and future place in history. To write history, as drawn from the recollections of Napoleon, with the privilege of having long periods of the Emperor's undivided time, could be a compensation for a successful historian with a reputation to sustain and an already established public demand for his work.

If Las Cases' presence involved no mystery, still he must have recognized position. His duties on St. Helena as a chamberlain would be largely honorary. They would be easily discharged. Meanwhile, his insights into the mind and memory of such a history-maker should be as rewarding intellectually as prospectively they would be financially.

Las Cases was accompanied by his 15-year-old son. This was convenient. It provided a page boy for the court in exile.

On shipboard and on St. Helena the presence of the two ladies in attendance added piquancy to an assortment of lives destined for a period of strange mutual involvement. One was the Countess Bertrand, otherwise Madame Fanny Bertrand. She was the wife of the grand marshal of the palace. She came honestly by her very English given name of Fanny, through British descent. The other, more glamorous and even theatrical in appearance, was the much-married divorcée, Countess Albine de Montholon.

This, then, was the little group of persons who, like Napoleon himself, were getting their first physical sense of future closeness; of having their lives indefinitely cast into a restricted pool of shared experiences much too quickly for them to adjust to the sudden and drastic change that had come to their individual ways of living. They would wait circumspectly for Napoleon to indicate his readiness to cease his introspective gazing toward the receding land shapes and go below. Courtly manners were the greater part of what values they had left to preserve. They were attendants to an emperor. To see him as a lesser personage would be to lessen their own self-esteem.

Except for Las Cases, the historian, and Napoleon, the maker of history, members of the company hardly would realize that they were sailing not only to St. Helena but into the pages of history. And only one knew the plot for the story of exile . . . a plot he earnestly hoped would be enacted but never become recognized or described.

19

On Stage with Napoleon

Now, WHILE the southbound *Northumberland* stands well off the Bay of Biscay, running a long reach in a series that will take her obliquely closer to her far-off destination, will be a good time to become further acquainted with the members of the Emperor's court in exile. We have as yet met them only briefly. Later they will become much better known from their actions and experiences at Longwood House on St. Helena. Humanly, we shall develop preferences and prejudices toward them.

But each and all, in character and personality, are products of their personal heritages, of their backgrounds, their times and their patterns of life. Hastily assembled though they were, all had been seen to have something recommending them to as competent a judge of human qualities as was the Emperor.

In other words, these are people of human frailties and strengths, joined to share, in confinement and for good or ill, the fate of one admired, self-centered man of genius. Napoleon Bonaparte, the object of their group and individual attentions, will live out the remaining years of his life under the peril to his future arising from past greatness. For a great dynast once deposed, must stay deposed or he may return to avenge his humiliation.

Napoleon's conquerors as yet would have an imperfect view of him in historical perspective. Almost alone in history he had been inclined to be trustful that gratitude of those he had put down and then restored to position under his guardian watch was the soundest basis for a policy of reconstruction after war. He was not at this time receiving nor would he henceforth ever enjoy the consideration he had given to most of his defeated enemies. Certainly the allies were not disposed to show him once more the leniency and freedom accorded him in the Elba interlude.

These adherents of the Emperor, who left Europe to be with him in his last and greatest ordeal — in circumstances where he would never identify his enemy — have been the subject of much examination and debate. This one was faithful to Napoleon; that one was selfish and inconsiderate. Another failed him in significant ways. Others were exemplary in their selfless devotion. Amongst the latter, Count de Montholon usually has been placed. Napoleon having described him as the most faithful of the faithful, the evidence was in his favor from the highest possible authority.

But that favorable estimation of de Montholon would only be formed after the days of outward passage on His Majesty's ship *Northumberland*. It was to come from a sick and querulous man, eager for a solacing attitude when no physical comfort and certainly no mental serenity were to be had. As Napoleon saw de Montholon he was tireless in his ministrations. Always, or nearly always, he was bright and amiable, respectful, considerate and never far away when Napoleon was gravely ill and humanly grateful for the care of an attentive nurse. True, the man might at times be careless with the truth. His eager services were clearly enough self-serving. His interest in Napoleon's money was observable. But, all in all, he was eagerly attentive. That was enough for the distressed Napoleon . . . and therefore for most chroniclers of events at Longwood House on St. Helena.

Not so charitable have been the judgments respecting other members of the court by writers of history. Some examined Napoleon's followers very critically. Montholon tended to be seen as through Napoleon's eyes. He was, at St. Helena, apparently redeeming a quite questionable past.

Blue bloods like de Montholon and Las Cases, discovering a certain affinity while at sea, since they were of more aristocratic lineage than the others, would not have known that historians would tend to extend a like preference for them, probably for a similar reason. It would be grounded in human respect for those descended from power and privilege. As for the commoners of the party, they would be less fortunate in history's judgment of their services. Henri Gratien Bertrand was one of these commoners, notwithstanding his Napoleon-conferred ennoblement. His blood had been proletarian and revolutionary red.

Bertrand had joined the National Guard in Paris as a newly-qualified engineer officer. Later he served in the French Army in Italy under the command of the fast-rising young General Bonaparte. He was promoted rapidly to become a brigadier-general after the Egyptian campaign's Battle of Aboukir. In 1804 he was appointed aide-de-camp to Napoleon and campaigned with him until after Wagram, where he had won distinction and the commander's gratitude as a builder and restorer of strategically necessary bridges. As every soldier knows, bridges often win battles.

In 1811 Bertrand was appointed governor of the Illyrian Province where, it is said, he was very popular. The years 1813 and 1814 saw him again in the field at the head of an army corps from Italy. He distinguished himself by ably covering Napoleon's retreat to Mainz.

In May 1813, when Napoleon's empire was beginning to crumble, Duroc, Duc de Frioul, was killed at the Battle of Bautzen and Bertrand in November was appointed to succeed him as Grand Marshal of the Palace. In this post he remained steadfast while other marshals deserted the Emperor in 1814. Predictably, he would go to Elba where he became Napoleon's Prime Minister. His loyalty he repeatedly proved beyond question of a doubt.

During the Hundred Days that followed Elba, Bertrand donned again his uniform of Grand Marshal of the Palace. He helped his master take possession of the Elysée palace. Committed utterly to the man who, by long odds, was the most inspiring leader the Army of France had ever known, he unhesitatingly elected to remain with Napoleon, even in defeat. In the course of events he would return to St. Helena in 1840 to be with the party that would accompany Napoleon's body to France. He was dead four years later at 71.

Fanny Bertrand was an aristocrat. In a French and English society that could intermingle at the top, she was the daughter of General Arthur Dillon, owner of a regiment of the Army of France that had been under the command of a Dillon during the whole of the 18th century. On her mother's side Fanny was related to Napoleon's first wife, Marie-Joseph-Rose Tascher de la Pagerie, better known as Josephine de Beauharnais.

During the Reign of Terror Fanny, like so many other daughters of the French aristocracy, lost her father by execution. She was permitted to reside in England where she had relatives and could feel secure in the period of The Terror.

Madame Bertrand has been described as pleasing in appearance rather than beautiful — an attractive, graceful young woman. Her wit sparkled and amused and she was innately kind of heart even though at times she could offend with a sharp and ill-considered remark.

Through kinship with the Empress Josephine, she was entitled to be counted one of the clan; sufficiently so, indeed, that Napoleon had promised her an honorable dowry and a worthy husband. For a time Fanny entertained a strong hope that with such exalted patronage she might become a princess. Instead she had had to content herself with a marriage to the neo-aristocratic Bertrand. But she acquired a title, nevertheless, and her marriage proved to be a happy one. Husband and wife remained mutually loyal, as we shall see, through the adversities of St. Helena as well as in good fortune.

But it could not be said that for loyalty or for any other reason Fanny Bertrand cherished the disciplines of adversity. She had appealed urgently to her cousin, Lord Dillon, and to the British Government to forestall her officer husband's announced intention to go to St. Helena. She had declared, in deep emotion, that Napoleon was a monster. She had even tried throwing herself into the sea, presumably not so much with the intention of drowning as to make her point. But all in vain. Her husband was adamantly loyal to his leader. Those who had taken charge of Napoleon's future could endorse General Bertrand as a suitable person to share responsibilities within the forthcoming household on the island of exile.

It had been suggested that Bertrand might go alone, but Fanny was too devoted a wife to hear of this. She was compelled to realize that Bertrand was determined to discharge a debt to the Emperor who had been friendly and generous to them both when he had money and favors to award. Respect for her husband prevailing over a womanly intuition that all would not go well at St. Helena, Fanny yielded to her resolute husband's decision.

It was not surprising to find Bertrand, Gourgaud and Las Cases amongst those in attendance on Napoleon. It is much less understandable that Napoleon should have acquiesced to the proposal of the de Montholons for a place in the royal exile's household. Two of Napoleon's most obviously loyal staff officers, Planat and Résigny, had been refused passages in favor of the Montholons.

Regrettably the records remain incomplete as to the person or persons who passed judgment — and for what given reasons they decided favorably — on the inclusion of these various volunteers. No suspicion having been directed at de Montholon, perhaps there was little reason for those with responsibility for Napoleon's care to be searchingly interested or even casually curious on the subject.

Until quite recently no revision of the Napoleon story was thought to be necessary on the much written-about closing phase of his life. Certainly blame should not attach to any historian on grounds of negligence toward the subject.

The discovery, coming many decades later, that analyses of Napoleon's hair raised utmost doubt about his having died a natural death, because the hair bore a tell-tale content of poison, was like the breaking of a code. Thereafter could be exposed to view the secrets of a spy plot. Until the code was broken the secret agent system was invisible.

It was not until Napoleon had abdicated for the second time that Charles Tristan de Montholon would place himself and his countess unreservedly at his command. This could have seemed strange inasmuch as the crises of war had not aroused a similarly fervid loyalty. Napoleon would one day say that the Montholons were at St. Helena only for what they could get from him. But by then he was accustomed to their ingratiating ways. His then existing retinue was small enough without allowing prejudice against such apparently charming and considerate companions to add to his loneliness. Yet at his time of power, when he had the choice of association amongst all the people in France, Napoleon had not favored the Montholons. It was strange, indeed, that amongst the very few attendants who would be available to him, the Montholons would gradually become first in numbers of meaningful ways.

While still aboard the *Northumberland,* Napoleon well could have wondered that young de Montholon seemed to bear so little resentment against him. After all, he would remember angrily ordering his discharge from his post as French envoy at Würzburg. It then had seemed to Napoleon, deeply committed as he was to details of his campaign against Russia, that it was unbearable to learn de Montholon had demeaned his office and thereby the prestige of his country by marrying so questionable a person as the twice-divorced Albine Roger. From the distance of Warsaw the Emperor regarded the romance of Charles Tristan and Albine with anything but a melting heart. He dispatched orders that undoubtedly blighted the young aristocrat's budding career as diplomat.

The Emperor might have recalled, too, that Charles Tristan de Montholon's father had died when the son was still very young. The mother married again. Her second husband was a brilliant royalist politician, Charles-Louis Sémonville. Craftiness was the trade mark of Sémonville in affairs of the several courts in which he served. A kindlier opinion would be that he was marvellously adaptable. It was this quality together with his facile mind that permitted him to pass through political walls as though they did not exist. Thus he remained welcome and influential to the policy-makers in the successive French regimes from Louis XVI to Louis-Philippe. It was an accomplishment of no mean order.

Sémonville was known to be an aide or agent of that arch-Bourbon, the Count d'Artois, brother to King Louis XVIII. Yet for considerable periods of time he enjoyed the favor and generosity of Napoleon. For his services to the House of Bourbon, the King had made Sémonville a peer in the new French House of Lords and a Grand Referendary. Thus he occupied one of the highest offices of state the Bourbon monarch could offer. On January 6, 1815 Sémonville was made grand officer of the Legion of Honor. The insignia he received bore Henry IV's portrait, not Napoleon's.

Charles Tristan was raised as Sémonville's son in every

apparent respect. He grew up bearing the compound name Montholon-Sémonville.

It is hardly likely that at Malmaison Montholon dwelt much on the fact that his father had been Master of the Buckhounds in the household of Louis XVI's brother, later to be Louis XVIII.

He most probably did not refer either to the trouble in Würzburg or the severe "indispositions" which had prevented him from serving actively in the military campaigns of 1812, 1813 and 1814.

As the Napoleonic war drew to a close in March 1814, the Count had accepted command of the National Guard, that is to say the home guard, in the department of the Loire. All went well and quietly there.

Napoleon did not like to have around him people who stole. So it is improbable that Montholon mentioned anything of the fact that he had appropriated to himself two lots of military funds during his stay with the Defence Establishment. But it was money belonging to the Napoleonic regime and Montholon, at the time of defalcations, was on the King's side. Under those circumstances it was not considered either proper or prudent to call such a person a thief.

Though Montholon would claim he won his honors of rank in the field, historians have testified that political rather than military consideration had produced his preferments.

Was the defeated Napoleon so distraught that he could accept de Montholon without experiencing any sense of serious misgiving? Would he not have given thought to the fact that this volunteer courtier, by reason of a mother's second marriage, had become the step-son of one of the most trusted servants of the Bourbon cause? Strangely these questions are without satisfactory answers.

We know that Sémonville himself at this time was out of grace with the troubled Emperor. Napoleon on occasion had befriended this servant of the Bourbons. He had made him a count in 1808. But much as he might have wished for the impractical development of an alliance of the old Bourbon and new Bonaparte families, Napoleon surely could perceive that Sémonville had never deserted the Bourbons and had the closest of ties with the Count d'Artois, an abler and more determined man than the claimant to a crown he himself would inherit. A brother of Charles Tristan's was an attendant to King Louis.

It is a pity that in some moment of confiding to Bertrand, to Las Cases or Marchand, the Emperor did not see fit to explain his unlikely addition of this Sémonville family member, Count Charles Tristan de Montholon, to his court in exile.

Was it perhaps enough that Count de Montholon-Sémonville was the scion of a family belonging to the old, the true French aristocracy and that Napoleon was pleased to be thus served by a blue-blood royalist? In manners and speech he would contrast favorably with the come-lately aristocrats of Napoleon's own creating. Yet the implications for harsh consequences that could go with associations so closely identified with Bourbonism seem never to have aroused a sense of caution in the man whom the Bourbons had tried so hard to eliminate.

Well before presenting himself and his wife at Malmaison as virtually self-appointed candidates to share Napoleon's clouded future, and regardless of where that might be, Charles Tristan had discreetly dropped Sémonville from his name. It was simply as Count de Montholon that he had once asked for relief from the arduous life of officer in an Army at war and had applied for and received the sinecure post of chamberlain at the court of the Empress Josphine.

Historians henceforth will do well to give attention to that fateful occasion of the meeting of the Emperor at Malmaison after his return defeated from Waterloo and his second abdication.Napoleon was assembling his personal resources for emigration. He was once more vulnerable to enemies, some of them new — his former friends — and some as old and implacable as Blücher who would not hesitate to shoot Prussia's enemy, the outlaw of the Congress of Vienna.

At Malmaison, gold specie, plate, art objects and similar portable possessions were gathered assiduously by the Emperor, in preparation for flight or for deportation. Some time before it was decided to proceed to the Bay of Biscay and embark for the United States, or surrender to the blockading British Navy, approval must have been given by the Emperor to this most improbable of recruits to accompany him into exile. Who decided that the de Montholons would qualify? It is a teasing question, for history later would turn on the fact that the ineffable pair, Charles Tristan and Albine, were ready and willing to go.

One account credits Maret, one of Napoleon's most constant supporters, as possibly recommending de Montholon. His friends knew him as an impecunious young officer, with a courtier's manners — and conscience — and a record of dodging the rigors of army life on the fighting fronts while achieving rank through Sémonville's influence. He had become a full colonel without having commanded even a platoon of soldiers. His many claims of hot engagements and war wounds were lively reading. According to Montholon, it was all gospel truth. Diligent search by various historians could substantiate so little that his accounts were indulgently dismissed as wishful imaginings.

Could it be that in his fate of being separated by the European feudal kings from his Empress Marie-Louise and anticipating an extra-marital life of indefinite duration, it was not Charles Tristan but Albine whom Napoleon chose? If so, the assignment of the pair to accompany the Emperor wherever they might go was a clever one. Without straining imagination, we may surmise that in this pretty and adventurous divorcée, now married to a volunteering officer who had been briefly a chamberlain to Josephine, Napoleon saw some probable measure of relief from the impending isolation from army, country and Marie-Louise.

Of course no historian past, present or future could do more than speculate on whether Charles Tristan's professions of deathless loyalty or Albine's eyes spoke the more persuasively to the sorely distressed monarch. But, obviously with imprudence, he had accepted an offer of comfort and companionship from what plainly was a dangerous source. He would entrust himself to the care of a Bourbon aristocrat whom he had once sacked and disgraced as he was on the threshold of a career in the diplomatic service of France. Albine was the woman he had thus ordained to be not fit for Montholon to marry.

It was a time of decision in which Napoleon's star of destiny was in unfavorable phase. By all accounts de Montholon was a young man of almost excessively pleasing personality and politeness. As for Albine, whose portraits portray prettiness if not beauty, there was visible qualification of a kind to be appreciated. In the frustrations of war against Russia, he may have been harsh toward a romantic young couple.

Napoleon, like many another of the greats of history, craved the attentions of the opposite sex. His conquests of the heart were at least as numerous as his victories in war. Mme. Bertrand and Countess de Montholon were the only ladies Napoleon would take from Malmaison to Longwood House. Mme. Bertrand was interested exclusively in her lawful husband. This fact would emerge from St. Helena memoirs along with suggestions that this fidelity at times sorely exasperated Napoleon.

Albine de Montholon was somewhat older than her husband, who was 34. She had married first an obscure Monsieur Bignon, who divorced her. She then was wed to a Swiss called Danile Roger. Both marriages were dissolved on grounds of her infidelity. When she with her free-booting husband started off on the journey to Malmaison to "follow Napoleon to the ends of the earth", she left behind two sons, one a Roger and the other a Montholon. The Montholon offspring was then only seven months old. She had an older son by Montholon, called Tristan. The exact date of this child's birth is not known, but officially it was supposed to have been toward the close of 1812. This may not be correct, however, as on July 9, 1816 Las Cases recorded that the boy should have been seven years of age. However that may be, the fact is that Albine was now the legal spouse of Charles Tristan de Montholon, a quite charming young man, if his surface polish was not penetrated to the grain of his actual personality.

Albine's third marriage was to be far more fateful than she could have had reason to suspect as she gave her vows of undying faithfulness to her newest husband.

The Countess Albine de Montholon's beauty, at the time she went aboard H.M.S. *Northumberland,* was not as freshly brilliant as once it had been, but a piquant face and her bright sophistication more than compensated. She knew how to dress and how to charm. She was gaily coquettish and competent enough in conversation. She had poise to cope with most social situations. Compliments and impertinences were met with the same delightful smile and a lively rejoinder. In short, she was the very woman to include in the drastically diminished court of the exiled Emperor. She was typical of the kind for which the courts of the Bourbons were celebrated. And not many of her kind would have volunteered to go.

For Montholon it was certainly helpful to be able to bring Albine to Napoleon's court. Montholon's other qualifications for inclusion in Napoleon's miniscule company of attendants were not especially visible. But it would have been surprising had he not exaggerated them a little when he first offered his services to his new master, a man still wealthy and still to be reckoned with — as witness that astonishing return from Elba.

Later when, in the year of 1819, the fourth year of Napoleon's exile to St. Helena, news from France must have brought word of the elevation of Charles-Louis Sémonville, by the King's favor, to be a marquis, some signal of alarm well might have sounded in the depths of Napoleon's mind. We have no indication that this was so. Montholon by then was thoroughly established. Rather than being compromised by such evidence of great regard given by King Louis to de Montholon's stepfather, the young man had become more trusted and depended upon than any other member of Napoleon's exile court. He was called the most loyal of the loyal and preferred above even so great a friend to Napoleon as Bertrand.

In the light of all we know we may today speculate on the possibility that Louis XVIII's appointee as observer at St. Helena, the Marquis Claude-Marin-Henri de Montchenu, had reported to Paris Charles Tristan's wholly successful penetration to a position of utmost trust. It was a perfect set-up for a secret agent with a mission vital to the security of the Bourbon succession. Satisfaction in its accomplishment could conceivably have expressed itself by proxy in the conferring of the title of marquis on the trusted senior Sémonville. Certainly no recognition could be given at that time to de Montholon by the King or by the King's spy-managing brother, the Count d'Artois. It was d'Artois who was master of scores of secret agents and a collection of assassins in Paris and elsewhere. As for Louis, he could not fail to have been conscious, every day of his renewed reign, of the danger that the hated Corsican usurper would return. Well might he have conferred on de Sémonville by proxy some measure of the gratitude owed to his aristocratic stepson. With such trustfulness established the rest of the agent's St. Helena task should be easy.

But in the year of 1815 all of these things were still obscurely in the care of the future.

Amongst the company St. Helena-bound from England, Charles Tristan de Montholon alone must have had some sense of mastery of the future. In the little cadre of royal attendants he could have no confidants — not even with the shallow Albine could he share awareness of his duty. He would have had forebodings of possible disaster. His patience and his nerves would be severely taxed over a long period of time. Such, by tradition, is the lot of the successful secret agent who has penetrated high into the enemy's councils.

It was altogether unlikely, however, that when outward bound from the familiar surroundings of his past, with the pleasant adventuress who now shared his life and name, de Montholon could have anticipated the full extent of his success. He would have been aware that Napoleon was a man of wealth. But he could then hardly have dreamed that when he, forever painfully in need of money, returned from his mission of duties in exile he would live — for a time — in luxury from legacies of gold conferred through his victim's Will. Seventeen years after his return to France he would partly recoup that gambled-away fortune with the proceeds of his book of St. Helena memoirs.

The book's author being remembered gratefully in France by all friends and admirers of Napoleon as "the most faithful of the faithful" at St. Helena, how could even as dubiously dependable a set of memoirs as Montholon then concocted fail to receive a reading? But as the Montholon *Histoire* was critically read, a public, ready to approve, became embarrassed by discovering he had plagiarized heavily from the accounts of historian Las Cases and Dr. O'Meara and presented the product as his own chronogically diarized memoirs. Even worse, he had gathered up Napoleonic papers at St. Helena and sold them in England, pocketing the proceeds.

Of those now on the *Northumberland,* as it bore Napoleon to St. Helena, nine would return with sad memories to the island 19 years after Napoleon's death. They were invited to be present at the reopening of his tomb. Montholon, as we shall see, would have the best of reasons for not being amongst them. At that time he was in England and deeply involved in a new mission as trusted agent for the royal French secret service. He was likewise the trusted right hand man to the Bonapartist pretender, Louis Napoleon, who was living exiled in England and plotting a coup that would win him the throne of France.

For King Louis-Philippe it would be unfortunate indeed if, in the midst of the predictable great outburst of emotional nostalgia for the personality and piping times of Napoleon I, this troublesome aspirant to become Napoleon III should land with a party on French soil, proclaiming the arrival of a new Napoleonic age!

Louis-Philippe must have been advised, from some dependable source, that the family to which he was related by birth had been well served by Montholon, and that he was an expert on rendering Napoleon harmless. Montholon then would have appeared trustworthy as a means to ensure that the Return of the Ashes could be politically safe to perform, with credit to the existing royal regime. He could also be depended upon to be in need of money.

In nice co-ordination, *La Belle Poule* sailed July 7, 1840 for St. Helena, to bring back the body of Napoleon for reburial in the *Dome des Invalides;* and well before it could return, Montholon, as aide de camp to Louis Napoleon, sailed on the fourth of August from England, with a small military party bearing a confused captive eagle. The mascot would be even more symbolic than the head of the expedition had visualized. The object was to land at Boulogne and provoke an uprising of the local regiment. The expected party was quickly captured and charged with treason. Louis Napoleon, sentenced to life imprisonment, was intended to be leniently buried alive in the fortress castle of Ham. For appearance sake, Montholon would have to go with him. His sentence was for 20 years but in something much less than "durance vile"; and he would be safely available until another need for his specialized services might arise. He had been needed in 1840 — but not at St. Helena.

De Montholon lived to the ripe age of 72. His chief place, insofar as history was to be concerned, would be as the attendant described by Napoleon as "the most faithful of the faithful."

20

Table Talk of the Last Journey

WHEN H.M.S. *Northumberland* was built according to the tried and tested plans of centuries, no one could have guessed she would make history in a passenger carrying role, while her exploits in British naval warfare would be of no particular renown.

Right aft, below the quarter-deck, lay the after cabin and next to it two sleeping cabins for the admiral, when the *Northumberland* served as a flagship. The rest of the area was taken up by the wardroom.

When Napoleon boarded *Northumberland* at Start Point, transferred from H.M.S. *Bellerophon,* he presumed the prestigious after-cabin would be exclusively for his use and so proceeded to occupy it. Admiral Sir George Cockburn, in command of the St. Helena fleet, found it necessary to tell him the cabin was intended for the use of all the senior officers and that he would have to make do with one of the sleeping cabins. It was the first of many indignities that would aggrieve the conqueror as an exile living under supervision and restraint, though technically not a prisoner.

Opposite Napoleon's cabin was the admiral's. Captain Ross, in command of the ship, gave up his cabin to the Bertrands, while the Montholons were given that of the admiral's secretary, John Glover. General Gourgaud, Count de Las Cases and his son all had to sleep on sofa-beds in the after-cabin until such time as provisional cabins had been constructed 'tween decks.[1]

The admiral and Napoleon were at table with their respective suites. The day was August 17, 1815. Captain Ross sat at the head of the table, with the Countess de Montholon on his left. This lady had been escorted to table by Sir George Cockburn.

Half-way down the board sat the Emperor, with Mme. Bertrand on his left. To the left of Mme. Bertrand was the Count de Montholon and at the end, Miss Amy Stranger. We do not know anything about the mission of this woman with the unusual name but on such a voyage the admiral was certainly permitted to have at least one lady guest on board, if he wished. Admiral Plampin, one of Sir George's successors in command of the St. Helena fleet, took advantage of this privilege in such a way that St. Helena society, led by the governor's strait-laced lady, was deeply shocked.

To the right of the captain sat the Count de Las Cases and General Bertrand. With them was Colonel Sir George Bingham, who was under orders to command the troops on St. Helena. Beyond this were two places reserved for various dinner guests. One seat was now occupied by the Rev. George Rennel and the other by the ship's second-in-command. Much to his annoyance General Gourgaud had been given the bottom place. The admiral's secretary, John Glover, sat sedately at the other end of the table, near the captain.[2]

They had reached the meat course and were being served lamb chops. Napoleon took his viand in his fingers and tackled it with evident relish. Vegetables and puddings meant nothing to him[12], and Corsican soldier and veteran campaigner that he was, he considered such tools as knife and fork quite superfluous for the eating of meat from a bone.

We have not been privileged to enjoy the small talk at table of Alexander the Great or of Caesar. There is an insight value in knowing what things were talked about in the Captain's dining cabin on the *Northumberland* while it was trudging toward an isolated volcanic rock, then nearly unknown. Because of this unwilling tablemate, accepting his position with a degree of relaxed dignity that made him popular with all hands aboard, the name of that island suddenly would be on every tongue throughout the civilized world. It would become the most famous isle in history, identified by association with one person, his years of exile and death in its rugged and restrictive confines. We may eavesdrop, thanks to the preserved written accounts of some who were there and who sensed that history travelled with the interesting man of sallow countenance, questing conversation and eyes that seemed large, luminous and of piercing penetration. Those eyes were the one feature of his physical make-up no one failed to remark.

We shall be ready to be awed by the global sweep of Napoleon's mighty comprehension of the world, of the Eighteenth and Nineteenth centuries, and so will be slightly surprised at what kind of things interested him at this time and place.

Still tearing at his chop, Napoleon conducts a cross-examination of the ship's chaplain, Rennel. An Anglican clergyman was for him something quite new.

"Do you have music during your services?"

"Why, yes, general. In that way we are the same as the Catholics."

"Do you have Extreme Unction, too?"

"Oh, yes."

"Do you also pray for the dead?"

"Yes, we do, general."

"How many sacraments have you? Seven?"

"Well, out of the seven sacraments of the Catholic Church we have only kept two, Baptism and Holy Communion, as these were the only sacraments that Christ himself instituted."

"Do you also believe in transubstantiation?"[3] Napoleon had always been a little troubled where Christianity was concerned. When the question cropped up, he often used to express sympathy with the religion of Mohammed. Mohammedanism seemed to him to promise, while Christianity only threatened.

The lamb chop — or chops — had disappeared, and the admiral saw his chance to join the conversation.

"I hope, Sire, that you have seen the newspapers *Peruvian* had with her."

(He probably addressed Napoleon as "Sire" and not "General", thus defying the orders of his government. But here on board it was he who was in command.)

"Thank you, yes, I have read them, admiral. I see that King Louis has now appointed new presidents of the provinces and city regions. I think I would have agreed to most of them."

"You have had a wonderful career, Sire."

"I made one great mistake. I should have been killed at Moskova (Borodino), where I lost so many of my generals. My career would then have been exceptional in world history and no one would have dared oppose my son as my successor.

"I was only thirty years old when I became head of the state of France. I had then a long, unbroken line of glorious military victories to look back upon."

"But we have not yet seen the end of your career, Sire. One day, perhaps, England may see fit to bring you back from St. Helena."[4]

"The French will never forgive the Bourbons for employing foreign bayonets to help them back to power," said Napoleon. "Just now France wants peace. But wait until those who now hear so much about the revolution and the empire shall have come of age. Ten or fifteen years is the most the Bourbons can hope for."

"It would be very interesting, Sire, to hear your opinion of your opponents, the King of Prussia and the Tsar of Russia."

"The King of Prussia was a poor wretch. His queen had more to her. She begged me to let him keep Magdeburg, but I had already made my plans. She was very elegant, and most attractive . . . as beautiful as a lady of thirty-five can be expected to be.

"But it was difficult to interrupt her. She always dominated the conversation and invariably returned to the subject of the discussion but with *grande convenance*. You could not be angry with her, for what she wanted was really of the greatest importance to her. I might have let her have her way but instead I told Talleyrand and Prince Kurakin to settle the Magdeburg business with her and I saw to it that the treaty with the Tsar was signed.

"I know she told the Tsar that I had not kept my promise, but he tried — perhaps in vain — to deny this. No, she never forgave me for Magdeburg. It was the queen who really held the power in Prussia. Tsar Alexander was very taken with her. He asked me if I could arrange for them to meet without being disturbed by the king. I did."[5]

"And what about the Tsar, Sire?"

"Alexander's character and Frederick William's were quite different. He was cleverer and much more active than the other European rulers, but incredibly false-hearted. He is witty, charming. But always remember, he is a real Byzantine."

"What about your other opponents, Sire?"

"Well, it's true that Louis has admitted that he has your Prince Regent to thank for his crown. But the Prince Regent is also indebted to the Count d'Artois, brother to the King. He handed you the finest fleet that France has ever had and, at the same time, gave you your supremacy at sea.[7]

"There is a story about d'Artois," continued Napoleon, "which is characteristic of that man and what he stands for. It clearly shows the difference between the house of Bourbon and what I represent. An Englishman, who had to do with the Count when he was in exile in England, had been visiting Paris and was about to return to England. He went to take leave of d'Artois and said that he hoped the Count and His Royal Highness would remember him as a friend, in spite of the fact that they were of different nationalities. 'What do you mean?' asked d'Artois. 'I only know of two nationalities, la noblesse et la canaille — aristocrats and the mob. My lord, I think we are of the same nationality, don't you?'[8]

"The Count d'Artois is a clever politician, the King is not. Soon after I became First Consul, the King wrote a letter which was handed to me by Third Consul Lebrun, who in his turn had received it from the Abbe de Montesquiou, the King's secret agent in Paris.[9] In his letter Louis accused me first of having taken too long in ceding him his throne. He went on to congratulate me on my policy, but said I could never make France happy without him. The letter finished something like this: 'You will always be too necessary to the State for me not to repay our family debt to you by high offices'."[10]

"Obviously he wanted you to play the part of another General Monk, Sire — he who prepared the way for Charles II's accession to the throne."

"The Count d'Artois introduced the matter much more diplomatically," Napoleon went on. "He sent Mme. de Guiche, a very beautiful lady, to call on Josephine, who was always available to members of the higher aristocracy. Josephine invited her to lunch at Malmaison and in the course of the meal Mme. de Guiche related how several days earlier she had happened to overhear the conversation between d'Artois and a confidant. This favorite had asked the Count how he thought they should reward Bonaparte for preparing the way for the house of

Bourbon's accession to the throne. The Count had answered: 'First we shall make him *Connétable*, with all that that entails, and then on the Place du Carrousel we shall erect a magnificent monument of Bonaparte crowning Louis XVIII.' "[11]

"Did you ever meet Mme. de Guiche yourself, Sire?"

"No, I did not. I gave orders that she should leave France immediately."

"What did you reply to the King, Sire?"

"I think I wrote something like this: 'I have always sympathized with you in your family's misfortune. Your Royal Highness should not think of returning to France, for you could only do so over the dead bodies of 100,000 Frenchmen. I would add that I shall always do everything possible to mitigate your lot and help you forget your misfortunes.' "

Napoleon was wrong. By the time the house of Bourbon had been re-established in Paris, not a hundred thousand but many hundreds of thousands were dead. But the return of the Bourbons was not the achievement or the crime — of the indolent King Louis. Artois, his younger brother, was the great intriguer. As the reactionary counter-revolution could not have been stopped anyway, it was a pity that the beautiful Mme. de Guiche never met young Bonaparte. She and her husband should have been directed to Bonaparte's office, and not to Malmaison. The Count d'Artois had not then the understanding he was later to acquire about how a cavalier like Napoleon Bonaparte should be handled.

Dessert had been served. Napoleon finished his meal quickly, left his half-filled wineglass and stood. At the same time all those present rose. When Napoleon first came on board, the British officers had paid no ceremonious attention to his premature departures from the dinner table. He was accustomed to going on deck for his evening stroll. This would last about an hour, and when the English had finished their port, the admiral used to join Napoleon. A certain accord developed between the two men as a result of these walks.[12]

After the exercise in sea air it was time for a game of cards in the after-cabin. It was usually Vingt-et-un, and for stakes, of course. For high stakes. On one occasion Napoleon won 80 gold napoleons. It happened to be his forty-sixth birthday.

Usually he was less lucky at cards. His chess before dinner was better. Certainly it was when he played against Count de Montholon. Napoleon was supposed to be a poor chess-player while Montholon excelled. Nevertheless, Napoleon would beat Montholon. It pleased them both.[13]

Montholon knew how to cheer Napoleon in many different ways. Later on Napoleon was to say to Gourgaud: "Mme. Montholon pays me some attention . . . I find her rather nice. She is not beautiful, but still . . . her husband does what I want and has no pretensions."[14]

The dinner talk on August 17 was not precisely as told here. The author has combined actual passages from the memoirs of Cockburn, Glover, Las Cases and Gourgaud respecting several occasions on the voyage. They are here used illustratively and in fair context to recapture something of the atmosphere of Napoleon's last journey. On the whole, it was a pleasant prelude to what would become the long and painful anticlimax in the life of the greatest commander since Julius Caesar. If Montholon brought the Emperor suffering, his wife, with the Count's consent, did what she could to relieve his hunger for feminine company.

Some years later, when Napoleon's virility no longer unsettled him so much, he was able to consider his relationship with Mme. Montholon in a more objective way. Some weeks before he died he confided to Bertrand: "Mme. Montholon is an intriguer who well knows her own interests. When you talked to her about pensions that she thought would never be paid, she wouldn't agree to anything; she only surrendered her heart in return for good bills of exchange."[15]

Still, Napoleon seldom appeared on deck before he had finished dinner, which was generally at five in the afternoon. He breakfasted in his cabin at ten or eleven o'clock, after which he read or dictated for a few hours. At about four in the afternoon he would play chess until it was time to go to dinner. After dinner came the stroll on deck, followed by a game of cards. At ten or eleven o'clock Napoleon would go to his bed, and the faithful Marchand, his head valet, would sleep on the floor outside his master's door.

Humble Marchand would see much and say little. None

aboard the *Northumberland* could suspect that one day his memoirs from St. Helena, long withheld from the press, would alter the written history of his master's life by the mere recital of unexceptional events with tedious faithfulness.

On August 24 the exiled party reached Funchal, on the Portuguese island of Madeira. While there a powerful sirocco suddenly blew up. The heat rose and grapes in the vineyards shrivelled. That sort of thing happened, through the vagaries of nature, every eight to ten years, with distressing damage to the island's economy and contentment. This time, however, the islanders knew whose fault it was. That man Napoleon never should have been allowed to come near their beautiful, bountiful and peaceful island!

The British Consul, Mr. Wilch, came on board and was invited to dinner. Peaches, grapes and figs, together with a large quantity of cattle and fowl, were loaded. This was hardly describable as prison fare. The fresh water supply was renewed.

The journey continued. The obliging admiral thought that Napoleon would like to see Pico del Teide on Tenerife. He altered their course to a setting between Gomera and Palma in the Canary group of islands, but mist and fog hid the summit.[17]

From time to time sharks were seen in the warm waters and on one occasion a dolphin was caught and its flesh added to the bill of fare. It was a diversion to watch the flying fish as they broke from waves and skimmed the water, hunted by swift porpoises.

A mulatto from Guadeloupe, nameless in history, fell overboard. This brief distraction from shipboard routine came almost as a relief from monotony. The ship luffed and braced her sails back. A boat was lowered and search made but it was too late for a rescue and the *Northumberland* resumed her steady trudge on her south by west course.

On Sundays church service was held on the battery deck. It is hardly likely that Napoleon took part. He could have fared worse when Neptune demanded his baptism and that of his following as the *Northumberland* crossed the Line on September 23. Fortunately for him he had the means to buy himself free from indignity. The Emperor offered 100 gold napoleons for the ship's company. But both Bertrand and the admiral protested. Napoleon should consider the effect on the crew. He morosely sulked and gave nothing. Going to exile, why should he be balked? Life was hard enough for the men of the *Northumberland* and he held nothing against them for his plight.

A certain amount of squabbling inevitably went on among Napoleon's retinue. Las Cases had given the Emperor to understand that Gourgaud had told the admiral that Bonaparte was not chief general on the 13 Vendémiaire during the royalist insurrection, as he had claimed he was, but that it was Barras. Gourgaud was told off for not having let Napoleon relate the story in his own way and Gourgaud in his turn took verbal revenge on Las Cases.

On another occasion Gourgaud had expressed his disapproval of the execution of the Duke of Enghien. Historian Las Cases considered the remarks disloyal. He even asked Gourgaud why he was following Napoleon into exile. Gourgaud thereupon grew suspicious of Las Cases.

Bertrand began to look askance at Count de Montholon and both ladies had now arrived at the stage of hearty mutual dislike. "Intrigues and deceit surround me. Poor Gourgaud, why are you sailing on this galley?" wrote Gourgaud in his diary.[18]

At the start of the journey the ex-Emperor appeared to have an unusually great need for sleep. It was a struggle to keep awake. After a few weeks at sea, however, he seemed restored. Never again would he enjoy such a feeling of physical well-being and good health.

During his strolls on deck he often encountered Dr. Warden, the squadron's head physician. He cultivated him for the sake of free consultations and medical inquiry in which he had an insatiable interest. He was skeptical about most medical practices of the time. Actually Napoleon had been assigned his own physician on board, a Dr. O'Meara, but Warden was nearly ten years older than O'Meara and was the senior physician of the ship. He would doubtless be the cleverer of the two.

"Well, how many have you bled today, doctor?"

Bleeding was a concern of Napoleon's. He had obviously certain difficulties in understanding why this method was so generally used and praised by physicians. Napoleon thought it would be more reasonable to conserve this valuable fluid for occasions when life for one reason or another was in danger. Warden had told Napoleon that new blood formed very quickly. Napoleon wondered whether the quality of blood depended on what one ate. Warden admitted this. The Emperor thought one should be very careful not to bleed members of the crew, as it was probable that their food was not especially healthful. Dr. Warden assured him that, generally speaking, the crew was in excellent health. He considered this due to the fact that at the slightest indisposition he made it a rule to open a vein. Out of a sense of mischief, Napoleon would not give up, however: Was it because of the bleeding or in spite of it that the crew members were still alive?[19]

Once Dr. Warden told Napoleon that one of his servants was sick. "Oh, bleed him, bleed him!" cried Napoleon. "To the powerful lancet with him; that's the infallible remedy!"

Bleeding for Warden was an indisputable blessing, but in terms of medicine Napoleon was not exactly of a trusting nature. He doubted the value of the remedy. Warden said: "But you have seen yourself, Sire, what a good effect bleeding has had on Mme. Bertrand."

"Oh, well, she recovered, for what good that was," growled Napoleon, and added for reasons not speculated upon except privately, "It would have been better had she died. How much blood did you take, doctor?"

"Altogether two pounds, Sire."

"And she's still alive! I must say, though, you did your best."[20]

Mme Bertrand was obviously not then in favor. From which it may be supposed the amiable Albine de Montholon was all the more so.

Dr. Warden considered that Fanny Bertrand had contracted an inflammatory fever. Gourgaud had heard that she had suffered from inflammation of the brain, encephalitis maybe, or perhaps meningitis. Aubry does not mention the source of his information but says that Mme. Bertrand had accidentally drunk a solution of sugar of lead.[21]

The business of bleeding seemed to worry Napoleon persistently. Warden had constantly to answer questions. "Could someone suffering from a tropical disease, which you maintain should be treated by bleeding, regain his full health, that is to say the health he enjoyed before bleeding, after a period of, say, eighteen months?"

"How long does it take for the veins to recover after bleeding?"

"How much can you take from a person without bleeding him to death?"

Questions are sometimes more revealing than answers. It is obvious that Napoleon had not the slightest confidence in the ingenious and simplistic method of curing people by reducing their blood volume. No doubt he put his questions in order to test the English physician's general knowledge of the art of healing. He was going to have to submit to English medical science from now on, since Dr. Maingaud, his own physician, who had attended him as lately as aboard the *Bellerophon*, had refused to go on to St. Helena.

Napoleon's faith in doctors was limited and in any event did not extend beyond the borders of France and Italy. Most people trust only doctors of their own nationality. When in 1818 Napoleon found himself in need of a dependable physician on St. Helena, he wrote to his relatives, asking them to send one in whom he could have confidence. Aboard *Northumberland* Napoleon would indulge his mild curiosity about the remarkable ways of medical men of his time. He would have no inkling then to what extent, at St. Helena, doctors and their prescriptions would affect his remaining years.

Bleeding was not the only resource of the English physicians. Blistering, for instance, had been found a good cure for most illnesses. Napoleon tried to learn more about this, too.

"When I returned from Egypt I had some trouble with my lungs. My physician, Corvisart, blistered me. Would you have done so too, Dr. Warden?"

"I think I would have bled you first, Sire."

Dr. Warden had been told by the French courtiers on board that etiquette did not allow him to put questions to Napoleon. He could answer, but he was not to ask.

However, on one occasion his curiosity gained the upper hand. He had observed already during their first week on board, that Napoleon looked worn and as if he were not getting enough sleep. Actually he had slept quite a lot — too much perhaps — during his first weeks as a prisoner of the British. Warden was bold enough to ask the Emperor directly if his sleep was sound. He knew he ran considerable risk of being snubbed for his question but to his great astonishment Napoleon looked at him with sorrow and resignation and answered in a friendly manner: "No, it is not. From my cradle I have been an indifferent sleeper."[22]

Warden was convinced that Napoleon had once enjoyed exceptionally good health, as he had withstood every kind of strain. The doctor considered that his health was still good, in spite of a drawn look during those first weeks on board. Otherwise, Napoleon would not have possessed that considerable *embonpoint* of his. To the average physician of the nineteenth century stoutness denoted health.

One thing is certain and that is that Napoleon had impressed his English hosts more and more favorably as they approached their journey's end. The admiral, who at first was casual toward the fallen ruler, had more respect for him as the days passed. A certain guarded and reserved friendship grew between them, despite the fact Napoleon had once and for all decided that Sir George was, if not exactly a shark, at least much like one.

Naturally the memory of Waterloo weighed heavily upon the Emperor and the fateful battle was often discussed.

Would it have been possible to avert the catastrophe? What mistakes had been made? Was it all the fault of that archtraitor, the Bourbon's Count de Bourmont? Had the outcome of the battle anything to do with the fact that in the afternoon, when the result seemed uncertain, a number of officers started shouting: "Every man for himself"? Could Marshal Ney have acted differently? In Napoleon's opinion the marshal had made many mistakes.[23] These were a few of the questions discussed.

Poor Napoleon! Waterloo had been all too carefully planned to bring about his downfall. Certain soldiers and politicians of France had joined hands to destroy him.

The Count d'Artois had managed to smuggle into Napoleon's staff one of his most reliable and tested agents, the Count de Bourmont. Bourmont took Napoleon's plans of attack and a parcel of other top secret documents and deserted to the Prussians a few days before the great battle. For this he was handsomely rewarded and finally made Minister of War to d'Artois when the latter had become Charles X. For this appointment of a traitor, along with other reasons, both King and minister were forced to flee in July, 1830.

De Bourmont had an excellent record in the service of the house of Bourbon. He had distinguished himself in the royalist army at Vendée by capturing Nantes among other targets. He was involved in the attempt to murder Napoleon on Christmas Eve 1800, when a cart loaded with gunpowder exploded in the rue Saint-Nicaise, just a few seconds too late in the plan to kill the fast-rising First Consul. Many innocent people lost their lives or limbs as a result.

Bourmont was arrested and imprisoned for four years. He managed to escape and joined the royalists again. In due course, however, he was granted a pardon by Napoleon and entered the service of Murat and Eugène, viceroy of Italy and father-in-law of King Oscar I of Sweden. During the first Restoration, Bourmont stood high in King Louis' favor. But when the King had to flee Paris during Napoleon's triumphant march from Elba, Bourmont went forth to meet the conqueror and offered his services, which were gratefully accepted by Napoleon. Fifteen years later Charles X was to declare in Council that Count Bourmont had never acted in any way unless by his order, given first as Count d'Artois and later as King.[24]

General Grouchy was another who enjoyed the favor of King Louis during the first Restoration. He was supposed to keep an eye on the Prussians and see that they did not take part in Waterloo. Grouchy went off with the whole of his corps out of sight of the Prussians. It was variously theorized that he had deserted and also that suffering illness at the time of Waterloo, Napoleon had given him less than explicit directions.

The practice of sending an agent as aide-de-camp to the enemy was resorted to by Charles X according to his own witness during the July revolution of 1830. Lafayette, leader of the military section of the July revolution, had an aide-de-camp who was an agent of King Charles.[28] The King naturally did not say who this agent was.

Napoleon himself was more or less *hors de combat* at Waterloo, suffering severe bladder difficulties. This was the man whose invariable policy was to conduct strategy of the battle as a personal "command post". In the decisive hours of Waterloo he fought a desire to drop off to sleep. He could not sit a horse for any length of time.[27] Yet he had been a general who delighted to ride and whose *joie de vivre* had once been at its highest levels of elation at the height of battles. By whom and by what means was this military genius made ill at crucial times? While Napoleon feared the possibility of poisoning he seems never to have suspected that his chronic illness was actually the work of a poisoner. He did not know that his unfortunate sickness during the crucial battles at Borodino, Leipzig and Waterloo was no mere ill health or due to stress but that he was even then, as science has indicated, victimized by poisonings. However, when after the victorious battle of Dresden August 27, 1813 he was pursuing the enemy, he became suddenly extremely ill and had to return to Dresden. He couldn't fulfil his victory. This time Napoleon realized that he had been poisoned. By what? By garlic in a stew, he explained to Daru, his intendant général.[30] He had never been able to stand garlic, Napoleon said.

If the Emperor really couldn't stand garlic, nobody should have dared serve him a garlic course. Even in the field he was served by his own trusted servants, who knew his habits, tastes and wishes.

There must have been a better explanation to the loss of the fruits of victory. In 1813 nobody could find a logical explanation to the fact that Napoleon thought there was a garlic smell from a course that couldn't possibly have been stuffed with garlic. In 1830 the famous German chemist Gmelin reported, garlic odor was characteristic of domiciles where there were arsenical-containing wallpaper pigments. Arsenic trioxide has in itself no odor, but in connection with organic bodies or enzymes it can be transformed into a gas, trimethyl arsine, with garlic odor.[31] We are forced to conclude that almost without grounds for doubt arsenic was the additive in the stew. The timing of Napoleon's illnesses was too convenient to his enemies.

Another subject constantly discussed on board the *Northumberland* was "the shameful treachery of the English". Napoleon, by his own account, had gone on board the *Bellerophon* of his own free will, under the impression that asylum would be afforded him in England; but he had been taken prisoner instead, denied habeas corpus, and carried off to an uncertain fate.

It was easy to see what the English intended to do, said Napoleon to his officers on a number of occasions. He was being sent to a distant island and isolated from the rest of the world, there to disappear completely in due course.

Had Napoleon been less of a soldier and more of a politician, he might have realized how unreasonable it was to think that the British government would want to shorten his life. He would have seen that their aim in deporting him to St. Helena was rather to lengthen his life by insulating him from the possible fatal consequences of the death sentence passed on him at the Congress of Vienna.

It was October 14, while the admiral and his guests were at table, that a report was received of land being sighted. Everyone went up on deck and there, far away on the horizon, could be seen a greyish mass rising out of the sea, soon to be hidden again by the sudden descent of the tropical night.

The next day, contrary to his shipboard habit, Napoleon was up early, armed with a telescope. Before him lay St. Helena, a huge wall of volcanic rock. It rose almost vertically out of the sea to a height of fifteen to eighteen hundred feet. Not a tree, not a sign of other vegetation was visible. Brown and volcanic red seemed to be the only colors of the island. As they approached a cleft in the rock, there were revealed a few houses, the steeple of a church and a fairly large building somewhat like a castle.

Napoleon, always a quick appraiser of geographical surroundings, lowered his telescope and went back to his cabin.[22]

There he met Gourgaud and muttered: "This is a terrible place. I would have done better to stay in Egypt; had I done so I would by now have been emperor of all the Orient."[26]

References

1. Glover 121, 126
2. Ibid 135, 115
3. Ibid 135
4. Gourgaud I:55
5. Las Cases I:738 et seq.
6. Ibid 435
7. Aubry 1, page 113
8. Las Cases I:437, footnote
9. Ibid I:199
10. Ibid I:200, footnote
11. Ibid I:200
12. Cockburn 41
13. Glover 129
14. Gourgaud II:147
15. Bertrand III:151
16. Cockburn 79
17. Ibid 52
18. Gourgaud I: 54-62
19. Warden 75-76
20. Gourgaud I:57-58
21. Aubry 1, page 122
22. Warden 80
23. Warden 144 et seq., Aubry 1, pages 20, 21
24. Boigne III:276
25. Aubry 1, page 126
26. Gourgaud I:63
27. Cabanés 279 et seq.
28. Garnier 280
29. Boigne II:238-9
30. Cabanès 207
31. Vallée et Consortes 67/143

21

A Guest of the Balcombes

DOWN IN THE HARBOR of Jamestown, the only town on the island, was a small inn, owned and run by a worthy gentleman called Porteous. Napoleon stayed at this inn when he went ashore from the *Northumberland* at 7 o'clock in the evening of October 16. The tropical sun was setting.

A crowd had gathered, trying to peer through the windows at the man they had long considered to be the Beast of St. John's Apocalypse.

This attention bothered Napoleon. He went off to bed, having arranged that the admiral should call for him early the next morning. They were to ride out together to the country house of Longwood, a neglected mansion thought to be suitable, for the time being, to shelter the Emperor and members of his establishment. It had seen better days. The location was scenic but the place was no substitute for Malmaison.

At half-past six the following morning, the admiral asked General Gourgaud to tell "General" Bonaparte he had called. Gourgaud was surprised and angry at this form of address, but went to tell Napoleon the admiral was waiting. At the same time he mentioned the severe breach of court etiquette.

"The admiral is an ill-mannered individual," growled Napoleon; but he went out to meet Sir George amicably. Outside the inn stood a magnificent black horse, saddled in red embossed with gold. Napoleon's temper improved. The question was how to mount. Gourgaud ran forward and gave the Emperor help.

They set off at a gallop and Bertrand had to hurry to catch up with them. There was one riderless horse. Gourgaud thought it was for him, but was told it was meant for a servant. Napoleon might be invited to lunch somewhere on the trip. It was important that a valet be at hand to wait on him. Civilian court etiquette was beyond Gourgaud.[1]

That same morning William Balcombe and his family were on the lawn in front of The Briars, watching the road that wound round the mountain, on which their house had a pleasant and peaceful site. William Balcombe was a merchant who held the monopoly on deliveries to the East India Company, for which St. Helena was an important supply base. He would now also monopolize deliveries to the exiled emperor and his household. He owned a banking-house by the name of Balcombe, Fowler and Cole. Rumor said he was the natural son of the Prince Regent.

It was also said that he was not wholly scrupulous, but he was obliging, cheerful and definitely inclined to a comfortable stoutness. In short, he had the qualities of a successful merchant and a pleasant companion.

So here he was with his family, gazing along the mountain path. His wife was with him, together with their two daughters, Jane and Betsy, sixteen and fourteen years of age respectively, and their two young sons of five and nine. They were a well organized and happy family. One of the boys, Alexander Beatson, the five-year old, was to become the grandfather of Dame Mabel Balcombe-Brookes, wife of a world-famous tennis champion, Sir Norman Brookes. Dame Mabel has written a delightful book about Napoleon's life on St. Helena, based on Betsy Balcombe's memoirs and the stories, which, orally transmitted, belonged to the family tradition. The book emphasizes especially the short but comparatively happy time Napoleon spent as the Balcombes' guest. Dame Mabel donated her grandfather's home, The Briars, to the French State in 1959.

On the path that wound round the mountainside, a small group of horsemen came in sight, only to disappear again behind a new bend. Suddenly one of the family, who happened to be looking through the family telescope, cried: "I can see someone wearing a little three-cornered hat. But he hasn't a grey cloak!" However, it was soon agreed the man with the three-cornered hat must be Napoleon.

Later that day the two physicians, Warden and O'Meara,

called on the Balcombes and were able to tell them that the Emperor had ridden off to Longwood. They were immediately pestered with questions.

Oh, no, Napoleon was better than he had been made out to be. No, he was not a monster. Indeed, he could even be pleasant and agreeable.

At about four in the afternoon there was commotion again at The Briars. The riders could be seen returning from Longwood. But now what? They were leaving the road and coming towards the house! Betsy ran off to hide. Her mother called her back, for Betsy was the only one in the family who could speak a little French.

The horsemen drew up at the gate; the admiral and his attendants dismounted and so did Bertrand, but the Emperor continued onto the smooth and well-kept lawn. He rode at a walk slowly towards the main building, the admiral and Bertrand on either side. The whole family was assembled to meet him.[2]

He certainly was impressive, thought Betsy — as long as he remained on horseback. He dismounted, not without difficulty, and when he took off his hat his reddish brown hair was seen to be drenched with sweat. He wore a green uniform with the grand star of the Legion of Honor pinned to his chest. He wore, too, his big boots and the white nankin trousers.

Deliberately Napoleon advanced towards the Balcombes.

"I have heard of you," he said glumly to Mr. Balcombe. And then, as though reviewing a company of honor gathered for his inspection, he took in the rest of the family and turned back to Balcombe.

"You have a beautiful wife," he remarked, after further scrutiny, "and beautiful daughters, too."[3]

He had been on horseback for an hour, but now he asked for a chair. Several were immediately brought to the lawn, and with a commanding gesture he bade Betsy sit by his side. She was a pretty girl. And she could manage a little French, as well.

An emperor's and consequently also a former emperor's conversation was usually one-sided. Questions, just questions. Plenty of them.

"Well, Miss Betsy, what is the capital city of France?

"Of Italy?

"Russia?"

"St. Petersburg," answered Betsy, "but it used to be Moscow."

At the mention of Moscow, Napoleon turned to her and demanded brusquely: "Who set Moscow on fire?" Poor Betsy started to tremble and dared not answer. Napoleon repeated his question more gently and Betsy was finally able to reply: "I don't know."

Napoleon burst out laughing and said: "Oh, you know quite well it was I who set fire to Moscow."

His good spirits must have made Betsy want to please their celebrated guest, for she added: "Yes but *I* think it was the Russians who set fire to the city in order to get rid of Your Majesty." A pat on the cheek and her ear pulled were her reward for adapting herself so well to the situation.[4]

After a few remarks on how attractively the house was situated, the Emperor got down to the reason for his visit. Longwood was as yet uninhabitable. it would have to be extended and repainted. He had no desire to stay another night at the inn, where he felt like an animal in a zoo, so he wondered if he might possibly live at The Briars for a while.

William Balcombe quickly replied that this would indeed be a great honor for his family. He would see to it that the house was evacuated straight away for Napoleon to move in.

The latter explained that that was not what he had meant. He would be more than grateful if he could have the small pavilion, which looked as if it were not being used for the moment.

This pavilion, which lay about twenty-five yards from the main building and which had originally been built for occasional balls, had really only one large room. There were, however, two small attics under the roof as well.

Balcombe could not see how the pavilion could possibly suit Napoleon. He suggested once more that the big house be evacuated. His offer was kindly but firmly refused.

The admiral then suggested that a tent should be set up to serve as a dining room. They would, as well, stretch a roof of sailcloth over a vine-covered arbor outside the pavilion and this could become a temporary study where Napoleon could read and dictate.

When they had agreed upon these arrangements, Bertrand

set off for Jamestown with orders from Napoleon to his retinue. Las Cases and his son were to move over to The Briars; the rest of his suite were to remain at the inn. The head valet, Marchand, was to bring Napoleon's camp bed, his portable desk of field service days and certain other things necessary for camp life. The two other valets, Noverraz and Saint-Denis, were to come with him. The rest of the servants were to remain in the town.

When Marchand arrived, Balcombe suggested that everything necessary for Napoleon's comfort should be provided from the house — chairs, beds, tables, curtains, carpets. In view of Napoleon's express orders that the family were not to be unnecessarily disturbed, Marchand contented himself with receiving one armchair, a table and a few odd chairs.

Mr. Balcombe insisted that Marchand should also have the finest chest-of-drawers in the house.

To go with the chest Marchand sent off to Jamestown to fetch a case enclosing a washbasin, which he had rescued from the Elysée palace. It was a magnificent silver affair, made by the jeweller Biennais.

He hung some pictures of the King of Rome and the Empress Marie-Louise, draped some cotton sheets around the windows, and all was ready for Napoleon to take possession of his temporary and make-do residence.

The Las Cases, father and son, each took over one of the small attic rooms. Marchand and the two other valets, Noverraz and Saint-Denis, had the side passage. Some mattresses on the floor were their only furniture.[5]

Dinner was to be sent from Jamestown, for which the major-domo Cipriani was to be responsible. When it arrived, it was cold. Camp life might be glorious but Napoleon did not like cold meals. The next day, therefore, Pierron, the chef, and Lepage, his assistant, were summoned. They were to prepare Napoleon's meals in a little hovel used by the slaves in cooking their own simple fare.

When Bertrand arrived back at the inn with Napoleon's instructions he was received with mixed feelings. Montholon was annoyed. It had been agreed that he alone should be head of the imperial household. Already Napoleon seemed to have forgotten this. He took his case to the admiral who was in command.

The admiral could see nothing to worry about. He had left Napoleon, happy and contented, at the Balcombes'. It would do him good to stay for a while with ordinary people and in the country where he could hear the lowing of the cattle. Montholon must await the court's arrival at Longwood.

As soon as the passengers' belongings had been taken off *Northumberland,* Napoleon and his adjutants were given their swords. The admiral kept back the pistols, but when he heard that Napoleon had no sporting-guns, he arranged for these to be sent immediately.[6] The ritual said something of the understanding between these two men of military life.

Sir George had considered it advisable to place sentries around The Briars under the command of a captain and a sergeant. But when he heard that the ex-Emperor was sensitive to this, he immediately withdrew them and gave orders that the captain should wear civilian dress and try to keep out of sight. It is quite obvious that the admiral did all he could to accommodate Napoleon, in line with instructions from his government.[7]

Napoleon's evenings with the Balcombe family were undoubtedly happy ones and they found him straight-forward and unaffected. He seemed to relax with them from the daytime role of Emperor which he felt he still must play.

However, by October 21 he was already urging his retinue to protest. "This is a terrible island and we are being kept prisoners here. You must all make your complaints heard."[8]

By the next day Las Cases and Napoleon had managed to draft a letter of grievances. It was to be signed by Bertrand as Marshal of the Palace and senior officer at the court of exile. Bertrand found the remarks and accusations ridiculous and recommended that the letter should not be sent.[8]

On October 24, Napoleon scolded Bertrand for not sending the letter to the admiral. At the same time he told Gourgaud that if the admiral should ask him whether the Emperor wished for anything, he was to reply that he did not. If Napoleon required something he would issue an order. Bertrand was told to have the letter of complaint to the admiral ready by midnight, but he managed not to have anything to do with it.[8]

While this argument was going on at The Briars, the generals and their ladies billeted down at the inn in Jamestown found an invitation from the admiral awaiting them. A visit to the mansion house would compensate them for the fact that Napoleon had commandeered their chef.

Bertrand continued to refuse to sign Napoleon's and Las Cases' protest, but he loyally obeyed Napoleon's orders to his officers to have nothing to do with the admiral. Montholon on the other hand, favored the letter. He put on his best uniform and waited upon the admiral, which Gourgaud discovered. Montholon was annoyed.[6]

On November 5, Napoleon again asked Bertrand if he had sent the letter. Bertrand said he had not done so as he thought the complaints unfounded.

"You are a ninny, Bertrand!" cried Napoleon.

"Your Majesty is wrong in not listening to my advice."

"*Silence, Grand Maréchal,*" roared Napoleon. "You would not have said that in the Tuileries. There I was always right."[9]

On November 20 Cockburn arranged a ball in honor of Napoleon. The guest of honor refused to accept. He allowed his retinue to go, but on their return reproached them and forbade that they should ever again accept an invitation from the admiral, either to dinner or to a ball.[10]

Las Cases considered the living-quarters assigned to Napoleon's servants at The Briars to be unfit for use. So he wrote to Colonel Bingham, asking him for an army tent. Napoleon did not like complaining to Bingham and reprimanded Las Cases. Not even Las Cases had yet realized that nothing was to be done and nothing accepted that was contrary to Napoleon's fixed idea that the English were doing all in their power to make life miserable and dangerous for him and his court.[10]

On November 23 those of his retinue who were living in Jamestown had been invited to dinner at The Briars. Bertrand set off before the others, but soon was back again to announce that the dinner had been cancelled. Napoleon had suddenly felt indisposed and could not receive them.

The next day Gourgaud went as usual to take Napoleon's dictation, but found the Emperor out of sorts and very tired, unable to keep going for more than a very short time. He had an irritating cough and seemed to be troubled by the light, for he asked that thick curtains should be drawn across the windows.[11]

In spite of the fact that Napoleon kept urging his staff to show their displeasure at their "imprisonment" and with the admiral's arrangements, and apart from the above-mentioned indisposition, on the whole he enjoyed good health while at The Briars. Later, when illness became hard to bear, he would often speak of the happy time he spent there in camp-like simplicity of surroundings but experiencing a happy, family atmosphere.

Betsy Balcombe tells us in her memoirs that Napoleon was always in the best of spirits and almost childlike in his happiness. In spite of the fact that high-spirited Betsy often tested his patience, he was never really angry with her and never alluded to his rank or right to respect. He used to join in their simple games even in Blind Man's Buff. He corrected the translations into French that the Balcombe girls had to do each day.

It seems quite possible that Napoleon did not always know whether he was playing the part of a great conqueror or just an ordinary, kind-hearted individual. Certainly Napoleon of The Briars was not the Emperor at the Tuileries. He was relaxed and humanly engaging in this brief holiday from being a great figure of history, resistant to captivity.

Napoleon cannot justly be considered to have been a drinker. On the contrary, he was before his time an advocate of temperance. In spite of this, his manner often resembled that of the confirmed inebriate, good and accommodating when sober, but much less engaging when the blood in his veins had been charged with alcohol.

Nothing has been related in the literature of history that Napoleon used opium or any other narcotic. In spite of this his conduct was sometimes so unpredictable that one was tempted to suspect him of narcomania, when we know for a fact that, for his time, he led a more than ordinarily sober life. There were not many narcomaniacs in Europe at the beginning of the nineteenth century, for there were not so many addictive drugs available in those days. On the other hand there were people who took daily doses of arsenic with the object of keeping fit. Such people were known as arsenophagists, or arsenic eaters. By degrees their systems became so accustomed to the poison they could take enough to kill an ordinary person and yet show no ill effects. They were to be found mostly in and around Tyrol, and even to this day a few of the unusual species are left. They could be recognized chiefly by their extreme corpulence. They seemed to be blown up. When Napoleon returned to Paris from Elba, there was surprise that he should have become in eleven months so noticeably corpulent. The change had meaning.

Although not much has been written about how such people behaved under the influence of the poison, we may assume that like all other narcomaniacs they suffered from withdrawal symptoms when deprived of their daily dose. They probably reacted very much as the alcoholic does when he cannot get his usual intake of spirits. To have taken on corpulence from such a cause, Napoleon would have acquired other characteristics of a user of arsenic.

As long as Napoleon stayed at The Briars he made no real excursions into the island. So, definitely, he was not harboring plans for escape. On one occasion, however, he did express a wish to go out riding. Horses were immediately fetched from Jamestown. Las Cases and Saint-Denis, his valet, got ready to accompany him, but just as the Emperor was about to mount, he happened to catch sight of the British officer on duty who, in accordance with instructions, was preparing to escort the party on this trip into country hitherto unknown to them. Napoleon forthwith cancelled the excursion and gave orders that the horses were to be returned to town immediately.[12]

The presence of a British officer could not have been the real reason Napoleon changed his mind so suddenly and returned the mounts. He must have known that the man had instructions to see that the Emperor was allowed to ride in peace and safety. If the circulation of blood to the imperial brain had been normal, Napoleon no doubt would have understood that the officer was not some sort of gaoler in disguise.

Just as Napoleon was about to set off, he must have formed an idea of some real obstacle to going, but resourceful as he was, he hastily improvised and excused — the presence of the escorting officer. Actually there is reason to believe that a compelling incentive to cancel the trip was that the ailing Napoleon could not hoist himself up into the saddle. During walks at The Briars he had regained considerable strength in his legs, but not enough for a horseman.

On November 6 Bertrand at last despatched the letter of complaint that Napoleon had dictated to Las Cases. It had now been softened into a comparatively mild account of how uncomfortable the Emperor was lodged, with no bath and no stable of his own, and that there were sentries stationed nearby.

The admiral's reply was very polite, but pointed out that he knew of no *emperor* on the island. That of course infuriated Napoleon.[13] He was always angry when, in some report or salutation, the British insisted on calling him General Bonaparte. However, it would appear that, unlike the most senior officers at St. Helena, the officer group in general made it a habit to address him verbally as *Sire* or *Your Majesty.*

In spite of indications that Napoleon had still not recovered muscular strength in his legs — a strength that had been missing during the fateful Hundred Days — he gave the impression of being in the best of health while staying at The Briars.* He showed a great desire for work and dictated his memoirs to his senior attendants. Las Cases wrote down his dictated account of the Italian campaign of 1796-97, Bertrand was given the Egyptian expedition, Gourgaud the Hundred Days, while Montholon got the Empire.

At the beginning of December Longwood was sufficiently renovated for the admiral to suggest Napoleon should move in. It seems, however, that it was not easy to persuade Napoleon to shift. Montholon had to make several attempts to change the royal mind before Longwood was accepted.[14]

Gourgaud mentions that de Montholon used his influence to please the admiral, with whom he was secretly on the best of terms in spite of Napoleon's instructions to the contrary.[13]

Something must have occurred on December 7, for Napoleon was very angry with de Montholon, calling him a rogue.[14]

Montholon seems to have been unduly interested in monitoring Napoleon's sexual relations during the stay at The Briars. Countess de Montholon was living in Jamestown, and at night sentries saw to it that all communication between The Briars and the town was blocked. But Napoleon had three valets, bright

---

*Napoleon's legs were too weak for riding during his Russian campaign. He seldom moved other than in a carriage or sleigh.

young fellows of about twenty-five to thirty, good-looking and enterprising. They would certainly have had no difficulty establishing friendships with young women on the island, and evidently there were more than enough to go round. But Napoleon resented being a subject of Montholon's attention to his amatory interests. As for de Montholon, master of the household, The Briars may have been considered too open to English observation and report to be a place where caution could be thrown to the tropic winds. Napoleon's wrath on one occasion certainly had some relation to his activities concerning the opposite sex, for he said of Montholon: "He may be cuckold as much as he likes, but he shouldn't spy on me."

On December 10 Napoleon at last moved to Longwood and a new and far less innocently rustic phase of his exile began.

References

1. Gourgaud I:65
2. Betsy Balcombe 112-14
3. Dame Mabel Brookes 17
4. Betsy Balcombe 115
5. Marchand II:36 et seq.
6. Gourgaud I:69 et seq.
7. Forsyth I:18
8. Gourgaud I:67
9. Ibid I:71
10. Ibid I:76, 77
11. Ibid I:78
12. Marchand II:41
13. Gourgaud I:73
14. Ibid I:83

22

The Move to Longwood

LONGWOOD SITS on a plateau 1750 feet above sea level and five miles from Jamestown. The place had been built by the East India Company as a summer residence for their vice-governor. It was never so hot there as in Jamestown, the mercury seldom rising above 64°-68° F. (17°-20° C).[1]

The trees were not of the sort that provided dense shade, but there was a park, about four miles in circumference. A native gum-wood or eucalyptus was the commonest tree species.

When Napoleon arrived on the island a camp had been pitched on the plain a good bit north of Longwood for the 53rd regiment of infantry and a section of artillery, the units assigned responsibility for Napoleon's protection. "For his custody" was the term used, out of consideration for the French king.

Sentinels were placed around the park — "to prevent all intruders", as Glover, Admiral Cockburn's secretary, put it.[2]

The purpose was indeed to protect Napoleon rather than to prevent him from escaping, which in itself was quite impossible. At an early stage, however, de Montholon had managed to make Napoleon believe the sentinels were there to make life disagreeable for him. When he had heard the Count describe the positions of the sentries, Napoleon cried out: "You may be sure they have instructions to kill me! They will say there was a mistake and I shall be bayoneted. Oh, I know the English."[3]

As soon as Admiral Cockburn's squadron had got Napoleon and his court ashore, building had begun in earnest at Longwood. All the carpenters, shipwrights and laborers in the squadron, together with all available manpower on the island, were kept busy extending and improving the buildings, which had become run-down through long disuse and neglect.

Every day a long line of sailors left Jamestown for Longwood. On their heads and shoulders they carried construction materials: timber, planks and stone, as well as furniture and household effects. Occasionally the soldiers of the 53rd Regiment helped out as bearers. Day in and day out, all day long, several hundred heavily-laden sailors and soldiers trod the pack-horse road up to Longwood.[4]

When at last Napoleon arrived to take over his residence, he made a tour of the main building and found everything to his satisfaction. The relieved admiral recorded his delight.[5]

The house could have been bigger. The Emperor was accustomed to spacious salons and chambers. An area of about 240 sq. yds. in the main building was to be for Napoleon's personal use. A similar area on the ground floor had been set aside for kitchen, pantry and other service quarters. In the attic were a few smaller rooms for the servants.

The Bertrands were at first to live in a small house called Hut's Gate a mile from Longwood, while the Montholons eventually would occupy a wing of Longwood House.

Later on the Bertrands were given their own newly-built house nearer to Napoleon. The gentlemen Las Cases had at the outset to be content with a small room next to the kitchen. Later a cottage was built at the back of the big house. It would include a small sitting-room, a bedroom for them both and a room for their servants.[6]

Napoleon's apartment consisted of an antechamber, a drawing-room, dining-room, library, study, bedroom and bathroom. It was not exactly an emperor's palace, but it was certainly not a prison cell. In any case they were uncommonly fine quarters for a lieutenant general. Napoleon chose to regard the establishment as a royal court.

As far as is known, the British never objected to Bertrand being called Grand Marshal of the Palace, or to Montholon and Gourgaud being aides-de-camp and the elder Las Cases as chamberlain. It will be recalled that not even a page was lacking at the Emperor's abbreviated court.

The servants likewise had court titles and the British took no exception to this as being pretentious or improper. There were valets, a major-domo, footmen, cooks, a lamp-trimmer and of course a collection of others without especial classification, as well as the personal servants of the rank. Each of those in waiting was provided with one or two servants of his own.

The most obvious indication of the fact that the British really regarded Napoleon as an emperor while, for political purposes, calling him a general at St. Helena was the government's obvious effort to provide a still more princely residence for him. A great palace of wood, in a style both tasteful and dignified, was pre-fabricated in England, and costly furnishings ordered. This palace was dismantled and shipped to St. Helena in marked sections for re-assembly. When Napoleon first started to. air grievances about his residence, the British tried to explain to him that a better one was being prepared and soon would be shipped. But Napoleon insisted that he would never accept this palace, for that would mean he had accepted imprisonment and exile as his permanent lot.

As a matter of fact, in his calmer moments Napoleon realized that the British had every intention of treating him favorably. On July 24, 1816, he said to Gourgaud: "The British government intends to treat us well."[7]

The close custody irritated him, he said. He might better have conceded that this was not only because of his return from Elba but necessary as official reassurance to the French royal family, always apprehensive that Napoleon one day would re-appear in Europe. A letter of the French Prime Minister Richelieu clearly testifies to this.[8]

Actually it was beyond practicability for Napoleon even to dream of escaping from the island. No ship could approach St. Helena without being observed by lookouts posted high on the mountains. Even had Napoleon been quite free to roam at will over the entire island, unescorted by a British officer of the guard, he still could not have left St. Helena without the permission and help of the commander of the British squadron.

Napoleon's freedom to come and go as he wished was indeed to a certain extent curtailed, but this was in part to protect him from attack and from obtrusive curiosity. O'Meara describes the security arrangements for Napoleon's safety and concludes that the natural obstacles to escape were in fact insurmountable. No one on the island could get near the sea except at Jamestown; in

any case not anyone so lacking in agility as Napoleon was at a
time when his body had become corpulent and his legs weakened
by what we now must recognize as arsenical poisonings inflicted
prior to his arrival at St. Helena.[9]

For a while it looked as though Napoleon had thought of
continuing at Longwood the simple country life he had been
leading at The Briars, and that he might decide to follow a
normal and relaxed routine.

He invited officers of the 53rd to dinner, as well as the
vice-governor, Colonel Skelton. A certain Captain Younghus-
band was also honored with an invitation to dine. The officers'
wives often were amongst the guests.

The Balcombes were sometimes by invitation at Longwood, as
well as Sir William Doveton, an estate owner on the island, and
his daughter.[10]

There were well equipped stables at the renovated Longwood,
with carriage horses and riding mounts. Gourgaud was appointed Master of the Horse. Count de Montholon was now truly
installed at the head of the imperial household. In this way
he effectually usurped Bertrand's position. Napoleon sensed
this and sent Gourgaud off to Hut's Gate to tell Bertrand that in
spite of Montholon's appointment he, Bertrand, was still Grand
Marshal of the Palace, an office of which "according to the
Constitution" he could never be deprived.[11]

Bertrand, much less sensitive to slight than the fiery Gourgaud, accepted his emperor's decision as final.

Only four days after his arrival at Longwood, on December 13,
1815, Napoleon, accompanied by Gourgaud, began cautiously
to try out his horse in the park around Longwood House.

A couple of days later his party rode as far as Hut's Gate, and
from there Napoleon thought he would try a roundabout way
home. However, when Gourgaud and he reached the limits of
the area in which he was allowed to move freely without escort,
he was firmly challenged by an English officer. This offended
His Majesty and angered him intensely.

Gourgaud must have mentioned the incident to the admiral,
for on the next day the latter informed them that the British
officer had been severely reprimanded. There had been a
misunderstanding.

Still Napoleon was not satisfied. He renewed his orders to his staff to find occasions to complain about the admiral and the British government[11]

As yet Napoleon seemingly still had to discover and remark that the climate of St. Helena was "detestable", for his health at that point was not the subject of any particular comments.

On December 20 the admiral paid one of his many visits and according to Gourgaud was most pleasant as usual. His purpose this time was to inspect the stables to see if further improvements could be made. "He is very honest with us," wrote Gourgaud in his diary.[12]

Nevertheless, Napoleon ordered Count de Montholon to tell the admiral that he was behaving very badly, indeed that he was a murderer. Gourgaud could not imagine that Montholon would do otherwise than pass on these remarks considerably modified. Napoleon must have thought so too, for he said later to Montholon: "I told you to speak harshly to the admiral . . . I am sure you were as gentle as possible."[12]

From that remark it may be judged that there were limits to Napoleon's credulity. No one in his retinue was as soft-spoken towards him as Montholon, none so eager to side with and encourage him in his anglophobia. Yet no one could keep on good terms with the English admiral as could Charles Tristan, a well-educated, aristocratic courtier.

Bertrand, on the other hand, tried to reason with Napoleon and make him cease these ill-founded quarrels, but at Napoleon's order he kept a reserved attitude towards the admiral.

At first, life at Longwood was comparatively congenial. Napoleon worked long hours with his memoirs. His staff was kept busy with the fairly onerous task of taking down his rapid dictation and writing it out in rough for his editing. After that they had to decipher his practically illegible corrections and, last of all, prepare a fair copy. However, Saint-Denis was generally made to write this, as he had such a neat and tidy style.

Work was then interrupted for meals, at which the conversation was pleasant, and there was time, too, for riding and outings by carriage. This was a routine and an atmosphere to which the restless emperor might have made his concessionary adjustments. But it could not continue.

On December 23 Napoleon fell suddenly ill. Gourgaud writes that "His Majesty is indisposed, keeps to his room and does not eat with us."[13] On the evening of the same day new horses arrived, brought by the admiral from Cape Town.

Dr. O'Meara had met the admiral and had been asked to convey the latter's respects to Napoleon and to tell him that a couple of letters had arrived for him from Europe. Following upon his instructions, the admiral had opened and read these letters. He had found them most insolent. The admiral wondered if Napoleon wanted the letters or whether he, Sir George, should keep them.

The admiral's good intentions were ill rewarded. Napoleon lost his temper and shouted: "What impudence and cowardice!"

The Emperor sent Gourgaud and Montholon to air their grievances to the admiral. When the latter saw these gentlemen approaching, he suspected nothing, greeted them in a friendly manner and asked if they would do him the honor of dining with him on the following Tuesday.

The two adjutants did not manage to state their errand on that occasion and were forbidden by Napoleon to accept the admiral's invitation.[14]

On December 26 a very upset Mme. Bertrand came up from Hut's Gate. Someone had told Napoleon that she had bought a teapot with Louis XVIII's arms on it and that she had been given four dozen towels by the English. She wished to deny these accusations and what is more, she had not requested Napoleon's servants to wait on her, as she was very sure that Montholon had said she had.

Napoleon was still indisposed and kept to his room; so Mme. Bertrand could not speak with him. The next day, however, Gourgaud told Napoleon that Mme. Bertrand had been shamefully maligned.[14]

There were signs of the coming cultivation by Count de Montholon of suspicious and divisive attitudes which would keep the court from a calm and amiable tropic somnolence.

Nothing is known of Napoleon's symptoms during this particular indisposition. They can hardly have been serious or worrying, as Dr. O'Meara, who lived at Longwood, was not called upon for attention.

Montholon and his wife must have behaved perfectly, for no complaints were heard about them. On the other hand Napoleon was not satisfied with the Bertrands. They came in late to dinner. They were, it would appear, selfish and concerned mainly with their own interests.[15]

There were sporting arms, shot and powder at Longwood. Otherwise life would have been too dull for a valiant soldier like Gourgaud. He managed to bag several partridge and turtle doves and was even able to rid the island of a pheasant.

The admiral called again the day before New Year's Eve to make sure that the Emperor lacked nothing. He was met by an unexpected volley of reproach: "Posterity will certainly reproach England for having left me for two months at The Briars, very badly lodged in a single room, without the possibility of a bath."[15]

As instructed, the admiral listened in silence to this upbraiding, bowed low and promised to remedy in the future what had been found fault with in the past. However, he could not possibly allow Napoleon to leave the domains of the large park at Longwood without an escorting officer. He would, however, instruct the escort to keep at a distance of, say 30 to 40 paces; that is, if Napoleon had objections to a British officer mixing with the French attendants.

On New Year's Eve Napoleon received a magnificent gift from the admiral, an elegant calash that Sir George had ordered from Cape Town. This might imply that the admiral had noticed that Napoleon was no longer the good horseman his illustrious past would have caused people to suppose. A carriage was perhaps the right way of getting the Emperor to break the isolation for which he now blamed the sentries and escorting officers.

By the beginning of 1816 a noticeable improvement in Napoleon's condition, both physical and mental, was remarked by his court members. He was again able to ride well, and even galloped so fast that on one occasion the escorting officer, whose name was Poppleton, and who was co-operatively dressed in the garb of a servant, could not keep up and lost sight of him.[16]

Poppleton's disguise was intended to mitigate Napoleon's irritation at being "watched over" by a British officer.

Already on New Year's Day itself Napoleon had astonished those around him by his calm and conciliatory attitude. He reviewed the past eventful year and suggested that the new one be marked by concord and unity. All the French at Longwood, he said hopefully, should live as one big family.

He could not have achieved composure completely, however, for soon after his fine speech he remembered that the food and service at dinner on New Year's Eve had been lamentable. Montholon was reprimanded for the way he ran the household. It was good that for once Napoleon had occasion to blame Montholon rather than scolding the ever-correct, and well-meaning Bertrand, a man of submissive loyalty.

On January 3 the admiral suggested that he and Napoleon should go riding. It turned out to be a veritable reconnoitring tour of fifteen or sixteen miles. On his return Napoleon said that he had managed to win the admiral over. The excursion had very much tired the Emperor, but he had undertaken it like a soldier. The next day he kept to his bed until 10 o'clock.[17]

On January 7, Mr. Porteous, the innkeeper, visited Longwood together with a Miss Robinson and her two daughters, one of whom Napoleon nicknamed *Bouton de Rose,* or Rosebud. Albine de Montholon immediately perceived the possibilities of the visit and was most attentive and obliging to this young lady. Napoleon suggested that the ladies should go for a drive in the fine new calash. He did not go himself, but allowed Gourgaud to take his place as their escort.

When they returned, Gourgaud noticed that Mme. Montholon was no longer interested in *Bouton de Rose.*[18]

Mme. Montholon was now four months pregnant. This may have had some influence on Napoleon's feelings towards her, for shortly after Mr. Porteous had left with his ladies, he began to pester Albine to such an extent that Gourgaud, although he did not particularly like her, could not help feeling sorry for her.

"You ought to know much about love, for they say that you have had lots of affairs. *A propos,* is it true that you have had three husbands and have been divorced twice?"

Mme. Montholon blushed, but Napoleon went on: "Monsieur Roger I know of, and Montholon, but who was the third?"

Poor Mme. Montholon managed to stammer: "I don't know why people think I should have had three husbands."[19]

It may be suspected that someone close to Napoleon evidently had been trying to open his eyes and have him understand that the Montholons were not a totally trustworthy pair. This person conceivably could have been Cipriani, a former security agent in King Joseph's secret police at Naples and now Napoleon's major-domo and his "spy".

Indeed, family loyalties at Longwood were fragile, despite Napoleon's fine New Year's speech.

On January 11 Gourgaud met Montholon, who was wearing civilian dress. A short while later Gourgaud met him again, but this time he had on his full-dress uniform. Gourgaud wondered what all this was about. Well, it seemed that Poppleton had to attend a court-martial at the military camp, and that was why Montholon had donned his uniform. There had always to be a soldier at Longwood.

Shortly after that Gourgaud caught sight of a group of colorful English soldiers with Montholon among them. Bingham was there, recently promoted to major-general, and a certain Admiral Taylor, together with three other high-ranking officers whom Gourgaud did not know. Gourgaud sensed that something was in the air and questioned Poppleton as to when he would be going off the the court-martial. "What court-martial?" asked Poppleton. He knew nothing of any court-martial. Gourgaud came to the conclusion that frequently Montholon was not to be relied upon and was far from being a loyal supporter of Napoleon's edicts.

The British officers had hoped to be received by Napoleon, which was why they were so splendidly attired. Unfortunately Napoleon could not receive them, explained Montholon. He was at present ill.

Gourgaud had heard nothing about Napoleon being ill. He went in to the Emperor and found him quite well. Thereupon Gourgaud could no longer contain himself and told Napoleon that in the future he would take no orders from Montholon. Napoleon begged Gourgaud not to get excited. The reportedly ill Napoleon ordered his horse to be brought. He was gone for a considerable time on his ride. On his return Gourgaud and Las Cases joined him in a long walk.[20]

There was no doubt about it, Napoleon at this time was well on the way to regaining his health, which had been especially bad during the Hundred Days. The fact of recovery was particularly obvious that day. He could both ride and walk without becoming exhausted. Good spirits were obvious, as well, from his animated and cogent conversation. During his walk with Gourgaud and Las Cases he discussed with apparent pleasure the British plans for building him a fine large palace. Napoleon argued thoughtfully and reasonably against his own past suspicions. He did not think the British intended to make him comfortable only to plot against his life. He reviewed his ambivalent attitude toward the new palace in the following monologue:

"If I accept, it could be taken that I mean to stay here always. It would ruin the hopes of my supporters. On the other hand the erection of such a place must mean that the British do not consider me as just an ordinary general. It would give the Prince Regent a very bad impression if we refused, and besides we are badly lodged at the moment. It is difficult to know what to do. I shall wait before deciding."[20]

On January 14 Montholon had thought fit to tell the admiral that Napoleon was very angry because he had been challenged by a sentry, who had even threatened to shoot. Napoleon insisted that the sentry be punished. The result was that General Bingham announced a court-martial for next day and called upon General Gourgaud as witness.

Gourgaud asked Napoleon for permission to witness at the court-martial. What court-martial? Napoleon had never requested that the sentry should be punished. He called for Montholon and reproved him severely. He said later: "Montholon is always lying; he's a scoundrel."[21]

The court-martial was cancelled. Napoleon had begun to manifest some of his old characteristics as when he would astonish those around him by unexpected generosity and mercy. Perhaps when well he did indeed possess the attributes of the truly great — the quality of modesty and consideration, without rancor or pettiness.

On the same day, January 14, 1816, Napoleon received a visit from Commander John Theed, master of H.M.S. *Leveret,* who brought welcome mail. Mme. Bertrand gave Theed a souvenir — a locket containing some of Napoleon's hairs. Generations later this locket came into the possession of Dame Mabel

Balcombe-Brookes. Voluntarily, she sent these hairs in 1962 directly to the Department of Forensic Medicine in Glasgow, where the eminent chemist, Hamilton Smith, accepted them for an activation analysis. The results may cast some light backward down the years into events and circumstances at Longwood at the time of the exile court.

Four of the hairs, the longest about 4 cm, the others 3 cm and 2 cm, were shown to contain a considerable amount of arsenic. The hairs were examined in 1 cm sections and these showed the following concentrations:

Hair No. 1: 60.0: 35.4: 25.2: 47.8 p.p.m. arsenic
Hair No. 2: 36.3: 76.6: and 3.5 p.p.m. arsenic
Hair No. 3: 33.5: 62.0: and 50.2 p.p.m. arsenic
Hair No. 4: 15.0: 23.8 p.p.m. arsenic.[22]

A normal concentration of arsenic in human hairs today is considered to be 0.8 p.p.m. In the early 1800's it was probably about 0.6 p.p.m. There is reason to suppose that this increase has been produced by the current custom of spraying vines and fruit trees with arsenic. In Napoleon's day the normal concentration was undoubtedly less. Regrettably, we do not know just when these hairs were clipped from Napoleon's head; nor do we know how far from the scalp they were cut. We do know they must have been taken at the latest on January 14, 1816 and were probably cut about 10 cm from the scalp. This would mean that while the exact date of arsenical intoxication of which these hairs are a proof cannot be determined, it probably included the period during the fateful Hundred Days from Elba to Waterloo or possibly even earlier.

References

1. Glover 225
2. Ibid 226
3. Gourgaud I:82
4. O'Meara I:15
5. Gourgaud I:84
6. O'Meara I:16
7. Gourgaud I:168
8. Lucas-Dubreton 98, 100, 102
9. O'Meara I:21
10. O'Meara I;23, Gourgaud I:85
11. Gourgaud I:85
12. Gourgaud I:87
13. Gourgaud I:88
14. Gourgaud I:89
15. Gourgaud I:90
16. Gourgaud I:95
17. Gourgaud I:94
18. Gourgaud I:96
19. Gourgaud I:97
20. Gourgaud I:98, 99
21. Gourgaud I:101
22. Forshufvud, Smith, Wassén 218

23

"The Servants Admit Harlots at Night"

ABOUT THE MIDDLE of February, 1816, Admiral Cockburn gave Napoleon good reason to be irritated. The admiral had actually issued orders that sentries should be posted around the buildings at Longwood after sunset, so that every window and every door would be watched. Napoleon could only interpret this as a device of the admiral's to humble his prisoner.

Napoleon sent for Dr. O'Meara and asked him to request the admiral to see to it that the sentries should remain out of sight.

Sir George was astonished. Surely it had been none other than Napoleon who had expressly asked for these sentries to protect him against any possible attempt at murder by the population, sailors or soldiers![1] Soon it was discovered that de Montholon was responsible. He had hit upon the idea of the risk of attempted murder and had acted on his own initiative.

The danger of murder actually had not occurred to the admiral, but Montholon having called his attention to it, the more he thought about it the more the sentries seemed necessary. For that reason he refused to give in to Napoleon and take them away.

Nor was the admiral content with posting sentries outside the doors and windows. He demanded also that Gourgaud should hand over his pistols to the officer of the guard.

One can understand Gourgaud's excitement and anger. He was going to corner Montholon. The sentries were the Emperor's business, but the pistols were his and no one was going to take those away from him, an emperor's aide, who looked upon the protection of his master as his personal duty.

Gourgaud forced Montholon to admit to Napoleon that it was he, Montholon, who was the originator of the hateful sentries.

201

Roared Napoleon: *"Il faut que vous avez l'âme basse pour vous faire notre geôlier* — You must have a very mean spirit to become my gaoler."

"Pourquoi prétendez-vous que je cours des dangers? — Why do you think I am in danger?"

"One of the natives or a sailor could murder you, Sire," Montholon offered.

"Ridiculous! Why, if it were necessary, one of my officers could sleep next to my room, but for God's sake don't be so concerned about my safety that you have to resort to sentries."

"Sire, your servants admit harlots at night," said Montholon.

"And what then! If this should reach scandalous proportions, you ought to be able to put a stop to it without calling for the help of the English. Do you want this place to become a monastery? Leave me in peace."

Both officers retired, but Gourgaud was soon to be recalled.

"Sit down, Gourgaud, and we can read a little English."

But Napoleon could not forget those sentries. What about this threat of murder? Was there any real reason for thinking that someone here on the island might have a grudge against him?

"No, no, they want to frighten me so that they can send a British officer with me when I go out riding.

"C'est une vraie femme de charge que ce Montholon — What an old woman Montholon is!

"Tell Montholon to come here!"

Montholon appeared and was again reprimanded. Napoleon finished by saying:

"The first of my servants who appeals to the British will immediately be discharged, even should it be my valet or Pierron (the chef).

"Tell the British officer to issue countermand orders and you, Gourgaud, be good enough not to give your pistols over to Poppleton again.[2]

"Shall we have a game of chess?"

Count de Montholon brightened, for he usually played against Napoleon.

"Well, Gourgaud, shall we two play chess?"

Montholon and Albine, who had come in in the meantime, were considerably taken aback.[2]

During the whole of Napoleon's exile this matter of sentinels stationed close to the house was to be the cause of more or less continuous disturbance. The admiral refused to change his orders and continued to insist that Gourgaud should deposit his pistols every evening with the officer of the guard. Gourgaud refused at first but was forced to obey. Napoleon suggested that he send the pistols to Cockburn direct without saying anything.[3]

As Napoleon's disapproval of Montholon increased, so Gourgaud became more and more indispensable. This would be a problem Montholon would have to take steps to overcome. Everything depended on Napoleon preferring him to all others.

Mme. Montholon might have been able to put things right for her husband, but her conspicuous pregnancy was certainly a drawback. Neither of the Montholons was in favor any longer. The Emperor now was partial to Gourgaud.

In a letter to a Mr. Finalyson, an official at the Admiralty, O'Meara would give a vivid description of the episode of the sentries at the windows. He thought it must have opened Napoleon's eyes to the unreliability of Montholon. Napoleon scarcely spoke to Montholon, wrote O'Meara, and when on one occasion Montholon was going to ride into Jamestown, Napoleon had said: "Well, Montholon, don't come back with lies as your news. Bertrand is going to town tomorrow and then I shall hear the truth."

When Montholon explained that one of the reasons he had asked for the doors and windows at Longwood to be guarded was that ladies of easy virtue made use of them to enter the house at night, he may have been telling the literal truth. But this reason won him no sympathy from those of the men at Longwood who had been unable to strike up a friendship with the few women in the ex-imperial household.

Anyway, the fact remains that Napoleon was very angry, and the reason for his mood of exasperation can hardly have been that the admiral wished to protect his life.

It is an excellent rule when faced with something apparently inexplicable, to ask oneself "où est la femme?". In this case, one might then suspect that it may not have been Montholon who was the real instigator of the strengthened night watch at Longwood. Perhaps, instead, it was his Countess.

Mme. Montholon tried to soothe Napoleon's bad humor about the sentries by engaging a girl from the island as an extra chambermaid. This solution had to do, although it was not ideal. The chambermaid, Esther Vesey, it would be found, was of the sort who easily became pregnant.

References

1. Gourgaud I:110; O'Meara I:71-72
2. Gourgaud I:110, 111
3. Gourgaud I:113

24

A Brave Soldier is Afraid, a Bodyguard Removed

THE MONTHOLONS' accreditation at the court of exile obviously was at first insecure. Napoleon had said he would discharge anyone who had anything to do with the English, were it the chef himself. In this respect Montholon had sinned.

However busy Montholon may have been, he had not yet managed to persuade Napoleon to realize that only he, Count de Montholon, young and well-brought-up aristocrat that he was, should be the indispensable member. In Napoleon's past, men like Bertrand and Gourgaud had served him well.

When the need is greatest, help is generally at hand. Especially this is so for one who knows how to help himself.

Suddenly and without the slightest warning, brave General Gourgaud fell seriously ill. He had without doubt the best constitution in the little French colony, but all the same it was he who first became a victim of what soon was to become known, for lack of other explanation, as the dreaded "climatic sickness". To what else could those at Longwood, who resented exile, attribute a mysterious occurrence of vomiting and illness?

The doctors diagnosed dysentery. It should have seemed a strange sort of "dysentery". But in those days nearly all illnesses that included diarrhoetic conditions were called "dysentery".[1]

Dysentery, bacterial in nature, is not usually dangerous for those in good general health. If one person is taken ill, his case is often followed by others. But none other in the court excepting Napoleon contracted it. It was obvious that this was not an ordinary variety, for O'Meara was confounded by it and did not want to take sole responsibility for the patient. He asked for a second opinion from the highest medical authority on the island, the naval squadron's head physician, Warden.

Warden came and decided that the patient's liver was out of order. Dr. O'Meara had paid especial attention to the accompanying serious nervous and cerebral symptoms.

The patient was greatly distressed and O'Meara, who must have seen many cases of ordinary dysentery, wrote in a report that he had never seen anyone as afraid of death as Gourgaud. On one occasion a cockroach had crawled up onto Gourgaud's sheet. The brave soldier was terrified. He cried out that here was the Devil himself, with claws and long teeth, coming to fetch him.[2]

Gourgaud also suffered from spasmodic jerks and often wept like a child, which well might mean that his eyes watered freely.

Gourgaud obviously displayed liver symptoms, considerable mental anxiety and distress, watering of the eyes, muscular spasms and diarrhoea. All these symptoms are typical of acute arsenical intoxication, but there is no mention of the doctors suspecting more than a particularly puzzling kind of dysentery.

Another fact indicates that Gourgaud was beset by no natural illness. He had several dangerous crises in the course of it. After the worst of them, however, which occurred on March 13-14, he recovered amazingly quickly.[3]

Arsenical intoxication or not, Gourgaud's serious illness came at a very opportune moment for the Montholons. They now had a chance to talk far more intimately with Napoleon and vindicate themselves of Gourgaud's many accusations. The best thing about Gourgaud's illness, so far as their interests were concerned, was that Gourgaud's mental health was to suffer for quite a long time.

The first criterion of good health, real, absolute health, is to be able to forget oneself. The worse the state of health, the less the patient can forget himself, the more egocentric and the more *envious* he becomes. The worse in quantity and quality the circulation of blood to the brain, the clearer are the symptoms of m ntal insufficiency. Such, for instance, as an urge to dispute. Gourgaud had begun to love to pick a quarrel. So sometimes did His Majesty. It is never good when the quarrelsome live together. Montholon could consider himself safe in the future.

Dr. Warden left us a rather interesting description of how things were done at Longwood, as observed on one of his professional visits to Gourgaud.

Warden was once unexpectedly invited to dine at the Emperor's table. He had arrived on horseback and was dressed accordingly, when he entered Napoleon's antechamber. There he was received by the Count de Montholon, in full-dress uniform. He was led into the drawing-room, where Napoleon was seated at a chess game with Bertrand.

Napoleon greeted his guest most courteously. Warden retired behind Napoleon and watched the social activity. There was a little conversation among those present, who kept their voices to a respectful whisper, something Warden had difficulty in imitating at once.

Just before dinner was announced, Montholon whispered to Warden that he was to sit between the Emperor and the Grand Marshal. There was usually an empty chair at the table. Warden supposed that it was there as a token of the separation from the Empress Marie-Louise.

The china dinner service was more beautiful than any Warden had ever seen, the silver heavy and richly-decorated with eagles. Dessert was served on golden plates.

A bottle of claret and a carafe of water were placed at each setting. No healths were proposed or drunk. Everyone drank when it suited him. He must not miss a chance, though, for immediately a diner finished eating, his wine was removed. Dinner lasted an hour.

It might be interesting to hear a little of the conversation.

"Have you visited General Gourgaud?" asked Napoleon.

"Yes, general." (He certainly did not use this address, but in order to get his book published in England, Warden had to write it so. He must have said "Sire". Without the "Sire" he would have risked being dismissed from the table.)

"How have you found him?"

"Extremely ill. Dysentery, Sire."

"Where is its seat?"

"In the intestines, Sire."

"What has been the cause?"

"Heat of climate on a constitution peculiarly predisposed. But remove the cause and the effect will cease. Had he been bled in the first instance, it is probable that the disease would have been less violent."

"What remedy is now proposed?"

"The functions of the liver and other viscera are deranged. To restore them therefore to a healthy action it will be necessary to have recourse to mercury."

"That is bad medicine."

"Experience has taught me the contrary, Sire."

"Did Hippocrates use it? I believe not. He had great faith in simples." Napoleon today would have been called a believer in naturopathic measures.

"He might, nevertheless, have derived great advantages from modern discoveries. I have been taught to assist Nature."

"And couldn't you do so without having recourse to such a dangerous mineral?"

"Experience has convinced me that mercury, provided it produces salivation, is infallible."

After the meal the little court moved into the drawing-room, where cards were laid out. Napoleon played carelessly, thought Warden. He seemed to take pleasure in losing his money. Perhaps he saw it as an unembarrassing way to continue to distribute royal largesse.

After a short while, however, Napoleon went back to his cross-examination of Warden, this time mostly concerning the soul and its purpose and connection with the mortal body.[4]

But Warden does not tell us that on that occasion Napoleon was heard to criticize rather strongly the idea, held by doctors, that diseases could be cured with the help of dangerous poisons. Las Cases mentions this, however, and we are told that the Emperor Napoleon considered that physicians, at least those of the simpler category, should be forbidden to use any poisonous medicine whatsoever. He had considered ordering that prohibition while he held supreme power, but had been advised against it.

"Such a measure," said Napoleon, "would certainly have been wise and would have done a lot of good. But people were not sufficiently educated; most of them would have considered such a law as the act of a tyrant, though it would have been intended for their protection."[5]

Napoleon bowed to the will of his people — then.

To this day the myth has persisted, as first ordered into

existence by Napoleon and cultivated by Montholon, that the Island of St. Helena was cursed with a bad climate and ridden with endemic diseases. How septic were those surroundings?

On the small island water came almost directly from the tropical downpours. The corps of engineers and the station doctors knew enough to protect it from pollution. Not only did the health of inhabitants of the island depend on its purity but it would go into the casks of naval ships and merchantmen that made of St. Helena a watering port of call.

The direct, antiseptic rays of the sun in equatorial latitudes is helpful in disease control. Moreover, St. Helena was recognized as a fully approved port of convalescence. Sick sailors were put ashore to recuperate and be picked up on their ships' return.

Dysentery could be brought to the island in that way and may have been in some degree endemic there as it was at times to most parts of the populated world of the seventeen and eighteenth centuries. Hepatic illnesses were likewise widely prevalent in that age, but probably not more stubbornly so at St. Helena than elsewhere.

The records do not show that of the approximately 50 members of the household contingent, all members included, that went with Napoleon to St. Helena or later joined him there, fatalaties occurred in other cases than that of Cipriani, of a child of a servant in the Montholon household and, of course, in the case of the Emperor himself. Two of these deaths must be traced to planned poisoning and the other may have been by misadventure, but quite probably from the same basic source and cause.

References

1. Kemble 251
2. Forsyth I:75, 76
3. Las Cases I:453
4. Warden 114-18
5. Las Cases I:427

25

Enter Sir Hudson: The Climate Worsens

On February 19, 1816, at the most acute stage of the crisis of the sentries at the windows, Napoleon felt unwell. He retired to his bedroom and kept to himself. However, he was sufficiently recovered on February 21 to go for a short ride in the park, though only at walking pace. On the sixth of March he had so far improved in condition as to be able to go riding as usual, according to Las Cases.

Those rides had started by being promising. Napoleon could once more sit a horse and break the vicious circle into which his health had fallen.

His former inability to ride a horse, noticed at Borodino and once more at Waterloo, was not surprising to anyone who had seen how difficult Napoleon found it to walk. During his first days on board the *Northumberland* the admiral sometimes had discreetly to support him under the arm, when he seemed more than usually unsteady on his feet.[21]

His legs were not only weak; they were also shapelessly fat, swollen. Now that we know Napoleon had been poisoned on various occasions when still in power, it is unnecessary to explain his disinclination to ride when he suffered from those accepted symptoms of arsenical intoxication, swelling of the ankles and calves together with fatty degeneration and weakening of the leg muscles.

Apart from a few days' "indisposition" in mid-February, mid-March and mid-April, the Emperor enjoyed fairly good health during the first four months of 1816, as proved by the fact that he went often for long horseback rides.[1] It should be noted that these "indispositions" characteristically occurred in the middle of the month.

As Napoleon regained strength in his legs, so his mental health, which had been a matter of concern during the first months of his exile, became noticeably better.

On April 14, 1816, the island's optical telegraph system announced that H.M.S. *Phaeton*, bringing Sir Hudson Lowe, the newly appointed lieutenant-general and governor of St. Helena, had been sighted.

The next day Sir Hudson came ashore in Jamestown together with his suite, among whom could be reckoned, beside his wife Lady Suzanne, Sir Thomas Reade, the governor's next-in-command, Major Gideon Gorrequer, his adjutant, Lieutenant-Colonel Lyster, head physician Alexander Baxter and some officers belonging to the Royal Engineers, a Major Anthony Emmet, a Lieutenant Basil Jackson, who appears to have been a truly sly dog, and a Lieutenant Wortham. The engineers were charged to plan and excavate a site for Napoleon's new palace.

Hudson Lowe has been much criticized in the literature on Napoleon's imprisonment. He died under an assumed name in 1844, in an out-of-the-way small town in Britain, despised by the world and especially by his own countrymen, in the supposition that he had made life an ordeal of wretchedness for Napoleon and had finished by "murdering" him with sadistic mental cruelties.

Had he really done this? The truth is more likely to be that Sir Hudson, according to instructions, was a cautious but usually compliant host to a too-frequently ill and decidedly difficult guest. But what did that matter, when this guest would write in his Will: "*Je meurs prématurement, assassiné par l'oligarchie anglaise et son sicaire: le peuple anglais ne tardera pas à me venger.* — My death is premature. I have been assassinated by the English oligarchy and their hired murderer. The English people will not be long in avenging me."

An assassinator was certainly present, but it was not Sir Hudson Lowe, prejudiced though his position in history became due to Napoleon's harshly worded declaration in his Will. It is important to remember that de Montholon assisted the Emperor in the drawing of that strange and recriminatory document. Was it Napoleon or his aristocratic assistant who chose the word "assassinated"?

If one reads the documents on Sir Hudson's government of St. Helena, which are largely set out in Forsyth's classical work on Napoleon's imprisonment, it becomes quite clear that Sir Hudson's reputation for harshness did not come from his own actions.

Sir Hudson became the scapegoat for the deeds of others — deeds directed towards making Napoleon appear wretched while alive, and letting him die at last as a pitiable remnant of his former self, unworthy to be seen as an immortal of French and world history.

There was a risk that the blood of Napoleon the martyr would be upon the one or ones said to have harassed to death the people's idol. It was therefore a good thing to have a scapegoat at hand. Sir Hudson was to be the victim of his position as guardian of the person of the Emperor in exile.

Suspecting nothing, Sir Hudson announced upon assuming his duties that he intended to call on his important prisoner early next morning.[2]

Those authors who have judged Hudson Lowe harshly have usually criticized the British government for their choice of governor on St. Helena during Napoleon's exile. To pass such a judgment is to be wise after the event. The British do not deserve blame for having chosen Sir Hudson. He had certain qualities that seemed to qualify him to play the host on St. Helena.

Sir Hudson spoke fluent Italian, which was Napoleon's mother tongue, and French, Spanish and Portuguese as well. He was almost of the same age as Napoleon, knew Corsica well and was acquainted with the distinctive Corsican mentality. Sir Hudson actually lived in Ajaccio during the British occupation of Corsica and had later become organizer and head of the Corsican Rangers, a group of Corsican bandits and deserters.[4,29] Today they might be known more kindly as commandos, guerrillas, partisans or loyalists.

He had experience in island administration from his appointment as military governor of Capri and Kefallenia-Ithaca. He also knew Elba well, his regiment having been stationed there after the evacuation of Corsica;[4] and he had fought in Egypt after Bonaparte's departure. In short, there was background for a great many congenial conversations between Sir Hudson and

Napoleon. Sir Hudson, moreover, was a fairly experienced diplomat as a result of his activity as agent on Sardinia in 1803 and in Sweden in 1813. He must have been successful in the latter post, for Charles John, Sweden's crown prince and acting regent, later sided with him and openly joined the coalition against Napoleon.

Sir Hudson Lowe's task on St. Helena was more than ordinarily hard. Just as one does not blame a doctor at a mental hospital for inability to get on close terms with a paranoid patient, so one can hardly blame Hudson Lowe for being unable to make friends with the angry and seriously ailing Napoleon, in spite of all the outward prospects for sympathy to arise.

Had Napoleon been physically and mentally fit, such as he was when Consul, singularly able to win the sympathy and friendship of the people, then relations between Hudson Lowe and Napoleon could have been very good — always provided, of course, that there should be no secret agent determined to do all possible to hinder growth of the friendship.

In the circumstances existing, these two leading characters in the drama of St. Helena were destined to become adversaries rather than mutually courteous officers and gentlemen of opposing forces thrown together by the vagaries of fate and fortunes of war.

Sir Hudson's first official act as governor of St. Helena was to call on the Emperor. He inquired of the English officer at Longwood, Captain Poppleton, about the best time for a visit.[3]

Poppleton told him that Napoleon used always to return from his morning ride at 9 o'clock. For safety's sake Poppleton had asked Napoleon himself if he could receive the governor at nine on the morning of April 16 and Napoleon had agreed.

Attired in full-dress uniform and accompanied by Admiral Cockburn and the whole of his staff, Sir Hudson rode ceremoniously over the plateau in the morning tropic sunshine towards Longwood. The party dismounted in the courtyard of the lodge's main entrance. The place seemed quiet and shut up. Presently Count de Montholon appeared and informed the governor that His Majesty was indisposed and did not intend to receive visitors.

Poppleton was called for. He could give no reasonable

explanation. It would have been better if Gourgaud had been asked. He could have explained what had happened.

It was true that Napoleon had told Gourgaud the day before that the governor could call at 9 o'clock the following morning. Napoleon had added that of course the governor's request was not in accordance with ceremonial proceedings at the ex-imperial court, but it would be received *tout de même*.

However, this conversation was interrupted by Bertrand, who said that it had been arranged that the admiral would introduce Hudson Lowe. This considerably irritated Napoleon, who had intended to take the opportunity to tell the new governor of the 'unworthy treatment' inflicted on him by the admiral.

Napoleon paced back and forth in his drawing-room, growing more and more irritated. Finally his imperial mind was made up: *"On ne m'a avisé de cela; si l'amiral vient, je ne recevrai personne* — I have not been told of this. If the admiral comes, then I shall receive no one."[3]

After half an hour spent in talking with Montholon and with Gourgaud, who had joined them after a time, the governor and his attendants departed. Sir Hudson was disappointed, but the admiral could not conceal his delight.

Apparently reluctant to return so soon and so unsuccessfully the whole official company rode over to the Hut's Gate to call on the Grand Marshal of the Palace. Bertrand tried as best he could to smooth things over. It was just that the governor's request had not been made through the right channels, he explained. And, of course, Sir Hudson properly should have asked the Grand Marshal of the Palace for an audience with the Emperor, to satisfy protocol. It was officialdom speaking to officialdom.

So now the governor had considerably greater cause for worry than simply that he had been refused audience; he had committed a breach of etiquette in high quarters. For such a gaffe in diplomacy one might be made to suffer all one's remaining years. Sir Hudson asked Bertrand straight out, and Bertrand could do nothing but confirm that, as a matter of fact, the governor had been guilty of *une fausse démarche*.[5]

Sir Hudson assured Bertrand that he had most assuredly not intended to inconvenience Napoleon. He had only wanted, as soon as possible, to affirm his readiness to serve.

And so the quarrel began which was to continue as long as Napoleon lived and in the end earn Sir Hudson a world-wide and undying reputation as his destroyer by what a later generation might call psychological warfare.

Following upon an invitation from the Grand Marshal of the Palace, the whole English company returned to Longwood at four o'clock on the afternoon of the next day. This time the governor was courteously and graciously received; not Admiral Cockburn, however. When the latter prepared to follow the governor into Napoleon's drawing-room, Noverraz, the valet on duty, shut the door in his face, after allowing the governor, who was a couple of paces in front, to pass. An intensely angry Sir George strode straight out, threw himself on his horse and spurred away.[6]

He was entitled to act as he did. He had handed over the command on St. Helena to Sir Hudson. Now it was the latter's turn meekly to receive the flailings of the island's unreconciled royal guest.

Napoleon was pleased with events. He had been able to teach the admiral a lesson and pay off some grudges. Posting sentries at his doors and windows, indeed!

Had the admiral insisted on entering, Napoleon intended to say: *"Votre conduite, indigne d'un militaire, attache une grande honte sur le front de vos descendants, jusqu'à la dixième génération* — Your conduct, unworthy of a military man, is a disgrace to your descendants unto the tenth generation."[7]

At the same time as the guard changed at the highest level, so it also changed in the Emperor's own household. Montholon was returned to grace — and this was to endure for the rest of the Emperor's life — while Gourgaud and Bertrand thereafter declined in Napoleon's esteem.

The governor had brought with him declarations for all in Napoleon's suite to sign. Either they had to undertake to submit to all the restrictions put upon the Emperor himself, or they were to be moved immediately to Cape Town for a period of political quarantine before being allowed to return to Europe. Count and Countess de Montholon were the only ones present who signed spontaneously. Montholon had declared he was there for the duration.

Bertrand did not want to commit himself for longer than six months. His wife had indeed been very badly treated, so the Grand Marshal was fully justified.

Gourgaud signed, but added a clause that angered Napoleon. He wrote that he was staying as a point of honor. Napoleon would have preferred for his aide to have stayed because of his undying respect and affection for his monarch.[7]

Napoleon thought that if he could but get the new governor of St. Helena to himself, he could have those hated sentries taken away. Why should he be guarded like a common felon in a jail?

It was not to be manageable, however. His guardian, the governor, dared not alter the protective measures Admiral Cockburn had installed.[8]

On April 29, Napoleon was again indisposed. He kept to his room, received no one and ate alone. This indisposition continued for a few days, lasting longer than those he had suffered thus far in his exile. On May 5 his symptoms had become more alarming, and Dr. O'Meara was called.[9]

The physician was admitted for the first time to Napoleon's bedroom — and by a back door. He observed that, in a room where the furniture was simple and shabby, including the ex-commander's iron camp bed. Only one item, other than a few portraits, bore witness to Napoleon's former exalted status — a washstand with basin and jug of silver.

Napoleon lay on a sofa, gloomy and depressed. He wore a white dressing-gown, wide white trousers and white stockings. His shirt was open, without cravat. On his head he wore a colorful checked cloth. Taking his ease, he could revert to Corsican ways.

Before O'Meara was allowed to enter the sickroom he had had to assure the Grand Marshal that he now regarded himself entirely as the Emperor's private physician. He was not an army doctor under orders from the governor. He was also made to promise he would say nothing to anyone about details of Napoleon's illness. Furthermore Bertrand had informed the doctor that etiquette demanded that no direct questions should be put to the Emperor. O'Meara should answer Napoleon's questions, but he was to ask none. These were hard instructions for an attending doctor to follow.[10]

Faithful to his promise, O'Meara does not tell us of Napoleon's symptoms on that occasion, apart from saying that the Emperor had an attack of gout.

Gout means at least one swollen foot and it could mean two. In fact, it could mean anything in the diagnosis of an early 19th century physician. It also meant severe pain. The cloth on his head could have signified a headache. According to Las Cases that was so.[15]

But Las Cases notes on the same day that Napoleon showed a marked change physically; his conversation dragged. Even his expression had changed; he thought he had a temperature and was obviously cold, for he had asked for a fire to be lit. And he could not stand the daylight.[11] Las Cases had noticed on May 2 that Napoleon's legs no longer supported him.[12] "Les jambes me refusent le service," said Napoleon.

This is the first time we learn that Napoleon showed in severity those symptoms on St. Helena that were later so often to recur during a great part of his captivity. Other symptoms also would appear, but weakness of the legs, a sensation of fever, headache and sensitivity to light, sensation of cold, especially in the legs, all of these would remain as the chief somatic symptoms of his illness in exile.

Las Cases was present on October 16, 1816 when Santini, lackey and porter, trimmed Napoleon's hair. Las Cases noticed a large lock of hair fell to the ground. He bent down and picked it up. He was historian enough to appreciate having it.[13]

This lock of hair was to come into the possession of a Russian family, one of whose members, Gregory Troubetzkoy of New York, gave Doctor Hamilton Smith at the Department of Forensic Medicine in Glasgow, permission to undertake an analysis. This was performed on 1 cm, 2 cm and 3 cm sections of some of these hairs. Under activation tests the irradiated hair revealed a high arsenic content, with values varying between 9.2 p.p.m. and 30.4 p.p.m. As the hairs were cut and not shaved, it is impossible to fix exact times for the different intoxications. However, the analysis of these hairs does signify that Napoleon was poisoned by arsenic over a period of about two months in 1816. The hairs were no longer than 2.1 cm at the most and cannot thus testify to a period of more than about eight weeks.[14]

On April 30 the governor paid another visit. He was received in friendly fashion by the Emperor, who lay stretched on a sofa in his dressing-gown.

It was not long, however, before both gentlemen began to disagree about the sentries, and Napoleon accused Sir Hudson in harsh terms.

"The admiral was undoubtedly instructed by his government to let me die little by little. I see that you have had the same instructions. An assassination is a costly business. Apparently they wish me to die more slowly."[16]

So far, of course, Napoleon was right; it would be much too expensive to murder him outright with, for instance, a couple of bullets. It does seem extraordinary, though, that the great man should not have realized the contrast between his fear of being murdered by the British and their generosity toward him; as witness the matter of willingness to provide for him the costly proposed palace, pre-fabricated in England.

Had the British really intended to allow Bonaparte discreetly to disappear without themselves appearing as villains, they could have done so without sacrificing enormous sums on his custody and on the princely upkeep of himself and his court.

They could, for instance, have had him fall or leap overboard one moonless night from the *Northumberland* or the *Bellerophon*. It would have been an unfortunate accident with overtones of suicide.

Why Napoleon never realized when he lived on St. Helena that it was the French oligarchy of the day that really desired his destruction can hardly be explained otherwise than in the possibility of his having received certain special information. There must have been there an agent of the Bourbons who cultivated in him specific attitudes of suspicion in order to protect his actual enemies.

A good indication of Napoleon's state of health at different periods on St. Helena comes from the notes on his riding excursions kept by members of his suite.

During the whole of the month of May, 1816 His Imperial Majesty did not once go riding, but on June 2, at nine in the morning, he mounted and rode a mile along the path down to Hut's Gate. The next day Napoleon lay in his bath for three hours — a bad sign — and was gloomy and depressed.[17] Thereafter he went out only by carriage.

Early on the morning of June 7, Napoleon announced he would go riding. After breakfast he changed his mind and went instead in his carriage. As a matter of fact Napoleon was to ride no more for several years. It was not until 1820 that anyone — except Montholon — was to record that Napoleon had again mounted a horse.

Considering riding as an indication of Napoleon's state of health, it is perhaps relevant to recall the fact that Napoleon retreated from Russia not on horseback, as artists would have it, but by sledge and carriage.

Caulaincourt writes in his memoirs that the Emperor then used to get out two or three times a day and walk by the side of his carriage. He would stumble forward, while the chief of the general staff, Marshal Berthier, Caulaincourt or some other staff member would support him under the arms.[18]

Even on the way to Moscow Count de Castellane, who was Napoleon's aide-de-camp, had noticed at Vilna that Napoleon seemed unwilling to ride on horseback. If he did, it was only at walking pace, and he had to be assisted into the saddle. Whenever he wished to go longer distances, he called for a carriage.[27]

It is worthy of recollection that just before the battle of Wagram — which was a Pyrrhic victory — the *officier d'ordonnance* Anatole Montesquiou had noticed that Napoleon found it difficult to walk; he had had to support himself heavily — *très lourdement* — on General Savary's arm.[28]

In the middle of July the prisoner of St. Helena began to worry about his teeth, which were later to become loose. Due to scurvy, O'Meara concluded as he examined the swollen gums. Due to arsenical stomatitis, we should say, on conclusive grounds.[19] Given the amounts of arsenic in the system that samples of Napoleon's hair revealed under analysis for that particular chemical element, it would have been strange had he not shown all or most of the symptoms above mentioned.

Napoleon was finding it more and more difficult to move about. On the nineteenth of September Las Cases noted that the Emperor's walk had become very heavy and that one foot dragged. "He seems to be getting weaker," went on Las Cases. "His face sags."[20]

During the first months of Napoleon's illness in 1816, the acute periods lasted a week at the most. After that the patient's spirits rose and the severe pain and attacks of shivering disappeared. On October 24, however, a period of sickness began which was to last for two weeks.

During the first year on St. Helena, neither Napoleon nor his suite seems to have noticed that the climate there was bad. But when Napoleon began to fall ill constantly, and when several of his court were often indisposed at the same time, it was said that the climate of the island was mortally dangerous.

Gourgaud and Las Cases frequently fell ill at the same time as Napoleon, and the health of the younger Las Cases gave considerable cause for worry. The boy suffered from periods of severe difficulty in breathing and palpitations of the heart (tachycardia). He fainted several times. Doctors Warden and Baxter, head physicians of squadron and garrison respectively, were summoned to Longwood to diagnose the boy's illness.

Indeed, it was as the French had suspected. The boy had a congenital heart defect which the climate of St. Helena affected very badly.[22] We, however, must assume that desired illness was induced. It was neither a serious hereditary malady nor one related to climate.

The "congenital heart defect" improved from time to time, however, in spite of the fact that the climate of St. Helena remained the same. Towards the end of 1816 the boy's condition became such that his father feared for his life.

Las Cases realized that the youth must get away from St. Helena and made plans for an honorable departure. On November 25 the gentlemen Las Cases went to Jamestown.

Not surprisingly for us but probably to the wonder of people at St. Helena, the change of environment was all that was needed for health. Father and son recovered rapidly as soon as they had travelled the small distance to reach the port and its environs. It cannot then have been the climate of St. Helena that was so adverse, but rather the climate of Longwood.

Palpitations of the heart and difficulty in breathing may be signs of so-called sub-acute arsenical intoxication.[23]

When the Las Cases left Longwood, the Montholons could hardly suppress their delight, noted Gourgaud in his diary.[24]

Said Napoleon to Bertrand on November 28, "Las Cases (departure) is a great loss to me and I am shocked at the delight that has been shown over his departure."[25]

The apparent reason for Las Cases' departure from Longwood was that he had intended to smuggle out a letter, sewn into his valet's coat, and for this the governor had had him brusquely arrested and taken away. The letter was quite innocent and would have passed the British censorship without difficulty. When Sir Hudson discovered this, he wanted to let Las Cases go back to Longwood. But Las Cases did not wish to go; his son's illness was at the moment of much more concern to him than Napoleon's memoirs. As a matter of fact he had a whole bag filled with manuscripts, which were to be the basis of his famous *Mémorial de Sainte-Helene*, later to be dubbed the Koran of Napoleon's devotees.

After the Las Cases had departed Longwood, their health so rapidly changed for the better that Dr. Baxter, who examined them some time after Las Cases' arrest, thought the accounts of their earlier ill-health exaggerated, but agreed that it was difficult for the younger Las Cases to run or walk uphill. Now Baxter, too, realized it was certainly not the climate of St. Helena that was the cause of their illness.

One thing is certain, though, and that is that the "murderous" climate at Longwood was definitely not good. But that dangerous climate was strictly confined to Napoleon's and Bertrand's houses. The health of the military, stationed some hundred yards away, was much superior.[26]

References

1. Las Cases I:452, 496; Gourgaud I:113
2. Bertrand I:13
3. Gourgaud I:122
4. Forsyth III:506-508
5. Gourgaud I:123
6. Marchand II:78
7. Gourgaud I:124-6
8. Bertrand I:19, 28
9. Las Cases I:544, 550; Bertrand I:19, 22, 24, 28
10. Bertrand I:27, 28; O'Meara I:46
11. Las Cases I:558, 559
12. Las Cases I:555
13. Las Cases II:442
14. Letter to the author from Dr. Hamilton Smith
15. Las Cases I:572
16. Bertrand I:19
17. Gourgaud I:145; Las Cases I:673, 676
18. Caulaincourt II:131
19. O'Meara I:77
20. Las Cases II:361
21. Glover 132
22. Marchand II:130, 131
23. Heffter 853, 854
24. Gourgaud I:200
25. Bertrand I:154
26. Forsyth I:29
27. Grunvald 32
28. Montesquiou 170
29. Masson (1) 213 et. seg.

26

Cockburn Relieved, Montholon Reinforced

ON NEW YEAR'S DAY 1816, Napoleon had expressed the hope that all in his company should live together in peace and harmony, like members of one big family.

As with everything else Napoleon had wished for during his unhappy captivity, this did not work out. But on June 18 a happy event occurred in the family: Mme. Montholon gave birth to a daughter, who was christened Hélène-Napoléone.

It was difficult to tell even then who was the little new-born lady's biological father. Anyway, Napoleon had to pay. There was a little confusion about the christening. There was no proper priest on the island, only English Protestants. Finally one of them had to baptize the little girl.

Hélène-Napoléone was a vigorous young lady. She was to live through the rest of that century and quite a way into the next. She would outlive two husbands, the first a Viscount de Gouedic and later on a Count de Bonfils de Rochon de la Peyrouse. To whom, in ancestry, she owed her health and longevity was for sundry reasons unattributable. Named as she was, for her mother, who would be surprised at the inevitability of judgments that Hélène-Napoléone resembled her distinguished namesake?

On June 17, 1816, H.M.S. *Newcastle* lay at anchor in the roads with the new squadron commander, Admiral Malcolm, on board. With him were three so-called commissioners, representatives of the rulers of France, Russia and Austria. They were to help with Napoleon's custody. In point of fact they tended to become distant on-lookers at the life of the inhabitants of Longwood. In sinecure roles, they were retained at St. Helena to report home that "the devil was still in chains". One had a more serious function than the rest, though he simulated naivete.

223

The French commissioner was Marquis Claude de Montchenu. Napoleon called him a *général de carrosse* and thought that Montchenu had never heard a dangerous gunshot. Actually the marquis had made a fine career for·himself before the Revolution in the royal French army on the strength of his noble descent. At the time of the Restoration he was made a *Maréchal de camp,* like so many other faithful servants of the royal family. He held, in fact, the same fine rank as de Montholon. During Napoleon's rule he had not held an official post.

It was Talleyrand who had made Montchenu King Louis' representative on St. Helena. Talleyrand whimsically predicted that Montchenu's presence on St. Helena would be quite certainly the death of Napoleon, Montchenu was so deadly dull.

The Duke of Richelieu, Talleyrand's successor as French President of the Council, wanted his own man on St. Helena, and offered Montchenu another post, but Montchenu stuck to his appointment on the grounds that his mission on St. Helena was of the greatest importance to France. And well it may have been.

On the whole, Talleyrand was quicker of comprehension than the Duke of Richelieu.

The Marquis de Montchenu has been portrayed as an almost comic figure by many authors who, ridiculously enough, have missed the point of the whole drama of St. Helena. He was, as a matter of fact, a very purposeful gentleman who had studied well his part of incompetent old blockhead. He actually wore a wig with a pigtail — unless, perchance, it really was his own hair, braided and powdered.[1]

That the Marquis Montchenu's mission on St. Helena was not considered by his superiors as merely conventional and unimportant was also revealed by the fact that he had with him a "secretary", a Captain Gors. It should not be taken for granted that the marquis necessarily was in charge. It could very well have been Gors. In any case, Gors was in the habit of adding his comments to the marquis' official letters.[2]

The Russian commissioner, the Count de Balmain, interestingly was of Scottish descent and is described as an elegant, cultured and likeable person. He was an officer and diplomat and seems to have been a good friend of Tsar Alexander who in turn once had been a very close friend of Napoleon's.

The Austrian Baron Stürmer has been described by Hudson Lowe as a chameleon, but otherwise a pleasant enough person. It is notable that all three commissioners withstood the "murderous" climate of St. Helena without being ill for any length of time. Stürmer left the island at the request of Hudson Lowe, who discovered that Stürmer and his wife, who was French, had visited Longwood without permission. The Russian left in March 1820 and took with him as his wife Lady Suzanne Lowe's eldest daughter by a former marriage.

Montchenu must have taken his mission on St. Helena very seriously, for he stayed until the bitter end. He and his shiny fine dress sword were certainly not necessary to stop Napoleon from escaping. He said himself, soon after his arrival on St. Helena, that Napoleon had not the least chance of getting away. Not even a dog, he thought, could have got out of Longwood at night without running into a sentry. There was always a frigate at anchor outside the only spot on the island, other than at Jamestown, where it was conceivably possible to land or embark.[3]

So Montchenu was able to assure the Duke of Richelieu that his fears of Napoleon escaping again were unfounded.

All the same, Montchenu stayed on as France's official observer. He cannot be suspected of having considered it his duty to protect Napoleon.

Montholon wrote in his consistently misleading memoirs that Montchenu and Napoleon were old friends from boyhood days and that their youthful reminiscences were the basis of a sort of mutual gallantry.

That was, of course, quite untrue. Napoleon never addressed a word to Montchenu whom, as a matter of fact, he never met. The first visit Montchenu paid the Emperor at Longwood was when Napoleon lay on his *lit de parade*. Montchenu came then, accompanied by the governor, to assure himself that Napoleon really was dead.

Une âne de vieille souche — an ass with a fine ancestry — such was the opinion of Montchenu that Napoleon privately expressed. Napoleon should have realized by then that such well-connected asses could be dangerous to an upstart.

When Montchenu arrived at St. Helena, he carried letters to Montholon and his wife.[4]

At the time of the commissioners' arrival on St. Helena, relations between Gourgaud and Montholon were fairly pleasant. They had discovered a mutual interest: to get rid of the "Jesuit", Las Cases. Montholon led Gourgaud to believe that Las Cases was an unreliable supporter of Napoleon.

On July 11, 1816, Napoleon and Gourgaud visited with Mme. Montholon. They found her reading La Fontaine's fables and the History of Mme. de Brinvilliers.[6] The sweet and lovable Marquise de Brinvilliers, so gentle and appreciated by those dear to her, poisoned most of them: her husband, her children, her lover, her father and both her brothers — all these together with an unknown number of ordinary people and patients of a hospital where she used the sick as guinea pigs. The Marquise de Brinvilliers was a sensitive person, so that often, when she saw her victims in pain, she would stop poisoning them. Thus she saved the lives of her husband, her children and her lover. But she was in a position legally to inherit from her father, and from her brothers. A man-servant, Jean Hamelin, known as La Chaussée, was ordered to attend to her brothers, but the marquise herself poisoned her father, Antoine Dreux d'Aubray.

Her methods were interestingly subtle. Every now and then she fed her father arsenic; but not enough for him to notice he had been poisoned. The doses were designed to undermine his health and cause numerous symptoms which confused his doctors. When they discovered they were baffled by the case of Antoine d'Aubray they suggested a change of air. So he left for one of his country seats, where he rapidly regained health. However, missing his gentle daughter, he invited her to join him. Whereupon he fell victim once more to the same mysterious, many-sided illness. He was taken back to Paris. His illness continued. His daughter offered to nurse him. So tender were her ministrations that Monsieur d'Aubray decided to re-make his will in her favor.

The ink had scarcely dried on Monsieur d'Aubray's signature when his daughter handed him a cup of "vin émétisé", that is a tonic wine in which tartar emetic, an antimony compound, was added. This drink had been prescribed by her father's doctor, but his daughter had laced the dose of tartar emetic so efficiently that Monsieur d'Aubray was immediately very sick, with continuous vomiting. This new illness was enough to bring him to his grave.

In all, d'Aubray's illness lasted eight months. The Marquise de Brinvilliers, whose crime was discovered, admitted she had poisoned him 28 to 30 times. At times her servant Gascon had given her father the poison. Yet, at the post-mortem examination, the doctors had judged that Monsieur d'Aubray had died a natural death.

Mme. de Brinvilliers would certainly never have been found out if her sister-in-law had not suspected something, if one of her accomplices had not accused her, and if she herself had not been imprudent enough to keep an exact written account of her poisonings.

There is much in the story of Mme. de Brinvilliers that coincides with the drama on St. Helena. We shall see how Napoleon, after enjoying relatively good health for quite a while, would suddenly relapse with the same illness as had troubled him previously. This new illness was to last eight months, and he was to be given about forty more doses of arsenic. During a period of ten days in which he was writing his last and famous Will, his health improved; but once the Will was signed he became suddenly worse than ever before. About a week later he was dead. This last Will was drawn up in favor of the one who had so tenderly nursed him during his final illness.

The resemblance between M. d'Aubray's ailments and death and that of Napoleon is so strong that it would have been quite extraordinary if the poisoning of d'Aubray had not in fact served as model for that of Napoleon. We are not privileged to know how it came about that the book about the de Brinvilliers case was at Longwood. It would be significant to know the relationship of book acquisition and ownership, in this case, to Montholon or another. We only know that it was there and that Montholon's wife was reading it at a time when Napoleon was being unsuspectingly poisoned.

Discussing the story, Napoleon thought that the celebrated case of Mme. de Brinvilliers' murder of her own father must have been fiction.

"I can understand a woman poisoning her husband, but not her father — what do you think, Gourgaud?"

"I don't think a woman could do either. Poison is the weapon of the cowardly."[5,6]

Thus Gourgaud outdid Napoleon in credulity. It is to the credit of their character that they could not believe that Mme. de Brinvilliers had poisoned both father and husband.

It was a pity that Montholon was not present at this discussion of the Brinvilliers exploits. His reactions, reported, might have been interesting. How the book came to be in the Montholons' hands is a question tantalizingly pertinent but forever unanswerable.

Napoleon soon came to regard Sir Pulteney Malcolm, the new commander of the St. Helena squadron, as a good and companionable man. Hudson Lowe may not have thought so, and possibly with good reason. A certain sympathy developed between Napoleon and Malcolm. This caused Sir Pulteney to seem less loyal to the governor, who would be held personally responsible for Napoleon's security.

By posting Sir Pulteney to St. Helena, the British government let it be known once more that they wanted to be on good terms with Napoleon. Sir Pulteney's wife, who accompanied him, was wholeheartedly an admirer of Napoleon.

There was a reason for a warmth of feeling toward the Emperor on Lady Malcolm's part. Her brother's life happened to have been saved by Napoleon's personal intervention. That young man was a captain of cavalry named Elphinstone. The day before the great battle of Waterloo a skirmish occurred at La Belle-Alliance in which Captain Elphinstone was very seriously wounded. He lay to all appearances dead when Napoleon chanced to pass by. The Emperor stopped and ordered his doctor to see if anything could be done for the fallen Englishman. Through this momentary and kindly interest of the Emperor, who we know was ill at the time, Elphinstone's life was saved and he was able to rejoin his family.[7]

Lady Malcolm's uncle was Lord Keith, who was in command of the fleet to which the *Bellerophon* belonged. He could thus lay a certain measure of claim to some of the honor of having taken Napoleon prisoner.

Lord Keith was not known for any foregoing Napoleonic

sympathies. He used to refer to the Emperor as "The Reptile". But after the incident of his nephew he changed his opinion and expressed his thanks to Napoleon on board *Bellerophon*. Further than this, his own daughter married one of Napoleon's most trusted aides-de-camp, General Charles de la Billarderie de Flahaut, a great charmer, with Napoleon's stepdaughter, Hortense Beauharnais, numbered amongst his conquests.

Napoleon's health was sometimes better, sometimes worse. Each time he fell ill the familiar symptoms would recur, though new ones might be added, such as blisters in and around the mouth, colicky pains, and pain in the side. On December 3, 1816, Bertrand noted that Napoleon's skin had become yellow, suggesting his liver was affected.[8]

On the night of December 14 Napoleon experienced very severe illness. He suffered muscular spasms and lost consciousness for a few seconds. His head ached so badly that he himself thought he would suffer apoplexy. Similar attacks accompanied by fainting occurred on December 18 and 28.[9]

O'Meara had reported to the governor in November that Napoleon, along with all his other ills, seemed to have developed pleurisy.[10]

O'Meara noticed on several occasions that Napoleon found it hard to keep warm. Very often fires were lit in his room, and *he liked to sit before a fire with his feet wrapped in warm towels*. He would also lie for hours in the relief of a warming bath. Yet that, in the latitude of St. Helena, was the season of tropical mid-summer.

It can be quite clear to us now that during the year 1816 Napoleon had begun to be the object of a more systematic arsenical intoxication. That he should be poisoned is in itself quite logical and consistent. After all, poisoning as a way of rendering a dangerous person *hors de combat* and, if necessary, of getting entirely rid of him has been used since the beginning of recorded history. The extraordinary thing in the drama of St. Helena is that no one seemed to notice or realize that Napoleon was being poisoned. Of course, there were always some. One member of the establishment had his suspicions. It was one thing, however, to suspect that Napoleon was being poisoned, but quite another to dare to open one's mouth about it.

Gourgaud on occasions certainly suspected a poisoner was at

Longwood. On September 9, for instance, Gourgaud complained that the wine gave him colic pains. Montholon agreeably remarked that he had noticed the same thing. Gourgaud suggested that the wine had been poisoned with lead.[11] They wanted O'Meara to analyze it.

It is quite probable that it sometimes occurred to the island's governor, too, that Napoleon might be poisoned. In any case, in February, 1817 the governor considered the removal of Montholon from Longwood. When Napoleon heard of this he said to O'Meara: "I should mind very much if I were to lose Montholon. Apart from the fact that he is so attached to me, he is very useful and always tries to anticipate my wishes. I know that it could hurt him very much to have to leave me, even if, as he has nothing to fear in France, it would be doing him a great service to allow him to leave this hopeless place and go back to his circle of friends. *He is of noble birth, so he could easily win favor with the Bourbons, if he wished to.*"[11]

Remarkable in the drama of St. Helena is the fact that Napoleon was quite aware that Montholon belonged to those who could naturally gain favor with the house of Bourbon. Surely he must have known well that his fiercest enemies, who had made repeated attempts on his life, were of that same dynastic company of people.

Napoleon, with a Bourbon aristocrat in his small household, did not comprehend his purpose. We may truly enough call Napoleon "the great". There are so few really great men in history we cannot afford to miss a single one. But let us realize that the illustrious Napoleon was human. He was at times dangerously credulous and quite unbelievably naive. But these qualities, after all, he shared with many others of the world's great, as history confirms. Noble origins impressed him.

References

1. Gourgaud I:152, footnote
2. Marchand II:415
3. Rosebury 98
4. Gourgaud I:156
5. Funch-Bretano and Gril

6. Gourgaud I:161
7. Marchand II:162
8. Bertrand I:156
9. O'Meara I:276, 281, 293
10. Bertrand I:145
11. O'Meara I:383

27

A Painful and Disappointing Year

ON THE MORNING of New Year's day 1817 there was a knock on General Gourgaud's door. Outside stood a happy and expectant group of children. There was Tristan Montholon, Napoléone, Henry and Hortense Bertrand and perhaps there were others.

When the ailing general opened the door, the children cried out in chorus: "Happy New Year! Happy New Year!"

Gourgaud was not unprepared; he brought out the toys he had bought in Jamestown.

Later Bertrand came in and wished Gourgaud, not a Happy New Year — for Bertrand was a reasonable and sensible fellow — but a better one. Montholon came, too, with his good wishes, though just at that time Montholon and Gourgaud were not the best of good friends.

Now it was Gourgaud's turn to go a-New Year visiting. For Mme. Bertrand he had a casket of China tea. On the box he had written: 'May your years be as many as the leaves in this casket of tea.' Mme. Bertrand and Gourgaud had become very good friends. In due propriety, of course.

It must have been with quite mixed feelings that Gourgaud received Montholon. A couple of days earlier Gourgaud had once more been made aware of the latter's double dealing. In Gourgaud's eyes the noble count definitely deserved the name Gourgaud had once given him, *Le Bas*, the mean one!

By this time Montholon had earned other names for himself. O'Meara called him *il bugiardo*, the liar, and the governor's adjutant Gorrequer sardonically honored him with the name *"Veritas"*, the Truth. There was a doctor on St. Helena called Shortt. Gorrequer referred to him in his diary as *il longo,* the long one.[15] His was a simple code of opposites, easy to decipher.

231

Poor Montholon! He was surrounded by people who distrusted him — Gourgaud, Bertrand, O'Meara, Cipriani, Gorrequer. In spite of this he kept his promise not to leave Napoleon. Montholon must have been a very courageous man, devoted to his mission. His situation must have been not at all agreeable, but he was nevertheless always gentle and polite.

The day before New Year's Eve Gourgaud had gone down into Jamestown, ostensibly to buy New Year presents. That may have been true, but his chief business was to say goodbye to the departing Las Cases. Gourgaud obviously was having trouble with his conscience. For the past six months he had actually made life highly unpleasant for Las Cases, intending to get rid of "the Jesuit", whom he considered to be unreliable and definitely no true admirer of Napoleon. One reason Gourgaud thought this was that Montholon had related to him much of a critical kind about Las Cases. It had affected their relations.

It was only when Las Cases was no longer of the household that Gourgaud discovered there were many things in Montholon's stories that could not possibly have been true.

On one of the streets in Jamestown, Gourgaud unexpectedly encountered Sir Hudson Lowe. Tentatively, Gourgaud asked permission to see Las Cases.

Of course! Why should there be any difficulty? Las Cases was at the Castle, the administration headquarters.

Arriving there Gourgaud discovered that Bertrand had thought of the same thing — to speak candidly to Las Cases. Bertrand had also brought him a letter from Napoleon. Longwood was not big, but easy contact between its chief inhabitants was made difficult by whisperings and suspicions. But now Gourgaud and Las Cases could talk freely, away from that atmosphere. Of course there had been misunderstandings and slander, too. When he had listened to his father and Gourgaud, young Las Cases summed up the entire situation with the words: "*Ah, ce sont les Montholons qui sont bien méprisables* — Ah, the Montholons are really despicable!"

The remorseful Gourgaud embraced Las Cases and his son with tears in his eyes.[2]

The letter from Napoleon, which Bertrand handed him, obviously pleased Las Cases. Napoleon trusted Las Cases and gave him his blessing, whatever he did, whether he returned to Longwood or preferred to further Napoleon's cause in Europe.

On New Year's day Napoleon sat for several hours in his bath. This can be taken to signify he was in pain and that his legs suffered from a feeling of icy coldness. Napoleon certainly itched and had various kinds of skin troubles, though no witness mentions this in specific terms. Indirectly we know that this was so, since Marchand mentions Napoleon's urge to brush his entire body. And, as well, we know this sensation to be part of the syndrome of sub-lethal arsenical poisoning.

However, by four in the afternoon of New Year's day Napoleon had made the effort to dress and go into the drawing-room. Presiding there with small reason for happiness, he received the good wishes of the little court.

"Well, Gourgaud, what are you going to give *me* for the New Year? I hear you are giving presents to everyone today."

"Sire, I can do no more than offer your Majesty that which I have once and for all dedicated to you, which is my life."

In return Gourgaud was given a telescope. Bertrand received a set of chessmen, Montholon a dressing-case in silver and a mosaic star of the Legion of Honor. The ladies were each given a valuable china cup and saucer, materials and Chinese gowns. All these Napoleon had acquired through Lady Malcolm with the help of one of her brothers, a director of the East India Company.

Montholon must have been given the silver dressing-case in private, as only Marchand would mention it, not Gourgaud or Bertrand.[3]

The children received candy and expensive presents. Hortense, for instance, was given a bonbonnière which Napoleon had once had from his favorite sister Pauline, and which had cost about a thousand gold francs. Little Napoléone and Hortense each was given a mug. The infant Henry had to be content with a soft shawl.

No diarist tells us what young Tristan de Montholon received. It is probable Napoleon gave the boy some especially fine New Year's gift — in secret. Envy rode high at Longwood.

What about the servants? Ah, no! They received no New Year

presents. That would have been against the current etiquette! They were merely servants.

In spite of surroundings that had the odor of imprisonment to the French, the little family party was quite successful. Napoleon's mood improved. He watched and smiled at the children's happiness and laughter.[4]

Yet that morning he at first had been inclined to cancel the whole New Year celebration. He was ill and in much pain. The past year had brought only disappointment, and the prospects for the year to come were not good.

It had started off so promisingly, but the year 1816 just ended had seemed bewitched. The riding excursions, which had done Napoleon so much good mentally and physically, could not long continue. He was having recurrences of that mysterious malady that had troubled him from time to time before St. Helena. It was to be hoped 1817 would be a year of more tolerable experiences. Yet . . .

That grandly envisaged work, Napoleon's History, which Las Cases and Napoleon had started so promisingly, was interrupted by the departure of Las Cases.

The new governor was a treacherous individual, who certainly intended to kill Napoleon by slow fire.

Gourgaud had become a great problem. When they first came to Longwood he had constantly bothered Napoleon with tales of Montholon's lies and deceit. After Gourgaud's serious illness, it was suddenly Las Cases who was the unreliable one. Gourgaud knew that he was a Jesuit.

And now Gourgaud maintained that Las Cases was reliability itself and that it was Montholon who had misled Gourgaud about the biographer.

Napoleon had realized the truth of this and had tried to persuade Montholon to leave off such foolishness; but Montholon denied having slandered Las Cases.[6]

On the eighteenth of November, 1816, Napoleon had tried once and for all to clear up the misunderstanding between Las Cases and Gourgaud. As we have Gourgaud's notes at our disposal, we can hear what Napoleon and Gourgaud had to say on that occasion in attempting reconciliation.

"Ah, Gourgaud, how are you?"

"Thank you, Sire, very well."

"Why are you always quarrelling with Las Cases? He is a man of great merit, another Talleyrand in miniature. All we have against him is the result of misguided envy. I agree that he makes himself a trifle ridiculous by maintaining that his family is as grand as the Bourbons, but I find this rather amusing. He knows England well, and we shall have to live there eventually.

"So I want you, dear Gourgaud, to be friends with Las Cases. I speak to you as a father to his son."

"Sire, Las Cases is too much of a Jesuit for me. He is treacherous and I am compromised," was Gourgaud's reply.

Napoleon flared up and gave his imperial word that Las Cases had never spoken derogatively to him about Gourgaud.

Gourgaud then appealed to Montholon to uphold him. Montholon started talking about his own merits as envoy to Würzburg, as general, as chamberlain, etc., and said that he did not wish Las Cases to be given precedence. In other words he preferred to talk of something else. But Napoleon must have known that Montholon was the source of the calumny from which Las Cases had suffered, for he accused him of it, in spite of the fact that Montholon had definitely denied that he had maligned Las Cases behind his back.

When a killing is being purposefully planned, a first thing to do is to see to it that there are no unnecessary witnesses.

For de Montholon there were still too many witnesses at Longwood. This was in spite of the fact that Napoleon had been helped to believe that the English wanted him dead. He had consequently isolated himself from all who had anything to do with the governor, the hand of the law on St. Helena. Napoleon's induced illness, too, had forced him to break off all social relationships with the officers of the British military station.

There were many French witnesses at Longwood and, what was even worse, some Corsicans. It was true only Napoleon's court had the right to enter his apartments and never servants of low degree. All the same, there were too many witnesses. They had to be reduced and obviously from the Bourbon point of view Las Cases, the historian who wrote Napoleon's History, should be the first to disappear.

Bertrand had said he meant to leave anyway, within a few months; Gourgaud, on the other hand, would have to be encouraged to go. After that there would be only the Montholons. Should Mme. Montholon prove difficult she, too, would have to be got out of the way, somehow. And then of the courtiers there would only be himself, Montholon, left. Exactly! But there was one mysterious figure at Longwood, not really allowed into Napoleon's bedroom, yet who was often to be seen there. He was a Corsican, too. It would be best to try to get rid of this Cipriani.

Of course, all this would take time. *Eh bien,* this was an important matter and no risks were to be run. The time needed would have to be taken.

Retrospectively the agents in the drama could consider they handled the Las Cases business successfully and well.

The attack had been planned along three fronts. Gourgaud was used to make life at Longwood miserable for Las Cases. The governor was supplied with information that made him suspect Las Cases and be prepared to strike at the first opportunity to exile him from the island.[14]

This had been obvious on October 5, 1816, when the governor forwarded to Bertrand an assortment of unjustified accusations against Las Cases. The governor did not mention where his information came from. It will be remembered that Napoleon had once and for all forbidden his suite to disclose anything at all about life at Longwood to the English.

The third front against Las Cases was the special Longwood climate, which acted so strangely but conveniently at exactly the right times. It attacked Las Cases senior fairly mildly, but was all the more severe toward his poor boy.

The governor was a great disappointment to Napoleon. He would not remove those sentries. He would not even change his mind when it was obviously hinted at what the whole thing was really about. On July 16 Napoleon and Sir Hudson had a long conversation. It started off in fairly friendly fashion. Napoleon was in a joking mood and repeated before every complaint: "Would you like to know what I think about that? Then listen!"

Well, about those sentries . . . And now we shall hear what we had long suspected.

"The way it is now, I can't have anyone to dinner, and suppose I wanted a girl or a mistress, she couldn't get in."

"But you haven't one," replied Sir Hudson.

"But I could get one."

"Oh dear, I'll have to report that to my government."

"But the question doesn't arise! Your government hasn't sent a corporal here but a lieutenant-general and as such you ought to know how to behave. You must want to revenge yourself on me for something."

"Me? No, why? I didn't ask for my appointment."

"You behave like someone out for revenge."[8]

The matter of the sentries was a touchy affair. The governor should have realized perhaps that on that point he could be accused with much more justification in fact than for that other imputation of Napoleon's, that Lowe wished to poison him.

It was not only Las Cases and Gourgaud who had fallen ill in the same way as Napoleon. Mme. Bertrand was ill from time to time, and Bertrand as well. This prevented their attending to Napoleon to the extent the Emperor desired. On September 19, for instance, Mme. Bertrand was so ill it was considered necessary to resort to that reliable old cure-all — bleeding. She was in great pain. Four days later both the Bertrands were ill. Both were bled. At the same time Gourgaud was rather sick. Furthermore, Mme. Bertrand was pregnant and a miscarriage was feared. There was no miscarriage, then. On January 17, 1817 she gave birth to a boy, Arthur. But there were more miscarriages later. Five, in fact. Arsenic, of course, is a recognized inducer of abortion.

With Napoleon sick, Gourgaud, Bertrand and his wife and Las Cases, too, Napoleon and those near to him began to think that this must certainly be some sort of dreadful climatic affliction.

Actually Napoleon, within himself, may not have been quite so sure that it was the climate of St. Helena that brought on the sickness. It was more likely to be the unending wind at the elevation of Longwood. It was the same wind as blew the world over. Ah, yes! It was the wind that caused the trouble.

He could recall an experience of this. When he fell ill at the time of the battle of Borodino outside Moscow in 1812, his surgeon-in-ordinary Yvan was able to tell him that his illness was due to the equinoctial winds.

Napoleon remembered it well. He had not fallen ill exactly at the time of the autumn equinox, but perhaps Dr. Yvan knew that it could start to blow early. It was actually on the fifth of September, 1812, two days before Borodino, with a pitched battle in the offing, that Napoleon found it necessary to call in his physician, Mestivier.

"Well, doctor, you see I'm getting old. My legs are swollen, I can hardly urinate. It's no doubt the dampness of these bivouacs."

On the night of September 7, 1812, Mestivier noted that Napoleon had a dry and persistent cough and that his breathing was labored. He could urinate only slowly and in strictured pain. The lower part of his legs and his feet were swollen. His pulse was feverish and irregular. The doctor diagnosed pleurisy. (Dr. O'Meara was to make the same diagnosis of similar symptoms four years later.) And on September 7, 1812 Napoleon had a frightful headache. On the ninth he was so hoarse that he could not speak. Dr. Mestivier did not realize, just as later Dr. O'Meara and Dr. Antommarchi in their turn, did not appreciate, that Napoleon's symptoms were remarkably similar to those of arsenical intoxication.

But Dr. Yvan thought the distressing illness was caused by the autumn winds. And also by fog, rain and the field bivouacs.[9] If Dr. Yvan had been alive in our time he would have had much greater resources at his disposal to cure his patient and would not have had to rely solely on those simple and robust but much respected methods of Napoleon's day. And yet his diagnosis of Napoleon's illness at Borodino — a chill — might have been accepted just as readily today, given the identical symptoms. Such is the subtle nature of arsenical poisoning. One of its consequences is an onset of deafness. In Moscow Napoleon astonished his staff by not hearing a cannonade that was perfectly clear to everyone else.[16]

So much for the past. In the reality of the present not all was bad. Mme. Montholon was no longer pregnant. This went a long way toward restoring good relations between the Montholons and Napoleon. Instead, Esther had become a problem.

And who was Esther? Esther Vesey? Well, it was certainly the fault of the sentries. Before they interfered, Napoleon had had great pleasure in meeting Miss Mary-Ann Robinson, the daughter of a Miss Robinson who lived in a little cottage not far from Longwood.[10] Miss Robinson had two daughters, the eldest about sixteen. She had red cheeks, large brown eyes and grace without shyness.[11] Napoleon called her "his nymph." "Le bouton rose" had blossomed forth.

The sentries were obviously a total obstacle to the development of the acquaintance between Napoleon and his nymph. The situation was therefore fairly painful, until Napoleon accepted an improvisation. This was Esther. She was also called Miss Vesey. As mentioned, she had been employed as extra chambermaid by Mme. Montholon.[12] Now it was the chambermaid's turn to be with child. So Napoleon wanted her to leave Longwood immediately.

Marchand offered to marry Esther. Napoleon disapproved. Marchand was stubborn. Napoleon called for Bertrand and asked him to fix the matter.

If Marchand married Esther, Napoleon reasoned, then the press would immediately take it for granted that Napoleon had made her pregnant. That was what all great men used to do — arrange that a servant should take the blame. No, this might come to the knowledge of the Empress Marie-Louise and give her a chance for divorce. Better that Esther leave the house the next day and alone. This she did on October 29, 1816.[13]

Bertrand interceded for Esther and pointed out that Napoleon had been seen fairly often with *La Nymphe*. But the Emperor was not impressed.

"To compare *La Nymphe* with Esther is ridiculous. First of all she is not a servant. She is not with child and she does not sleep under the same roof (as I do). I stopped seeing her eight months ago."[13] Exactly. Rather more than eight months had passed since the admiral had hit upon the unhappy idea of posting sentries all 'round the house at night.

As mentioned, it was Gourgaud and Montholon who had

collaborated to get rid of Las Cases. And appropriately, Gourgaud had had to do the work. But Las Cases had not been away from Longwood for more than a month, when Gourgaud found occasion to challenge Montholon to a duel.

The immediate reason was that Gourgaud had happened to observe Albine de Montholon slipping into Napoleon's bedroom at half past seven on the evening of December 15, 1816, when the latter, in a state of undress, had opened the door to her.

Half an hour later Gourgaud had met Montholon who was looking for his wife. Gourgaud did no worse than to reassure Montholon by telling him the Countess was safe in Napoleon's bedchamber. Confused, Montholon stammered: "Oh, I didn't know, but I don't mind."[17]

Four days later Gourgaud was told that Napoleon had decided that in future Gourgaud was to take his meals alone in his room. He discovered that Montholon was behind this imperial decree and realized that he was not viewed favorably in the highest quarters for failing to be wise enough to keep his eyes and mouth shut. He could hardly have been called discreet. But one did not attempt to provoke a duel with a reluctant man like de Montholon by being discreet.

The duel was averted by joint effort of Bertrand and Napoleon. But a break in relations between Gourgaud and Montholon was now definite and the rift was wide and deep.

References

1. Gourgaud I:178
2. Ibid I:250-251
3. Marchand II:149; Gourgaud I:256; Bertrand I:172
4. Marchand II:150
5. Bertrand I:87, 321
6. Gourgaud I:163
7. Ibid I:194, 194, 163
8. Bertrand I:84
9. Cabanès 193-198
10. Marchand II:62
11. Las Cases I:336 footnote
12. Savant 272
13. Bertrand I:140
14. Ibid I:132
15. Kemble 2, pages 287, 290
16. Montesquiou 242
17. Gourgaud I:234

28

One Drama and Three Producers

WHEN REFERRING TO the classic authors on Napoleon's captivity, one is struck by the lively descriptions of the disorder and arbitrariness existing on St. Helena depicting it as a minor hell. From the island's experience emerged a stimulating literary epoch in which author vied colorfully with author to recount the misery and privations of life at Longwood:

There was sometimes a shortage of water at the court's lodge, so Napoleon could not get a proper bath; this though the island was often nearly drowned by the tropical rains.

Sometimes there was no food in the house and very little fuel. There was not even enough wine!

During the last quarter of 1816, we are told from the records, 3724 bottles of wine were delivered to Longwood. During the first quarter of 1817, 3336 new bottles arrived, during the second quarter of 1817, 3258 bottles of wine were received. By this time the number of inhabitants actually had declined.

Money was so short that Napoleon had been compelled to slash expenses and to sell his table silver as bullion to a Jamestown merchant.

Suffering terribly from all this inconsideration and pettiness, embarrassed by sentries in red uniform, the legendary Napoleon rode around until he finally collapsed from fatigue and exhaustion due to a fearful cancer of the stomach caused by the cruelty of his captors.

There were rats, horribly big rats on St. Helena; rats without respect even for the Emperor's glorious hat. What a terrible fate! But was it not typical of perfidious Albion.*

---

*The expression "Perfidious Albion" was Napoleon's own, used to describe England's policy. It was a cutting weapon in his "psychological warfare" technique.

To crown it all, the Frenchmen of Napoleon's household were not altogether of the highest class. Take Bertrand, for instance. A conceited, stupid, narrow-minded engineer. His wife was no better, more English than French, conventional and touchy. She could not even come in punctually for meals. She thought the imperial court was an inn!

Napoleon's doctor, O'Meara, was dishonorable and a spy of the governor. Las Cases, the Jesuit, had only joined Napoleon to pick his brains for a book he planned. When he had collected sufficient for eight volumes of a good book, he made off, to concern himself henceforth with finding a publisher who could make the work a world-wide success.

As for Gourgaud, he was the bane of Napoleon's life, what with his envy of Montholon and his claim to respect and honor, merely because on two occasions he had directly saved Napoleon's life and thus obliged the Emperor to retain him. But surely the worst of them all must be Dr. Antommarchi, the Corsican, Napoleon's last physician-in-ordinary. Ignorant, proud, ill-mannered, false, and altogether so insufferable that Napoleon could not bear to look at him.

So went the gossip of St. Helena into history. What was the source of it all? Do we have far to look in order to form a shrewd guess? A clue of identity comes readily.

According to these classic accounts, it was only the Montholons who behaved decently and with *savoir vivre* towards Napoleon. The Count and Countess were not upstarts but aristocrats who showed that they knew how to behave. Unfortunately Madame the Countess was also beset by the same dreadful climatic sickness as Napoleon. What a good thing it was that faithful Montholon could keep going and wait on his Emperor, when all others had failed him. But Mme. Montholon had to leave, and so Napoleon was forced to endure the last two years of his life without those special attentions that only a woman of quality can give to such a royal menage.

Montholon, however, most faithful of the faithful, always remained ready at the Emperor's side, right to the bitter end. It was only fair that, amongst the attendants, he should be the principal beneficiary of Napoleon's will. He had been *so* faithful! Later he was to stand at the side of the future Napoleon III at

Boulogne, when the latter wanted to attempt a counterpart of Napoleon I's triumphant march from Elba.

When the English statesman, Lord Rosebery, in his classic *Napoleon, the Last Phase,* published in 1900, had to decide who was the more reliable, Dr. Antommarchi or Montholon, he did not hesitate in favoring Montholon. That man was an aristocrat: "His memoirs were like their author, gentlemanlike."[1]

Today, now that we can know what underlay events at St. Helena, the classic accounts of Napoleon's captivity seem rather grimly amusing. It is not difficult today to see the common pitfall, carefully prepared by Montholon, into which, one by one, so many St. Helena authors fell. For that matter, some still write history under the influence of the Montholonian version. The pitfall was smooth and attractive, as was its maker. The bait: *Histoire de la captivité de Saint-Hélène, Leipzic 1846.* Its author: Count Charles Tristan de Montholon.

That the chroniclers of St. Helena could not discover the real plot in the drama depended probably not so much on their lack of clear-sightedness as on the fact that they had never been told of the standing rule in all political drama, that there should be security agents in the background, good men and dependable, with orders to kill if necessary. Internationally, that is how it has always been. We know it has remained so into modern times.

But another reason the chroniclers found it hard to follow the drama of St. Helena was that there were at least three different producers — namely, Napoleon, the Count d'Artois, represented by Marquis de Montchenu, Montholon's close friend, and the British Government, represented by Sir Hudson Lowe.

The British Government, who owned the stage and who fully realized Napoleon's worth as a counter in the political game, that historic political contest between France and England, wanted Napoleon happy and flourishing under their hospitality. It was urgent that Britain protect Napoleon from any consequences of the death sentence passed on him at the Congress of Vienna and from the danger of a mad or determined killer. The British military were further alert to prevent any other state — America, for instance — making off with him in some melodramatic coup, possibly to repay a sentimental debt to the army of Lafayette.

The British interest in keeping Napoleon safe and well is

strikingly illustrated by certain policital events after Napoleon's death. At the Congress of Vienna in 1822, negotiations led to England finding herself alone against the other countries of the Holy Alliance, who had decided that France should intervene with her army in Spain, one of England's fields of interest and influence. Had England then been able to say that she held Napoleon alive and securely, and at will could land him under protection on the shores of Europe, the French king, at least, could have been counted upon to reconsider.

In 1830 France took possession of Algeria, under protest from England. In covert terms Britain had threatened that the occupation of Algeria, which the French were planning, would have serious consequences, for which the French government would have to take full responsibility.[2] King Charles X, for years patron to Montholon, was not intimidated. Britain's preferences could be ignored. But supposing the English then had held Napoleon, alive and well, and ambitious to stage another — and better — Hundred Days! To him, as King Charles X, the Count d'Artois' long and eventually successful campaign against Napoleon was paying a highly satisfactory rate of return in terms of diplomatic reward.

Obviously the British government could not publicly proclaim that they had carried off Napoleon to use him as a weapon should the old traditional quarrel between England and France flare again. Officially, England had taken the burden magnanimously upon herself to protect the world from that notorious troublemaker and spiller of blood, Bonaparte.

Sir Hudson Lowe had received a memorandum from the British War Department with instructions as to the custody of Napoleon.[3] There are in it, still available for this generation of historians to read, several paragraphs detailing the steps to be taken to prevent Napoleon Bonaparte's escape; but there are also some that plainly show that "General Bonaparte's" personal safety was truly a concern of the British government. It is also quite clear that Napoleon's exile was to be made as endurable as possible consistently with keeping him as agreed.

Let us look at some of the rule book paragraphs.

Para. 11. "The General must be always attended by an officer appointed by the Admiral or Governor, as the case may be." If the general should be permitted to move beyond the boundaries where the sentries were placed, the officer was to be attended by one orderly at least. As it was quite impossible for Napoleon to escape from St. Helena, that paragraph can only be interpreted as intended to ensure protection against any possible attempt on his life by persons living on the island which Nature had constructed strangely like an ancient and impregnable rock-walled fortress. It would serve to pacify the Bourbons who lived in fear of Napoleon's escape and a return to France. There were many French officers as far away as America who continued to plot various plans to use for an attempted release of Napoleon from custody.

Para. 20 says that persons in the military corps at St. Helena who were foreigners or were otherwise deemed unreliable, were to be conveyed from the island.

The next paragraph says that if there were any civilian foreigners on the island who could be calculated to be potentially instrumental in "General Bonaparte's escape" — read, also, "death" — measures should be taken for their removal.

It is difficult to understand how any foreigner among the military or civil population could be instrumental in Napoleon's escape from a captivity which with reason could be considered completely escape-proof. On the other hand one fanatic might wish to free the world from Napoleon, that wild beast of effectual allied war propaganda.

Para. 25 says that medical persons should be directed to assist Napoleon's own doctor, should Napoleon be attacked by any serious indisposition.

Para. 17 in the instructions says that the Governor and the Admiral are "strictly instructed" to forward to His Majesty's Government any wish or representation that the General might "think proper to make to the British Government". The Governor and the Admiral were not in such cases at liberty to exercise any discretion.

For safety's sake Lord Bathurst, Secretary of State for War and the Colonies, wrote a few lines personally to Admiral Cockburn and later also to Hudson Lowe to emphasize the importance of treating Napoleon as well as possible. They were not to impose any restrictions other than those necessary for the task that the

Admiral and Governor "must ever keep in mind — the perfect security of General Bonaparte's person. Whatever, consistent with this great object, can be allowed in the shape of indulgence, His Royal Highness is confident will be willingly shown to the General."[4]

There is no reason to believe otherwise than that Sir Hudson came to St. Helena with the best intentions of following his government's instructions, that is to say, of watching over Napoleon's life and making his circumstances as a captive as pleasant as possible. He did not succeed; of that there can be no two opinions. But it was certainly not the governor's fault that he was a guardian rigidly conscientious about his great responsibility. Quite obviously he was not chosen for his qualities as a social host or as a riding companion for Napoleon. There was between the two men an insurmountable obstacle to good understanding. In fact there were two if we count Montchenu as well as Montholon. They manipulated events both methodically and efficiently to prevent any reasonable contact between the two chief characters in the drama of St. Helena.

In 1828 Basil Jackson, who will come later into this chronicle, was to meet Montholon in his magnificent Chateau de Frémigny in France. Some mutual reminiscences from the days of St. Helena were recalled. Montholon spoke well of Governor Lowe and maintained that his task had been an impossible one. "Not even an angel of God could have acted so that we were satisfied." By "we" he meant, of course, Napoleon and himself. Jackson then complained that Montholon had resorted to slander and lies in order to defame Sir Hudson. Montholon answered: "That was our policy: what would you wish?"[5]

It seems that the main reason for Napoleon's suspicion of the governor was that Napoleon was wholly convinced he intended to poison him. The Emperor must have received some secret and false intelligence, that produced such suspicion. It was not an atmosphere in which friendship was likely to flourish and flower.

For instance, after the governor had taken leave of him following his visit on April 30, 1816, Napoleon said: "What a repulsive and ominous expression that governor has! Better not finish your coffee if you have let such a man out of your sight for one instant." He continued, "My dear, they could have sent me some more dangerous man than a gaoler." He could have meant an assassin — a poisoner.[6]

Napoleon's instructions that he would take no medicine or drink from any British hands but only from his valet or from such as faithful Montholon can be appreciated as the product of a sense of alarm.

On August 18, 1816 a scene was enacted at Longwood illustrating well the great difficulty Sir Hudson had in keeping on reasonably good terms with his captive.

Sir Hudson, Sir Pulteney Malcolm, Sir Thomas Reade and the governor's adjutant, Major Gorrequer, had come to Longwood. Napoleon had just gone out for a short walk and was seen to turn off towards the stables. The governor asked if he could see the ex-Emperor.

"He is not at home," was the reply.

"Really? But we have just seen him."

At that moment they saw Napolon going toward the main building. The governor and the admiral went forward to meet him, but he walked on. They caught up with him, one on each side. No one said a word.

They walked around the house, and then the governor announced that he had reason to complain about Bertrand's discourteous reception of him several days earlier.

Napoleon did not answer. They circled the house again. Then Napoleon suddenly started:

"*Eh bien*, the Grand Marshal does not want to have anything to do with you; that's all there is to it.

"He has been *Grand Officier de la Couronne*, he has been in command of armies. He fought at the head of his army corps when you were still only a colonel on the general staff.

"You address him and speak to him — not as a corporal in a troop of regular soldiers but as a corporal among soldiers once under your command, deserters and traitors every one of them.

"The Grand Marshal has been insulted and doesn't want anything more to do with you. There is no one here with me who would not prefer four days on bread and water to a conversation with you."

"Indeed, really," put in Sir Hudson. (He knew at least one of

Napoleon's following who had nothing against a conversation with the governor.)

"We used to be able to buy openly in the shops. You have stopped that."

"But that was Admiral Cockburn," put in Admiral Malcolm.

"No, Admiral. That's what you've been told by Monsieur Lowe. It is not so, you shouldn't believe him. Doubtless Monsieur Lowe is not so stupid as to try and look as though he were never wrong, but he is no more than a clerk, who has done nothing but scribble and balance accounts the whole of his life.

"Monsieur Lowe tells me that I am not to talk politics to people who are introduced to me.

"*Parbleu, Monsieur Lowe,* that is too much. You don't know me. My body may be in the hands of wicked persons, but my spirit is independent. I am as proud here as though I were at the head of 400,000 men or distributing royal crowns from my throne.

"You talk about reducing expenses for us. I find such pettiness painful and undignified."

Napoleon had much more for which to accuse Sir Hudson. The governor had not forwarded some books because they were addressed to "The Emperor Napoleon".

"And who gave you the right to question this title?" cried Napoleon.

The admiral tried to explain that the British government had expressly forbidden both the governor and himself to address Napoleon as Emperor. The governor had no choice.

Sir Hudson listened in silence to the greater part of Napoleon's complaints. At last he ventured to say:

"But, Monsieur, you don't know me."

"*Eh, parbleu,* where should I have met you? I haven't seen you on any battlefield. You were only fit to hire assassins."

Calmly and without losing his self-control, Sir Hudson assured him that he had never himself asked for the appointment he now held, but rather wished to be relieved of it.

"You are right in asking to be sent home. That would be a good thing for both of us.[7]

"You say you have your instructions. But the executioner also has his. He just carries them out. You have your instructions, act on them and leave me in peace. If you don't want to provide us with food, then don't. As long as we are near the 53rd regiment, they will see to it that we do not starve."

"That's nothing to do with me," replied the governor.

"Without a doubt the executioner is laughing at his victim's screams," shouted the ex-Emperor.

Now the governor had to laugh. He left. When he met Captain Poppleton, he said: "My goodness, Napoleon really is in a bad temper."[8]

The admiral took his leave of Napoleon — very respectfully, however.

Afterwards Napoleon had told Las Cases that the governor had been no more discourteous than to take his leave abruptly. Napoleon also admitted that he had treated the governor badly during their encounter.

If Napoleon's boorish behavior on this occasion was not due to mental insufficiency, quite natural considering the intoxication by arsenic to which he was being subjected and its consequent effect on his mind, then it arose from false intelligence. Perhaps it was due to both.

References

1. Rosebery 22
2. Dareste IX:558
3. Forsyth I:15-19
4. Ibid I:15
5. Rose II:552
6. Las Cases I:553
7. Las Cases II:206, 207; Gourgaud I:174; Bertrand I:106
8. Bertrand I:107
9. Forsyth III:146, 147

29

Another Depressing New Year

THERE HAD BEEN a military ball on St. Helena on New Year's Eve, and the Bertrands, the Montholons and Gourgaud had attended. They did not come home until six in the morning of New Year's Day, 1818.

At three in the afternoon Napoleon summoned Gourgaud. He wanted to hear what it had been like at the ball. He lay only half-dressed on his couch, as he did so often nowadays. He was in a bad mood.

"Your *domestique* Fritz is a spy — Poppleton says so."

"I suspect, Sire, that Montholon says so. He wants to get into Fritz's room."

"You insult me, I believe you are angry," Napoleon cried.

This time Gourgaud did not dare contradict, but kept his silence. Napoleon grumbled on a bit and rang for a valet to help him get dressed. There was to be a New Year's Day party.[18]

The day before, Napoleon had hinted to Gourgaud that Mme. Bertrand was expecting magnificent New Year gifts. Someone had of course whispered this in his ear. We can be quite sure that this someone was neither Bertrand nor his wife. It was the special talent of de Montholon to initiate such rumors.

When at last the expectant company had gathered in the drawing-room of Longwood — there were only the Bertrands, Count de Montholon, Gourgaud, and the children — the surprise was sprung. *"Grande surprise"*, wrote Gourgaud. The only New Year gifts distributed were small baskets with sweets for Mme. Bertrand and the children. The Countess de Montholon was not there. She thought she might momentarily go into labor.

At eight o'clock the company sat down at table. Napoleon was melancholy. He made an attempt to lighten the gloom by delivering a monologue on the spirit of rebellion in France at the moment and the impossibility that his rivals, the Bourbons, could remain.

After supper the party went into the drawing-room. There was no air of festivity and at half past nine Napoleon retired. A depressing celebration of the arrival of the year 1818.

It was indeed a very sad year that lay behind Napoleon this New Year's Day. It had been another year when none of his hopes had been realized. His illness had made it increasingly hard to sustain the legend of Napoleon the Great. That was, at least, how things were on St. Helena. What was happening to the legend of Napoleon in Europe was something no one had told him. Had he known that already in 1817 the reviving legend of the Emperor's greatness had begun to be a dreadful political explosive menacing reactionary Europe, he might in spite of everything have felt a strong revival of customary confidence on this New Year's Day.

Napoleon, like so many other great men, took it for granted that it was his own brilliant series of actions as conqueror and civil administrator that had earned him his towering reputation. But behind the incipiently flourishing new Napoleonic cult in Europe was certainly no newly-awakened and positive admiration for Napoleon's conquests or for his person. Rather the era of Napoleon held a nostalgic appeal chiefly through the dissatisfaction of the literate public with the policies of the Holy Alliance.

Napoleon was becoming a figurehead for progressive political forces because he had been superseded by less popular rulers, the Bourbons and the other hereditary and despotic monarchs of Europe. He could be turned once more into a fabled figure immensely gifted to lead. Was he not the brilliant Bonaparte, the one who, as a 27-year-old general, had brought the mighty Emperor of Germany to his knees? Might not the slender Bonaparte on the bridge at Arcole become the St. George of the approaching decade of the 1820s, who would liberate the cartoonists' distressed maiden Marianne from the Bourbon dragon?

Napoleon's health had varied greatly during 1817. On some

days he would be in a comparatively good temper and filled with a desire to work. He would dictate diligently. Then suddenly he would suffer a recurrence of illness. For those around him such a relapse might often mean only that Napoleon was depressed.

During March, April and half of May the Emperor was in relatively good health of body and mind. During July and August, too, he enjoyed recovery from an illness in the latter part of May. But with the end of September a long, serious illness began. It would continue with little surcease from distress as long as his physician, O'Meara, remained on St. Helena, which is to say, until the end of July, 1818, when the dramatic episode would come to its close.

It was on September 26, 1817 that, with unbroken illness beginning, Napoleon complained to his doctor of a great tenderness in his legs. They were badly swollen. Depressions made in the fluid-filled flesh around his ankles remained. He complained of nausea.

While O'Meara was with him, Napoleon's breakfast was brought in. It consisted of two radishes, a small piece of buttered toast and a cup of *café au lait*.

Two days later the doctor was again called in. The patient's ankles were grossly swollen, his appetite bad. He had eaten nothing for twenty-four hours.

O'Meara was so concerned about the condition of Napoleon's legs that he asked permission to consult the chief physician of the island colony, Dr. Baxter.

Napoleon thought that would be useless. Baxter could hardly prescribe anything else but that medicine which was denied to Napoleon, exercise on horseback. As long as the governor insisted that Napoleon should be accompanied by an escorting officer when out riding, it was unthinkable to Napoleon that he might start to move about once more.[1]

On October 1 Napoleon had a new complaint, a dull pain in the right hypochondriac region, that is to say, in the region below the false ribs — more specifically, in the region of the liver.

Such *douleurs hypochondriaques* or hypochondriac pain is often referred to in the history of Napoleon's illness. Authors lacking in medical knowledge finally took it for granted that Napoleon's pain was *hypochondriac,* that is to say, the product of his imagination. It was a complete misconception further complicating the mystery of what, medically, afflicted the Emperor.

On October 1 Napoleon had also noticed a strange sensation of cold and numbness in his right shoulder. His old hacking cough troubled him. His gums had begun to swell and he had become unable to sleep.

On the third of October the pain in the hypochondrium was more pronounced and O'Meara noticed a distinct swelling of the region. Napoleon thought it had been there for the last two months. He had assumed that it was only fat, but now when it was painful to the touch, he supposed his liver was inflamed.

Doctor O'Meara again asked Napoleon for permission to consult Dr. Baxter — without result.[2]

Of course O'Meara suggested medicines, principally the widely-used calomel, but Napoleon would not hear of drugs. He took long, warm baths, which helped — for a little while.

The doctor suggested an anti-scorbutic diet; that was a language Napoleon, inherently a naturopath could understand, and he began to drink lemon and orange juice freely. But his "scurvy" did not improve; rather the opposite.

Today we might conclude that the doctor at that point should have realized something was wrong with his diagnosis of scurvy. But in those times doctors regarded scurvy as a much more complex illness than is done today. It was known, for instance, that it was an illness common to the sea and coastlands; so it actually was thought to be caused by rain and wind.[3]

O'Meara was quite certain the climate of sea-girt St. Helena was responsible for Napoleon's illness. And, to the detriment of his future, he was indiscreet enough to cross deeply-rooted British policy on St. Helena as a place to confine Napoleon, and blame the climate.

On October 11 the pain in Napoleon's side and shoulder had become worse and heart palpitations had set in.

When the doctor called the following day, he found Napoleon sitting with his legs in a container of hot water. The Emperor seemed to find it very hard to keep his legs warm.

When appointed by Napoleon, Dr. O'Meara had had to promise to tell no one, least of all the English, anything concerning Napoleon's health. However, there are some reports from O'Meara to the senior doctor, Baxter, among Governor Lowe's papers. But since Baxter was bound by the medical vow of silence, O'Meara would naturally have considered himself justified in sharing with the chief physician on the island information about the condition of so important a patient.

Because of these reports, some authors have called O'Meara traitorous. He would surely have been more of a traitor to Napoleon had he not sought help, when he himself had failed to diagnose and successfully treat his patient's illness. It is unlikely that any doctor of that time could have diagnosed chronic or sub-acute arsenical intoxication; and certainly very few had ever seen the kind of acute intoxication that killed outright.

Madame de Brinvilliers undoubtedly would have known the symptoms of chronic and sub-acute arsenical intoxication. So did some at the court of King Louis XIV. But their knowledge and that of the lovely marquise had not been acquired at medical faculties. Her expert was an apothecary-chemist named Glaser; and her lover, Sainte-Croix, had had lessons while in the Bastille from a well-known Italian poison-mixer called Exili. His real name was Eggidi and he was an Italian aristocrat.[6] Many traditions from the court of Louis XIV certainly were still current in that of Louis XVIII.

Respecting O'Meara's inability to diagnose Napoleon's illness correctly, for which he frequently has been blamed, I may refer to a conversation I once had with the head of the Paris Police's forensic laboratory, Professor Henri Griffon. Discussing the symptoms of Napoleon's illness on St. Helena, we had no difficulty in agreeing that Napoleon's main illness was arsenical intoxication. This seemed to us both to be beyond further need for debate.

I then asked Professor Griffon, who had had especially wide experience of cases of poisoning with arsenic, if he could explain why so many doctors, including those of modern times, had published works on Napoleon's illness and death in which they had consistently overlooked arsenical intoxication.

Professor Griffon's reply was that he had never found in any case of murder by arsenic a doctor who had diagnosed correctly and in time. Therefore it must be conceded that none of Napoleon's doctors fairly could be blamed for not having understood his illness. They simply were not trained to read the symptoms of poisoning. This was unfortunate. Had the doctors of Napoleon's St. Helena had such training, one or two deaths from "peritonitis" and "cancer" might have been exposed, one or two abortions prevented and many cases of "dysentery", "gout", "scurvy" and "consumption" might have been treated correctly by removing the cause, i.e., the poison-mixer.

We may recall that during the last six months of 1816 Napoleon had been unable to ride. His walks had become fewer and shorter. Finally in 1817 he became too ill to go out in his carriage. Now, in 1818, it was necessary to find some worthy explanation for the fact that he was so seldom to be seen outside his apartments. A scapegoat must be found. Conspicuously available, the luckless Hudson Lowe was blamed because Napoleon could neither walk nor drive, still less ride. It was Sir Hudson's cruel insistence that Napoleon was not to go riding outside the safe area of Longwood without an escorting officer that was really the reason Napoleon now was slowly but surely dying. Napoleon stuck to his accusation and later confirmed it in his famous Will. But as to the Will, as we shall see, it is always necessary to remember who helped Napoleon prepare it.

Many influential Englishmen on their way from England to India or the Cape and vice versa used to stretch their legs on St. Helena, while their ships took on water and provisions. Napoleon would have benefited by meeting and impressing them and winning their sympathies. He had possessed great charm when fit in body and soul.

But now he was not well. He was too ill, in fact, to receive travelling visitors, much less make the effort to impress them.

Lord Amherst had arrived on April 13 for a lengthy stay.[4] Admiral Malcolm thought Napoleon should receive so important a peer, Great Britain's ambassador to Naples, as he returned from a mission in China. Napoleon was very doubtful.

On June 28, just before leaving, the Ambassador paid the necessary visit to the Grand Marshal to request an audience.

It was settled that Napoleon should receive Lord Amherst on the first of July.[5] On June 26 Napoleon had not felt well, but on the 27th he had dined with Bertrand and Gourgaud.

On July 29 he sat at table with Montholon and passed a bottle of wine to Gourgaud. The latter found the wine had a strange flavor and said so to Napoleon.

"That rogue Reade could poison me; he has the key to the wine cellar!" shouted Napoleon.

"Your Majesty would be wise not to drink the wine alone," ventured Gourgaud.

"Why?"

"No one would dare to poison as many as we are. There would be too much talk; the poisoners would be punished."

"Nonsense, the fact is I would then really be dead."

It was Gourgaud's fate that none of all the wise and cautionary things that he said to Napoleon on St. Helena was accepted by the Emperor. Gourgaud often warned Napoleon that Montholon was a shady and dangerous character. The result was that Napoleon became suspicious — of Gourgaud.

Moreover, Gourgaud was the only one at Longwood who dared to say that Napoleon might be poisoned, but all his warnings went unheeded as stupid Gourgaud nonsense. Napoleon was obviously inclined only to call something a poison when it killed immediately. Because he had not died from drinking wine he had no fear that treated wine ultimately could be his undoing.

Count Charles Tristan de Montholon, chief of the Longwood household, kept the key to the wine cellar. It is highly unlikely that Sir Thomas Reade possessed a duplicate key.

Whatever might have been the matter with the wine that Gourgaud regarded with suspicion, he was in any case very sick during the night. So was Napoleon. Consequently Lord Amherst's visit had to be put off. Bertrand was sent to Plantation House to announce that Napoleon did not feel well that day, but that he would receive his caller next day, providing he was better.[7]

On July 1 at 2:30 p.m. Napoleon summoned Gourgaud; Lord Amherst was expected at 3 p.m. At that moment Montholon turned up — dressed in civilian clothes. He had obviously not expected Amherst to come. Napoleon rebuked him for not being in full-dress.

"Parbleu, what does this mean, Noverraz! Why haven't you fastened gold buckles on your shoes?" cried His Majesty.[8]

Gourgaud found Napoleon irritable and out of sorts. Was it because a British ambassador was coming? To receive an ambassador should have presented no problem to a man who had been accustomed to the routines of European royal duties.

When an individual has become unbalanced, excitable, nervous, depressed or angry without any apparent psychical reason, it should be assumed his brain cells have been affected by some poison, such as alcohol, narcotics, arsenic or by self-intoxication through faulty functioning of the kidneys or disturbance of the internal organs of secretion.

For one who feared Napoleon might come to some unwelcome sort of an understanding with Lord Amherst, it would be very fortunate that the Napoleon mood should be thoroughly disgruntled.

About the wine. Special wines not usually enjoyed by the rest of his suite were put aside for Napoleon. Every now and then, however, possibly impulsively, he would present a bottle to someone he wished to honor; to Mme. Bertrand, Gourgaud, Las Cases. Whether or not it was due to the wine, it so happened that those guests of his often fell ill, like Bertrand. Poisoning a Frenchman is easiest done with wine. For who can be successful in shaking a Frenchman's high regard for the virtue of wine?

Lord Amherst arrived with a considerable retinue. There was a Captain Maxwell, Amherst's secretary Hayne, a diplomatic secretary Ellis, Reverend Griffith, a natural scientist named Able, a Lieutenant Cook, one of the ambassador's sons and two doctors.

The whole company assembled in the billiard-room and Lord Amherst was conducted ceremoniously by the Grand Marshal into the drawing-room, where the Emperor — General Bonaparte to the British — was waiting.

Napoleon's officers had been instructed, when conversing with members of Amherst's party, to belittle the governor and protest against enforced restrictions on Napoleon.

Gourgaud played his part by asking the guests what it was really like in China. Bertrand held forth on the campaign in Egypt. We do not know what Montholon said to Lord Amherst's secretary.

Napoleon had decided that for his part, he would not air his grievances in front of his guest. The conversation lasted an hour and a half, but toward the end it began to get out of hand. The governor had actually tried to prevent Napoleon from acquiring a bust of the King of Rome.

Amherst apparently asked if Napoleon had actual evidence of such obstruction, for his reply is recorded: "I have no physical proof, but I have a moral certainty about it."

Lord Amherst must also have asked Napoleon why he did not wish to see the governor, for Napoleon answered:

"I don't want to see the governor because I don't want to submit to the restrictions he has forced upon me. Neither England's parliament nor her king is sufficiently powerful to force me to live together with my gaoler. As I am in their hands, they may do with me what they will, but they may not defame my character.

"I don't want to go out as I don't want to submit to the restrictions and because sentries have been posted as an insult to me and my officers."[9]

When his lordship and suite had returned to Jamestown for dinner with the admiral, followed by a visit to the theatre, Napoleon was still highly excited. He tried to play chess with Gourgaud but could not sit still.

"Oh, I can tell you that at this moment the governor is getting what he deserves. At first I hadn't meant to mention his name to his lordship, but in the end I couldn't help it. The ambassador said that he had wanted to meet me for 25 years. He was in Turin until the Armistice of Cherasco in 1796. He had a love affair there. I forced him to leave."

What a misfortune! In trying to get rid of those sentries who had prevented him from meeting his nymph, Napoleon was fated to have sought help from the wrong man.

Napoleon's hope that his supporters would unite and work together to glorify his deeds, in their speech and written words, had also gone awry during the past year.

Gourgaud was the problem. In spite of fatherly advice and imperial commands to keep on good terms with Montholon, Gourgaud was finding it hard not to speak ill of both the Count and Countess. He had become deeply envious of Montholon and from mail lately received had cause to worry about his mother's welfare. He was much changed as to appearance and vigor after his serious illness and would never completely recover. He kept suffering periodic relapses.

Gourgaud certainly had cause for dissatisfaction. After all he was a Napoleonic general and Montholon only a *Maréchal de camp* of the Restoration, but in spite of this, perhaps due to his blue blood, the latter had of late been better placed at table than Gourgaud. Montholon was paid twice as much, too. Gourgaud pointed out the unfairness to Napoleon, who denied it, however.

"But everyone here knows that he is paid twice as much as I am," maintained Gourgaud.

"*Eh bien, oui,* I give his wife the same as I give him," explained Napoleon.

That set off a serious quarrel, which ended by Napoleon declaring he preferred Montholon to Gourgaud. Gourgaud was plainly quite crushed, whereupon Napoleon softened and invited Gourgaud to dine with him at lunch.[10]

Those who have criticized Gourgaud in their accounts of St. Helena and have described him as an ill-mannered, quarrelsome whipper-snapper, have failed to appreciate the fact that in the presence of an undisclosed security agent, directing developments along a chosen line, all personal relationships would be seen as subject to abnormal pressures and influences.

The authors of Napoleonic history, unaware of the poison plot, of course made no allowance for this in writing of events at St. Helena. Gourgaud, too, was unaware; otherwise he would never have allowed himself to become entangled in hopeless situations or have so long hoped that his honor, greater loyalty and good intentions must in the end prevail and be appreciated.

The Marquis de Montchenu set a trap for him. He was shrewd enough, however, not to fall into it.

At Montholon's suggestion Gourgaud met Montchenu on September 13. Montchenu had hitherto been very haughty toward Gourgaud. When Gourgaud informed Napoleon of this, the latter had offered him cold comfort by telling him that Montchenu considered Gourgaud and those like him as lower class, "*roturiers*" — plebeians.

This time, however, Montchenu was kindness itself. The

marquis had thought it a pity that Gourgaud should have to live like a hermit in chastity and virtue. He just wanted to tell him that he had heard from a reliable source that General Bingham's wife was very *"complaisante"*.[11]

But the hook was perhaps a little too obvious. Gourgaud did not take the bait. Life was complex enough for the young general. He had no intention of complicating it further.

Napoleon, too, had realized that Gourgaud found it difficult to adjust to the boredom of inaction at Longwood and had suggested that he take a mistress; for instance, the mulatto girl who worked at the Bertrands'. Gourgaud was able to tell Napoleon that he had actually thought of the same thing, but that the alert Mme. Bertrand always hid the girl when she saw Gourgaud approaching.[12]

Napoleon's own love life did not run as smoothly as before.

In the middle of the summer of 1817 Mme. Montholon's figure began to thicken once more. She had often to leave the dining-room, and was even ill at the imperial table.

Meanwhile, however, Esther had given birth to a son. Bertrand had seen Esther and the little boy and had been astonished to note that he had blue eyes. Both parents, Esther and the given father, Marchand, had brown eyes. This promoted idle speculation with which to while away time.[13]

On September 12, a Friday, Esther returned to Longwood.[14] She must have been appreciated there, although she was only a chambermaid to Mme. Montholon, who was lodged in one wing of the building. On October 4, a Saturday, Marchand showed Napoleon a portrait of the King of Rome which Marchand had made by copying from the many pictures of the King that were to be seen at Longwood. This contrived portrait was painted on the false bottom of a small box. In this way the portrait was protected from profane eyes. The box with the concealed portrait was to be a gift from Napoleon to his Esther.[15]

Four days after Esther's return, Montholon complained to Gourgaud that for some time Napoleon had not bothered to see Countess Montholon.[16] This was good news for Gourgaud, but of course it was not true. Bertrand notes on September 14, "He (Napoleon) visited Mme Montholon."[17]

Esther could not replace Albine Hélène.

While Montholon seemed anxious to win Gourgaud's friendship, he purposefully worked at getting rid of Gourgaud. That man not only told Napoleon the truth but even kept a diary. Moreover, he talked loosely about the risk to Napoleon's life through poisoning.

On October 4, 1817, Charles Tristan called on Gourgaud for a confidential discussion on how the land lay. It is interesting to hear something of what Montholon said on that occasion.

"His Majesty will never leave this place. He is much too delicate . . . I don't know how his illness will end, but in the meanwhile it is making life at Longwood very tedious. There will soon have to be a medical consultation before he can eat, before he can shave, etc. I am tired of writing and re-writing his Observations, which will anyway rot away, buried in a corner of the garden together with his other manuscripts."[15] Montholon, so often untruthful when he spoke of what was happening and what had happened, could be grimly right when he spoke of the future.

In spite of everything, Napoleon struggled to retain dignity. During 1817 he was often not well enough to eat in company with his following, but when he did no carelessness was permitted.

The servants who waited at table all had their particular duties and a livery to correspond. The major-domo set the table with china and silver brought from the Tuileries.

During the meal both the valets, Saint-Denis and Noverraz, stood one on each side behind Napoleon's chair. These two dignitaries served only the Emperor. His guests were waited on by the lackeys.

When it was time for dessert, it was the chef himself who came and served it.

During his illness Napoleon was too weak to do other than eat alone in his room. Then the routine was much simplified, but not wholly at the expense of finesse. Under the personal surveillance and command of the major-domo, his meals were brought to his door. There they were received by the lackey on duty and served by the first valet Marchand, assisted by the lackey.

Imperial grandeur had to be maintained — even when breakfast consisted only of two radishes, a slice of toast and a cup of coffee.

References

1. O'Meara II:236-37
2. Ibid II:255 et seq.
3. Richter-Collin V:535 et seq.
4. Bertrand:I:216
5. Ibid I:238, 240
6. Funch-Brentano 8
7. Gourgaud II:165-6
8. Ibid II:168-9
9. Bertrand I:240
10. Gourgaud II:40-42
11. Gourgaud II:250
12. Gourgaud II:162
13. Gourgaud II:184
14. Gourgaud II:250
15. Gourgaud II:272
16. Gourgaud II:251
17. Bertrand I:272
18. Gourgaud II:326

30

Only Two Originals Remain

"THIS NEW YEAR'S DAY has been very dreary," wrote Bertrand in his diary for the first of January, 1819.

Napoleon had got up that morning in a melancholy mood. He went straight to his bath and remained there for the next few hours. He must have been either in pain or suffering that old icy chill in his legs, a complaint which had been better for several months past.

His officers came to wish him a Happy New Year. They were shown into the bathroom. There was room, for now there were only two — Bertrand and Montholon.

Gourgaud had left Longwood and so had Doctor O'Meara. The major domo, Cipriani, no longer came to the bathroom door with breakfast. He had been in his grave since February of 1818.

William Balcombe, Napoleon's only lay friend on St. Helena, could not come to pay his respects, either. He, too, had left the island.

Although the Emperor was not well, he refrained from cancelling the New Year party, which was timed for 3 o'clock.

The Bertrands and the Montholons with seven children, four belonging to the Bertrands and three named Montholon, were there. Before sitting down to table, New Year gifts were distributed. For each of the children there was a golden coin, a double napoleon. After they had eaten, the youngsters were each given a small box of sweets produced by the chef. The boxes as well, each decorated with the Emperor's and Empress's monograms, had been made by Pierron.

Napoleon's spirits rose when he saw the children's eager appetites. He was especially amused by little Arthur Bertrand.

He entertained his guests in the drawing-room for a time following the meal, then retired to his bedroom at 5:30 p.m. He was too ill and depressed to celebrate entering on a new year.

It is easy to understand why Napoleon felt particularly pessimistic on that New Year's Day. From rising hopes he had once again been cast down to renewed pain and inevitable anguish of soul.

Towards the end of 1818 it had actually appeared that Napoleon would quite regain his former health.[1] A few days before the end of the year he suddenly had a relapse into that illness that so often had plagued him. The St. Helena chroniclers of his captivity early called it climatic sickness. Historians naturally made use of the term in referring to his malady.

Certainly, it was a climatic sickness; not a special Helenic disease, but a sort that had every now and then raged at court — particularly in the climate of the courts of the Medicis and the French Bourbons. It had claimed many lives at the court of Louis XIV and even the court of Louis XV had felt its ravages. In the case of the King it is just possible that it was given the name of "smallpox".

At Napoleon's brilliant imperial court in Paris it was, as far as is known, only the monarch who, particularly at decisive moments, was attacked by this so-called climatic sickness. It came regardless of where the court happened to be — in Russia, Saxony, Belgium or Paris.

When Napoleon had fallen ill again at the end of 1818, there was no doctor accredited to his court. O'Meara, his physician in-ordinary, had been arrested in July of that year and removed from the island.

The governor had immediately appointed another doctor at Longwood, a Dr. Verling, so that Napoleon need not find himself without medical assistance should he be ill. Dr. James Verling has been described as a cultured and courteous person, who was supposed to be clever in the arts of healing. He spoke both French and Italian and at the age of twenty-three had submitted as thesis for his doctor's degree a treatise on jaundice.[2]

As O'Meara had found Napoleon's liver affected, and had often seen that his skin and the whites of his eyes were yellow, the governor's choice of doctor indicated a consideration for Napoleon's health.

But Napoleon stubbornly refused to accept Dr. Verling. He was an army doctor and under the governor's command. An Englishman as well. He could have had army orders to poison his patient. It was necessary to keep a sharp watch for poisoners.

It was not difficult for Marchand to make out what this time had caused Napoleon's relapse. He had sat with his feet in a flannel bag, trying to warm them. After that he had put on his silk stockings, his thin cashmere trousers and the shoes with the thin soles and gleaming gold buckles. Not only that, but he had gone out in the chill of the evening. Naturally he caught cold.

By now Napoleon ought to have known that the chill of the evening was dangerous. The Empress Josephine had gone out in it with Tsar Alexander at the end of May, 1814. She had caught cold and died. Whether it was the chill of the evening in her case or the danger of seeking Tsar Alexander's sympathy and help that brought her to the grave can be overlooked in this connection. It can be safely presumed that the Count d' Artois' *police occulte* were in any case extremely interested in the understanding that had so obviously developed between Tsar Alexander and Napoleon's former wife and still trustworthy friend, Josephine.

Of course there were courtiers of the old reliable Bourbon variety close to Josephine. For instance, our friend Montholon. On December 21, 1809, he had been appointed chamberlain to the Empress Josephine, only a few days before her divorce from Napoleon. As a modern detective in films might say, "very interesting!" There were other Bourbonists at Josephine's compact court.

Napoleon had at last concluded that Gourgaud was of no further use in his retinue. Gourgaud had become quite impossible to deal with. It was of course the murderous climate of St. Helena that had robbed him of his sanity. The man could finally see no good in the Montholons, whatsoever. He had even become obsessed with the idea that Montholon was a traitor and that he had become a serious threat to the court. If Gourgaud continued to challenge Montholon to duels, the Count, as an aristocratic officer and a gentleman, would finally have to accept for the sake of his honor. So weak and dandified a person as Montholon ought not to duel with the aggressive Gourgaud — this even though Gourgaud could not have been in his normal form, due to the many relapses of his unshakable sickness.

On December 18, 1817, Gourgaud had been summoned to Napoleon. It was some time since Napoleon had paid any attention to him at all. But now he had a special reason.

"If you fight Montholon, you will not intimidate him," began Napoleon. "You insult Montholon, and as recently as yesterday you said that Mme. Montholon was ugly. You speak of those who are faithful to me behind their backs. You are a bad character, like Mr. Lowe. Even Bertrand tells me that he can't get on with you. If you find it dull, why don't you go hunting with Archambault and Noverraz? Why don't you make friends with Marchand or Cipriani? But you despise those who are friendly towards me."

Montholon was now exerting a most extraordinary influence over the once so self-sufficient Emperor. Gourgaud, who had often risked his life in Napoleon's service, little by little had been pushed aside. From his place of honor at Napoleon's table, he had been sent down to the farthest place. Finally he was banished altogether, ordered to take his meals alone. And now he had been told to seek his companions among the servants in the house. In the Gourgaud-Montholon contest for Napoleon's favor, the Montholons had won.

But once more, as so often in the past, Napoleon's anger was quick to subside. Only a short while after quarrelling fiercely with Gourgaud, he tried to console the faithful friend whose loyalty and vigor at arms he could not easily forget.

Later that evening Napoleon was directly obliging to Gourgaud, calling him *Monsieur le Baron, mon premier officier d'ordonnances.*[3]

On the twentieth of January, 1818, Napoleon again had tried to make peace between the rivals.

"They are all attention to me; they would go hungry for my sake." Then he added, somewhat strangely: "After all, I like only people I have some use for — and for as long as I have it."[4] Gourgaud would feel this was a warning of possible discharge.

Napoleon was not wholly exceptional in considering a friendship on such terms. Seldom, however, does anyone so honestly admit it. The Emperor concluded: "I care nothing for what people think."

"But, Sire, the Montholons are traitors to you," Gourgaud was bold to say.

"If they betray me, they will be acting as so many others have. You begrudge them because they like me. If you liked me, you would wait upon them . . . You and the governor are making things difficult for me. What right have you to complain that I see only Montholon, or because I take my meals with him?"[4]

Montholon had never admitted, at least not to any mere onlooker, the tricks by which he reduced Gourgaud's worth in Napoleon's view. However, on one occasion Napoleon made a significant remark. He accused Gourgaud of having followed him not through devotion but through fear of being hanged if he were to stay in France under the restored Bourbons. Gourgaud had links with the Duke of Berry — the second son of the Count d'Artois — and had betrayed him by going over to Napoleon. To Gourgaud it was a sensitive subject.

In other words, Gourgaud had done just about what Montholon might equally be seen to have done, on the face of things. *Quod licet Iovi, non licet Bovi* — that which the Count may do, the Baron may not.

It could only have been Montholon who, certain of being believed, had given this false information from the Bourbon royal court. No one else at Longwood had been there.

In vain Gourgaud tried to convince Napoleon he had never had close relations with the Duke of Berry.[5] Napoleon was not to be convinced.

On January 21, Gourgaud met Mme. Bertrand, and she told him Napoleon now and then visited the Montholons in secret. She confirmed what Gourgaud had suspected, that they received large sums of money from Napoleon — more than 50,000 golden francs a year.[6]

The Montholons certainly did receive considerable sums while Napoleon lived, quite apart from the moneys inherited under his Will. We know that on June 15, 1819, Albine de Montholon was favored by the Emperor with an annuity of 20,000 francs a year, to be paid from the funds administered by Prince Eugene for his stepfather.

On June 28 Montholon received an additional 24,000 francs. This money Napoleon's mother was to pay from her large fortune, an estate which had devolved through gifts from her son. At the same time Montholon received a cash sum of 144,000 francs in the form of a cheque, to be honored by Napoleon's brother, Joseph. These sums were directed to the Montholons, in addition to those that the Countess had received in return for her companionship with the Emperor.[7]

Napoleon's generosity to the Montholons seems unduly great, even considering *les petits soins*, those little attentions. But if we consider the donations as contributions towards the education of the Montholons' daughters, then Napoleon's actions can be comprehended and considered appropriate enough. There is every evidence that at this point Napoleon was deeply involved with and partial to the Count and Countess. For the ailing and rejected Gourgaud, this was bitter medicine which was certainly no remedy for his injured feelings.

On the second of February, 1818, Gourgaud had had enough, and he made his formal application to leave:

"I have always done my duty. I do not please Your Majesty. I do not want to be a burden to anyone. I ask to be allowed to leave."

Napoleon was angry and pointed out again that he had the right to treat the Montholons as he wished, and this without criticism from the general. The deeply resentful Gourgaud blurted out that he had reason to believe Napoleon had children in common with the Montholon couple, which did not exactly pacify Napoleon. And yet the angry Emperor was reluctant to declare a full and final break with so tried and proven a friend.

"If I should sleep with her," he asked, "what harm could that do?"[8]

Napoleon repeated that he wanted Gourgaud to make a greater effort to be friendly with the Montholons. Gourgaud replied that Montholon and his wife had calumniated him too much for friendship to be possible, and that he would address himself directly to Montholon for satisfaction.

"If you threaten Montholon, you are a bandit and a murderer!" shouted Napoleon. "I forbid you to challenge Montholon. I shall fight in his place. I will condemn you."

Gourgaud was unyielding. He knew what was required of his honor. Napoleon tried other tactics. "You realize that if you duel you will be killed." It was a strange change of front in the discussion. There was no question as to who ran the greater risk in the duel Gourgaud sought.

When he saw that nothing could be done, Napoleon apologized to Gourgaud. "I pray you, forget what I have said," were his humble words.[8] Gourgaud promised to spare Montholon, provided he was given a written order from Napoleon not to fight the count. Only so could his honor be saved in such insulting circumstances.

Napoleon now realized nothing could be gained in preventing Gourgaud from leaving St. Helena. He insisted only that the latter should give as the reason for his departure not the conduct of the Montholons but his own ill-health.

In January, 1818, Napoleon had asked Bertrand what he thought of Gourgaud. Bertrand admitted that Gourgaud was often wrong, but pointed out that his mind was affected (Sa tête n'est pas à lui"). But, he added, "We don't know the extent of influence the mercury has had on him."[9]

Bertrand was a clever fellow. He suspected that Gourgaud had been poisoned — poisoned by his doctor. Such things could happen. Bertrand may be forgiven for not realizing what poison was responsible and who had administered it, but thought instead of the doctor and the mercury he prescribed as medicine.

It was not impossible that the administration of mercury had been to a certain extent harmful to Gourgaud, but at least the doctor had not ordered the medicine for Gourgaud when he was well but only when he had become ill. It is not known what sort of mercuric medicine Gourgaud took. He probably received what were called blue pills, which consisted chiefly of pure mercury. They normally would pass more or less unchanged through the stomach and intestines and therefore probably did not do much harm. Another possibility is that Gourgaud was given calomel, the nearly insoluble and therefore relatively safe mercurous salt. But, as has been said before, calomel can be converted to extremely poisonous salts by administering at the same time certain refreshing drinks, in themselves rather harmless. But in such case the effects would be very dramatic; the consequences of the poison would be immediately obvious in anyone who was not already too debilitated to afford a contrast in conditions.

We have only very brief accounts of Gourgaud's symptoms. He himself wrote to Sir Hudson Lowe a few days before he left Longwood and complained that his health had been very bad for the past two years. He had often had recurring attacks of dysentery and pain in the liver.[10] Marchand also mentions Gourgaud's continual relapses,[11] and Gourgaud repeatedly noted in his diary that he was ill.

But it is quite plain that Gourgaud's illness was peculiar to his residence at Longwood. Almost immediately upon his departure from the midst of the exile establishment, his physical condition rapidly improved.[12]

Whatever his mental state, Gourgaud was not as deranged, however, as the historian apostles of the Napoleonic cult would have it.[13] He told the governor that Napoleon's illness had nothing to do with the climate at St. Helena, for Gourgaud had seen him suffer from the same kind of illness while in Russia.[14]

Returned to France, Gourgaud further said that Napoleon, when protesting that he was short of funds at St. Helena, had 240,000 francs in gold, mostly Spanish doubloons, at the same time as he sent silver plate from Longwood to be sold in Jamestown.[15] Napoleon, it would seem from Gourgaud's report, had been engaged in a bit of what would now be called the strategy of deception.

For his statement, the honest Gourgaud became referred to in Europe as a liar. Yet the protocol of May 8, 1821, signed by Bertrand, Montholon and Marchand, testifies that the deceased Napoleon left in cash, 300,122 francs in gold. It could not possibly have come from the sale of incidental possessions, such as silver plate, from his Longwood household.

In his *Histoire*, Montholon states that Gourgaud left Longwood for reasons of health and with Napoleon's full permission, and that he had been told to contact the emperors of Russia and Austria and tell them about the cruel treatment meted out to him at St. Helena.

Gourgaud, we are asked to believe, would be especially suited to such a delicate mission for, according to Montholon's account, he was an old friend of these rulers. Montholon does not disclose so much as a word of his quarrels with Gourgaud. In 1846, when Montholon wrote his book, the political wind blew from quite a different quarter to that of 1818. It still would be unwise to offend the fierce Gourgaud.

References

1. Marchand II:205
2. Cabanès 334
3. Gourgaud II:316, 317
4. Gourgaud II:336, 337
5. Gourgaud II:316
6. Gourgaud II:338
7. Gourgaud II:338, footnote; Bertrand III:151
8. Gourgaud II:350-55
9. Bertrand II:64
10. Forsyth III:391
11. Marchand II:183
12. Forsyth II:249
13. Forsyth II:256
14. Aubry I, page 366
15. Forsyth II:260

31

The Murder of Cipriani

GOURGAUD'S DEPARTURE reduced the number of witnesses of the drama of St. Helena as directed by Montholon, its actor-producer, to three: Bertrand, Cipriani and O'Meara, apart from the two ladies of the court.

Cipriani was not just one of Napoleon's ordinary servants. He was a boyhood friend from Corsica. On Corsica there were no in-betweens. You were either a friend or a foe, and whatever you were you were very much so. Napoleon and Cipriani were true friends. Both had belonged to the Salicetti stable. Salicetti, member of the convention and political commissary, had pushed Napoleon forward at Toulon in 1793 and in doing so had sent him on his way to fame. Salicetti, of course, was a Corsican, too.

When Salicetti and Napoleon separated, each to go his own way, Salicetti eventually became Minister of Police and War for King Joseph in Naples. Cipriani had remained with Salicetti until the latter was poisoned to death in 1809.

After that Cipriani left the police and became a citizen of Genoa, where he started a shipping company.[4] His real name was Franceschi, not Cipriani. But as Franceschi and as King Joseph's security agent, he had played many tricks on the English under the command of Hudson Lowe, then a colonel. On coming to St. Helena, because he wanted to avoid reminding the English of such unpleasantness, he switched and used his given or Christian name as his surname.

The return of the Bourbons not suiting Cipriani, he had joined Napoleon on Elba. There, at least in name, he was the major-domo that later he became in fact on St. Helena by truly performing the functions of that office.

Gourgaud often had felt he was being watched by Cipriani,

and this embarrassed him. He considered that the title of major-domo was only a cover for Cipriani's real office as the exiled Emperor's Minister for Foreign Affairs and of the Police.[1]

Cipriani assumed it to be part of his duty to keep watch on Montholon and his lodgings.[2] This was a task he would not have considered either onerous or hazardous to his health.

On Wednesday, the twenty-fourth of February, 1818, without warning, for he had been in perfect health, Cipriani suddenly was seized with terrible pains. He had to be carried up to his room. Dr. O'Meara supposed the intestines, for some mysterious reason, had become inflamed; but obviously it was one of those intestinal inflammations that O'Meara seemed fated never to understand, for he called in two other physicians, Dr. Baxter and Dr. Henry. Cipriani was heavily bled, but not even that helped. We can assume that Cipriani had fits of shivering and felt very cold, since they placed him in a hot bath.

Next day although the pain had eased, his condition was worse. O'Meara realized that the end was near, and on February 26, at four in the afternoon, Cipriani died.[10]

Death was due to an inflammation of the intestines, said O'Meara.

It was a very sudden and rapid inflammation that overcame Cipriani who, suspecting nothing, was carrying out his duties as usual. It took him but two days to die.

Cipriani was not an aristocrat. There would therefore be no post-mortem examination: so risk of discovery was non-existent, provided there was no one in the vicinity who thought for himself. As a matter of fact just such a person was on the island.

William Balcombe could not accept the doctor's diagnosis of Cipriani's illness. According to oral tradition passed down in the Balcombe family, Balcombe was convinced that Cipriani had been poisoned. From the same source we know that Balcombe had sought and received permission to exhume the body of Cipriani. But strangely the coffin could not be located, in spite of the fact that Cipriani had only recently been buried.[3,9]

As Dame Mabel Brookes very rightly states in her book on St. Helena, there were two other suspicious deaths at about the same time. A small child, about whom we know nothing, and a children's nurse died in the same way as Cipriani.

If, as Balcombe believed, Cipriani's death was the result of poisoning, it is not impossible for the arsenic to have been added to some sweetmeat or cake. If so, we need not attribute these two additional deaths to anything but carelessness or misadventure.

The sweets should have been kept in a safe place. All we know about the poor child is that its mother was in service to the Montholons. So also had been the dead nursemaid.[5] Marchand says that the nurse, until seized with illness, had been in excellent health.[8] The climatic illness of St. Helena appeared to have its severest manifestations in the household of the Count and Countess de Montholon.

Not quite a year later Marchand fell ill of the same sort of violent sickness as brought Cipriani to the grave.[7] Marchand himself thought that his illness was identical to that of Cipriani. The valet, a competent artist, was innocently sitting designing motifs for the court ladies' embroidery work when suddenly he was seized by a very severe pain in the stomach, which forced him to bed. His pulse was violent and irregular and he had fits of shivering, but no temperature. Dr. Verling, who attended him, did not bleed him immediately. It could have been this fact or something else, but for whatever reason, Marchand escaped the same fate as the hapless Cipriani. After three weeks' convalescence Marchand was once more up and about.[6] He would survive in the household, with Montholon, until the death of his master. The illness is notable for two reasons: it effectually removes Marchand from suspicion of being the poisoner of St. Helena, and it causes one to wonder if, in the absence of his memoirs, this or any other generation would have had evidence upon which to base a revision of Napoleonic history.

References

1. Gourgaud II:281
2. Forsyth I: 294
3. Brookes, oral communication, ef. Brookes 203, 204.
4. Marchand II:184
5. Las Cases II: 79; Marchand 11:185
6. Marchand II:210
7. Marchand II:208
8. Marchand II:186
9. The Sun-Herald 4.2.1962
10. O'Meara II:387-9

32

Two Other Witnesses Leave St. Helena

AFTER CIPRIANI'S DEATH, Napoleon was left with only two friends other than Bertrand and Montholon who could be regarded as of his own class — Balcombe and O'Meara.

William Balcombe left the island on the 18th of March, 1818. He explained his departure as due to his wife's ill health. She could no longer stand the climate of St. Helena. This was odd since then, as now, where she lived the climate could be considered exceptionally favorable.

Mrs. Balcombe, of course, could have sickened quite naturally, but Balcombe's departure did not come amiss to anyone who wanted Napoleon to himself, and one or two bottles of the Emperor's special wine almost certainly would find their way to his cherished friends at The Briars. Balcombe himself probably drank whisky, if we know him rightly.

In any case, Mrs. Balcombe was thought to have fallen victim to that increasingly famous local climatic sickness, which at last was given medical recognition by being identified as hepatitis.[1]

Napoleon considered the departure of Balcombe to be a bad omen. He saw this change in his purveyor as plainly confirming his growing suspicion that someone wanted to poison him.[2] He would be bound to suspect it was that detestable Hudson Lowe.

Long afterward, in an article written for the press[3], Dame Mabel Balcombe-Brookes said that it was a firmly-rooted and traditional belief in her family that when Cipriani died, William Balcombe became entirely convinced of what he had long suspected; *Napoleon's illness was nothing less than a systematic intoxication with arsenic.* The most urgent reason for his departure to London was that he wanted to inform the Prince Regent — his natural father — of his suspicions.

We may well pause here to consider how differently history might have been written and even the events of history changed if Balcombe had "broken" the Napoleon poisoning case in 1818. But his reported mission was wholly unsuccessful, and why should it not have been?

Perhaps even then there existed spirtual kin to those sharp-witted writers of 1961 who, when the author, on a basis of Napoleon's symptoms and a chemico-forensic analysis of strands of his hair, wrote that he had been poisoned by arsenic, found this proof worthless. The reluctance to accept an amendment of firmly established historic assumptions was strong and rigid. The rationale was that arsenic would be present "because arsenic tends to accumulate in buried corpses". Even if this were true in certain circumstances, it could have nothing to do with the poisoning of Napoleon. His body was never in contact with the earth. It was enclosed in two hermetically soldered metal coffins, and there was not a hair on it when it was placed in these coffins. The strands of hair that the author caused to be analyzed had been taken before the body was doubly enclosed and sealed for first burial in a subterranean vault.

In cases of poisoning by arsenic, the victim should lose weight; Bonaparte most certainly did not.

In the presence of intoxication by arsenic there is insomnia and agitation; Bonaparte was often extraordinarily sleepy and apathetic.

All this is what was so confusing in cases of arsenical intoxication. Doctors in those days did not realize that the patient's symptoms could swing from one extreme to the other and that arsenical intoxication produces different results depending on the size of the dose and the resistance of the recipient. Doctors in those times were aware of only a few of the acute symptoms.

This symptomatic oscillation between one extreme and the other is common to a number of toxics. Opium can be laxative or constipating, stimulating or soporific. The same applies to alcohol and sleeping tablets, the most common poisons. Poisons are capricious.

Balcombe's report resulted — according to family tradition — in his being forbidden to return to St. Helena, and he was for a long time kept in the background, later to be sent to Australia; fortunately for him it was not as a convict but as Colonial Treasurer.[4]

However, William Balcombe's visit to London seems to have had a certain effect on the development of the drama of St. Helena.

One event in this drama of special interest to historians was the removal from Longwood and St. Helena of Dr. O'Meara, who had become so indispensable to Napoleon.

The attempt to get rid of O'Meara, who as a doctor could not have suited the plans of the Bourbon agents, was made in principle along the same lines as were so successful in getting rid of Las Cases and Gourgaud — the man was slandered behind his back.

In the middle of October, 1817, Napoleon had been made to suspect O'Meara, but after a lengthy conversation with the doctor, Napoleon once more accepted him as his attending personal physician.

More success was met with insofar as the governor was concerned. Montholon called O'Meara a rascal in the presence of Sir Hudson and protested that he had seen through him from the beginning.[5] Montholon also gave Sir Hudson news of Napoleon's illness which was wholly contrary to O'Meara's reports.

Pursuing his vendetta, Montholon said the reason Napoleon had kept to his room for quite a while prior to O'Meara's departure was solely because he wished to protest against "the restrictions". So Napoleon had turned day into night, slept the greater part of the day and wandered around his apartments at night. He could also walk in the billiard room during the day, as this was not open to observation.

The truth was that Napoleon's loyal doctor had as his principal worry the fact that his patient's legs at times no longer supported him. It was often difficult for him to move.

When the governor had become quite convinced that O'Meara was unreliable, he wanted to have him taken off the island. But his proposals to that effect to Bathurst, Secretary of State for the Colonies, were rejected, until on May 16, 1818 O'Meara's recall was ordered.[6]

In a private letter to Sir Hudson, Lord Bathurst told the governor to see that it became known that the reason for O'Meara's posting away from St. Helena was not any personal quarrel between Sir Hudson and O'Meara, but due to the things Gourgaud had revealed in London.[6]

There can be some basis for that explanation, but perhaps the real reason for O'Meara's recall could not be disclosed. As late as April 29, 1818, Bathurst had rejected the governor's request that O'Meara be removed from Longwood.

In a letter of May 5, 1818, whatever Gourgaud had told him, Bathurst still had not changed his attitude concerning the doctor.

On May 10, Henry Goulburn, Bathurst's Under-Secretary of State, interrogated Gourgaud in London, but it was not until May 16 that orders to remove O'Meara from Longwood were issued and forwarded to St. Helena.

Balcombe had left St. Helena only a few days after Gourgaud sailed. So he could have arrived in London close on Gourgaud's heels and there stated his suspicions.

One seeks in vain in Gourgaud's disclosures for some reason to deprive Napoleon of his trusted physician-in-ordinary. Gourgaud blamed O'Meara for believing that Napoleon's illness was a result of the climate of St. Helena. But O'Meara was not with Napoleon at Borodino and Waterloo, as Gourgaud had been. Under all the circumstances O'Meara had made a quite excusable mistake.

Around the sixteenth of May, Bathurst must have had a new and very strong motive for changing his attitude of the twenty-ninth of April and for taking measures which he realized would appear ruthless and tyrannical . . . a motive important to the main reason for keeping Napoleon on St. Helena. It could have had something to do with Napoleon's physical safety. Whether or not they were based on fact, Balcombe's disclosures or surmises invited caution. Bathurst could not himself judge of their reliability. The experts had probably turned a cold shoulder to Balcombe and his suspicions. But perhaps Bathurst had learned not always to rely on experts.

The governor had certainly told Bathurst what Count Montholon had said about Napoleon's illness being caused by Dr.

O'Meara poisoning his patient with mercury medicines. The governor did not know that Napoleon's symptoms had developed long before O'Meara had set foot in his sickroom, for Napoleon had forbidden his retinue and his servants to disclose anything about what went on in the French colony at Longwood. Above all, everything that concerned Napoleon's illness was a top "state secret"..

At first Bathurst paid no attention to Montholon's relayed gossip, but when Balcombe arrived and said that Napoleon was being poisoned (not with mercury but with arsenic) one may surmise that Bathurst no longer dared to take the responsibility of having Dr. O'Meara remain on St. Helena.

When the time came for the Balcombes to visit Longwood and say good-bye to Napoleon — Mrs. Balcombe could not go due to illness — Napoleon seemed depressed over their departure. Betsy thought so. Though by then he was most of the time more or less depressed, anyway.

Napoleon accompanied his guests out into the garden, which looked out upon the Atlantic, and said: "While you sail to England, I shall be left to die here on this wretched rock. Look at these dreadful mountains; they are the walls of my prison. You will soon hear that Napoleon is dead."

Betsy gave way to crying. Napoleon took out his handkerchief and wiped away her tears, after which he offered the same monogrammed handkerchief to her as a souvenir.

After dining, when the Balcombes were getting ready to leave, Napoleon asked if he could give Betsy some farewell present. Betsy asked for a lock of his hair. Napoleon called for Marchand and told him to snip off a lock for each of his guests and one for Mrs. Balcombe, too.[7]

Mrs. Betsy Balcombe-Abell wrote in her memoirs, published in 1844, that this lock of hair was the only souvenir she then had left of all that had been given to her by Napoleon.

The lock of hair was eventually inherited by Dame Mabel Brookes. Dame Mabel's grandfather was, as has already been said, Betsy's brother; Betsy died childless.

In 1962 Dame Mabel, co-operating with the author's request, allowed Dr. Hamilton Smith at Glasgow University to analyze a few hairs from the lock for a possible arsenic content.

280 ASSASSINATION AT ST. HELENA

It is not known how far from the scalp Betsy's lock was cut and for that reason no exact dating can be given for the intoxication by arsenic proved by the lock of hair.

Some time, however, between January, 1817, and March 10, 1818 the arsenic revealed in the analysis must have been deposited in the hair. The arsenic is stored in the hairs in such a way that there can be no doubt that it was deposited biologically, which is to say, through the digestive and blood systems. The highest arsenic value in these hairs was 26 p.p.m., the lowest 6.7 p.p.m. The hairs were examined in 1 cm sections. A deposit of 26 parts per million in a section of Napoleon's hair was a reading of at least 32.5 times more arsenic than was normal and 'legitimate'. As has been said, a normal value today is 0.8 p.p.m.; at the time of Napoleon it was certainly much lower, an estimate being 0.6 p.p.m.

Unhappy O'Meara! He knew that Montholon had lied, but the doctor never revealed the count's reasons. It was hard to believe at that time that an aristocrat could be a liar. So the historians concluded that O'Meara must have been an unreliable person. O'Meara's published journals must have been unpleasant reading for Montholon.

Dr. O'Meara was arrested on July 25, 1818 and taken from Longwood. Napoleon's health immediately improved. This was a quite normal result of leaving off medicine, explained Dr. Verling, the physician who was appointed by the governor to Longwood immediately after O'Meara's removal.[8] But Napoleon had never taken medicines. It is far more likely that without a doctor present, the poisoning could not continue. A doctor *must* be there — a matter of safety for the poisoner!!

O'Meara little knew whom he had touched when he said of Montholon: "Had he not been false and vile, he would have been a nobleman."[9]

O'Meara's journals were dangerous documents to Montholon; they had to be counteracted and O'Meara must become re-garded as an unreliable witness. In this Montholon succeeded extraordinarily well. In his famous *"Histoire de la Captivité"* he writes that he rushed into O'Meara's room after his arrest and managed to extract the doctor's journals from their hiding place.

Here reproduced for the first time, this portrait by Jean B. Isabey was commissioned by Napoleon. It is in the Weider collection of Napoleonic relics. Napoleon favored Isabey with a snipped lock of hair. Hairs from it, analyzed for arsenic content, helped testify to the fact that Napoleon was poisoned as early as 1805, possibly starting at the time of the arrest of the Bourbon Duke of Enghien.

The education of the little King of Rome – 1812

V. de Parages

Jules Girardet

The first riding lesson of l'Aiglon

Winter overtakes an eastern campaign

Where Napoleon landed at St. Helena, the stone steps today are as they were in October, 1815.

Built as a country villa resort for senior officers of the East India Company, Longwood House has been restored, after years of neglect, through the dedicated efforts of Gilbert Martineau, French consul. For a time used as a stable, now a public museum, it has been restored to what it had been when Napoleon was its unwilling occupant.

Nineteen years after Napoleon's death and entombment at St. Helena his casket was opened. Former attendants present, aged by nearly two decades, were astonished to see that the Emperor's unembalmed body was almost perfectly preserved. Arsenic may have checked the processes of decay in the triply enclosed and sealed coffin.

Nostalgia for la gloire de France of Napoleon's first and second empires swept the nation in a great emotional response to "the return of the ashes," from St. Helena in 1840. The elaborate catafalque was in itself symbolic of the lost grandeurs of the man whose imperial style reached back to Charlemagne, Caesar and Alexander the Great.

Author Weider, with sons Louis, Eric and Mark, planted a Canadian tree at the site of Napoleon's grave in "Geranium Valley". Here seen on steps of Longwood House.

David Chandler, foremost modern authority on campaigns of Napoleon, seated in Napoleonic ceremonial chair, holds the hat Napoleon wore in the Russian winter of 1812. Items illustrated are from the Weider collection, Montreal.

LOUIS MARCHAND
First valet to Napoleon

*His careful St. Helena diary notes, 140 years later,
helped reveal a secret assassination*

Portrait by Martinet

COUNT CHARLES TRISTAN DE MONTHOLON
Bourbonist major-general and Napoleon's *maréchal de camp*

*The ending of the St. Helena story was known to him
long before it happened*

Portrait by Milliet

COUNTESS ALBINE DE MONTHOLON
Wife of General de Montholon

'She gave her heart only for
good bills of exchange.' — NAPOLEON

Miniature by Bordes

COUNT HENRI GRATIEN BERTRAND
Grand Marshal of the Palace

*Into exile as into battles with total
devotion to a difficult taskmaster*

FANNY (née DILLON) BERTRAND
One of only two court ladies at St. Helena

Her faithfulness was an aggravation to the
master of Longwood

Drawing by Chasselas

BARON GASPARD GOURGAUD
Aide de camp to the exiled emperor

*Napoleon forbade him to duel with his enemy,
de Montholon*

**CAPT. FREDERICK
LEWIS MAITLAND**
Commander of
H M S *Bellerophon*

*The captive Napoleon
was a captivating guest*

EMMANUEL LAS CASES
Historian and chamberlain at
Longwood House

*He departed when he and his son
contracted Longwood's unexplainable
illness*

Napoleon's party boards the *Bellerophon* at
Rochefort, bound for England and St. Helena

THE EMPRESS JOSEPHINE'S MALMAISON

*There Napoleon, when defeated at Waterloo,
assembled his attendants for exile*

LIEUT.-GENERAL SIR HUDSON LOWE
Governor of St. Helena

*Humorless and rigid, he was unfairly blamed
for Napoleon's premature death*

NAPOLEON ON BOARD HMS BELLEROPHON, July 1815 – *From the painting by W. Q. Orchardson*

CHARLES X (le duc d'Artois)
Friend to Count de Montholon

*Tireless plotting recovered
the Bourbon throne from Napoleon*

HAMILTON SMITH, B.Sc., Ph.D. C.Chem.
Senior lecturer in forensic medicine
(toxicology) at the University of Glasgow

*He enlisted atomic science to confirm positively
in many tests Forshufvud's suspicions of the
sustained arsenical poisoning of Napoleon*

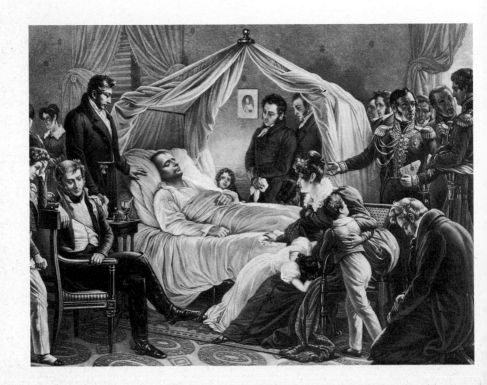

LONGWOOD HOUSE AS IT APPEARED IN NAPOLEON'S TIME

Work in the garden was prescribed as good medicine for the prisoner of St. Helena but other prescriptions decided the fate of history's greatest military genius. Longwood, rarely visited due to irregular transportation, is a museum in which the attempt has been made to present the 'palace' just as it was during Napoleon's occupancy.

NAPOLEON'S LAST HOURS

In this famous artist's conception of the death of Napoleon, more is pictured of significance than the painter realized. Bertrand and Mme. Bertrand are seated with children near them. Marchand stands under the canopy near the bed. Illustrated clutching the Will he helped prepare and which made him wealthy is Gen. Montholon, gesturing toward Napoleon. Kneeling is the second valet and groom, Noverraz, whose souvenir of hairs shaved the day after his master's death, would become evidence in the "new post-mortem" at Glasgow University. On the bedside stand is shown a wine glass of the kind that, in Napoleon's last days, contained a "refreshing" drink called orgeat. It was used to activate physician-prescribed calomel into deadly mercuric cyanide.

1797

1802

1813

Stomach disorders together with chills, eyesight and hearing impairment, itching skin and, in particular, steady accumulation of fat on the victim's frame are all classic symptoms of chronic arsenic intoxication.

These complaints Napoleon had along with weakness of the leg muscles which ended his previous strenuous riding for exercise. He developed stoutness in spite of unusually abstemious habits of eating and drinking.

These illustrations portray the gradual change from his characteristic gaunt appearance before he aspired to the throne of France and began to show progressive disfigurement by unnatural fat. Irradiation test of hairs prove he received in the last year of his life more than 40 separate sub-lethal ingestions of arsenic. These, the authors reason, were intended to reduce his leadership abilities at strategic battles and gradually identify him as a person with a deep-seated and critical illness. Until the author of the Forshufvud theory pursued his suspicions, no one saw in Napoleon's strange obesity the evidence of a poisoning conspiracy. He died in 1821 — supposedly of a cancer of the stomach, normally a cause of extreme emaciation.

1815

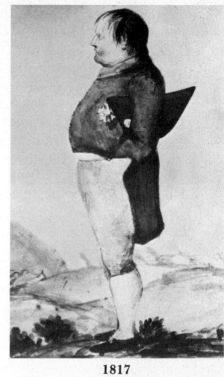

1817

1819

1820

THE DUKE OF REICHSTADT

*The death at 21 of Napoleon's forcibly estranged son
was suspiciously similar to his father's*

But how maddening! They were written in Italian. (In fact they were not, although certain of Napoleon's expressions had been quoted just as they had been uttered.)

However, Montholon could not read them. He showed them to the Emperor, "who pointed out many errors". We are not compelled to believe that.

Unwittingly, Montholon had shown he possessed the qualities of an aggressive secret agent in dealing with an emergent situation.

It must have pleased Napoleon to see that his health was beginning to improve, but the difficulty now was to keep up the myth of St. Helena's murderous climate.

As always, Napoleon had an idea. He gave his two remaining officers orders to say at every opportunity that the Emperor was very ill.

"Such tricks are always successful in the long run," he explained to Bertrand.[10]

If anyone asked why Napoleon did not go out, his officers were to answer that the Emperor was distrustful.

If anyone asked why he did not want a doctor, they were to answer in the same way.

"This is an unfailing method with excellent results. It's what Talleyrand used to do. He uttered only one sentence during a discussion and repeated it. You should repeat it three times, once at the beginning, once in the middle, once at the end. Always come back to the main point."[11]

Of course Bertrand was the only one to obey this imperial order, and he did so according to that supreme rule for a courtier, *Le Roi veut* — the King desires. Montholon made his own interpretation of the rule.

Bertrand was a poor actor. Towards the end of 1818 the governor met Bertrand. Bertrand said his piece, according to instruction. The governor was not to be fooled. He told Bertrand that others, who had seen Napoleon, had watched him recover rapidly. Dr. O'Meara had been feeding Napoleon with mercury and this was actually why Napoleon had been ill.[12]

The governor must have heard this from someone very close to Napoleon, as all that concerned the Emperor's health and care was held in secret by Napoleon's strict order. We may guess who the governor's informant was — especially as his "information" could be proved false.

From time to time O'Meara had prescribed medicine for Napoleon, but his patient regularly refused to accept such remedies. Only once did Napoleon try a small dose of calomel out of curiosity. He became so ill that any further use of the stuff was forbidden.

The governor's explanation of Napoleon's ill-health could not last long. At the close of the year 1818 Napoleon would have a relapse of his illness, even though no doctor had visited him.

Thus de Montholon emerges in clear and distinct view as a liar. But he can be seen, too, as an agent with a severe problem. His plan calls for the Emperor to accept medicines prescribed by a doctor. Napoleon rejects on principle all medical potions.

References

1. Brookes 211
2. Bertrand II:105
3. Sun-Herald 4.2.-62
4. Brookes 245
5. Forsyth III:77
6. Forsyth III:399, 400
7. Aretz 255
8. Bertrand II:151
9. Forsyth I:184
10. Bertrand II:192
11. Bertrand II:162
12. Bertrand II:208
13. Aretz 152

33

The Napoleonic Cult Revived

THE DIRECTION OF EVENTS concerning Napoleon, with which Montholon, under the guidance of the more experienced Montchenu, was charged, obviously was aimed at estranging Napoleon from the English, at depriving him of his attendants, destroying his health, his capacity to think and work, and turning him into a miserable invalid.

Without doubt these Bourbon security agents had made great progress.

Despite illness, Napoleon's direction of policy at Longwood had been by no means a fiasco. His frequent apparently irrational behavior bore rich fruit internationally. It is the irrational in human behavior that gets attention in the press. Napoleon's living legend was further nourished abroad.

In England, traditional enemy of France, a Napoleonic cult flared amongst the public in 1816 with the publishing of a book by Dr. Warden on Napoleon's captivity, which was called "Letters from Saint Helena". A vast number of editions came out. It was part of the first trickle of printed account that would precede a veritable flood of books on Napoleon.

In 1817 the unsigned *Lettres du Cap* had been published in London. If he was not actually the author, Napoleon certainly collaborated in their preparation.

Striking evidence of the intensity of the English Napoleonic cult was the arrival at Portsmouth in November 1818 from St. Helena of a cutter called *Mosquito* with the great but incorrect news that Napoleon had escaped from St. Helena. There was rejoicing over the whole of London, both in the City and in the districts less renowned. Many streets were illuminated by torches.[1]

It may be judged with what concern the spontaneous demonstration of sympathy toward Napoleon was received in the countries of the coalitions that had aligned against him. The zeal for precautions against his return would be reinforced. But none of this inspiration toward utmost custodial care would add anything to Napoleon's safety from a poisoning program. The malevolent plan was well advanced toward leaving the Emperor exposed to subtler and more deadly danger than he or his guardians realized or even suspected from the direction it came.

The French government enforced a censorship on the press, but in leading quarters the jubilation over the false report became known and was the cause of much agitation.

The Duke de Richelieu repeatedly urged the French ambassador in London to remind the British government that Napoleon was a dangerous individual and on no account should he be allowed to escape. "That devil of a fellow has an amazing influence on all who come in contact with him; just look at the crew of the *Northumberland*," Richelieu was to write.[5]

In England new fuel was added to the sacrificial fires of the Napoleonic cult with the printing in London of *"Manuscrit venu de Sainte-Hélène d'une manière inconnue."* Napoleon thought he recognized the author as his old antagonist, Mme. de Staël, who had in fact reconsidered her opinion of Napoleon when she saw what had come after him. Actually Napoleon's guess was not far wrong, for the author was a friend of hers, a certain Lullin de Chateauvieux.[1]

Napoleon could not direct any propaganda in France itself. The press was ordered to say nothing at all about St. Helena. French Napoleonic propaganda was nevertheless taken care of very effectively in the house of Bourbon and their ultra-royalist supporters in higher circles, who opposed anyone suspected of having Napoleon's cause at heart.

The really effective propagandists against the Bourbons were unintentionally the king's brother, the Count d'Artois, and the latter's two sons, the Duke of Angoulême, and the Duke of Berry; not to mention Marie-Thérèse, Duchess of Angoulême, Louis XVI's daughter and the only surviving member of the royal family after their imprisonment in the Temple tower. She was understandably filled with hatred of everyone who had had anything to do with the Revolution. She had become known as *Madame la Rancune* — Madam Revenge. In other respects she was a practising Christian.

The Duke of Berry was all for starting a royal chase, this time after the marshals of France. Eight of them, at least, should be put to death.[3] He was finally satisfied with one, a Marshal Brune, whose sympathies were by no means those of a Bonapartist. But he was an old revolutionary and a protégé of Danton's, was of simple birth and so had no influential relatives. He had been made a marshal in 1804 but fell out of favor in 1807, to be reinstated once more in 1815 during the Hundred Days. He was chosen by the royalists for an example in Avignon. His body was cast into the Rhone.

A victim was also needed as a warning for Toulouse. There was some doubt as to whether to choose Rémusat, the prefect, or the former mayor, but it was thought still better to have a general and General Ramel was picked. He was seized by a gang of royalists collected for this purpose, shot in the stomach, run through with bayonets and diced into small pieces by sword.

In Nîmes a General Lagarde fell victim to the royalists' vengeance and in the little town of Uzès twenty Bonapartists were shot in front of the town authorities.[3]

A General La Bédoyère had joined Napoleon in 1815 without previously having reached an agreement with d'Artois. After Waterloo he realized the necessity to escape from France, for coming as he had from the higher aristocracy, he was now considered a traitor by the royalists.

Bédoyère was caught, however, and condemned to death. His wife went on her knees before the king, but her prayers were rejected. But the good ruler of his people was not entirely heartless. He comforted her with the assurance: "I shall have masses said for the repose of his soul."[2]

His widow had to pay for the firing-squad; twelve men at three francs each.

La Bédoyère was only twenty-nine. His execution made good Bonapartist propaganda. An engraving was distributed over the whole of France, which depicted on one side how Napoleon had generously listened to the prayer for mercy of a Countess Hatzfeld for her husband, accused of espionage, and on the other how King Louis XVIII had refused the plea of Mme. La Bédoyère. Under the engraving were the words: *Le tyran pardonne– le bon père ne pardonne pas*– the tyrant has mercy, the good father none.

It was indicative of the development of the Napoleonic cult in France that Stendhal, who can hardly be accused of being anyone's supporter, dedicated his *Histoire de la Peinture en Italie* in 1817 to the Emperor.

On New Year's Day 1819 Napoleon would have been entitled to feel well pleased with developments, insofar as his policy was concerned, had he only known what results were being obtained in France. His political aim was to undermine the position of the Bourbons. He never knew that they, in a very different way, were busy ensuring that he, the caged eagle of France, would not emerge from captivity. The danger that Napoleon might win the sympathies of those who guarded him and escape or be released could only be removed by his death.

As for the British, their direction of the drama of St. Helena had failed in every respect.

The governor's instructions and his efforts were aimed at winning Napoleon's sympathy and friendship. All Napoleon's wishes should be granted so long as security was not endangered. The work on Napoleon's new quarters — his "palace" — was making progress, but the project was large and transport difficulties were even greater. The attitude of desire to build goodwill must have been obvious to Napoleon, however. It would be equally apparent to those in Paris who feared and hated him. Strangely, Napoleon himself did not exploit his opportunity to divide his enemies by charming his captors.

How hopeless it was for the governor to make friends with Napoleon is illustrated by the following incident.

The Emperor complained about the position of Longwood House on a high interior plateau where the climate, especially in summer, was "unbearable". In 1817, therefore, Sir Hudson started negotiations with a Miss Mason, who owned a residence called Pleasant Mount. It was supposed to do full justice to its name. There everything Napoleon said he missed at Longwood, shade, water and a lovely outlook, should be found. Miss Mason agreed to let the house for 100 pounds a month. Sir

Hudson wrote to Bertrand and offered Pleasant Mount as a summer residence for Napoleon. The governor received no answer to his letter.[4]

References

1. Lucas-Dubreton 126
2. Lucas-Dubreton 41
3. Lucas-Dubreton 30-38

4. Forsyth II:200
5. Lucas-Dubreton 100

34

A New Physician Arrives — and Leaves

THERE WERE NO SPECIAL festivities at Longwood on New Year's Day, 1820. As had become the custom, everyone of suitable standing at the imperial court had been invited to dinner.

Those present included what remained of the old guard, that is to say, Montholon, the Bertrands and their children. There were also three newcomers, two priests and a surgeon.

No expensive presents were exchanged on this New Year's Day, but each child was given a golden coin bearing Napoleon's image.[1]

The first priest was Father Buonavita. The second priest, Father Vignali, had been trained in medicine and was supposed to become Napoleon's physician-in-ordinary. After Napoleon had examined him on the subjects of bleeding and blistering, he appointed the physician to be abbé instead.

The other doctor had been sent to Longwood to be Napoleon's surgeon-in-ordinary. He passed his examination better and was appointed physician-in-ordinary. His name was Antommarchi.

It seems that on this particular New Year's Day Napoleon had not had to lie for so long in his bath. His health had noticeably and remarkably improved. This was most evident from the fact that he now could walk daily in his garden and even sometimes help with its new lay-out.[2] He had not ridden during the past year nor during the two preceding years.

The Emperor rested, bathed and went for walks — that was the usual daily routine, wrote Dr. Antommarchi in his memoirs. He was convalescent, with good hopes of complete recovery.

During the past year, as in his previous year of exile, Napoleon had had a number of sad trials, but his health had been better than in 1816, 1817 and the first half of 1818.

288

In the middle of January, 1819, however, Napoleon had a severe relapse of the "climatic sickness", and for a while it was thought he would die. On the night before Sunday, January 17, he is said to have suffered from a sudden and violent headache, with pain in the shoulders, fits of shivering, difficulty in breathing and dizziness. He fainted and remained for a time unconscious.

Bertrand feared the worst and sent an appeal to Dr. Stokoe, one of the physicians to the navy. There was a good doctor on hand, Dr. Verling, but since he was under the command of the governor, he could not be called.[3]

Dr. Stokoe was on board H.M.S. *Conqueror,* which lay at anchor off Jamestown. But the letter of urgent summons could not go directly without first being sent to the governor's mansion, Plantation House, which lay at the end of a four-mile long winding road out of Jamestown. The governor had to be awakened so that he might read the letter before allowing it to go on to the admiral who was staying at The Briars. So the dragoon, who acted as courier, had to ride back the long, hilly road from Jamestown to The Briars, there to rouse Admiral Plampin.

The admiral read Bertrand's letter and ordered his secretary to add a few lines: "The admiral wishes the captain to see that Dr. Stokoe proceeds immediately to Longwood, where he is to consult with Dr. Verling. Buonaparte is very ill."

The letter was handed back to the courier, who set off down the winding road towards the harbor of Jamestown.

It was dawn before the officer on duty in the castle had had a boat manned for the *Conqueror.* Once on board the captain and later Dr. Stokoe had to be roused.

When Stokoe finally came ashore there was the business of a horse to be saddled before he could start off along the five miles of road ascending to Longwood.[3]

It was not until seven in the morning that the doctor arrived . . . much too late for a doctor. The patient had managed to overcome the crisis medically unaided, probably after a good deal of vomiting. Moreover, he had been put into a hot bath and had broken into a heavy sweat. Thereafter the pain had become bearable. When the doctor arrived, Napoleon was resting and could not be disturbed.

The doctor was invited to breakfast by Mme. Bertrand, and there Stokoe was asked by Montholon if he would act as physician-in-ordinary to Napoleon. A condition was attached that he cease being an English military doctor and act only as Napoleon's personal physician. Stokoe accepted, subject to his military superiors giving their permission. In due course Stokoe was called in to the patient.

Stokoe found Napoleon lying on a couch, his skin yellow and his face drawn. There was still pain on one side, and when pressure was exerted on a certain spot, the pain became more acute. Stokoe thought he recognized the symptoms his friend O'Meara had spoken of, and considered that Napoleon was suffering from a chronic liver affliction.

Toward evening, the Emperor again felt ill, and Montholon set off for Plantation House to ask that Stokoe be sent immediately to Longwood. Bertrand wrote a letter directly to Dr. Stokoe for the same purpose.[4]

Montholon astonished the governor's adjutant Gorrequer by declaring that there was reason to expect a new attack of the same sort as that of the previous evening, and that the possibility of apoplexy (cerebral haemorrhage) should not be overlooked.[5]

This time the governor was not unduly perturbed by Montholon's report, which has been taken to prove that the governor was a ruthless man. Actually he had probably received more accurate reports than Montholon's from Longwood from the agent he finally had been able to install there. This agent will be mentioned later.

On the afternoon of January 19, Stokoe was again called to Longwood. He stayed the night with the Bertrands, and at two o'clock in the morning he was called to Napoleon's bedroom. The Emperor was once more suffering a severe headache and his pulse was very irregular. Stokoe suggested bleeding. At first Napoleon refused, but at five o'clock the headache had triumphed over his scruples and the doctor was allowed to cup him. This was followed by some relief. Dr. Stokoe drew up a bulletin in which he said Napoleon was suffering from an affection of the liver due to the climate. As the British contention was that tropical St. Helena, on no less authority than the Duke of Wellington himself, was a suitable place for the intrepid Napoleon to be exiled, the verdict could not fail to be disappointing to the authorities.

Before Admiral Plampin, who succeeded Malcolm in command of the St. Helena squadron, gave permission to Stokoe to attend Napoleon for the third time he asked him a few questions, which must have been set by a doctor.

"Let us admit, then, that General Buonaparte is suffering from chronic hepatitis. You say that he has suffered from this for the past sixteen months. On what grounds do you believe this?"

"On the information he gave me."

"Have you seen signs of it yourself?"

"I would not like to make a positive statement, but from his expression and the look of his tongue I believe that the liver is affected."

"Was there a swelling on his right side?"

"No."

"Did you look?"

"Yes, and I saw nothing abnormal. But when I pressed the hypochondrium (the region of the liver) he complained that I hurt him."

"But do you think the liver is hypertrophic (enlarged)?"

"I did not notice that the liver was swollen. Nor were his ankles and feet. I palpated them."

"What makes you think that General Buonaparte suffered from dizziness and fits of fainting on the night of January 16 to 17?"

"General Buonaparte himself said so, and so did those who were near him."

"Who?"

"A valet with Count Bertrand and Count de Montholon."[6]

This cross-examination confirms the governor's view that Napoleon had actually to a great extent recovered after O'Meara's removal. His ankles and feet were now back to normal size, which according to various witnesses had been far from the case in O'Meara's time.

Napoleon's illness of the night before January 17 was probably an acute arsenical intoxication. Perhaps the poisoner had accidentally administered too strong a dose, or else Napoleon had had an extra glass of treated wine. It was Saturday evening.

Esther was expected. Apparently Montholon had known when he talked with Gorrequer that a relapse was to be expected.

Stokoe wrote in his third bulletin that he was now quite convinced that the Emperor suffered from an affection of the liver. The doctor recommended that a physician be stationed at Longwood to carry out a regular mercury cure. It had been observed that Napoleon was most generous toward his physicians-in-ordinary.

One can quite understand that the governor, well-informed as he was by his security agent, became alarmed. Was the same ridiculous and dangerous comedy about to be re-enacted, with another mercury intoxication as a result?

We must respect the governor's memory because he did not allow himself to be deceived indefinitely. He realized that Napoleon's illness could be due to poison. But it was a pity he did not realize that mercury was not the only poison in the medical almanac . . . nor physicians the only poisoners.

The governor decided he would not consent to Stokoe being appointed O'Meara's successor to reside at Longwood. On the other hand he gave permission for Stokoe to attend Napoleon should he be called for when Napoleon became ill.

When Stokoe reported to the admiral after drawing up his third bulletin, in which he maintained his diagnosis of the Emperor's liver affection and had considered it necessary to open one of the patient's veins, his report was received with much skepticism. The doctor was subsequently regarded as a not very reliable person.[7]

Stokoe grew alarmed and suspected that secret forces were at work trying to ruin him professionally. He told the admiral he no longer wished to be Napoleon's physician. He wanted to return to Longwood only to announce this in person. Permission was granted on condition he did not spend the night with Bertrand but instead use the escort officer's room.

Early next morning Stokoe was received by Napoleon, stated his business and added that he intended to try to get sent home. Napoleon then handed him a cheque for a thousand pounds, a letter of recommendation to the Empress Marie-Louise and another to the rest of Napoleon's family, and instructions for the printing of a small work with pertaining documents.[7]

Stokoe stayed with Napoleon for two hours. But the doctor had orders not to stay at Longwood too long as he was scheduled to meet the admiral at The Briars not later than 10:30 that morning. Stokoe, in fact, did not report to the admiral until 12 noon.

The doctor had expected that the admiral would want to hear all about Napoleon's illness, but Plampin listened half-heartedly and interrupted:

"Why were you so late?"

"General Bonaparte asked me to stay with him for a while."

"Do you override my orders just to satisfy a whim of General Bonaparte's?"

"I was waiting to see the effect of a warm bath."

"Was General Bonaparte so ill that your presence' was absolutely necessary?"

"I can't say that he was very ill, but he did ask me to stay."[8]

The chroniclers of the drama of St. Helena, especially the French, have been horrified at the subsequent unfair treatment received by Stokoe at the hands of the St. Helena oligarchy. It has been thought that Stokoe was persecuted because he had diagnosed Napoleon's illness as being due to the climate and had said so. But formally it certainly was not for that that Stokoe was brought before a court martial, found guilty of insubordination, always a severe crime in the eyes of the British military authorities, and condemned to removal from office.

The judgment can hardly be called unfair. There was an accusation against Stokoe not mentioned at the trial, presumably so as not to reveal the source from which information had come. He had in fact accepted a bribe from Napoleon to act on his behalf and so had lost his required status of disinterest through monetary reward and the receipt of a letter of recommendation to the Empress Marie-Louise.

It was part of the Marquise de Brinvillier's famous practice of killing off her dear and wealthy relatives, that a physician should be at the victim's bedside and prescribe the final deadly poison. The physician's dosage would naturally be corrected appropriately as opportunity permitted.

When, as seemed likely, Napoleon was being persistently

prepared for despatch by the same old tried and tested method, no careless slips were to be permitted. A doctor must be in attendance. Who would suspect a physician of deliberately administering a deadly potion?

And now the British security service had played a nasty trick on the French, certainly not for the first time in the history of British-French relations. Dr. Stokoe, whom Napoleon had at last been persuaded to accept, had been dismissed almost as quickly as he had arrived.

Seeing how things had turned out, Montholon must have realized that his eagerness to get Stokoe appointed as Napoleon's physician would not be good for his own reputation with the governor. Thus he tried to cover his position by writing to tell Sir Hudson that it was Bertrand whose initiative lay behind Stokoe's appointment.[9]

Stokoe himself, however, clearly and definitely states that it was Montholon who asked him to be Napoleon's physician-in-ordinary.[10] The fact that Napoleon now was without a doctor was worrisome, particularly to Montholon.

On April 1, 1819, the count made special efforts to have Dr. Verling appointed as Napoleon's physician. Dr. Verling was to receive 12,000 francs a year in salary and as much again in cash for his pocket. That would be considerably more than he was paid as a British army doctor. The only condition was that Verling should sign a declaration that he would be "l'homme de l'Empéreur" and not "l'homme du Gouverneur".

Of course Dr. Verling would have to examine Napoleon's liver — an important but not wholly unique privilege for a physician-in-ordinary. There was not much likelihood that a prudent English army doctor would discover anything wrong with Napoleon's liver, remembering all that O'Meara and Stokoe had had to go through. (Just the same, a couple of years later an English army doctor Shortt was to make an eager attempt to point out that the Emperor's liver was enlarged. He was soon helped by his colleagues to realize he had never seen anything of the sort.)

There was just one thing Montholon wanted to make clear, and that was that Verling could certainly exaggerate his diagnoses a little. But Montholon himself believed — "like everyone

else at Longwood" — that it was apoplexy, cerebral haemorrhage, that actually threatened Napoleon's life. However, Dr.
Verling was to keep this confidential information of Montholon's
strictly secret.[11]

As Montholon's predictions, unlike his accounts of things,
were often found to be reliable, his words on this occasion would
indicate that it was still not settled whether Napoleon should die
of a "scirrhus at the pylorus", or more simply *à la* d'Aubray,
Mme. Brinvillier's father.

After Stokoe had left, therefore, Napoleon found himself
once more without a physician. This does not seem to have
affected his health, for he was actually in fairly good condition
during the greater part of 1819.

He would seem to have had occasional pain, especially in the
hypochondrium, that is to say, pain in the liver. He was still
excessively fat. Normally, a pain in the region of the liver would
in the first instance suggest gallstones. Why not in the case of
Napoleon?

For a day or so he would be out of sorts; but that need not have
meant that he was given an extra large dose of arsenic on those
particular days. It might have meant that he was not given the
dose he now was used to having, a dose which caused him no
direct discomfort, arsenophagist as he had unwittingly become.

By studying the accounts of Napoleon's walks and his riding
excursions, it is possible to get a fair idea of his condition and
general health. Characteristically his legs were almost useless
when he was really ill.

On February 9, 1819, Bertrand noted that Napoleon walked
for two whole hours with Mme. Montholon.[12]

On April 29 Governor Lowe asked Montholon how His
Majesty was. The dauntless count replied that Napoleon was ill
in bed. But according to Bertrand, Napoleon and he on that day
went for a walk in the garden.

The improvement in his general health should have made
Napoleon see that the climate of St. Helena and the "restrictions"
had nothing to do with the weakness in his legs that had
prevented him from walking and riding for more than two years.

The island climate and the "restrictions" were of course his
main propaganda themes, which he constantly repeated, good

pupil of Talleyrand that he was. He hoped that, by dwelling on these topics, he might be set free. The world should also be told that the English did not even give him the necessaries of life. They should know that he was forced to turn the faded material of his glorious uniforms and sell his silver to buy food for his household.

The story of the governor's meanness could not be used unchecked forever. It soon become common knowledge that the British government, through their governor, had paid out impressive sums in maintenance of the exiled French court.

Of course there was the residence. It was cramped and damp and there were rats. Arsenic had been suggested to get rid of them, but the resultant stench from their dead bodies was feared.[13] The governor often and readily admitted that the Emperor's residence was not suitable. He offered to carry out any provisional improvements required, pending the completion of the projected new palace.

The basis of truth in Napoleon's propaganda against the English was indeed meagre. But does any political propaganda require a great content of truth at all? Napoleon's complaints were to be very effective in Europe.

In order to maintain the myth of the Helenic climate's deadliness, even when he was in comparatively good health, Napoleon ordered his retinue and household to continue to say that he was sick. So that no Englishman could contradict this, he isolated himself entirely from them and walked in his garden, which was screened from prying eyes, whether at dusk or early in the morning.

With the idea of helping Dr. Stokoe in his trial at Jamestown at the end of August and beginning of September 1819, a fairly entertaining comedy was put on at Longwood, which was intended to show that Napoleon had been and still was in need of Stokoe's services.

Napoleon arranged that the escort officer had no opportunity of seeing him, which he had been ordered to do to provide daily verification of Napoleon's continued presence. The British then would think that the reason Napoleon was not seen must be that he was seriously ill.

When the governor did not get his written regular report that

Napoleon was in fact at Longwood, he tried to get some sign of life from him by addressing letters and parcels to him. Sir Hudson Lowe knew that it infuriated Napoleon to be addressed as "General Bonaparte", a form decreed by the great powers and laid down in the governor's instructions. Sir Hudson, however, had hit on the idea of addressing his letters and parcels to "Napoleon Bonaparte". That occasionally had been successful.

The question of his imperial title, which Napoleon did not want to give up, was rather a delicate one. Until late in the drama of his assassination he did not consider his political career ended with his stay on St. Helena. Regarding this as only an episode in that career, he consequently did not want to renounce even by inference his grandest title. After all he had been anointed as Emperor. He himself had made kings who ruled and were accepted. How many of Europe's reigning monarchs could say as much?

The English, on the other hand, had to consider the French king, Louis XVIII, who was actually at the moment a reigning monarch. Napoleon could not be given a finer title than that held by King Louis. Moreover, England had never recognized Napoleon's imperial regime even at the zenith of its strength and glory.

The governor personally was not averse to calling Napoleon an Emperor, His Majesty and Sire, and he certainly did so when there was no Englishman listening. But that which is written is written. He confided in Montholon once in January 1819 and explained to him that his instructions prevented him from addressing Napoleon in the way the latter wished. Montholon, apparently such a keen supporter of Napoleon at Longwood, consoled the governor by saying that, for his part, he found it extremely childish to address someone as Emperor who no longer held a throne.[14]

Anyway, the governor now wrote "Napoleon Bonaparte" on letters and parcels. This time he was not successful. The orderly officer handed them over to Montholon. Montholon could not accept them, pleading that he did not feel well.

Although the governor had long since broken off relations with Bertrand, whose information seldom corresponded to Montholon's, orderly officer Captain Nicholls had now to turn to the Grand Marshal. The latter read the address and pointed out that it was not formulated in a manner acceptable to His Majesty.

So Captain Nicholls returned to Napoleon's residence and found the head valet, Marchand. Marchand refused to accept the parcel. All dispatches, he said, had now to go through the hands of the Grand Marshal of the Palace.

Three days later, on August 11, Captain Nicholls returned with a Major Harrison and tried again to get the dispatches to Napoleon. Colonel Wynyard — perhaps he was only a lieutenant-colonel — came too, and tried through closed doors to persuade Marchand to hand over the parcel to the Emperor. This naturally had no effect on Marchand.[15] The captain and the major had not been admitted either. They went around outside the house, knocking on all closed doors.

The next day the same officers returned, but this time the captain had hit on the idea of leaving the packages in the anteroom to Montholon's bedroom. Montholon sent his black servant to the captain with the packages. Montholon still felt unwell and regretted he could not be of service.

In the evening Captain Nicholls tried giving Montholon a private letter from Major Gorrequer. Not even that was successful. The count was much too indisposed to read private letters. On the next day the same comedy was re-enacted with the same actors. On August 14 the comedians were reinforced by Sir Thomas Reade, the island's chief of police, and Dr. Verling. They hammered and knocked on all the doors. Nobody answered.

Day by day the same farce was repeated until on August 19 Bertrand finally accepted the packages, now three in number. At eleven o'clock on the night of the same day, Bertrand wrote to the governor to say that he had indeed handed the packages to His Majesty. When His Majesty had caught sight of the address on the wrappings, however, His Majesty had thrown them into the fire unopened.

On August 20, by order of the governor, two physicians, Verling and Arnott, presented themselves at Longwood. They offered their services to "the sick Napoleon". They were told they might be received, provided they first signed a number of documents, among them a contract in which the physicians renounced their duty of obedience to the English authorities. Arnott set off to tell the governor of the conditions for even looking at Napoleon.

Bertrand added: "This must be a joke! Imagine sending Dr. Arnott here without first having removed all obstacles to his becoming Napoleon's physician! And then all this knocking and banging on the doors, day after day."[15]

While this comic cat-and-mouse game was being enacted at Longwood, H.M.S. *Abondance* was approaching St. Helena, returning Dr. Stokoe, who had now to defend himself before a court martial at St. Helena on the charge of having been tricked into drawing up faulty bulletins on Napoleon's state of health. Dr. Stokoe had asked for transport home. He got it — there and back again.

On August 21 the governor announced most respectfully that Stokoe was now back on St. Helena. Napoleon had expected him and on the next day Bertrand sent word to the governor that Napoleon was very ill and wanted Stokoe sent for immediately.[15] Napoleon often showed that he could remember services rendered. He may also have been a trifle curious as to whether Stokoe had managed to transmit the documents he had received.

Marchand tells us of his conversation with Colonel Wynyard:

"I have a message for General Bonaparte from the governor. Please announce me," said the colonel.

"Colonel, sir, if you have a message for His Majesty, you must address yourself to General Montholon or to the Grand Marshal, according to the rules to be observed for correspondence with the Emperor."

"One of them is ill, the other is not at home. My orders are that it is you who must announce me to His Excellency or else take charge of my message for him. Do this, please, and you will save the General a great deal of unpleasantness."

"I know my duty too well ever to do such a thing."

"I shall go over to the officer of the escort and wait there for your answer."

"Colonel, my decision has already been taken. The Emperor is ill and I do not intend to mention to him a request that can only be unpleasant."

Having got rid of the colonel, Marchand went straight to

Napoleon, who was in his study humming a merry tune, always a sign that he felt well disposed to the world.[16]

Who could really begrudge Napoleon this small and somewhat mischievous diversion? His strange internment under British care on St. Helena offered few situations in which his innate need to dominate could find the slightest satisfaction. Deprived of so much else of the trappings of power, he still had protocol as a weapon of harmless but irritating effect and in Marchand, no doubt equally bored, a willing participant in petty gamesmanship. To this the foremost military strategist of his or any other age had been reduced.

References

1. Marchand II:244
2. Bertrand II:416
3. Frémeaux 1, pp. 90-2; Forsyth III:103
4. Bertrand II:246
5. Forsyth III:104
6. Frémeaux 1, p. 111-12
7. Bertrand II:247-8
8. Frémeaux 1, p. 122
9. Forsyth III:105
10. Frémeaux 92, 97
11. Forsyth: III:153-54
12. Bertrand II:297
13. Marchand II:216
14. Forsyth III:106
15. Bertrand II:378-85
16. Marchand II:220-21

35

Madame Montholon is Sent Packing

PERHAPS NAPOLEON's thoughts turned kindly toward Albine de Montholon on New Year's Day, 1820. She had left Longwood and St. Helena on July 2, 1819.

Something was strange about her departure. Montholon let it be said that his wife had had to leave St. Helena for reasons of health, and that Napoleon had wept at her departure. This observation was not so bad in itself, nor unfounded either, but a trifle banal and *a priori* quite suspicious, coming as it did from Montholon.

Slightly more interesting and credible is the information that she had left St. Helena in order to continue in Europe the affair she had begun with one Lieutenant Basil Jackson, a young man of twenty-four summers, some fifteen years younger than Albine. But it would be risky to believe wholly in this explanation either. Mme. de Montholon left St. Helena first; Jackson left later, and by order of his superior officers, who wanted an eye kept on her in Europe, too.[1]

But it was never the case that Jackson had fallen hopelessly in love with the now slightly overblown Mme. Montholon. He first visited her bed chamber on a "secret mission". He was allowed to remain until four in the morning, but then he had to leave in order to report to his superiors on everything that had happened at Longwood. His duties as security agent in contact with Mme. de Montholon lasted for six months.[1] It well could have been he who had revealed how Napoleon had tried to use Stokoe when the latter visited him in mid-January, 1819.

It was Sir Thomas Reade, chief of police on the island, who told Mme. Bertrand about Jackson on May 8, 1821, while they were planning the cortege that was the following day to accompany Napoleon's coffin to his stone tomb in Geranium Valley. The contest was over and Mme. Bertrand (née Dillon) could resume her real identity as an English lady.[10]

During the same conversation with Mme. Bertrand, Sir Thomas declared that the Montholons were *le ménage le plus fin, le plus roué qu'ils aient jamais connu* — the craftiest pair they had ever come across.

Napoleon first came to know about the British plot for a liaison between Albine de Montholon and Jackson in February 1819. The informant, the Russian Commissioner, Count Balmain, made the disclosure in a conversation with Bertrand.

"They say she has thrown herself at him," said Count Balmain. "It looks as though she were madly in love with him. She is rather man-mad and would like to go on being desirable.

"They say, too, that she is harming you at Longwood and is spoiling everything. She is not careful what she says. Too much escapes her lips. And then she is afraid, too late.

"Jackson writes down everything, every day, and every day he talks for two hours with the governor, who never gives as much time to anyone else . . . You should talk to Montholon and warn him about Jackson."[1]

On the same day Napoleon spoke about Jackson to Albine Montholon. She had nothing but praise for the lieutenant: Oh, no! He was such a nice young man, very polite and uncomplicated and rather stupid.

So perhaps it was not so dangerous after all. Napoleon appears not to have begrudged Albine a new interest, now that his own ardor had cooled.

A month went by, but then Napoleon again must have received some worrying information, for now he definitely ordered: Either the Montholons must give their word of honor not to have anything more to do with that fellow Jackson, or else they must leave — though in good and proper order.[2]

The Jackson affair must anyway have had something to do with Napoleon's sympathies or policy. On the same evening that the ultimatum was voiced, Mme. Bertrand was given a valuable little box with Napoleon's portrait, set with diamonds, while the Grand Marshal received four clasps.[2]

At the imperial request Bertrand once more spoke to Mon-

tholon about the Jackson business. Something new must have
turned up, for Montholon was very nervous. "He quite lost his
head," noted Bertrand. Montholon said that he wished to leave
St. Helena immediately.[3] One might well wonder why Montholon was so alarmed. Perhaps he felt spied upon and insecure,
knowing — as do we — that British security service agents can be
very dangerous. But it was a decision which, given effect, would
interrupt a long-sustained plan.

The threat to Montholon and his important political mission
was warded off by getting Napoleon to see that the countess
should be the one to leave the island. This would automatically
cut the connection with Jackson. A touch of climatic sickness
would not come amiss in getting Albine equally to realize that she
should go home.

On April 5, 1819 Napoleon issued a decree that Montholon's
countess should return to Paris, but that her husband should
stay.[4] And, believe it or not, Albine de Montholon went down
with a severe attack of climatic sickness; so much so in fact that
she had a miscarriage as well.[5] It was a most extraordinary and
fortunate coincidence. In practical terms, it would remove the
hazard to Montholon's plan and increase the danger in which
Napoleon was to exist.

However it happened, on April 14 Napoleon had become
convinced that the Countess de Montholon should be given a
sum of money when she left as "compensation, for her dowry."

Napoleon, insofar as can be judged, seems to have kept to his
old naive idea that loyalty surely could be won by kindness and
generosity. Not even such flagrant examples as his experiences
in the case of Bernadotte, Marmont, Berthier, Sémonville,
Bourmont, Murat, Augerau, Ney, Constant, Roustam, Corvisart, Yvan and various others had made clear to him the flaws
in such a philosophy and that loyalty did not predictably emerge
from purses or promotions.

On April 18 Montholon had been able to calculate an
appropriate amount for his wife's "dowry" — 500,000 golden
francs. Such a sum in modern terms would have a value of at
least five million francs.

The following day Napoleon spoke to Albine herself about the
matter. She could indeed assure him that Montholon had not

over-estimated. She, herself, thought that an additional substantial annuity would not be out of place.

"But I would then be penniless!" cried Napoleon.[6]

When Albine de Montholon left Longwood and St. Helena on
July 2, 1819 she took with her a cheque for 200,000 francs,
recently made out and signed, together with an entirely new
letter of pension for 20,000 francs or more a year. And as an
extra token of regard she carried the beautiful golden box with
Napoleon's portrait, set with large diamonds.[7]

So that no one should doubt that it was Mme. Montholon's
sudden ill-health that was the reason for her departure, which
had been arranged by Napoleon out of consideration for her
well-being and to his great sorrow, Montholon sent a message of
farewell to her through the governor — when she had already
sailed. "The Emperor openly mourns your departure deeply: he
has shed tears for you, perhaps for the first time in his life," read
the governor. Sir Hudson must have shaken his head: Odd
people, these French.[8]

Montholon told the servants a pretty tale about the reason for
Mme. Montholon's departure, which Marchand faithfully recorded in his diary. That it was in the interests of the Montho-
lon-Montchenu team to get Mme. Montholon away from
Longwood as soon as possible can be gathered from
Montchenu's description of Albine at the time. He called her *La
vipère dangereuse* — the dangerous viper.[11]

Officially, she left on July 2, but how could that have been
possible? It was not until May 26 that Count de Montholon asked
the governor for permission to send his wife back to Europe —
on account of her state of health, and to his great distress.[9]

Montholon asked that she should be allowed to travel directly
to Europe, thus avoiding the usual political quarantine in Cape
Town. But that was not so easy! Sir Hudson could not promise
anything of the sort; he was not in a position to do so. But he
offered to write to London immediately and ask for permission
to send Mme. Montholon home by the most direct route.

Two days later he wrote to Lord Bathurst on the matter.

A letter took about two months to reach London. A reply,
therefore, would not be received in less than four months. Mme.
Montholon's visa for her direct journey to Europe could not be

expected before September 28 at the earliest. But the record shows she left on July 2.

This fact can only be explained by the possibility that Montholon had managed to get a visa far more quickly than was usual.

References

1. Bertrand III:200, II:295-6; Gonnard 21, 37
2. Bertrand II:317
3. Bertrand II:318
4. Bertrand II:327
5. Bertrand II:345; Forsyth III:164
6. Bertrand II:333
7. Marchand II:213, 214
8. Forsyth III:168
9. Ibid III:161
10. Bertrand III:200
11. Gonnard 2, page 164

36

A New Physician and Two Priests

WHEN CIPRIANI DEPARTED this life so suddenly without having — *nolens volens* — received the Last Sacraments of the Church, and then could not be given a Catholic burial, the faithful Catholics of Longwood, headed by Mme. Bertrand, thought this was truly dreadful and said so.

To mitigate insofar as possible the harm done, Cipriani's death certificate attested that he had died within the Catholic Church. Perhaps that would do.

For the sake of order, though, Bertrand — probably at the suggestion of *Mme. la Maréchale* — wrote a letter to Cardinal Fesch, Mme. Letizia's half-brother, in which he asked him to arrange for a French or Italian Catholic priest to be sent to St. Helena as quickly as possible.

Bertrand begged the cardinal to deign to see to it that the priest he sent was an educated man, under forty years of age. The priest should also be a kindly man.[1]

When Dr. O'Meara was sent away from Longwood, Napoleon had asked relatives in Rome to provide him with a good physician, one on whom he could totally rely. And so, on the twentieth of September, 1819, at six o'clock in the afternoon, two doctors and a priest arrived at Longwood. The priest was quite old enough. Too much consideration had been paid to Bertrand's request that the priest should not be under forty years of age. This one was sixty-seven, and had already suffered his first cerebral haemorrhage. He shook and he trembled. But he was certainly kind. Moreover he had a beautifully appropriate name — Buonavita.

Napoleon's relatives had also sent a major-domo called Coursot, who had been in service with Duroc, the former Grand

Marshal of the Palace, and a chef whose name was Chandelier and whom the Princess Pauline had released.

Next day Napoleon received the newcomers at four o'clock in the afternoon. The young physician Vignali did not shine at the interview. As his qualifications were likewise on the spiritual side, he was appointed priest with the title of *abbé*.

The old priest was a still greater disappointment to Napoleon, who remarked, "He is a reciter of masses."

A few days later Napoleon was to say of Buonavita: "The cardinal has sent Buonavita in order that we may bury him here."[2]

Napoleon was also surprised at the cardinal's choice of surgeon. Among his qualifications, Dr. Antommarchi claimed he had been the pupil and assistant or prosector of Professor Mascagni, a very famous anatomist. Antommarchi had helped him in his production of an important illustrated anatomical work and intended to complete the project now that his master was dead.

Of course it was a good thing that Antommarchi was such a skilful anatomist, but Napoleon, under the circumstances, would have preferred a physician whose skills related to the living rather than the dead. Later a skilful dissector might be an asset, of course. But it was a strange appointment.

After Bertrand had talked with Antommarchi, Napoleon felt more at ease. Young Antommarchi, it seemed, had also had certain experience as a practising physician and had been recommended as such by Mme. Letizia's chamberlain, Colonna, who knew Antommarchi very well.[3]

After the formal but not unpleasant conversation with Bertrand, Antommarchi had to endure an inquisitional and quite disagreeable cross-examination by Montholon. "I understood nothing of the conversation," wrote Antommarchi in his diary. He certainly could have known nothing of the special position Montholon held at the court of exile. Would he ever find out?

When Antommarchi was to examine his patient for the first time, he was very kindly received. He noted that Napoleon was hard of hearing, which the latter ascribed to the climate. It is known today that arsenic gradually affects the hearing, but neither doctor nor patient was aware of this. But the climate after all was not such a bad guess; as now we know, it was just a matter of the particular kind of climate to blame.

Napoleon complained to Antommarchi about his liver, and mentioned that he had felt a dull pain in his stomach and had had difficulty in sleeping. Antommarchi was not alarmed. It could scarcely have been anything but the sort of thing that everyone suffers now and again, when general health is not at its higher levels.

Antommarchi suggested treating Napoleon's complaints with baths and exercise, which would indicate that Napoleon's trouble at that time was a general poor condition. Nowadays too we would suspect Antommarchi of being something of a genuine physician with respect for the natural curative forces operative in the human system. His master Mascagni, a very great man, was certainly not an obedient son of the medical high church. It was just such a physician Napoleon really needed, but if he was going to be judged by his help in the matter of aggravating Napoleon's "climatic sickness", then Antommarchi was no good at all. That was how Montholon described him in his famous memoirs and directly to Napoleon himself. Open air exercise, indeed!

Early on the morning of September 28, six days after their first encounter, Antommarchi met Napoleon out in the garden.

"You see, doctor, I have already started obeying instructions. I got up at dawn and went for a walk to get some fresh air."

Napoleon was clad in a white dressing-gown, wide white trousers reaching down to his feet, red slippers, with a scarf round his head and shirt open at the neck.

The next day Napoleon had obviously forgotten the doctor's instruction, for Antommarchi found him in bed in the morning. He had been sitting there reading all night. He complained of severe pain in the liver. Books lay tumbled on the floor and spread over the bed, all in great disorder. Antommarchi asked the valet on duty how he could leave the Emperor in such a state and why he did not tidy up. Tidying up, it appeared, was not allowed as long as Napoleon was in his room. So his liver pains could not have been so bad that night.

On October 6 Antommarchi visited the governor and answered his questions on Napoleon's state of health. It was indeed chronic hepatitis, just as O'Meara and Stokoe had suspected.

"Do you think so?" asked Sir Hudson.

"All the symptoms indicate chronic hepatitis."

"General Bonaparte must feel very well, anyway, in spite of this trouble."

"Yes, but the climate is detrimental and it could be dangerous."

"This is about the most healthy district I know of," replied the governor.

"Is that why it was chosen?"

"Without doubt, without doubt."

This was true, just as the governor had said. On their own the English would certainly never have discovered what was the matter with the climate of St. Helena. Most climates seem wonderful to the English. On the other hand the French were born to expect more from the weather, and those from Corsica still more so.

Few at St. Helena at that time may have known that it was Napoleon's honored adversary, the Duke of Wellington, who strongly recommended the island for exile purposes. He had been at the station and knew its climate favorably.

Doctor Antommarchi had managed to persuade Napoleon to dictate less and walk more, but he was still not pleased with the result. He prescribed even more physical exercise.

"And where could I take that, doctor?"

"Out in the garden, Sire, in the fresh air."

"Among the red coats? Never."

"Here in the garden, Sire. Dig and hoe."

"Dig?" A moment of reflection, then, "Ah, you are right, doctor."[4]

The major-domo was told to order wheelbarrows, spades, hoes and other garden tools. And so work began which was to last for nearly a year and which, without doubt, did Napoleon a great deal of good, now that for some unknown reason of policy his climatic sickness was improving while an interval of suspended "treatment" by the unseen hands intervened.

It would of course be interesting to hear a sound explanation of why the "climatic sickness" did not re-appear simultaneously with Napoleon's new physician-in-ordinary. It is quite obvious that there had to be a physician present for the final stage of Napoleon's liquidation. Actually, O'Meara was not in any way suitable for the last phase, because he held such a skeptical opinion of Montholon. But now another physician as required having arrived at Longwood, Napoleon's health was improving.

Possibly the heads of the royal French security service had begun to doubt the wisdom of disposing of Napoleon too soon. Napoleon might be more dangerous dead than alive.

Perhaps Napoleon's system had become tolerant to the strongest dose of poison prescribed by the security service, and he was recovering in spite of it? Surmise, just surmise.

In any case, the patient's health continued to improve even after the arrival of this new physician-in-ordinary.

Napoleon's work in the garden was mostly to consist of directing the operations, but even so he got a certain amount of exercise, for he had to be everywhere. An entirely new garden was laid out. Here he did, at times, work along with the rest.[5]

Napoleon's increasing energy was also evident from the fact that he took up hunting once more. He did not actually seek out his quarry, but if it happened to be in the neighborhood he was quick on the mark.

When the governor was told of the work on the gardens at Longwood, he put four Chinese laborers at Napoleon's disposal and offered to provide all requisites. Here was activity suitable to a benign climate. Besides, an Emperor interested in seeing how the garden grew would be easier seen for reporting purposes.

Montholon remained faithfully at Napoleon's side. He was convalescing after rheumatic fever and had been bedridden for a very long time. That, too, might have had a good deal to do with the improvement in Napoleon's health, and it could certainly have attracted dangerous suspicions if the climatic sickness had come on again just as soon as Montholon was able to rise from his sickbed.

Everyone at Longwood had to go out and dig except the chef. Work began at daybreak. Napoleon went around in the nankin coat and wide trousers made of the same material. He wore red slippers as usual. On his head he wore a huge straw hat as protection against the sun. So that the English assigned to confirm his physical presence would not easily recognize him, his valets, Noverraz and Saint-Denis, were attired in the same way. It was part of the minor mischief in which the Emperor indulged his desire to tease and frustrate his watchful guardians.

By ten o'clock the heat was too great and lunch was served in the shade of a Seville orange hedge. It consisted of soup, a vegetable and some meat, with coffee. The meat course was generally fowl, roast mutton or grilled spare ribs of mutton.[7]

Napoleon ate with a good appetite and was in excellent spirits. Over the coffee he would entertain his guests, Bertrand and Montholon, by telling stories of his eventful life. Sometimes Antommarchi was also invited, and sometimes one of the priests. It was a pleasure to hear Napoleon talk, wrote Marchand. He never had to search for words; they poured forth as water from an unfailing spring.[6]

His appetite, the composition of his meals and much else speak for themselves; there was nothing seriously wrong with Napoleon's health at the time work on the garden was going on.

References

1. Las Cases II:791
2. Marchand II:234
3. Bertrand II:395-97

4. Antommarchi 2, page 59
5. Forsyth III:210
6. Marchand II:247

37

Once More to Horse

CONSTRUCTION OF THE gardens proceeded for the greater part of 1820. Napoleon's strength of body and spirit increased.

By May he was so far recovered that he started in secret going for short rides on horseback. For these, it had been possible to get hold of an especially suitable mount, a pony once the property of Lord Charles Somerset's daughter.

The peer was governor of the Cape and had visited Longwood in January 1820, but had not met Napoleon. He had tried to, but when the Emperor had caught sight of him on horseback together with the governor and his staff, he had retired indoors.[1] It was not advisable for others to see how well he was in St. Helena's murderous climate.

To start with, Napoleon rode in what was known as the wood, where the trees were very sparse. As his only companion he took with him Archambault, the groom. They set out at six in the morning and stayed out for a couple of hours.

Antommarchi had been very keen on urging Napoleon to ride. As far back as October 1819, he had told Governor Lowe how important it was that Napoleon should go riding every day, and the governor had quite agreed. Apart from any benefits the exercise would contribute to his royal charge's health it should make easier a regular confirmation of his charge's continued presence on the island.

But Napoleon then had refused to go riding. It was because the governor had posted sentries around the place, said Antommarchi. This was what Antommarchi had heard at Longwood, although the governor had long since removed the obstacles that those at Longwood maintained existed to Napoleon's riding excursions. Napoleon could ride wherever he liked

312

on the island, with the exception of the town and the fortifications. It was impossible to gallop there anyway for the purpose of healthful exercise.

But Napoleon did not want a British officer trailing him when he rode out. That regulation, too, was cancelled by the governor. All Sir Hudson now desired was that the escort officer should be able to note once a day that he had seen Napoleon alive and apparently in good health.

Antommarchi had obviously not been informed about all this by any of the French at Longwood. It certainly was a strange place to which the good physician had come.[2]

As a result of this conversation with Antommarchi, the governor had written to Lord Somerset and had asked him if he could procure four especially suitable mounts. Two of these should be of middling size, strong, lively and sure-footed. They had rather to be good-looking than especially thoroughbred or fast. The other two could be ordinary mounts, one of them particularly suitable for a lady. It was the gentler horse Napoleon used to ride in May 1820.[3]

It could seem now that the direction of the drama of St. Helena had slipped out of both Montholon's and Napoleon's hands and had landed in the governor's. Everything went smoothly; no more complaints were to be heard from Longwood.[4]

That the English were overjoyed at having got the situation under control is made clear in a letter that Bathurst wrote to Sir Hudson on June 2, 1820.[5]

The Secretary of State for the Colonies had been told about Napoleon's newly-awakened interest in the laying-out of the gardens. He wanted the Emperor to know therefore that the British government would be very much pleased to contribute to the realization of Napoleon's present project. The governor had been instructed to order from England, the Cape or any other British possession any trees or shrubs Napoleon might wish. Everything possible would be done to see that the plants arrived in first-class condition.

The governor was delighted, and also very much surprised. He had changed nothing important in his conduct nor in the administration of his office, but now no more complaints.[6]

It would seem that an excellent explanation for this could be that Napoleon's mental health was well on the way back to normal, now that his "climatic sickness" had released its hold on him. He had abused his constitution under the pressures of his inordinate ambitions, but those same ambitions had been born in part of innate abnormal energies. His physique was such that he should not have died at 52.

In August 1820 Napoleon's riding excursions had become more extensive and he would go for long rides with Bertrand and Montholon. Sometimes Mme. Bertrand rode with them. Napoleon's mount was saddled extravagantly in red and gold. Usually he wore a uniform but only informal garb when out riding. He kept to that area around Longwood that had been wholly reserved for him, but it was extensive enough.

However, September 18 saw a change, and Napoleon, accompanied by two grooms, ventured out of the Longwood reserve for the first time in four years, to undertake a real excursion. It lasted for two and a half hours.

The governor must have been overjoyed. He had always hoped Napoleon's life on St. Helena would with time develop into a freer pattern.

But the governor was not to rejoice over his triumph for many hours. On the evening of that same day Napoleon was laid low by a serious relapse into the familiar and nauseous climatic sickness.

His head ached terribly, he had difficulty in breathing, he suffered an icy chill in his feet and legs, a weak, rapid and irregular pulse. His illness lasted three days, after which he began to improve. There were now dark rings under his eyes, the whites were yellow and so was his skin, though his face had a greenish hue. He had completely lost his appetite, and his old torpor and somnolence had returned. All this according to Antommarchi's journals for September 18 to 21, 1820.

Antommarchi knew nothing at all about the symptoms of arsenical intoxication. He could not know that Napoleon's illness had to do with poisoning. But he noted a number of symptoms observed in his patient, and in that way managed a description that could have come straight out of a modern textbook on toxicology of the symptoms of acute arsenical intoxication, induced by a strong but not lethal dose of the poison.

There was quite a lot of talk about poisoning at Longwood, and in September 1819 the foreign commissioners and Lowe had a discussion concerning the Frenchmen's apprehensions. Montchenu was able to say, however, that he had spoken to Montholon about this danger and Montholon had replied: "We don't believe anything of the kind ourselves, but it is always a good thing to be able to say."[7]

Anyway, Montchenu managed in this way to get Lowe and the foreign commissaries to realize that Montholon for one could not imagine that Napoleon might be poisoned.

On February 13, 1820 something happened in France that was to cause royalists' hatred of everything to do with Bonaparte to flare up with renewed and violent force. On that day the Duke of Berry was murdered by a Bonapartist saddlemaker called Louvel. The Bourbon dynasty had thus been sterilized, it was thought. At the time it was not generally known that the Duchess of Berry was pregnant.

Next in succession to the throne of the weak King Louis XVIII stood his younger brother, Count d'Artois. The latter's eldest son, the Duke of Angoulême, married to Mme. la Rancune, was childless after many years of a marriage which was said to have been unconsummated.

The Duke of Berry was only forty-two years old and his wife was twenty-two.

The scapegoat for this serious crime — the worst that could be committed, since it was a crime against God's deputy, the King and his House — could be no less a person than Decazes, the President of the Council, who was accused of being a crypto Bonapartist. It was to Decazes' disadvantage that he had been advisor to Mme. Mère, the Emperor's mother, and that he had advocated a policy of moderation and good sense. Although he had been much appreciated by King Louis, he had to withdraw into the background.

The day after the murder of Berry there was considerable rioting in Paris. The noblest lifeguards rode through the city's cobblestone streets carrying Berry's bloodstained shirt as a banner and demanding Decazes' head, while former soldiers of Napoleon led counter-demonstrations, crying "Long live the

King, the King of the birds, Napoleon the Eagle."[8]

Richelieu was once more made President of the Council and Napoleon became again the spectre of French politics. Ever since the Emperor's return from Elba, the Count d'Artois had called him *Le Revenant,* the Apparition, returning to haunt the affairs of the living.

Just as he had been during the royal family's many years of exile, d'Artois was now to become the most active leader of Bourbon politics.

It was the Count d'Artois who, from exile, had organized the many open attempts at the murder of Consul Bonaparte; it was he who was behind the smuggling of trusty royalist agents into Napoleon's court and staff[9]; it was he who prompted the Count of Bourmont's coup at the battle of Waterloo; it was he who saved the Count de Montholon from a well-deserved court-martial when the latter had embezzled some military funds.[13]

During the time he was next-in-succession, Artois had his own shadow government, complete with Minister of Police, the ultra-royalistic Jules de Polignac.[10] The latter, many believed, was the natural son of Artois. If one were to refer to the portraits of those two gentlemen, the correctness of this gossip could not easily be denied.

King Louis is generally described as a pious and a good man. But he was not altogether soft and gentle. We have already heard of his grimness toward Mme. La Bédoyère. Molé, Minister of Justice under Napoleon and Minister of Naval Affairs under King Louis, tells us a story from the King's cabinet which Molé thought very unpleasant. A drunken guard had shouted *"Vive l'Empéreur!"* He was reported to the colonel. The colonel handed the poor boy over to his comrades for punishment. They beat the Bonapartist to death. King Louis would not agree to the colonel being punished. He thought it a good thing that the boy's companions had administered justice.[11] With so little pity for a poor youth, whose only crime was that, being drunk, he became loose-tongued and aggressive, it is not likely that the King would have pity on the imprisoned Napoleon.

At St. Helena, on October 4, 1820, Napoleon must have felt fairly recovered from his latest attack of endemic sickness, for on that day he once more set out on a long ride. This time he was off to Sir William Doveton's house on Mount Pleasant.

While Sir William was out taking his morning walk in the brilliant sunshine, he caught sight of an approaching party of horsemen.

The Count de Montholon separated and rode forward to ask if the Emperor could rest a while in Sir William's garden. This wish naturally was granted, but when the Englishman saw how tired Napoleon seemed, he suggested he should come inside to be more comfortable.

As Napoleon reached the steps, Bertrand extended his arm and helped him up the short flight into the drawing-room. There he sank down on a couch, grateful for the rest.

From this position he conversed with Sir William, his daughter and with his little grand-daughters whose ears, a little later, His Majesty playfully tweaked as he gave each a small piece of licorice.

In the meanwhile Montholon had borrowed a table and laid out the lunch the party had brought along. Sir William was invited to join the meal. Lunch consisted of a cold pie, potted meat, cold turkey, curried fowl, ham, a salad, dates, almonds, oranges and coffee. Napoleon drank Sir William's health in a small glass of champagne. There were no grilled spareribs this time.[12]

After the meal Napoleon, as was his custom, wanted to know about the drinking habits of the family. He never ceased to be amazed at English drinking.

"How often do you get drunk, Sir William?"

Sir William admitted only that he drank an occasional glass of wine. Napoleon then asked Sir William's daughter how often her husband got drunk. Once a week, perhaps?

"No," she replied.

"Once a fortnight?"

"No, Sire."

"Once a month?"

"No, Sire, it is some years since I saw him so." Napoleon's only reply was "Bah!" By which he meant "Rubbish!" Then he changed the conversation. These were obviously no genuine Britishers.

He rose, took Bertrand's arm, and descended to the party's waiting mounts.

The governor was curious to hear what Sir William thought about the Emperor's health. "From every appearance but his pale color, it might be concluded that General Bonaparte was in good health. His face is astonishingly fat and his body and thighs very round and plump . . . He looked as fat and as round as a China pig," added Sir William. Indeed, obesity and good health in those days were commonly measured as coinciding qualities.

The good man must have thought that the fact that Napoleon could not walk unaided had nothing to do with his health.

With the necessary help, Napoleon mounted and rode homeward. At Hutt's Gate, a little more than a mile from Longwood, however, he was exhausted and had to go the rest of the journey by carriage.[12] This would be the last time the once tireless rider would sit a horse.

References

1. Forsyth III:209
2. Forsyth III:192-93
3. Forsyth III:194
4. Forsyth III:230
5. Forsyth III:238
6. Forsyth III:231
7. Forsyth III:187
8. Lucas-Dubreton 149
9. Boigne III:276, 277
10. Ibid II:344, 374
11. Lucas-Dubreton 142
12. Forsyth III:242-45
13. Masson I, p. 123

38

Montholon Writes Prophetically

N<small>APOLEON</small>'S ATTACK ON September 18, 1820 was the beginning of a long illness which would cruelly and inexorably deprive him of strength and of his will to live.

Time after time, for more than seven months, he was to endure days of severe and acute illness, when he must have suffered agonizingly. On those especially painful days he displayed symptoms of typical arsenical intoxication of an acute nature: palpitations of the heart, a weak and irregular pulse, very severe headache, an icy chill in his legs extending right up to his hips, pain in the shoulders and back, pain in the liver, a persistent dry cough, loosening teeth, a coated tongue, severe thirst, skin rash and pain in the legs, a yellow skin, yellowed whites of the eyes, shivering, deafness, sensitivity of the eyes to light, spasmodic muscle contractions, difficulty in breathing and nausea — they were all there, today's accepted, recognizable symptoms of arsenical poisoning. But still it was the damnable climate of the island — a place British seamen were sent to regain health from sieges of illness — that was blamed for the Emperor's decline.

In between these periods of acute illness, Napoleon was by no means well, though he suffered less and could carry on something of a conversation and take short rides in his carriage. He ate, but with little appetite.

From time to time he vomited and suffered diarrhoea, followed by periods of stubborn constipation.

Napoleon was once more to experience distressing difficulty in urinating, which had troubled him on previous occasions of ill health and had partly incapacitated him at Borodino and Waterloo.

While Napoleon's appetite decreased, his girth expanded. During O'Meara's time his body was described as smooth as that of a child[1]. Not even this typical and depressing symptom of a long drawn-out intoxication by arsenic was to be spared the unfortunate Emperor during this new phase of his illness. Henry, the young and obviously not over-endowed English doctor who was present at the post-mortem, was to consider this symptom as one of his postulated indications that Napoleon had led a chaste life.[2]

Information as to the symptoms shown during Napoleon's last long illness exists today in Dr. Antommarchi's journals, in Dr. Arnott's accounts and reports to the governor, in Bertrand's diaries and in Marchand's memoirs. All these eyewitness accounts of Napoleon's condition essentially agree. At the post-mortem a number of discoveries were made which further confirm the accuracy of these accounts.

But one witness, Montholon, in his "memoirs", gave testimony that was absolutely contrary to the others. His seemed a different viewpoint from which to observe the tragedy. Not surprisingly, his accounts will be found to differ remarkably from others that have come to posterity.

Montholon through his stories managed to create such a confusion of reports around the drama of St. Helena that the most extraordinary diagnoses of Napoleon's illness found their way into many of the innumerable works published on Napoleon's captivity and death. Gastric ulcer, rheumatism, tuberculosis, malaria, Maltese fever, gout, gonorrhea, syphilis, *Dystrophia adiposo genitalis* (an illness causing eunuckoidism), epilepsy, appendicitis, cancer, scurvy, dysentery — these are some of the diseases the doctors concerned have advanced in their writings as the cause of the Emperor's protracted and disabling illness.

One day in November of 1820, on his way to Longwood, the governor unexpectedly encountered Napoleon. The latter came from the opposite direction, riding in his carriage, which was drawn by four horses. With him were Bertrand and Montholon.

When the equipage caught sight of the governor, it swung away along another road. Nevertheless, the governor managed to get what he felt was quite a good look at Napoleon. As the

governor recorded what he saw, the Emperor wore a round hat
and a green overcoat, buttoned high at the neck. He was paler
than when Lowe had last seen him, but the governor thought he
had not lost weight. He also thought that Napoleon appeared to
have a "looseness of fibre" and seemed incapable of any effort.
He had a pale and colorless look.[3]

During O'Meara's time Napoleon, when ill, would withdraw
from the outside world. But now he would ride out. He may no
longer have wished to play games with his guardians and was
resigned to his fate.

When Marchand came into Napoleon's bedchamber on New
Year's Day, 1821, and opened the shutters, he was greeted by
Napoleon from his bed:

"*Eh bien, mon fils,* what are you going to give me for the New
Year?"

"My hopes, Sire, that your Majesty will soon get well and leave
this climate, which is so injurious to your Majesty's health."

"It will not be long now, my boy. The end is near. I cannot last
much longer."

"Oh, but your Majesty, that was not what I meant."

"It will be as Heaven wishes," said Napoleon, and got painfully
out of bed.[4]

As a matter of fact there is another witness who upholds the
statements made by Dr. Antommarchi and other witnesses, and
who completely repudiates Montholon's version in his memoirs.
The name of this witness is Charles Tristan de Montholon and
his testimony was in the privacy of letters to his wife. He did not
expect that they would become a legacy to history, although it is
likely that he wrote them knowing they would be opened and
read — and interpreted — by others than Albine.

We have already shown that Montholon was often unreliable
when speaking of what was or had been happening but, on the
other hand, could be fearfully accurate about what was going to
happen.

What he wrote to his wife was extraordinarily prophetic of
what the other witnesses would observe as happening a few
months later.

In a letter to his wife dated December 5, 1820, Montholon
wrote, among other things: "The Emperor's illness has taken a

turn for the worse. To his chronic ill-health has now been added *une maladie de langueur*, a wasting illness, which is very characteristic; he is so weak that he can no longer perform any vital function without feeling extremely tired and often losing consciousness. His stomach has been unable to retain anything for several days . . . he is constantly lethargic. He has had three vesicatories applied and the flesh beneath the last one was pale and lifeless *(cadavéreuse)*. His pulse can hardly be felt. His feet and legs are constantly wrapped in flannel and warm towels and are just as icily cold . . ."[9]

No other witness has stated that Napoleon's illness had thus drastically changed character in December, 1820.

But Montholon knew that Napoleon had contracted *une maladie de langueur*. If instead of *maladie de langueur* the synonymous expression *maladie de cachexie* is used[5], the inference to be conveyed may be clearer. The word cachexy suggests in the first place cancer. It was cancer Montholon meant, for in the official royal French communiqué on Napoleon's death, it was stated that Bonaparte had died of *une maladie de langueur*.

Montchenu, however, who was certainly as aware of Napoleon's real illness as was Montholon, said on the day of Napoleon's death in the following May: "Of five doctors there is not one who knows what he died of."[6] But Montholon knew — *five months previously*.

Montholon also knew in December, 1820, that Napoleon would reach a state in which he vomited constantly. But the records show it would not be until the end of March that this was noticed by Dr. Antommarchi and the other credible witnesses.

Still more significantly, according to Montholon's letter, too, a vesicatory was applied to Napoleon in December, 1820, which did not act normally and which caused the tissue beneath to become necrosed (dead). It was not until April 30, 1821, that Bertrand saw the results of vesicatories so strange that they did not cause the usual blistering, but turned the flesh beneath cadaveric. Bertrand notes three vesicatories on April 30, 1821. One of them had altered the flesh beneath to a deathly white.[8]

So Montholon knew on December 5, 1820, with amazing exactness what treatment Napoleon was to undergo four to five months later!

How are vesicatories made to cause necrosis? That was something that was already known in olden days. Caligula is said to have murdered a rival in just such a way.[13] Arsenic trioxide is mixed with the substance of the vesicatory. It is as simple as that.[7]

In the same famous and highly significant letter, Montholon hinted at the fact that Napoleon had not more than five or six months to live.

Montholon wrote several such mysterious letters to his wife.[9] He mentioned, for example, that he was acting as the Emperor's night nurse nearly three months before he began such duties. In a roundabout way he said, five months before Napoleon's last will was signed, on December 20, 1820, that he would receive two million francs as a gift from Napoleon. (He was right.)

On February 28, 1820, he wrote that Napoleon's work on the garden would soon finish, seven months before this actually occurred. In the same letter he mentioned mysteriously that the rains that would come would affect the properties of calomel adversely. Insofar as we know, Napoleon was given calomel only twice, the second occasion being on May 3, 1821. Calomel together with the slightest humidity causes severe colic, wrote Montholon in that letter.

Modern knowledge allows us to be somewhat startled by this first intimation of the fateful part that calomel would have in the death of Napoleon. We can suppose that Montholon had calomel, its properties and its functions very much on his mind at that time. Why else would he describe the peculiar properties of moistened calomel to his distant spouse?

These letters could suggest that the Countess de Montholon was aware of the plot to murder and was an accomplice in the act. Such a conclusion, going as it does against so much else that is known, would be rather too hasty. Even were the letters addressed to Montholon's wife, they almost surely were meant for other and more perceptive eyes. Her mail was certainly watched and censored before she herself opened it. It is also very probable that she allowed her father-in-law, the Marquis de Sémonville, to read the letters of his beloved adopted son. Sémonville, it must be recalled, was a favorite of the Count d'Artois. The latter thus, with apparent innocence, could be informed about Napoleon's illness. It was information that could be used officially for certain measurements and actions. As, for instance, the ordering and dispatch of Napoleon's leaden coffin, which was actually ready and waiting on the spot when Napoleon died — a made-to-measure product of remarkable properties.

The valet Saint-Denis describes an occasion when Napoleon seems to have been given rather too strong a potion.

It was about two months before Napoleon's death, at the beginning of March, 1821. Napoleon and Montholon were sitting in conversation in the parlor, when the Emperor rang and asked for his dinner to be served. It arrived very shortly thereafter. Pierron served the meal, assisted by Saint-Denis.

Napoleon had scarcely finished his vermicelli soup when suddenly he felt extremely sick, and threw up all he had eaten. After a time he took another plate of soup, which he kept down together with the rest of the meal. Saint-Denis says nothing to indicate that Montholon, dining with Napoleon, suffered any ill-effects from the soup.

On the next day, at the same time, exactly the same thing occurred. Saint-Denis wondered what it could have been in Napoleon's stomach that would cause the first plate of soup to be brought up each time but not the second.[10]

A reasonable explanation might be that just before his meal Napoleon had been given a dose of poison, perhaps in a pre-meal glass of watered wine, which was then so activated by the hot soup that it produced the effects of a stronger dose, setting off reflexes that caused vomiting. After that the amount of poison in the stomach was so reduced that vomiting no longer occurred with the second plate.

The periods of severe and acute sickness in 1821 occurred at monthly intervals, precisely as Montholon had said they would when he negotiated with Stokoe about the latter's appointment as Napoleon's physician-in-ordinary.[11]

A good idea of the fluctuations in Napoleon's health on St. Helena can be got by studying the portraits that were made of him there. During the years 1816 and 1817 he so degenerated in appearance that finally he resembled a total inebriate, in spite of the fact that he was very moderate in his consumption of wine and never took distilled spirits. After Napoleon had been working for a time in the garden, he looked like any other healthy fifty-year-old. He was certainly rather stout even then, but his general carriage spoke of well-being and good health.

According to the testimony of his own strands of hair, Napoleon was poisoned on about forty occasions during the severe illness which began on September 28, 1820 and lasted until he died.[12] Antommarchi's journals record that Napoleon had twenty-nine especially severe relapses from the end of September 1820, to the middle of March 1821, between which he made some degree of recovery. His naturally strong Corsican constitution struggled in his behalf.

On the days when Napoleon felt better, he went for short drives in his carriage. The English noticed then that he had to be helped up into the calash and was assisted down on his return.

References

1. Marchand II:210
2. Dr. Henry's post-mortem report, Lowe's Papers
3. Forsyth III:248
4. Marchand II:282
5. Larousse médical ill., column 662
6. Masson (2) II:110
7. Marchand II:290
8. Bertrand III:182
9. Gonnard 1 p. 63
10. Saint-Denis 262-63
11. Forsyth III:107-9
12. Forshufvud, Smith, Wassén 218
13. Douris 151
14. Antommarchi 1, I:407

39

Montholon Impugns Other Witnesses

THE GOVERNOR WAS now fully aware that Napoleon was ill enough for first naval doctor Shortt and Dr. Arnott to be called for consultation, in line with his official instructions.

Napoleon, unable to conceive of the governor's offer of medical help as being prompted by consideration and goodwill, feared it was a plot. Montholon's plan for keeping unnecessary witnesses out of the way was working to perfection. It was still not time for the English doctors to appear on the scene.

From Montholon's point of view Antommarchi was certainly not the right doctor for Napoleon. The doctor was no orthodox physician; he shared Napoleon's skepticism about the advisability of disturbing, by the administration of some chemical, an organism fighting for its existence. It is significant that, after the St. Helena period, Antommarchi would retire to Cuba — as a homeopath.

In his memoirs Montholon describes Antommarchi as an imbecile.

On January 27, 1821, Montholon called on the governor and told him about his concern for Napoleon's illness and its right treatment. Vignali, the physician-priest sent by Cardinal Fesch, could neither read nor write, Montholon testified. And as for Antommarchi! He may have been a good anatomist and a good doctor, too, but all the same he was proving quite useless. What was worse, Napoleon had of late found him quite disagreeable (supposedly as much so as Gourgaud had become before he had been released from service).[1]

Not only was Antommarchi ignorant; he put on airs and thought himself as important as if he were in charge of the island. (Montholon knew the governor's weakness.)

And now Montholon suggested that the governor should find another doctor for Napoleon, but not one under the command of the British government or the Bonaparte family. The French government should be approached. Paris had the very best physicians. This time Napoleon's family ought not to be mixed up in it. "Bonaparte" had definitely said this, went on Montholon.[2]

In this representation to Sir Hudson we must try to understand anxious Montholon and his set objectives. Appointment to St. Helena of a reliable French royalist physician would have been an enormous relief to Montholon. Such a man could arrive at the end of April.

The governor, however, was not convinced of the advisability of getting a doctor from Paris for Napoleon. He himself trusted Antommarchi and he had often given proof of this.

Otherwise Montholon was right when he said that Napoleon had seemed dissatisfied with Antommarchi on several occasions. Not because he considered him a bad physician, but because he was never there when most needed. That, indeed, was true. Antommarchi was often called away on different errands, just when Napoleon needed him at his side. It is very possible, indeed certain, that someone unidentified sent Antommarchi on those errands, someone having a quite remarkable ability to foresee when Napoleon would suffer his attacks. Someone with the typical qualities of a security agent, skilled in planting seeds of doubt that would yield a harvest of favorable decisions.

Apart from Antommarchi, there were now only two witnesses left at Longwood with the right to enter the apartments of the Emperor — Bertrand and Marchand.

At the beginning of 1821 there developed a serious rift between Napoleon and the Bertrands. The reason was said to have been that Madame Bertrand had now expressed a definite desire to be allowed to return home. She had been and was still very ill, and as usual she feared a miscarriage. She had already had many, though previously she had borne her children without difficulty. Indeed, she would again do so as soon as she got away from the abortive climate of Longwood. Her many days of illness prevented her from attending upon Napoleon to the extent that he wished.

Napoleon was very angry with Mme. Bertrand for wanting to leave St. Helena. He had not been angry with Albine Montholon. She was even paid to go away. She had had only one miscarriage, at a time when it would remove her reluctance to leave. Previously she had quite escaped the climatic sickness. *Quod licet Iovi, non licet bovi* may be applied once more; what the light-footed Mme. Montholon could do, *Mme. la Maréchale* could not.

There were further reasons for displeasure with Mme. Bertrand. On January 29, for instance, Mme. Bertrand had accused Montholon of no longer coming to see her. Napoleon spoke to Bertrand about this.

"You probably imagine that Mme. Dillon (Fanny Bertrand's mother) was a respectable woman," he suddenly said to Bertrand.

"Why, yes, like anybody else," replied Bertrand courteously.

"Do you really know what sort of a person Mme. Dillon was? When she was no more than fifteen years old, she was the mistress of the Prince of Guéméné."

"It is true, Sire, that it was Mme. Dillon, but your memory is at fault, Sire. It was General Dillon's first wife, whose name was Rothe and who was the mother of Mme. de la Tour du Pin."

"You are wrong. The Empress Josephine told me."

"In that case, Sire, she mixed up the two Mesdames Dillon."

"*Eh bien,* it must have been Montchenu who told Montholon," said Napoleon.[3] And so he revealed how Montholon had managed to start something designed to estrange Mme. Bertrand and Napoleon and in so doing perhaps eliminate the Grand Marshal himself.

On January 31, Antommarchi went to the Grand Marshal for advice. Napoleon had summoned Antommarchi at 1 o'clock in the night and told him that he no longer required him as his physician. He could remain as surgeon, but Napoleon had written to ask for another physician. The Emperor had added that he had actually nothing to complain of in the way Antommarchi had carried out his duties. But he was displeased with his behavior. The doctor was advised that he should see Montholon a little more often and try to get on well with him, wait on him, make a fuss over him.

Antommarchi's speech was coarse. He should learn to speak more courteously[4] and to use the phrase *Monsieur le Comte* liberally when he addressed de Montholon.[12]

Poor *Mme. la Maréchale!* Once more, in February, the fourth or fifth miscarriage in four years!

Apart from her miscarriages, Fanny Bertrand showed many other signs of the dreaded climatic sickness of Longwood. She vomited, vomited and vomited again. One cannot help wondering if she had not been put under medical supervision and found ready for antimony, naturally with the help of an adjusted prescribed dose. To poison with antimony, a doctor must be available. Tartar emetic has a recognizable taste which would act as a warning, unless the recipient was made to understand that it was medicine she was being given. Medicine also tasted nasty, but medicine could never be dangerous. Everyone knew that one should be careful with food and drink that tasted bad. And everyone knew, too, that medicine that did not taste nasty was of little benefit.

The governor was truly worried. It now appeared that it could not have been O'Meara's remedies, after all, that had caused Napoleon's 1816-1818 illness, for he was now quite sure that Napoleon took no remedies. It was Montholon himself who had said O'Meara had stuffed Napoleon full of mercury. It was a pity Sir Hudson's social position did not allow him to cross the gap and talk directly with Marchand. Because then he would have learned what really had happened with Napoleon's medicines. "Everything the doctor has prescribed for internal use we shall throw in the fire," Napoleon had said to Marchand.[5]

The people at Longwood complained about the house. But that was something that would soon be put right. The governor called on Montholon and asked him to suggest a lay-out for the plantations around the new palace. Where did he wish the stables to be? He need only say the word and it should be as he wished.[6]

Well, of course, the iron railings that had been put 'round the house would have to be removed, explained Montholon. Those "iron railings" referred to a magnificent fence, such as was always to be found around a gentleman's house and garden. No, that fence had to be taken down or else it had to be moved much farther away. Otherwise Napoleon would think he was caged in. It was a costly fence, ordered especially to a certain length. It could not be increased without great loss of time.

However, the governor admitted that there was something to be said for Montholon's point of view, and promised to consider the matter.

Some time later, when discussions about the new house were re-opened, Montholon told the governor that he thought that there should be a trellis in front of the house. Why, yes, that should be easy to arrange. And the fence must be taken down. That would not be difficult either. Oh, and the whole lawn must be re-made, in order to slope more gradually.[7]

The governor gently pointed out that to re-level the lawn would mean an enormous amount of work. He would have been pleased to consider such a wish while work on the terracing was going on. He pointed out that he had sent plans of the lay-out before work had begun on the terracing. It was a pity that any criticism had not been forthcoming then. Nevertheless, he would consider the matter and see what could be done.

But, continued the governor, why couldn't Napoleon in the meanwhile move in? It was so much better than the old house; more space, airier and with plenty of rooms. Absolutely free from damp, which had been complained of in the old house.[8]

No, explained Montholon, that was not at all possible. Napoleon had been in bed and suffering a high temperature for the past two days.

The governor was concerned and asked Montholon what he thought about the Emperor's illness.

As usual, Montholon was ready with an explanation. Napoleon himself thought his illness was caused by the medicine that Antommarchi had given him.

It is uncanny to perceive that everything in the drama of St. Helena seemed to proceed on a set plan, precisely as though instructions had been issued from a central headquarters to those concerned on the spot.

The previous illness, from 1816-1818, was caused by O'Meara's medication. O'Meara had been sent away. The illness that began in the autumn of 1820 was due to Antommarchi's medication. Such talk might seem to Paris cunning and effective, but on St. Helena it was obviously not wise. Sooner or later the English there must learn that Napoleon always had refused to take any medicine. So medicine was not the trouble, nor could the doctor then be blamed for the evil effect on Napoleon of prescriptions he never swallowed. Yet, persistently, Montholon wanted it believed that it was the doctor's remedies that had made Napoleon ill. On the other hand Marchand, who seldom left his master's side when the latter was sick, thought Napoleon was ill because he refused to take any remedies.[5]

Once or twice Napoleon was persuaded to take some "new medicine". He was very much afraid of the old, well-known medicines. And so, for a couple of weeks in January, he did actually take an infusion of cinchona.[9] During this time Napoleon's health improved, probably in spite of rather than due to the cinchona, and he managed to keep in comparatively good health for nine days after he had finished taking the quinine.

The governor was interested to hear what Napoleon, according to Montholon, thought had caused his illness. He was equally anxious to hear what the doctor thought.

To this, too, Montholon had his reply ready. Dr. Antommarchi thought that Bonaparte's chief trouble was in his digestive organs and his heart. His stomach was not in a condition to digest his food properly and his heart did not keep the blood circulating at the right rate. This latest defect was, however, nothing new for Napoleon, Montholon assured the governor. Napoleon had always had bad circulation and everyone near him knew this, explained Montholon.[10]

Indeed, this congenital weakness had already been observed by Corvisart, Napoleon's physician-in-ordinary, when Bonaparte was only a young general, went on *il bugiardo*. Corvisart had warned Bonaparte against sitting still, for he would then become horribly fat, as his blood would not circulate as it ought to.

Napoleon had started to put on weight rapidly as First Consul and especially as Emperor. Now his blood flowed so slowly that you could hardly notice it, even in the arteries. It was because of this that his legs were icy cold. Antommarchi had discovered a remedy for this, but after a couple of days the icy chill returned. This sluggish circulation would explain why Napoleon was so calm. Lately he had suffered from such indifference and apathy that he did not even read the newspapers. He had also quite forgotten what had happened during the last twelve months.[10] All this was presented as gospel, according to Montholon.

A little earlier in the same conversation, Montholon had complained that Napoleon was a truly bad patient; he absolutely refused to take any remedies.[11] The hard-pressed Montholon found it difficult to be consistent when repeating what he had been told to say. At times the truth spilled out, by inadvertence. In one and the same conversation he blames Napoleon's illness on the doctors' remedies and complains that Napoleon refuses to take any remedies at all.

Montholon's account of Napoleon's defective circulation had certainly been prepared long before ever Montholon was to use it. It was just another indication that events at St. Helena were being directed from Paris and that the prompters included some able and experienced doctor.

References

1. Forsyth III:253-5
2. Ibid III:256
3. Bertrand III:54
4. Ibid III:54, 55
5. Marchand II:195, 196
6. Bertrand III:61
7. Forsyth III:263
8. Ibid III:265-66
9. Bertrand III:32, 40
10. Forsyth III:267, 268
11. Ibid III:266
12. Marchand II:301

40

Time for Antimony: Montholon Plays Nurse

IT TOOK MME. DE BRINVILLIERS eight months to poison her father to death. By the middle of March 1821 the last phase of Napoleon's intoxication with arsenic had lasted for nearly six months. If the Marquise of Brinvilliers' plan was to be followed, it would soon be time to pass on to the next poison, antimony, but rather cautiously.

There was so much to be arranged before it was time for the calomel and the dangerous "humidity" that Montholon had referred to in one of his letters. The Will, for instance!

Mme. de Brinvilliers had managed to get her father to re-write his will in her favor and at the expense of her brothers' and sisters' interests. How had she done this? Why, she herself arranged to nurse her father, look after him and minister to him so tenderly as he lay on his bed of pain, that he could not know how to thank her enough. And then it occurred to him that he could re-make his will.

When the will had been drawn up, that was the end of the honored and distinguished Monsieur Dreux d'Aubray. All his glory of prestigious appointments vanished as his pretty daughter handed him a goblet of emetic wine, which is to say, wine mixed with tartar emetic. A week later he died.[1]

Of course it was a physician who had ordained the drink; and naturally the marquise had suitably increased the proportion of tartar emetic.

At the beginning of March, 1821 Napoleon started recovering fairly rapidly from his last acute sickness of late February. On March 10 he felt so much better that he was tempted to go out riding. Nothing came of it and he only went out in his carriage, but it was pleasant all the same.

On the next day he talked for a long time with Bertrand and Antommarchi and was obviously in good spirits, for he explained to Bertrand that he no longer thought that the English intended to get rid of him. They were going to see to it that he was removed to England and placed somewhere in a beautiful park.[2] The period of euphoria was unusual.

And then came March 17. Montholon had been told by Napoleon to see to arrangements allowing him to go out every day in his carriage. That morning, just as on those days immediately preceding, Montholon came to fetch Napoleon for his outing.

The Emperor did not feel especially like getting up, but when Montholon told him that the carriage was waiting outside and that it was a lovely day with no wind, Napoleon rapidly ate a light breakfast of some meat in aspic and allowed himself to be dressed in his long pantaloons, green frock-coat, red slippers and the round hat with the enormous brim that shaded his now sensitive skin from the burning sun. Thus dressed, he went out to the carriage, leaning on Montholon's arm.

Just as he was climbing in the carriage, he was suddenly seized with shivering and icy chill and had immediately to be helped into the house and to bed.[3]

Contrary to his usual practice, Marchand made notation of what Napoleon had eaten: meat in aspic, or perhaps he meant jellied consommé. He wrote it down — as a reminder.

Learning of shivering and icy chill, one wonders if this was not symptomatic of one more in the series of arsenical poisonings determined by hair analyses to have occurred in Napoleon's last year on St. Helena. The meat jelly certainly could have been treated to produce the sudden severe illness. Anything can be poisoned with arsenic trioxide, which is tasteless and odorless. A first-rate poison!

His valets covered Napoleon with an extra blanket and heated towels, which they wrapped around his legs. The chill had spread right up to his abdomen, so they fought it with hot towels there, too.

After a while the ailing monarch broke into a heavy sweat. (This is the way the system normally should react, trying to cleanse the blood of poison.) He began to feel better towards afternoon, but in the evening he again had a similar though less severe attack.

When that attack came on, Antommarchi was not at Longwood. He had been asked to accompany to Jamestown Buonavita, who was leaving the island. Buonavita was old and frail. Surely it would not be right to let him go down to the town by himself! Antommarchi, suspecting nothing, declared himself willing to go with the old priest. Napoleon felt better at the time Antommarchi and Buonavita set off.

However, Napoleon was very upset that his doctor was not there when he had his second attack of the day. Later he angrily refused to see Antommarchi. It was obvious, as Montholon had explained to the governor, that Antommarchi was never around when Napoleon was ill. But Montholon was.[3]

The next morning Napoleon arose at nine and had breakfast. The Grand Marshal had called to hear how His Majesty was, but he was not received. Instead Napoleon summoned Montholon. On that day, too, Marchand noted what Napoleon had for breakfast. Presumably as a reminder. A biscuit and a small glass of malaga wine.

After breakfast Napoleon was helped out into the garden and sat down on a bench. There he was seized by the same sort of sickness as on the previous day, but fortunately felt relief when he had brought up his breakfast. His features were much distorted, noted Marchand. Hot towels!

The doctor was there and prescribed a remedy, but Napoleon would hear of no such thing.[4] On the next day, nearly the same thing happened. The doctor was clearly present at Longwood when the attack came in the morning. Later Montholon came and kept Napoleon company. Either he or Napoleon had realized that the doctor ought to be consulted once more, but then of course he was not there. We might venture to guess that someone had suggested he attend to Mme. Bertrand. If she were not sick that day, she might be. She used to be ill at any time. Dare we guess who had caused the doctor to be away just when his master was about to need him most urgently?

On the morning of March 20 Napoleon had been helped out into the garden. While there he caught sight of a peach, which seemed to him to be ripe. It was not, but with plenty of sugar it was edible. Shortly afterwards Napoleon vomited. The peach was innocent, but what about the sugar? Marchand also noted this down. As a reminder.

These constant attacks, morning after morning, looked bad. Madame Bertrand was really worried. She questioned the doctor, who likewise was troubled. Gastritis, perhaps an inflammation in the gastric mucous membrane, he suspected had developed.

Now the generals Bertrand and Montholon conferred with the doctor. It is at this "council of war" that the word *émétique*, tartar emetic, an antimonial salt, is mentioned for the first time in the history of Napoleon's illness.

Émétique? Impossible! That could never be suggested to Napoleon; after all, it was one of those remedies Napoleon had wanted to ban from use when he had held the power of Emperor of France and King of Italy.

However, the next day a solution had been found — a drink; one in which had been added a very slight amount of tartar emetic.

Only the previous day Napoleon had expressly forbidden Antommarchi to suggest any medicine.

"Keep your remedies, I don't want two illnesses — the one that ails me and the one that you will give me," he growled.

Montholon was right; Napoleon was impossible as a patient. And time was getting on.

On March 21, however, as a result of the decision reached at the "council of war", Antommarchi dared to recommend to Napoleon a slightly emetic drink.

"What! An emetic drink? Isn't that medicine?" Napoleon asked.[5]

Someone must have convinced him it was not, for Napoleon then actually agreed to try this remedy.

And now what sort of beverage should be chosen? An emetic wine, like that chosen by the Marquise de Brinvilliers? It was decided to serve the prescribed remedy as an emetic lemonade.

Next day, March 22, prior to being medicated, Napoleon felt a little better. His pulse was more regular and he was able to shave himself. But he was still troubled with difficulty in breathing.

At 11:30 a.m. he was given his emetic drink. It was served in two doses. The effect was violent, wrote Marchand.[6] Napoleon was seized with violent vomiting but brought up nothing but mucus. Towards afternoon he became calmer and fell asleep in his chair. He wanted to be in the dark. His optic nerves obviously were so affected that he could not bear light.

We might well wonder what dose he was given since the results were so dramatic. Just an eightieth part of a gram, according to its prescriber, Dr. Antommarchi.[7] Let him believe this who can. Without the slightest doubt Napoleon had been given — unknown to Antommarchi — a very much stronger dose, as the described reaction indicates.

Antommarchi was puzzled. He could not blame the attack of the previous day on the very weak dose of tartar emetic prescribed; it must, of course, have been Napoleon's illness which had persisted in spite of the physician's remedy. So he urged Napoleon once more on March 23 to drink an emetic lemonade. Surprisingly, Napoleon must have been persuaded that the doctor's reasoning was wise and sensible. He agreed and tried the magic potion once again — with the same result. During the night Napoleon suffered a series of violent sweats. His flannel shirt repeatedly was changed.

The next morning he asked Marchand to bring him a small bottle and some licorice water, flavored with aniseed. He poured a little of the licorice water into the bottle and asked Marchand to fill it up with water.

"This drink," said Napoleon, "is the only one you may serve me in future. You must never give me anything to drink that I have not agreed to beforehand."[6]

By this injunction Napoleon ought to have managed to escape the antimony phase of his liquidation, which had become impossible to fulfil along the lines already hinted at by Montholon in his letter to Albine of last December. Undoubtedly Montholon was finding it hard. Napoleon was impossible as a patient. At least, he was so long as he had that "physician".

Then something happened which was on the face of it quite inexplicable. Noverraz, the strongest of all at Longwood, healthy, young, full of life, became the next victim of the climatic sickness. And this occurred on March 24, the very day Marchand suffered a relapse, albeit less serious, of his climatic sickness. Just as Cipriani and Marchand had done, Noverraz fell sick very suddenly and violently while going about his duties. A liver crisis, said the doctor. An extremely violent liver crisis, he added. Noverraz was *hors de combat* for the next six weeks.

Who, now, was there remaining who could step in and take over the Noverraz duties as night nurse?

Obviously there were several to choose from. First of all, the third valet, Saint-Denis. Then there were Pierron, Coursot and Archambault. The duty fell to none of these. Instead Count de Montholon himself volunteered to nurse Napoleon. What loyalty! What solicitude!

Napoleon was extremely touched. One might have thought, however, that Montholon would have given proof of even greater loyalty and solicitude had he instead allowed one of the staff, experienced and trained in domestic duties, to take on the responsible task of nurse to the Emperor precariously balanced between life and death.

When Bertrand heard of Montholon's grandiose gesture, he was unwilling to be outdone and suggested to Napoleon that both his officers should nurse him. Napoleon refused. However, during the day Bertrand would be allowed to relieve Marchand for an hour or two, so that the latter could get something to eat.[8]

But Napoleon's health did not improve, in spite of the attentions of the new nurse, who was on duty from nine in the evening until two in the morning. Antommarchi was worried. He really believed that a course of tartar emetic would break the back of the illness and suggested to Marchand that they continue giving that same emetic drink in spite of what Napoleon said. Marchand refused to co-operate.[8]

On March 27 Bertrand came in on his usual morning visit and was received kindly.

"Eh bien, Monsieur le Grand Maréchal, how do you feel?"

"Perfectly well, Sire. I could wish it were the same for Your Majesty. How are you finding your tartar emetic drinks? Are they doing you any good?"

The effect was explosive. Napoleon rang for Marchand.

"Since when, Monsieur, have you taken the liberty of poisoning me by putting emetic drinks on my bedside table? Haven't I told you that you are not to give me anything I have not previously approved? Haven't I forbidden this? Is this the way you repay my confidence? You knew all about it! Get out of here!"

Marchand protested that he was absolutely innocent and told of his conversation the previous day with Antommarchi, but added that he believed the latter innocent as well. *"L'affaire se sera passé à l'office* — This must have occurred in the pantry," explained Marchand.[10]

Napoleon's wrath turned from Marchand and he began to shower abuse instead on Antommarchi. The blame falling on him, he was therefore banished from Napoleon's apartments for two days, while Napoleon gave orders to Marchand to throw everything that stood on the bedside table out of the window.

During these days Napoleon's condition was very bad. His illness had obviously changed character and some new factor had crept in. His head ached severely, the sensation of icy chill no longer remained in his legs but had spread over his entire body. What caused Antommarchi the most anxiety was that the abdomen had become so swollen and painful when touched. The fever did not leave as previously it had done. Napoleon suffered exceedingly from thirst, which he quenched with licorice water. The patient yawned frequently and was generally restless. His pulse was irregular and he was extremely weak. From March 24 until April 4 his abdomen remained swollen and very sensitive.

There is reason for us now to suspect that this "slightly emetic" and — in the proportions prescribed by the physician — comparatively harmless lemonade, was so strongly reinforced by someone as to cause the perforation of the stomach wall later to be observed when Napoleon's autopsy was held. Antimony has the nasty property of capability to corrode the stomach wall; arsenic has not, unless taken in the form of solid arsenic trioxide.

On March 25 Antommarchi was so worried about his patient's condition that he asked Napoleon if he could call in Dr. Arnott. Yes, he could, but the Englishman was not to set foot inside the sickroom. He might want to administer poison.

Dr. Arnott gave his opinion that Napoleon's fever was not dangerous. The fevers which very occasionally cropped up on St. Helena were not at all dangerous. As Napoleon was not delirious, the fever was nothing much. This time the illness had nothing to do with Napoleon's previous liver complaint, said Dr. Arnott.[9]

Antommarchi's English colleague suggested the following treatment:

1. A large vesicatory to be applied over the whole abdomen.
2. A laxative to be given.
3. Vinegar to be sprinkled often over the patient's forehead.[10]

The governor thought that Dr. Arnott was a very good doctor. So did Montholon. Antommarchi, who had been so worried by the new turn in Napoleon's illness had taken, was a bad doctor, in Montholon's opinion.

We can, however, see that at this point Napoleon's illness had changed character. A new factor had to be accounted for. Antimony, the French *antimoine,* was an ancient and tested method for killing monks *(des moines).* Now it was being tried and found effective on someone of higher rank as well.

References

1. Gril 25
2. Bertrand III:95
3. Marchand II:284-85
4. Ibid II:286
5. Antommarchi 21st March 1821
6. Marchand II:287
7. Antommarchi 22nd March 1821
8. Marchand II:288
9. Bertrand III:105
10. Marchand II:289

41

A Sick Body but a Sound Mind

FROM WHAT HAS BEEN seen of Antommarchi as a physician, it must be conceded that he was a comparatively good one. He had managed to improve Napoleon's health very considerably during 1819 by sensibly suggesting physical labor and horseback exercise, It is true he had forfeited his credit when Napoleon again fell ill, but who could criticize him? When Napoleon's illness changed in character and serious abdominal symptoms became evident, Antommarchi realized how dangerous this was, while Arnott, his colleague, found nothing directly alarming in these new developments.

But Montholon had come to the conclusion that Antommarchi was a bad doctor and extremely ignorant. He thought Arnott ought to be called in as physician instead. Dr. Arnott had the governor's confidence; he was considered a sensible and judicious man without dangerous ideas of his own.

For a long time Napoleon would not hear of an English physician, answerable to the governor, entering his sickroom; but in the extremity of his suffering at last he consented.

"*Eh bien,* it is really more to satisfy those around me than for myself that I will see him," said Napoleon.

"Bertrand, tell him that you will see him and that he is to work with Antommarchi. Tell him about my illness and let him come in."[1]

This was half-triumph for Montholon, who had so long wanted Antommarchi changed in favor of an expedient physician. Montholon had told the governor outright that Napoleon's turn for the worse was due to the doctor's prescriptions.[3]

Of course Montholon could never disclose his real reason for wanting Antommarchi out of the way. Antommarchi was a

341

trained anatomist, at a time when anatomy was the basis of all medical training. It embraced as a study both normal and pathological anatomy. In other words, Antommarchi was about as good a pathologist as it was then possible to be, and he knew how to effect a post-mortem. Such a man was a threat to the planned finale of the drama of St. Helena. Eventually he would have to be removed from the island, just like Cipriani, Gourgaud, Las Cases, O'Meara and even Albine de Montholon.

As a matter of fact, it is rather strange that none of Napoleon's doctors fell victim to climatic sickness. Yet it was perhaps prudent not to alarm the medical men as to their own safety.

Montholon's schemes to be rid of Antommarchi were thwarted by the governor's dispositions.

Sir Hudson was afraid that something was afoot when he heard from Longwood that Napoleon had accepted Arnott as his doctor. And so he drew up a set of special private instructions. These might be worth a moment's examination.[3]

"Dr Arnott must ascertain whether he is sent for at the express desire of General Bonaparte himself, or called upon merely by Count Montholon or Count Bertrand; or, if it is at the request and desire of Dr. Antommarchi, he has been sent for.

"Should it appear that he has been sent for at the desire of General Bonaparte, he will ask to see him in company with his own surgeon, Dr. Antommarchi.

"Should he have been sent for by one of the Counts only, he should ascertain whether General Bonaparte was aware of his visit and ask to wait upon him in company with his own surgeon.

"If he should find General Bonaparte has not been rendered aware of his visit, he will decline to see him, unless on a specific application from Dr. Antommarchi, and an assurance from him, that his advice is really required.

"Should he have been sent for by Dr. Antommarchi, it will of course be understood, it is with the knowledge of General Bonaparte himself, and they will attend upon him together, but in either or none of the above cases, will he enter into any communication with Counts Montholon or Bertrand on any points connected with General Bonaparte's illness.

"His language at the same time to Count Montholon or Count Bertrand, upon this point, should be so decided as to leave them under the impression, that their intervention in any shape or way whatsoever, is considered by Dr. Arnott as quite unnecessary, whilst General Bonaparte's own medical attendant is at hand.*

"Should Count Montholon or Count Bertrand endeavor to force Dr. Arnott's attendance upon General Bonaparte, without his own surgeon being present, Dr. Arnott will object to the visit, accompanied by them alone, *and report forthwith to the Governor;* and he should not alter this revelation in consequence of Dr. Antommarchi's casual absence, but say he will wait for his return or else he will send for the Medical Officer close by at the Camp, to be present with and assisting him, until Dr. Antommarchi may return."[3]

These private instructions from the governor to Dr. Arnott were, no doubt, an unforeseen obstacle to Montholon's plans. "The wishes of Count Montholon are directly contrary to the instructions given me in the Governor's private memoranda," reported Arnott to Major Gorrequer, the governor's A.D.C. on April 1, 1821.[25]

It is obvious from these instructions that the governor thoroughly trusted Antommarchi but, quite rightly, not Count de Montholon. He withheld his trust from Count Bertrand — unfairly so, in light of the facts.

Late in the evening of April 1, Antommarchi called for his colleague Arnott in the orderly officer's room and suggested they visit Napoleon.

Arnott reported to the governor: "I accompanied him and was shown into a completely darkened room where General Bonaparte lay in bed. The room was so dark that I could not see, but I took hold either of him or of someone else. I felt his pulse and the condition of his skin. I gathered that the person in question was very weak, but there was nothing to indicate immediate danger."[2]

In this shady drama Montholon at last obviously had got hold of the right doctor.

On the next day at nine o'clock Arnott paid his second visit.

---

*This instruction would later be disregarded by Dr. Arnott.

The Emperor lay reclined in bed, pale and unshaved. He received Arnott in friendly fashion and said he had heard about him much that was good. There is little doubt as to the source of such praise. This remark is not surprising, considering Montholon's intense campaign for a change of doctors.

Arnott had to promise solemnly not to report anything about Napoleon's condition to the governor.

After examining the doctor on his knowledge of the anatomy and functions of the stomach and intestines, the Emperor began to talk about his ailments.

"I sometimes feel a severe sharp pain here, which seems to cut me like a razor. Do you think the pylorus is affected? My father died of this when he was thirty-eight; is it not hereditary?"

Arnott examined the area in question and was able to assure that though there was an inflammation in the stomach, the pylorus was not affected. The pain Napoleon felt was due to gas in the intestines. It had nothing to do with the liver. If the Emperor would not get quite so upset at the mention of the word medicine but would be good enough to take the remedy prescribed, all discomfort soon would disappear.

Those of us who know the end of Napoleon's story can likewise safely say that Napoleon's pain on April 2, 1821, had nothing to do with the pylorus — without denying that even an Emperor could have suffered from gas in the intestines. It is quite probable that those razor-like pains were connected with the perforation of the stomach wall fortunately covered by the liver capsule, as discovered at Napoleon's post-mortem. At the time of Doctor Arnott's first visit this perforation must have been *covered* by the pressure of the enlarged liver against the stomach and the perforation. A temporary healing was established. Stomach contractions could have caused extremely acute pain.

The Grand Marshal of the court acted as interpreter. Montholon had managed to procure a physician who understood nothing of what Napoleon said, and with whom Napoleon, therefore, could not communicate. Thus "the doctor's orders" could in reality be Montholon's, and the patient's supposed words could be incorrect. O'Meara and Stokoe, Napoleon's two previous physicians, had spoken the Emperor's tongues of Italian and French fluently.

The patient at Longwood might be faring badly but things there were progressing to de Montholon's satisfaction. Montchenu, too, must have been pleased.

When Napoleon heard Dr. Arnott's pronouncement he said to Bertrand:

"Tell him that I have never before suffered from my stomach. I may have vomited once or twice, but on the whole my stomach has always behaved as it should."[4]

The Emperor was not correct in this claim, as the record testifies. He was recalling the days before he crossed the Bourbon path to a Restoration.

And so to the remedy, the medicine. A few pills to get the stomach working. The doctor might have been expected to prescribe calomel at this stage, as Montholon had predicted in a letter to Albine — informatively through the official courier channels. But the time for that medicine was not yet.

However, if we refer to one of the sacred handbooks in medicine of those days, we shall find an acceptable explanation as to why Montholon's calomel forecast did not apply to this particular visit.

In Richter-Collins' comprehensive, eight-part book we read that "*Murias hydrargyrosum* (calomel) should therefore never be used at the start of an inflammatory fever . . . but only after sufficient cuppings and other weakening expedients have been resorted to, by which the way has been prepared for its use."[5]

The pills then prescribed by Dr. Arnott were supposed to have consisted of alum, soap and oil of caraway. They were to be taken morning and evening, two pills at a time.

Antommarchi would not approve this prescription. A dispute arose between the doctors, which was easily solved by Napoleon. He assured them that in any case he had not the slightest intention of taking the pills in question.

On the next day, April 3, Napoleon again suffered a fever, with icy chill in his legs and a severe headache. The attack came on at night. During the day, his condition had improved, but the night must have been a hard one, for in the morning Napoleon told Bertrand that he had felt as though he had put on Deianira's shirt, the poisoned garb which was the cause of Hercules' great torments.[9]

Without a doubt — even on St. Helena — Napoleon had many clear moments, but this time the light was only half sufficient. He felt as if he had been poisoned but he could not understand that to feel poisoned doubtlessly meant quite simply that poison had been used. Montholon had been on duty that night as nurse.

The "fever" Napoleon suffered in the night had not quite left him when the doctors Arnott and Antommarchi called the next morning. Arnott, however, was armed with a thermometer. Napoleon's temperature was 35.5° C.[6] A sensation of fever and shivering without an increase in temperature is usual in cases of poisoning. Obviously neither of the doctors knew this — or perhaps they did. To know is one thing, to speak out, another.

Antommarchi could not but consider that Napoleon was actually in danger of death. Arnott could not agree, but in spite of this Antommarchi felt obliged to tell Montholon and Bertrand of his fears. They should inform Napoleon that his last hour might easily be at hand and that he ought therefore to see to it that his affairs were in order.

At three o'clock on the morning of April 4, Montholon was relieved by Marchand. The night had been a troubled one, with difficulty in breathing, nausea, vomiting, dizziness and pain in the abdominal region. Severe sweating followed and then relief. By morning all was calm again.[7]

The next night was much quieter, and from that day a period of slow but marked improvement in Napoleon's condition could be observed. We have reason to believe he had decided to draw up his Will. It was a time when surcease from pain would be helpful and, indeed, desirable.

Concerning those days and the days immediately following, Bertrand noted that Napoleon "sometimes took as medicine a pill and infusion of cinchona." But both doctors and day nurse Marchand were worried because Napoleon absolutely refused to take any medicine at all. Since Bertrand was not present at Longwood at night, he must have got his facts from someone who was in Napoleon's sickroom at the time, and as there can be little doubt that it was Charles Tristan. Bertrand's information in this case may not have been reliable.

For a while Napoleon was still troubled at night with fresh "fever" peaks and also with certain acute but very temporary discomforts, but with morning would come relief. The days were comparatively calm.

Antommarchi saw Napoleon day and night, Arnott only during the day. The doctors could therefore not agree as to what really was the matter with their patient. The symptoms of suffering that Antommarchi noted at night were generally no longer present when Arnott called. Arnott began to be suspicious of Antommarchi. This, we may be sure, was the intention.

On April 7 Napoleon got up — most probably with help — shaved, washed and sat in an armchair to read the newspapers.[8] When he had washed, he looked once more at his reflection in the mirror and said, mournfully, "Sorry sight that I am!"

This was the countenance that once had been a privilege of Europe's ablest portraitists to copy and interpret. Time and poison had worked a sad change.

That afternoon Bertrand asked again if he could wait on Napoleon at night in place of Montholon. "I have spent so many nights in your company as aide-de-camp, I would like to spend a few with you as your valet," begged Bertrand, who perhaps sensed something amiss in the care of his Emperor.[9]

Napoleon remained firm. He wanted Montholon as nurse at night — no one else.

Strange things began to happen. A few days after April 7, Marchand noted that he had offered Napoleon an entirely new drink. He had found it on the patient's bedside table. The new drink, he learned was called *orgeat*. On April 29 Napoleon was still under the impression that it was made from barley, as its name implied (*orge* — barley).

At first brewed from barley, orgeat, from the 18th century had been made instead from sweet almonds. Typically in orgeat a few bitter almonds would be added for spice and the whole was made more aromatic by adding orangeflower water, which was agreeable to the taste and carried a pleasant perfume. From this point on the drink orgeat will figure prominently in the final phase of the story of Napoleon's death.

When Marchand first offered him the orgeat, Napoleon had eyed him rather suspiciously and said: "I presume that you have not been mixing anything in my drinks."[23]

Well may he have questioned the orgeat. But still stranger things were to happen.

At 7:30 in the morning of April 9 Napoleon called for Bertrand. The Grand Marshal found the Emperor wild with rage. Antommarchi should have been there at six o'clock but he had not come until half-past seven.

The unfortunate physician had been with Napoleon from eleven the previous evening until midnight. He had been called again from one o'clock until two in the morning and from three o'clock until four. Antommarchi, fatigued, had then gone to bed and had asked his Chinese servant to waken him in time for his next visit to Napoleon. The servant had also fallen asleep.

But Napoleon had been given a better reason for Antommarchi's omission. The doctor had spent the night with Mme. Bertrand — who had so stubbornly refused Napoleon the same favor. Napoleon might well have been angered.

"He spends all his time with Madame Bertrand," announced Napoleon. *"Eh bien,* let him spend all his time with his strumpets ... rid me of that stupid, ignorant, conceited and dishonorable fellow.

"I want you to call for Arnott, so that he can look after me in future. I'll have no more to do with Antommarchi."

This scene took place in the presence of Antommarchi and Bertrand. Napoleon repeated five or six times that Mme. Bertrand was a prostitute. He went on: "I have made my Will: To Antommarchi I bequeath the sum of twenty francs to buy a rope with which to hang himself. He is a rogue."[10]

It was another triumph for the Montholon method.

Antommarchi was thrown out and Napoleon continued to entertain Bertrand with tales of Mme. Bertrand's infidelity. He laid especial emphasis on how much she had degraded herself by taking this doctor as her lover. Now Mme. Bertrand had seduced and brought misfortune on Antommarchi exactly as she had previously done to Gourgaud. Thus Gourgaud was classed as the lover of *Madame la Maréchale* more than three years after he had left the island! Gourgaud never had a chance to take up this imaginary role of lover. There is in the record no suggestion other than a sick man's rantings that relations between Mme. Bertrand and Gourgaud were other than strictly proper; their closest bond was their common contempt of the Montholons. Gourgaud had a very strong conception of honor, which may have been awkward and irksome for others but which withstood the pressure of the imperial court, where sexual morality was undoubtedly lax.

Montholon, on the contrary, had tried to get his arms around Mme. Bertrand, but with no success at all.[11]

Antommarchi had made one great mistake, in Napoleon's view. He had not paid enough attention to Montholon.

The method used to get Gourgaud out of the way was effectual although so far as the general was concerned it had had to be reinforced by several attacks of the familiar climatic sickness. Antommarchi had the good luck to avoid this and so did the other physicians. This should explain why Antommarchi was correct in treating Napoleon's outbreaks of rage and the accusations he made as symptoms of his illness. In spite of all that was said about him, Antommarchi was definitely a competent doctor. He was to be adjudged as less than that in history because of Napoleon's enmity and Montholon's plottings for his removal. When Napoleon was sufficiently intoxicated, either with arsenic or antimony, he became as wax in Montholon's hands. Napoleon as invalid now often spoke the words formed by Montholon.

It could seem that Montholon now had reached his goal. Antommarchi had been banished from Longwood and there was room at last for the Parisian physician Montholon had asked the governor to procure. Perhaps it was too late to get him to come to Longwood, but the main thing was that Antommarchi should go, so that there would be no pathologist present on St. Helena when Napoleon's body was due to be dissected. It was not unheard of for a pathologist to expose a poison killer's carefully prepared ministrations.

Indeed, the trap had been successful. Antommarchi went straight down to Plantation House to ask the governor to arrange a passage for him home. Sir Hudson was not there, but Major Gorrequer accompanied the doctor into Jamestown. There he was able to see the governor in The Castle. It was not difficult for the latter to realize Antommarchi's dilemma, but he begged him to reconsider. Had he been unable to agree with Arnott? Antommarchi assured him this was not so.[12]

If we assume, now, that Antommarchi was an able practitioner of the healing arts, what about the governor, himself? Had he not also been in his own way a healer when he procured gardening tools and horses for Napoleon? He managed to persuade Antommarchi to stay on and made a point that seemed to have the desired effect on Antommarchi. *"Signor professor,"* said Sir Hudson, "it is necessary always to consider the temperament of the patient *(il genio della persona)* and circumstances of the case."[12]

Antommarchi returned to Longwood. Although he kept aloof, his presence would frustrate Montholon. The anatomist represented danger.

Faithful and forgiving, Bertrand as usual tried to pour oil on troubled waters. When he had climbed into Mme. Bertrand's bed the night Napoleon so furiously spoke of he had not observed any Doctor Antommarchi there. So he was fairly sure of the facts. There must have been a misunderstanding!

He went in to Napoleon and pointed out that the doctor was a good and reliable man but that he must have been badly advised. Napoleon on the other hand was quite convinced: *"Je pense qu'il s'est conseillé tout seul* — I think he has been advised by himself."[13]

On April 11 Arnott came to pay his usual morning visit. He asked where Antommarchi was. He was ill, was the reply. That afternoon, when Arnott called again, he heard that Antommarchi was still indisposed. During the night Napoleon called for his physician. There was no physician. The next morning no doctor called. Napoleon expressed surprise that Arnott showed so little interest. Why didn't the doctor come?

Bertrand told Napoleon that Dr. Arnott had not refused to see his patient, but that he wished to be summoned especially each time he was wanted.

What had happened was that Montholon had managed to get Antommarchi dismissed, but had not reckoned with his host. This time Sir Hudson had outwitted him and had secretly instructed Arnott not to visit Napoleon unless he had Antommarchi with him. Clearly, the governor respected Antommarchi and had reservations about the scheming head of the household, Montholon. In this case Sir Hudson differed from his country's future Prime Minister Rosebery. In his book on Napoleon's last days, Rosebery wrote that Montholon could be trusted. Why? Because he was an aristocrat. The Corsican commoner, Antommarchi, on the other hand, was quite unreliable.

Bertrand himself thought that Napoleon was much too ill not to need a doctor close at hand.

A quarter past ten. Still no doctor.

Napoleon lay in silence. After a long time: "What time is it?"

"Half past ten, Sire."

"Call Montholon, if he is there."

Napoleon relapsed once more into silence. Nowadays that was how he and Bertrand kept each other company. Napoleon had obviously begun to consider his long-time aide untrustworthy. Perhaps he had always been so!

"What time is it?"

"A quarter to eleven, Sire."

"Marchand, call Antommarchi," Napoleon shouted.

The next minute Antommarchi was there.

"What sort of concoction do they want me to take?" began Napoleon, as if nothing had happened.

"It is a solution of salt with five grains of opium, Sire." (1 grain = 1/20th of a gram.)

"What's that for?"

"It will check your vomiting, Sire."

"Must I drink it?"

"If your Majesty feels a desire to vomit, do so; your Majesty can drink half the solution and see what happens."

At eleven o'clock Montholon appeared. All Napoleon had to say to him now was: "Go and have lunch."

At midday Napoleon had his own lunch, roast meat in hot wine. Evidently his stomach had begun to behave more normally.[14]

At eight in the evening the doctors were again supposed to call. Arnott arrived too late, but was not lectured for it. Antommarchi was the one who must be punctual.

At three o'clock in the morning, just as Montholon had been relieved by Marchand, Napoleon again vomited. Yet he had been able to keep down the previous day's lunch and dinner. At this time his indispositions always were visited on him at night.

Those nightly attacks of nausea were important enough.

Napoleon had indeed begun to draw up an entirely new will. This he did during the day. As long as he felt ill at night, he could realize that he had to press on with the task.

It is difficult to say exactly when the work on the new Will began. On April 9 Napoleon had made his sardonic bequest to Antommarchi — twenty francs for a rope, as Napoleon had said.

On April 9 or 10 Napoleon asked Montholon, in Marchand's presence, if he thought that two million francs would be enough for Montholon to buy back "the forfeited family estates in Burgundy."[15]

The night of April 12 was quiet, the first for a very long time. Montholon knew the reason. He had at last managed to get Napoleon to take one of Dr. Arnott's "tranquillizing drinks". His comment would explain Napoleon's quiet night, far more probably due to the suspension of poisoning.

And now others began to notice that Napoleon was actually recovering. When the doctors called on April 14 he soon changed from the usual topic of his sufferings and began to discourse at length to Arnott on Abercromby's expedition into Egpyt.[16] Bertrand translated.

On April 13 Bertrand had gathered that Napoleon and Montholon were busy with some sort of written work. They were closeted together and were not to be disturbed. Bertrand found Napoleon very much better that day; he sat up for a while in his chair with the doors and windows open.

Bertrand asked Napoleon what they were doing. *Eh bien*, they were writing a letter to the Prince Regent. Napoleon was also busy with a pamphlet on the English oligarchy in which he pointed out how unhappy the British people really were. What did he want of the Prince Regent? . . . *Eh bien*, he was asking him to see that his body should not remain in London but should be sent on to France, *"sur les bords de la Seine"* — to the banks of the Seine.[17]

Exactly: *"L'oligarchie anglaise,"* and *"les bords de la Seine,"* those would become familiar expressions from Napoleon's Will, paras. 5 and 2. *"Je meurs prématurement, assassiné par l'oligarchie anglaise et son sicaire* — I die prematurely, murdered by the English oligarchy and their hired assassin . . . It is my wish that my ashes repose on the banks of the Seine, in the midst of the French people whom I have loved so much." Anyway, whether or not it was really Napoleon's Will, the last phrase was certainly in Napoleon's style. Otherwise there are many reasons for suspecting that the Will that Napoleon said he himself wrote was, like so much else on St. Helena, written in the manner already mentioned: the hand was that of Napoleon but, as to much of what was contained, the mind was Montholon's.

Para. 8 of the Will makes it quite clear that the house of Bourbon and its jurisdiction were represented in the writing of Napoleon's testament. There we have it in black and white that Napoleon was not murdered, according to the Bourbon ideal of justice. He was executed.

A murdered man does not receive the Last Sacraments before the blow. Napoleon would receive them immediately before his execution by calomel. It is also right and just that sentence of death should not be carried out before the guilty party has confessed. If no confession was forthcoming spontaneously there were numbers of ways in those days, as now, for obtaining it by force.

In Para. 8 of his Will Napoleon confessed to a crime which, according to the French law then in force, definitely should be punished by loss of life. In that paragraph Napoleon actually takes upon himself the blame for the death of the Duke of Enghien, a Bourbon of the Condé branch. He states that he did not regret the execution of the duke and says that under similar circumstances he would do the same thing.

Of all the arbitrary and, as many think, fatal decisions Napoleon made when in power, the arrest and execution of the Duke of Enghien, even though he had conspired against the then current legal government of France and enrolled in an enemy force, was the most damaging to his reputation. It was the only "crime" Napoleon admitted to and defended in his Will. In the eyes of the Bourbons the murder of a member of their house was a crime especially deserving of punishment by death. In Napoleon's case, any other killings could be conceded to have been incidental to a military and political career of such great motion and power.

By allowing himself to be lured into incorporating this confession in his Will, Napoleon provided the royal house with a legally unimpeachable weapon. He had validated his own sentence of death. Examination of the hand-writing in the Will suggests that Paragraph 8 concerning the Duke of Enghien was inserted in the space between Sections I and II after the page had been finished.

On April 15, Bertrand found Napoleon tired and weak, but he would sit up now and then. He had shaved and washed and had worked long with Montholon in the privacy of his bedchamber.

That evening he entertained Arnott by reading chosen extracts from his Will. But he said that they were from a letter he had written to the Prince Regent. Then he produced a beautifully bound volume on Marlborough's campaigns and begged Arnott to accept it on behalf of his regiment. At the same time he took the opportunity to praise the British soldiery.

It was on April 15 that Napoleon signed his Will proper. On the same day Bertrand once again asked Montholon what he and Napoleon had been doing so privately together. As usual Montholon's answer was hardly to be relied on: Napoleon had been telling Montholon how he thought France and the rest of Europe would receive the news of his death.

All the same, Bertrand must have suspected that some sort of will was brewing, for he went so far as to presume that Montholon would not besmirch Mme. Bertrand's good name and would moreover behave like a gentleman.[18] Montholon assured him that he had always looked upon Bertrand as a brother, which the good Bertrand probably interpreted in one way and Montholon in another. Brothers are often unbrotherly.

Later in the evening of April 15, Napoleon's strength was at a low ebb.

The main Will had been signed. Fortune had allowed him a few days' comparative respite from his illness, said Napoleon; while he worked on the important document, his nights had become noticeably calmer. Indeed, Napoleon ought to have felt relieved and at peace, as the threat of death appeared once more to have been averted.

But the very next night he was to suffer a relapse. Marchand, who as usual relieved Montholon, had to heat towels to revive the circulation in Napoleon's icy cold legs. Dr. Antommarchi was called and was upbraided for not keeping a serious mien on the previous evening when Napoleon had praised the British soldiers to Arnott.

On the morning of the 16th Napoleon once more closeted himself with Montholon. Marchand was summoned, however, as Napoleon vomited twice in quick succession. He asked Marchand then to bring him a glass of the wine especially reserved for him, which Las Cases had sent from Cape Town. Marchand took the liberty of advising him against this and Montholon agreed with Marchand that Napoleon should not take a glass of this wine. But the latter was obstinate and got his way. He dipped a biscuit in the wine and sucked on it.

Again Marchand was ready to jot down the circumstances — as a reminder. Napoleon suffered another attack of nausea and was sick.[19]

Shortly thereafter the doctors came on their visit. Napoleon admitted then that he had drunk a glass of Constance wine, against Marchand's advice, to revive him a little, and wondered if the doctors thought it was the wine that was to blame. Arnott believed that the glass of wine had caused the vomiting.[19]

It is obvious that head valet Marchand, unquestionably devoted to his master, was himself trying to discover what it could have been that caused those sudden attacks of illness.

It would almost appear that Marchand suspected Napoleon was being poisoned, without being able to understand how.

On April 17, two days after the signing of the main Will, Antommarchi asked Montholon what he and Napoleon were really up to, closeted away for several hours. Naturally Montholon could explain; there was nothing secret about it. Napoleon had been counting his golden snuffboxes and had also drawn up an inventory of his other treasures. The doctor asked if he had not made his Will yet.

"No, he has not," answered Montholon. "Were the Emperor to die now, not one of his retinue or servants would receive a centime."[20] It was not for nothing that Montholon was called "The Liar" at Longwood House.

Napoleon had vomited again on the night of April 17, but he was better in the morning. He sat in his chair with the windows and doors flung open as on the three previous days, and called to the sun: *"Bonjour, soleil! Bonjour, mon ami!* — Good morning, Sun! Good morning, my friend!"

At half past five the next afternoon (April 18) Napoleon summoned Bertrand and said: "I have made my Will. I have written everything myself. Sign here and affix your seal. Do this now and don't ask questions."[22] An imperial order had to be obeyed. Bertrand did as he was told and witnessed a will of which he knew nothing. Was Napoleon at that time sufficiently lucid for his Will to be considered valid? According to Montholon, Napoleon had himself declared that he was *malade du corps mais sain d'esprit* — sick of body but of sound mind.[21]

Could he really have been of sound mind when he would describe Mme. Bertrand as a whore? Anyway, the troubled Bertrand signed his name.

During his conversation with Bertrand, Napoleon had been in bed. Suddenly he arose. Bertrand rushed forward to help him, as was his custom. Napoleon pushed him aside and walked with firm steps unaided to his chair. "We thought it was Sixtus V casting away his stick and intoning the Te Deum," wrote Bertrand.[22] (Sixtus V, Pope of the counter-reformation, threw away his crutch on hearing he had been elected Pope.)

When the doctors came for their evening visit they were surprised to see Napoleon sitting easily in his chair without supporting himself on the arms. He was happy and talkative and ordered his dinner. He was served chopped meat and fried bread, which he ate with a good appetite. Later he asked for a little consommé and thought that he would like some *gigot* (roast leg of mutton).

Unfortunately there was none and he was served roast turkey instead. It was not exactly what he wanted. Had Bertrand any *gigot*? No, he had not, but later that evening Bertrand would be able to get some.

In the small hours of the morning Napoleon drank an infusion of cinchona, with the result that he brought up all he had previously eaten. He then became a little suspicious.

"Tell me, Dr. Arnott, is this quinine solution made here or in the town?"

"In the town, Sire."

"Did the apothecary come at the same time as the governor?"

"No, Sire."

"Did Thomas Reade get hold of him?"

"No, Sire, the man was here before the governor came. He is employed by the East India Company and is most trustworthy."

He probably was. But cinchona would effectually hide the metallic taste of tartar emetic.

Here was another indication that Napoleon was aware of the possibility that someone might want to shorten his life by poison; but always he looked in the wrong direction.

References

1. Marchand II:292
2. Forsyth III:274
3. Private suits etc. L.P.
4. Marchand II:293
5. Richter-Collin I:117
6. Frémeaux 2 p. 63
7. Antommarchi, Arnott 4th April 1821
8. Antommarchi 7th April 1821, Marchand II:296
9. Bertrand III:108-9
10. Bertrand III:110
11. Bertrand III:168
12. Forsyth III:276-7
13. Bertrand III:112
14. Ibid II:113, 114
15. Marchand II:297
16. Ibid II:298
17. Bertrand III:117
18. Ibid III:122
19. Marchand II:302
20. Bertrand III:123, 124
21. Marchand II:381
22. Bertrand III:126, 127
23. Marchand II:296
24. Bertrand III:128
25. Arnott Letter, 1821; Lowe's Papers

42

Legacies and Bitter Almonds

MONTHOLON HAD REASON to feel satisfied with Napoleon's Will. It was now specified — and only he and *perhaps* Napoleon knew of this as yet — that he should receive two million gold francs, with a purchasing power equivalent to at least twenty million and perhaps as much as forty million of today's French francs.

The words were plainly written: *"Je lèque au comte Montholon deux millions de francs comme une preuve de ma satisfaction des soins filiaux qu'il m'a rendus depuis six ans et pour l'indemniser des pertes que son séjour à Sainte-Hélène lui a occasionnées* — To Count Montholon I bequeath two million francs as proof of my satisfaction with the filial care he has bestowed upon me for the past six years and to make up to him for the losses cause by his stay on St. Helena."

We now are in a position to appraise that filial care. The Marquise de Brinvilliers had bestowed the same kind upon her father. On the other hand it is less obvious what great losses Montholon was supposed to have sustained by following Napoleon. That enterprise had already yielded a dividend not to be despised. It is most probable that Montholon owned nothing before he joined Napoleon, or in any event that he owed more than he owned. He could hardly have been a gentleman of sound financial means when in 1814 he larcenously diverted two lots of military funds, to a total of 6000 francs.

But on April 15 Montholon may not have been entirely satisfied. Napoleon certainly possessed other assets than those with which his main testament was concerned.

Napoleon had given a few millions in gold to the Empress Marie-Louise in 1814. There ought to have been at least a couple of millions worth claiming there. A codicil to the Will could be drawn up about that. It was not difficult to persuade Napoleon;

by this time Montholon would have known how to handle and how to prepare him. A codicil was added and a further 100,000 francs went to Montholon.

Napoleon's stepson, Prince Eugène, had charge of a certain amount of money that really belonged to Napoleon. At least two millions were to be had there. Another codicil was added. A further 100,000 francs to Montholon.

Bertrand, who had been the chief beneficiary in Napoleon's earlier Will, would now have to content himself with half a million. Marchand was left 400,000 francs. But by the first codicil Bertrand had been left a further 200,000 francs and Marchand 50,000. In codicil No. 2 Bertrand was left as much as in codicil No. 1.

Then Napoleon — apparently quite of his own accord — set about writing a third and a fourth codicil. In the fourth codicil a certain amount was withdrawn from Montholon. All codicils are dated April 24. Events of that day, the day when the stream of gold directed towards Montholon was in part diverted, are especially interesting and important to examine.

Napoleon, as mentioned, once more could sit up for part of the day and was no longer in such severe pain. Those razor-like stabs had obviously left him and he began once more to interest himself in reading and discussing what he had read. Here Bertrand's task was evident; he could listen and he afforded the opinions of a courtier.

By April 21 Napoleon was so much better that Marchand prophesied that if he continued to recover at the same rate, he would be able to go out in his carriage within a fortnight. Marchand tells us that on that day his master dined as he had at the Tuileries.[1]

Napoleon had been very busy all day. From four until seven in the morning he had dictated, sometimes to Marchand, sometimes to Montholon. Antommarchi was curious and wondered what was going on. Marchand's answer was evasive.

At 9 o'clock in the morning Napoleon fell asleep and slept until half past ten. At 11 o'clock the doctors called. They warned Napoleon not to overstrain his strength. When the doctors had left Napoleon arose and lunched at midday. His appetite was good. Then someone read to him from Polybios' description of the battle of Cannae and continued with Caesar's arrival in Greece before the battle of Pharsalos, after which Napoleon dictated his reflections to Marchand. At 2:30 p.m. he fell asleep and slept for two hours. He was wakened by the doctors when they paid their afternoon call. In future they were not to come until 5:30 p.m., Napoleon decided.

At 6 p.m. the Emperor dined. He was served cream of rice soup, mutton chop, chipped potatoes and apple meringue.

The meal was not a success. The soup was tasteless, thought Napoleon. He brought it up almost immediately. Falling into a bad temper, he started to pick a quarrel. With whom? With Antommarchi, of course, that unfortunate individual. He should have known the menu was badly planned.

"Montholon ought to direct you with his stick, as they do in the army," cried Napoleon.

"You have become involved with a woman; but what about your *character?* You are not nearly as good as Arnott. I don't know whether he is a good doctor or not, but he knows how to behave. He shall look after me in future."[2]

Poor Antommarchi — a scapegoat, whose real and incurable fault lay in the fact that he was a qualified doctor and a pathologist into the bargain and consequently dangerous! He had certainly not poisoned the soup nor the wine, but his presence did not suit Montholon now, with the climax of the long-sustained drama possibly at hand.

Bertrand must have tried to make Napoleon feel some gratitude towards his doctors, especially towards his physician-in-ordinary, now that his health was beginning to improve. "Oh, no," interrupted Napoleon, "you cannot say that my doctors have cured me, rather they have delayed the cure."[2]

It must have been very painful for Bertrand to witness Napoleon's brutal and unjust treatment of Antommarchi and it was quite understandable when these two later had a confidential tête-à-tête, that they both questioned as to what sort of intrigues were afoot.

Bertrand then heard — for the first time — that Napoleon had asked Antommarchi to convince Mme. Bertrand that she should become Napoleon's mistress. Mme. Bertrand was often ill and was then attended by Antommarchi. So he could talk to her confidentially. A doctor's orders should obviously be obeyed, but Antommarchi had refused to give Mme. Bertrand the orders Napoleon wished.

Also for the first time Bertrand learned that someone had told Antommarchi, on the very day after he arrived at Longwood, that Bertrand was a nobody and no trusty follower of Napoleon. It was said that he had only come because otherwise he would have had to share the fate of Marshal Ney and General La Bédoyère and be shot. And the Grand Marshal's wife gave herself to every English officer who passed her house. She was a most contemptible woman.[3]

Antommarchi had never mentioned this slanderous talk to Bertrand before. However, now it all came out, and it may be remembered that Antommarchi had noted that his first meeting with Montholon was very unpleasant and that he had not realized at all what the brazen Count was getting at.[4]

When they called on the morning of April 22, the doctors were told by Montholon that Napoleon had slept soundly from midnight until five in the morning. At 5 o'clock he had asked if it was midnight and had then fallen fast asleep again.

When the doctors saw their patient, they were told quite a different story.

"Well, and how did Your Majesty sleep last night?" Antommarchi asked.

"Badly," answered Napoleon. "From 9 o'clock yesterday evening until 3 o'clock this morning I woke up every half hour and had to clear my throat. But I slept well from 3 o'clock until nine this morning."

He added that he had eaten a little in the morning, but that he had not been hungry. As soon as he drank a glass of wine, he felt a desire to vomit. The doctors prescribed a solution of gentian to strengthen the stomach, one or two tablespoons to be taken in the morning.

Napoleon bade his doctors goodbye. It was time for Mass. The day was Easter Sunday.[5]

On this day Napoleon had a long conversation with Bertrand, which lasted from 6 o'clock in the evening until 8 o'clock. He mentioned his wills: there were three, said Napoleon, and he must have meant the main Will and the first two codicils, that turned a golden rivulet toward Montholon. Those two codicils, therefore, were drafted at least two days before they were dated.

Napoleon now told Bertrand why he had written that he died in the Catholic faith, although he had never before held it in the right veneration. It was, he said, a gesture to common morality.

One cannot help being impressed by the Count's ability as security agent. What consummate skill to be able to make Napoleon convey in his Will that he was an obedient son of the Catholic Church!

But here Montholon also reveals that he was acting on orders, for no one with justice can say Montholon was a better Catholic or more spontaneously inclined to obey the Church than Napoleon. It is wholly unlikely that he was suddenly and personally moved to an act obliquely proselytizing for the Church.

"*Je meurs dans la réligion apostolique et romaine* — I die in the apostolic and Roman faith." By managing to get that famous paragraph included in Napoleon's Will, Count d'Artois, through his agent, was doing the Church a considerably greater and more efficient service than when, as newly-crowned King Charles X, he would order the sentence of death on anyone who dishonored and insulted the Host.

That pious paragraph in Bonaparte's Will savors of Bourbonism. Members of that house were always careful that people should not die just anyhow but in good accord with the rules of the Church. Just before Ferdinand, King of both the Sicilies, who was very much a Bourbon, ordered the liquidation of Napoleon's brother-in-law Murat, ex-king of Naples, the latter was presented with a document for signature in which it was stated that he died a good Catholic. Murat tried right up to the end to avoid signing it, but did so at last. It both qualified and formally prepared him for immediate execution.[12]

Ever since the middle of March Napoleon had been actively antagonistic to Antommarchi. Now, no longer confident of living, he asked Bertrand to see to it that Antommarchi would perform an autopsy. Arnott could be present as an onlooker. In his lucid moments, therefore, Napoleon realized that Antommarchi was trustworthy and clever.[6]

Napoleon went on to explain to Bertrand why he had written in his Will that he had been murdered by the governor. Well, in the first place it was the climate that had been the death of him, and in the second place there were those "pinpricks", by which he meant the posting of sentries. This had prevented him from getting fresh air until it was too late. Murdered was a strong term to use in the circumstances. It would tend to confuse history and impose an undue further strain on relations between France and Britain.

Either Napoleon was fully aware that these accusations were entirely false — he had displayed the same physical symptoms on several occasions when he had been ill in Europe, where sentries had never prevented him from going out — or else the circulation of blood to his brain was very poor when he drew up this accusation.

Napoleon certainly excused quite badly this famous paragraph in his Will. Even if Montholon had suggested the accusation and successfully enforced it, Napoleon could not bring himself to admit as much to Bertrand. One thing is certain; it was in Montholon's interest that such a paragraph should be included. One cannot be too careful in a task as delicate as his. Should something go wrong and someone — Antommarchi, for instance — discover the real cause of Napoleon's death along with the nature of his long illness, there had better be a scapegoat at hand. Sir Hudson Lowe was placed in position as this scapegoat, once and for all. Harsh words in the Will ensured that.

Napoleon told Bertrand that he had appointed three executors, Bertrand, Montholon and Marchand. He obviously did not consider a more precise explanation necessary as to why he had chosen Bertrand and Marchand, but the inclusion of Montholon required some explanation to his faithful friends. It appeared that he wanted to repay Montholon for his loyalty, though Montholon owed him nothing. Also, Montholon had forfeited 300,000 francs when he joined Napoleon. So it was now Napoleon's hope that Bertrand and Montholon thenceforth would get along better together.

We can only surmise what the patient Bertrand thought of this suggestion . . . after all that Montholon had said and done to degrade Bertrand and his wife.

Further, Napoleon was pleased to inform Bertrand that he was to receive a million francs under the Will. Montholon would receive the same. Strangely enough, at the opening of the Will, it would be read that Bertrand was bequeathed 500,000 in the main document, the only will of any practical worth, while Montholon inherited two millions.

This confusion reinforces in the author's view a long-held suspicion that Napoleon's mind was not wholly lucid while Montholon "collaborated" on his Will. We know that Napoleon's sight and hearing had become very poor under the debilitating effect of his illnesses.

Antommarchi was not mentioned in the Will, nor was Mme. Bertrand. As far as Mme. Bertrand was concerned, Napoleon's excuse was that no ladies were mentioned in his Will. As a matter of fact, she was the one lady left at his little court.

Napoleon knew he had nothing against Antommarchi as a doctor and that he should have remembered him in his Will. He admitted as much to Bertrand. He would, however, put this right by a special codicil.

Unhappy Napoleon! He found it hard to explain to Bertrand why he had left nothing to Antommarchi. He didn't know. It was Montholon who knew.

Vignali, the physician Cardinal Fesch had sent and whom Napoleon had thought more suitable as house chaplain, had been left 100,000 francs in the main Will. Marchand got 400,000 francs, the other valets and Pierron 100,000 francs as well. Archambault, the groom, was to have 50,000, and Coursot and Chandelier, the servants who had arrived at the same time as Antommarchi, 25,000 francs each.

Antommarchi was destined to be scapegoat No. 2, in the same way as poor O'Meara. But then Antommarchi was a pathologist and Napoleon had declared that he wished for an autopsy. The world must have confirmation in black and white that Napoleon personally had not the slightest respect or regard for Antommarchi.

Two other personal enemies of Montholon, Gourgaud and O'Meara, similarly were omitted from Napoleon's Will, further supporting the conviction that the Will was partly Montholon's work. Left to his own inclinations, and having remembered servitors of much less value to him than faithful Gourgaud and O'Meara, who backed their opinions with courage, Napoleon surely would not have failed to reward them.

On April 23 Napoleon was busy for three or four hours writing a fourth codicil. When he mentioned this to Arnott, the latter presumed that Napoleon had dictated it. "Oh, no," Napoleon assured him, "I have written the whole thing myself." One may believe he did. Montholon was certainly not present when this codicil was drawn up, for Napoleon now withdrew monies that he had previously given to Montholon. Paragraph 7 of the codicil actually states that the 9000 pounds Sterling already given to the Count and Countess de Montholon by Napoleon should be reckoned as part of the total sum bequeathed to Montholon under the Will. In Paragraph 8 of the same codicil Napoleon annulled the pension of 20,000 francs granted to Mme. Montholon. In future the Count himself was to be responsible for that provision. Montholon, indeed, could not have assisted in the drawing of such a provision.

On the next day, April 24, Napoleon signed the four codicils. There is no record anywhere that Montholon tried to prevent the signing of the fourth and for him so unfavorable codicil. Perhaps he should have done so, since much would seem to indicate that Napoleon was beginning to emerge from the Montholonian entrancement. The day before, for instance, he had said to Bertrand: "I am well aware that Montholon courts me for an inheritance." On the same occasion he called Mme. Montholon *une intrigante qui connaît ses intérêts* — an intriguing woman who knows where her interests lie. He made a measure of redress concerning Mme. Bertrand before her husband, saying, "Mme. Bertrand is not self-seeking."[7]

Montholon was away that day. Marchand does say it was on April 27 that Montholon first put in an appearance in the evening, but it must have been on April 24 if Antommarchi's and Bertrand's notes are to fit in. Either Marchand's memory was at fault or else the publisher of his memoirs mistook a 4 for a 7.

However, Montholon turned up at 11 o'clock at night. When Napoleon saw him he said: "Well, my boy, it would be a pity if I were not to die now, when I have put my affairs in such good order."

"Sire, only Your Majesty could think of such a thing," replied Montholon, courteous as ever.[8]

Marchand retired and left Napoleon in Montholon's care.[8] It seems again as though Marchand had his special reasons for mentioning this, as a reminder, or perhaps as an apology when he saw what happened later.

That night Montholon's solicitude for his benefactor was not of the best. We shall not accuse Montholon of seeking to revenge himself for the fourth and unfavorable codicil which had been signed the previous evening. That was probably not the case. Montholon may not have been a vicious man. He was a security agent and as such had his own justification to act wickedly. His monarch was legally enthroned in France. Napoleon was the enemy of his king. It behooved him now to have caution. Who could tell what Napoleon would do the next day?

As the Will stood it was self-accusatory of Napoleon, still generous to Montholon and it could hardly be more satisfying to the Bourbons. Any change now could only worsen it. This was a crucially favorable time.

It started at four in the morning, that which, once the Will had been signed, was inevitable if the Brinvilliers method of surreptitious elimination was to be followed. Doctor Antommarchi was summoned; Marchand, who had relieved Montholon, called him.

The doctor noted: vomit of black, viscous matter mixed with semi-digested food and granular black blood. Later in the morning Napoleon was able to sleep a little. Here we may prepare ourselves, in the interest of understanding, to accept the fetid atmosphere in which the doctors and nursing attendants function as they care for a desperately or, indeed, terminally ill patient. We must address ourselves to the symptoms for they portray the truths that now, with the Glasgow scientist's analyses at our disposal, permit us to read clearly what the doctors in the sickroom could not understand in 1821.

At a quarter past eight vomiting began again, blacker this time and with clots of coagulated blood. The doctor thought that the stomach was ulcerated. At two in the afternoon the patient had a bowel movement, mixed with a large quantity of "black bile", which we may suspect to have been simply blood. A haemorrhage, then, was doubly evident.

In the evening Napoleon was a little better, but when the doctor's back was turned he ate a little fruit and drank some wine. Pierron, the butler, was severely blamed for this when Antommarchi found out, but it was too late. Napoleon had another of those "fever" attacks, recognizable by now, with fits of shivering and icy legs, as symptomatic of arsenic or antimony intoxication. But in this instance it was obviously not arsenic, or rather not arsenic alone, for arsenic does not cause such haemorrhaging. On the other hand, haemorrhage is a typical result of tartar emetic, the antimony salt.

This time no doctor had prescribed tartar emetic, at least neither Arnott nor Antommarchi, who both kept careful note of their prescriptions.

Bertrand noted that on that day Napoleon had vomited more than ever before. On the same day Napoleon suddenly asked Antommarchi if there were any bitter almonds on the island. When Dr. Arnott arrived, the question was repeated. An answer was forthcoming. There had been no bitter almonds on St. Helena, at least not for the last three years.

Arnott was also questioned about other matters, but time and again Napoleon returned to the same theme: Are there any bitter almonds on the island?[9]

Someone or something had aroused Napoleon's interest in bitter almonds. Who can that someone have been? Obviously, someone who had been alone with Napoleon. Marchand? No, for when Marchand relieved Montholon Napoleon was extremely ill. He could have been in no state then to talk about bitter almonds. But some related discussion must have taken place at night. This unaccountable curiosity about bitter almonds had been aroused so suddenly that both Bertrand and Arnott, like Antommarchi, had found it worth noting in their journals.

On the other hand Montholon must have known that bitter almonds were not especially wholesome. His brother had been valet to the Duke of Fleury, King Louis' favorite during the King's long exile. Soon after the restoration, Fleury died as a result of having drunk a whole carafe of orgeat. It was a beverage containing, amongst other things, bitter almonds.[10]

That day something else happened that Bertrand clearly

thought worth mentioning. Bertrand's little four-year-old son Arthur handed in to the imperial household some peach stones someone had asked him to collect. Bertrand does not say who that person was.

What use could anyone have for peach stones? They were poisonous; they contained hydrocyanic acid — like bitter almonds.

As a matter of fact the peach stones were not needed, for a little later that day a whole case of bitter almonds arrived at Longwood. The governor had sent them, wrote Bertrand.[11]

Bertrand thought so; but we need not. We know, of course, that scapegoat No. 1 in the drama of St. Helena was called Sir Hudson Lowe, but at no time did he concern himself in detail with what the French had to eat and drink. That was the culinary responsibility of the head of the imperial household, Count de Montholon. The governor occasionally had tried to appear interested, for instance, when he sent up a large shipment of coffee as a gift to Longwood. But then the recipients had said they feared the coffee was poisoned. What would they have said, then, if the governor had started to send up bitter almonds?

We might almost hazard a guess that the bitter almonds arrived at St. Helena by the same boat as Napoleon's elaborate leaden coffin, although we would not have the slightest written proof for such a suspicion.

References

1. Bertrand III:133
2. Bertrand III:131-34
3. Bertrand III:135
4. Antommarchi (2) page 11
5. Bertrand III:135
6. Bertrand III:137
7. Bertrand III:151
8. Marchand II:316
9. Bertrand III:163
10. Montesquiou 407
11. Bertrand III:166
12. Dupont 345

43

The Last Sacraments

DURING THE NEXT FEW days Napoleon's condition remained on the whole unchanged, except that with each passing day he grew weaker.

The symptoms were those of his continuing so-called climatic sickness, that is to say, fits of shivering, icy chill in the legs spreading sometimes to his body, a weak and irregular pulse, nausea. One new symptom could be noted, however, not typical of arsenical intoxication but rather of poisoning with antimony — a constant vomiting that produced only mucus mixed with blood.

Nothing is mentioned as to whether Napoleon had any difficulty in passing water during these days when he was so ill; on the other hand he seems to have needed to urinate very often. This is also suggestive of a change of poison. A lessening in the secretion of urine is typical of intoxication by arsenic; an increased secretion suggests antimony poisoning.

The patient also developed troublesome hiccups and talked inconsequently, so that it seemed as if he did not understand what he was saying. He would repeat the same thing, over and over again.

On April 28 Pierron had been to Jamestown where on the previous day a schooner had put in with provisions. Napoleon called for Pierron to give him news.

"Did the schooner bring oranges?"

"Yes, Sire!"

"Did you bring any with you?"

"Yes, Sire."

"Let me have one."

They brought Napoleon two of the newly-arrived oranges. He

369

found them sour; they were sugared, but he still thought them sour.

"Did that ship bring lemons?"

"No, Sire."

"Almonds?"

"No, Sire."

"Pomegranates?"

"No, Sire."

"Grapes?"

"No, Sire."

"Wine?"

"Yes, Sire, but not in bottles."

"Didn't that ship bring anything?"

"Yes, Sire, cattle."

"How many oxen?"

"Forty-three, Sire." (Pierron knew how to answer Napoleon. An answer had to be ready when he asked, or he became very angry. As to whether the answer was correct or not, he need never know.)

"How many sheep?"

"Two hundred, Sire."

"How many goats?"

"None, Sire."

"How many hens?"

"None, Sire."

"Yes, but didn't she bring anything? Did she bring nuts?"

"No, Sire."

"Nuts come from cold countries, almonds from hot, I believe. Didn't the ship bring lemons, pomegranates and almonds?"

Pierron was allowed to leave. It was only for a short while. Then he was summoned again and Napoleon wanted to know what that schooner had brought. The same questions, the same answers.

"Didn't that ship bring anything?"

Pierron was again permitted to leave, but soon he was recalled. Then he had to stand there again and answer the same questions.

"Didn't that ship bring anything?"[1]

On the next day, April 29, Napoleon asked for a drink of water flavored with wine. He suffered much from thirst these days and nights.

He was certainly given his thoroughly watered wine, but his attendants — who they were at just that moment is not known — advised him to drink lemonade or orgeat. The doctors had especially recommended this.

So far, so good. Orgeat now stood on Napoleon's bedside table, *recommended by the doctors*, and bitter almonds were to be had, available for powdering. So now the lethal drink could be prepared according to all the rules of the art. The orgeat that Marchand had found on the bedside table on the seventh of April was a sort of neutered orgeat. One who had an interest in having it used would serve this end by putting it there to accustom Napoleon to the drink and, moreover, so that everyone could realize orgeat was quite a harmless, customary drink, refreshing in the mouth of a man whose stomach churned with frequent vomitings.

The doctors had indeed recommended orgeat. But that casts no shadow of suspicion on them. In the practice of medicine in Napoleon's time orgeat had long been considered a suitable refreshment for a well-to-do patient. It was thought to have strengthening properties, too.

For two hours, from one o'clock until three in the afternoon, Napoleon repeated the same series of questions, at intervals of only a few minutes.

"Which is best, orgeat or lemonade?"

"Orgeat is heavier, less of a thirst-quencher, Sire."

"Which do doctors advise?"

"Whichever pleases you most."

"Orgeat is made of barley, isn't it?"

"No, Sire, it is made from the milk of almonds."

"Do they make cherry juice?"

"Yes, Sire."

"Apple juice? Pear juice?"

"No, Sire."

"Almond juice?"

"Ah, oui, l'orgeat."

"Nut juice?"

"No, Sire."

"Nuts come from colder countries, almonds from hot, don't they?"

"Yes, Sire."

Then he would be silent for a little while, only to start again: "Which is best, orgeat or lemonade?

"What do the doctors advise?

"Orgeat is made from barley, isn't it?"[12]

It is rather remarkable that only Bertrand specifically tells us that Napoleon was given orgeat during his last days. Both Marchand and Antommarchi note that Napoleon liked to drink *eau de fleur d'oranger,* Seville orange-flower water, a perfume that is actually used in orgeat.

One thing is very certain; it would have been easy to give orgeat and say it was orange-flower water, as they offer the same odor and Napoleon's sickroom was always kept dark. The poisoning had made Napoleon extremely sensitive to light and his seeing ability had become affected. When orgeat was given, it would have been easy to make both him and his attendants believe it was nothing more than orange-flower water.

Montholon could not really have thought things out properly by that night of the 24/25th of April, when Napoleon suddenly again fell very ill. He was worse than before. The cash assets! Napoleon's cash assets! Who would get those?

But Montholon managed to make good that omission on April 29 in a fairly daring and liberal way. He drafted two letters. One was to Napoleon's banker Lafitte, the other to a Baron La Bouillerie, who administered part of Napoleon's fortune. The letter to Monsieur Lafitte was as follows:

> Monsieur Lafitte, shortly before I left Paris I handed into your keeping the sum of nearly six million, for which you gave me two receipts; I have cancelled one and have told the Count de Montholon to submit the other to you, so that when I am dead you may hand him the above amount together with 5% interest accrued from July 1, 1815, after deduction of any payments you may have made at my command.
>
> I wish the auditing of the accounts to be done by you, the Count de Montholon, Count Bertrand and M. Marchand

together, and when this audit has been compiled, I hereby acquit you of all responsibility for the next amount in question. I also handed over to you a box with my seal. I ask you to hand over the same to the Count de Montholon.

There being no further reason for this letter, I pray to God, Monsieur Lafitte, that He may keep you deservingly in His holy care.

Longwood, the Island of St. Helena,
This 25th day of April, 1821.
NAPOLEON

The other letter, the one addressed to Baron La Bouillerie, simply requested him to hand over the accounts and the cash to the Count de Montholon.[2]

On April 29, the day on which Napoleon time and again put the same simple questions for a couple of hours on end — thereby showing plainly he was not fully in command of his mind — on that very day he was supposed to have dictated these precisely worded and businesslike letters giving power of attorney to Montholon. It is wholly incredible that in his described condition on that day he could have done so.

But fortunately for history, since the events are of deep significance, we know from Marchand's memoirs what actually happened. Montholon went to Marchand with the two drafts and asked him to make fair copies. They had been dictated by Napoleon, said Montholon, and now he wanted them re-written so that he could present them to Napoleon for signature.

Marchand took them and pointed out that the date was incorrect. This day was the twenty-ninth of April and the drafts were dated the twenty-fifth. Nevertheless, Marchand obeyed the orders of his superior to the letter and made the fair copies, which Montholon then took in to Napoleon. It was urgent, said Montholon, for it was not certain in what state Napoleon would find himself on the following day.

That the letter to Lafitte was a forgery is also clear from the fact that Napoleon never deposited some six millions of francs with this banker. The real amount was about three and a half millions. If Napoleon had been then of sound enough mind to compose the letter as Montholon had drafted it, he would have remembered what amount he had on deposit with his banker.

The figure quoted was guesswork.

Marchand writes in his memoirs: *"Ces lettres sont de la facture du Comte de Montholon* — These letters are the creation of the Count de Montholon."[2]

The mild Marchand was not wholly gullible. He thought the incident worthy of noting although he refrained from raising an alarm at so inopportune a time for a parallel crisis in the house.

Bertrand was much concerned that Napoleon was leaving nothing to Antommarchi. He asked Montholon to see to it that a letter signed by Napoleon was sent to the Empress Marie-Louise, in which Antommarchi was recommended for a pension of 6000 francs.

Later that day (April 29) Bertrand asked Montholon if he had managed to obtain that signature. No, the Emperor was not in his right mind. Montholon explained that under such circumstances he could not be allowed to sign anything, for then it might later be said it was Montholon who had drawn up the Will and not Napoleon.[3]

How entirely true that was! On April 29, the day Marchand testifies the letter of gift was dictated for signature, Napoleon was not only quite out of his mind, he was also, as has been said, both deaf and blind. His deafness was nothing new, Bertrand tells us, but he had never previously noticed Napoleon to be as deaf as he was that day.[4] Moreover, when Bertrand stood before Napoleon and the latter had his gaze fixed upon him, Napoleon still did not see that Bertrand was there.[5] That was his physical condition on the day when — unknown to himself — he is supposed to have dictated the cogent letter bequeathing all his ready assets to Montholon.

But on April 28 he had been even more mentally deranged, according to Arnott. On that day vomiting had been at its severest and the patient had been very tired. Antommarchi noted that Napoleon had a fever, Arnott said that he had none. Arnott had a thermometer and so we must believe him. What Antommarchi thought was fever must have been those attacks of shivering that accompany arsenic and antimony intoxication. His vomit was mixed with blood and also contained black clots of coagulated blood. The red blood in the vomit must have come from the oesophagus or the pharynx, where tartar emetic easily produces bleeding corrosion. The black clots would indicate gastric haemorrhage.

When he called at Longwood on the morning of April 30, Bertrand was told that Napoleon was once more of sound mind. He felt, therefore, he should take this opportunity to ask the Emperor what he should do with the shorthand notes he had made during their conversations.

Napoleon did not hear what he said. Bertrand shouted as loudly as he could, but in vain. Napoleon turned on him an unseeing, shifting gaze, shut his eyes and did not reply to his question.[6]

Had Napoleon, in a state of mental aberration, told Bertrand to burn his notes, it is probable the grand marshal of the palace would have done so — exactly that. Unpredictable or not, Napoleon was still the emperor to whom Bertrand had sworn eternal loyalty and obedience.

Had Bertrand's books been destroyed, much that we now know to be the truth about Napoleon's sufferings and death on St. Helena might never have been brought to light. Certainly nothing Montholon would write would be as revealing as the cryptic Bertrand notes.

That day Napoleon's vomiting was less violent and the vomit no longer contained so much black matter. He was generally calmer, but wanted nothing to eat. He absolutely refused to take any medication, but it had been possible to get his permission for three vesicatories to be applied, two on the thighs and one on the abdomen.

Vesicatories? Could these, then, be the vesicatories that Montholon, on December 5, 1820, so predictably mentioned as later to be applied? He foresaw it at a time when Napoleon enjoyed comparatively good health between his periods of sickness from October 26 to November 1 and from December 28 to 30, 1820.

Antommarchi noted that day (April 30), among other things, that Napoleon complained of a burning sensation in the pharynx. This was consistent with what could be expected. It was a symptom especially typical of antimony. The reaction was not at all that produced by arsenic-trioxide.

At 9 o'clock that evening, however, came a new and severe

attack, with shivering, difficulty in breathing, general restlessness and anxiety, a feeling of icy coldness, weak and irregular pulse and copious salivation. These symptoms continued until, toward midnight, Napoleon became quieter.

What had happened?

Bertrand as well as Antommarchi tell of that acute attack which started at nine after a comparatively quiet day. Both mention that the vesicatories were removed on Napoleon's demand. Under the vesicatory on the abdomen the flesh was observed to be white. In other words it was precisely as Montholon had pictured it to be — but, prematurely — on the fifth of December, 1820: cadavéreuse", or in other words, necrotic.

Clearly a mortifying poison had been mixed into the substance of the vesicatory. It is easy to believe it was arsenic. Had the drama proceeded so far that it had become too risky to administer further arsenic orally? Here the use of arsenic might have been discovered by visual evidence at the autopsy. There is no evidence that the condition of the flesh under the vesicatories aroused any comment, much less suspicion in the group of attending doctors.

An hour or so after the vesicatory had been removed Napoleon felt better. But first he had thrown up a considerable amount of mucus. In cases of acute intoxication the body tends to react by vomiting, regardless of how the poison had been absorbed into the blood stream.

Before the vesicatory had been removed Antommarchi thought for a time Napoleon was dying.[7]

Again during Montholon's accustomed watch later on the night of April 30/May 1 something happened to induce a reaction. Napoleon broke into a cold sweat, had difficulty in breathing and once more vomited a black substance. By inference from these symptoms, Napoleon had received another dose of tartar emetic.

This occurred during what normally would have been Montholon's night watch. But just that night Montholon had arranged for a replacement, and Bertrand had finally had his wish granted. He was to watch over his beloved leader. Now that the business of the Will was finished Bertrand could step in. It would therefore be seen that it was not only when Montholon was on night duty that the Emperor fell ill.

No shadow of suspicion can fall on Bertrand, however. It was not he who arranged for the drinks Napoleon had on his bedside table. The man whose duties, by definition, made him responsible for them was the head of the imperial household, de Montholon.

Tartar emetic now was important. It is less easy to poison with calomel and orgeat if the victim is not prepared in a special way. Experiments have proved that if canines are given only calomel nothing happens. Given only orgeat in reasonable amounts, they may even be inclined to relish it. But if both are taken, violent vomiting occurs, which saves the dogs from fatal poisoning. But if the dogs are given tartar emetic for a time — and they vomit after each dose — and are then given calomel and orgeat, they will keep down the mixture and will die of *squirre* at the pylorus, a hardening of the lower stomach orifice, and *cancerous lesions,* cancer-like ulcers. In light strength, tartar emetic erodes the mucous lining of the stomach, in that way suppressing the vomiting reflexes. In strong doses tartar emetic can perforate the stomach wall, with danger of peritonitis. This was Napoleon's malady at the end of March 1821.

Carlo Buonaparte died of a *squirre* at the pylorus. On December 5, 1821 Montholon had known that Napoleon would die of *une maladie de langueur* — a languishing or wasting illness.

Tartar emetic was not to be skimped now. On May 2 Napoleon was still weaker. His pulse was very rapid, up to 108 beats. Troublesome hiccoughing had started the day before, which greatly distressed the patient. This continued and grew worse on May 2. On that day Napoleon ate nothing.

May 3 was characterized mainly by Napoleon's extreme general weakness and by prolonged spasms of hiccoughing. He was given a teaspoon of ether. This soothed the hiccoughing spasms and he was able to sleep a little. His complexion changed often. At intervals he had the pallor of death.

The Emperor developed a burning thirst, Marchand tells us. Bertrand and Antommarchi confirm it.

Marchand gave Napoleon a drink of sugared water mixed with a little wine.[11]

From Bertrand we learn that on May 3 the Emperor was served "a little of wine with sugar, a sort of syrup".[8]

Antommarchi remarked that the Emperor drank quantities of orange-flower water mixed with sugared water. Montholon, in his memoirs, years later, would say that almond-milk and orange-flower water were the Emperor's own medicines and that on the twenty-third of March, 1821 he asked for orgeat (which Montholon says he dissuaded). This gentleman wanted it on the record that Napoleon, in his last days, drank freely a harmless orangeade.

None testified that someone gave Napoleon orgeat to drink on May 3, 1821. But, we know from Marchand that there now was an orange flower drink customarily to be seen on the bedside table. This had been so ever since the beginning of April. Marchand and Napoleon had been surprised by the arrival of the refreshant. It was, without bitter almonds, a harmless beverage. But on April 25, it will be recalled, bitter almonds arrived at Longwood, an important ingredient of the true orgeat. We may meditate without help upon what possible use they would have other than in the preparation of orgeat.

Antommarchi would have been unable to see what sort of beverage was given to his patient. The sick-room was quite dark, for Napoleon's eyes were sensitive to light. But the odor of the beverage would be noticeable. It would tend to perfume the atmosphere with the pleasing suggestion of orange blossoms.

Bertrand was informed that Napoleon was given, on the third of May, *before receiving a calomel dose,* a kind of syrup drink. Heavily sugared, orgeat of course would be a syrupy drink. Our conclusion must be that Napoleon on that day of the death-blow swallowed willingly a sort of beverage that looked like a syrup and smelled like orange-flower water. We may satisfy ourselves that, indeed, orgeat was the only substance figuring in this tragedy likely to look syrupy and have the odor of orange-flower water. The point is important to establish since that was the reagent of death.

What sort of beverage Napoleon was given *after* he had swallowed his calomel dose is of no importance. A few moments later, the deadly poison would be in his blood.

On the fateful third day of May Dr. Arnott, of his own accord or at the suggestion of Montholon, realized Napoleon's life was in danger. Drastic measures must be taken.

The patient had not had a bowel movement for a couple of days — not since the morning of May 1.

Arnott explained to Antommarchi that they could not let the patient lie there, day after day, without a proper evacuation.

The fact that Napoleon had eaten almost nothing for more than a week seems not to have eased Arnott's anxiety. He would have to explain such a lapse from sound medical procedure at some time and place within his profession. Of that he would be most uncomfortably aware. In the circumstances he had more need to give Napoleon a purgative than his mortally ill patient had need to receive it.

If a bowel movement must be induced, the best way to do so would be with calomel. It must be secretly administered to Napoleon without his noticing it.

Calomel! Montholon had already realized as long ago as February 8 of the previous year that calomel in the presence of "humidity" would put an end to Napoleon's work on the gardens. So now calomel soon would further fulfil Montholon's prophecy of December 1820.

But Antommarchi had not been reckoned with. Calomel? Never! Not so long as Napoleon was as weak as he was. It would kill him, protested Antommarchi.

"Then we must use an enema instead," said Arnott. Antommarchi would not hear of such a thing. Napoleon was much too weak to submit to the strain an enema would impose.

"Well, then, we must use calomel," declared Arnott. The doctor had his own good reasons, which he put strongly to Bertrand. On the record, Napoleon had been allowed to lie for three whole days — in fact, it was only two — without a bowel movement. This could show lack of responsibility by his attending physicians.

Napoleon was now without doubt in the greatest danger, Arnott reported, and nearly everything was against him; nevertheless, both as a doctor and for the sake of his own self-esteem and good repute professionally, Arnott must precipitate a bowel movement. If the members of the Medical Faculty were to hear that Napoleon had been allowed to lie for three days without a bowel clearance they would not understand, concluded Arnott.

Still Antommarchi refused to be persuaded. He considered Napoleon, at that point, far too weak to support an induced movement. The question could be raised again when Napoleon was a little stronger.

The doctors began to quarrel quite heatedly. Bertrand ordered them to withdraw to where they might discuss the problem thoroughly and, in a more seemly manner, attempt to reach agreement.[8]

At 2:30 the governor called on Montholon. He had heard that the doctors could not agree and wished therefore to suggest that the admiral's chief of doctors, Thomas Shortt and Charles Mitchell, should be called in for consultation. Montholon and Bertrand agreed with the governor. Antommarchi had no objection and asked the escort officer to summon both doctors of the St. Helena Station.

Doctors Shortt and Mitchell obviously had been standing ready, for they appeared almost immediately.

It is on the record and worthy of note that the four doctors met in Montholon's apartments. The Count acted unofficially as convenor and moderator. The result of the consultation was that the three English doctors approved calomel and Antommarchi still held out doggedly against its use. In the end three against one proved decisive.

So at last, *on the recommendation of three doctors and with the permission of the Count de Montholon,* Napoleon was to be given his calomel dosage. The amount was fixed at ten grains, that is to say 0.6 grams.

That was what, under any circumstances, could be called an heroic dose. There was on this third day of May, 1821 not much left in Napoleon of the hero of Arcole and Lodi. He had become extremely weak, his once amazing life force all but destroyed.

A normal dosage of calomel, according to English custom of the times, was *two grains divided into several doses.* German and Swedish doctors administered calomel in dosages of only one grain, or a tenth of what the desperately ill Napoleon was to receive.

Naturally there is no reason to suspect that the St. Helena doctors wanted to dispatch Napoleon's life with calomel. But their conference took place in Montholon's apartments. The

Count was the only non-professional person present. He was in a position to tell the doctors how one of Napoleon's earlier illnesses had progressed. If at the conference he related the same story as he later published in his famous *Histoire* or *Récits,* it is quite possible he would influence the doctors in their decision.

In his *Histoire* Montholon tells the story of a dangerous attack of dysentery Napoleon reportedly had suffered on some vague and unspecified occasion. "For three days we were extremely anxious," wrote Montholon. "Although the illness did not become worse, his life was still in danger as long as calomel had not achieved that which the doctors called its effect."[13] So we are encouraged by Montholon to believe it was calomel that had saved Napoleon's life at that other dangerous time. But where and when? Montholon ministered to the Emperor only on St. Helena. There is no entry of so remarkable an occasion as he described.

Marchand also mentions without date an occasion when Napoleon apparently had a severe attack of "dysentery" and when for a while there was actually cause for anxiety. But the illness passed over quickly, writes Marchand, adding that Napoleon proudly proclaimed that he had recovered without taking the doctor's medicine.

Now all that was required had been duly prepared and was in position to effect Napoleon's execution. The orgeat — genuine orgeat — was there and he was to be given the immense dose of calomel — and, note well, by doctors' orders.

But, hold! One more detail remained before he could be given the *coup de grâce.* In best Bourbon custom it was considered correct that, if possible, every execution should be performed only after the victim had been prepared for death by a priest and had been given the Last Sacraments. Moreover, Napoleon had said in his Will that he died in the Catholic religion. Well, then, he must die a sanctified death with the Last Sacraments duly uttered because otherwise the rest of his Will might not be regarded as more credible than an undemonstrated claim to religiosity.

Early that afternoon of May 3, the door to Napoleon's sick-room was opened slowly and carefully and the valet Saint-Denis whispered to Marchand, who was sitting watching by Napoleon's bedside, that he wished to speak to him.

Marchand tiptoed out of the room. Outside, not only Saint-Denis but also the priest Vignali were waiting. The latter told Marchand that Count de Montholon had called for him and told him Napoleon wished to see him.

Napoleon was in no state that day to take any initiatives whatsoever. The diaries agree that he was quite passive.

But the priest would assume it was Napoleon, and not Montholon alone, who had summoned him.

Abbé Vignali had come not in priestly dress. He wore his everyday clothes but he carried something under his coat which had caused Marchand to suspect that he was out on some religious errand.

Vignali asked to be left alone with the sick man, so Marchand left the room and the priest went in. Marchand lingered outside the door to stop anyone entering and disturbing the rites.

It was a good thing he did, for shortly afterwards the Grand Marshal of the Court arrived and sought to go in.

"What are they about?" asked Bertrand.

"Abbé Vignali requested to be alone with the Emperor. I suppose it is some religious rite which he does not want witnessed."

Half an hour later Vignali emerged. The Last Sacraments, he said, had been duly administered to the Emperor.[11] By grace of Bourbon decision, it would appear, Napoleon the agnostic was to die after appropriate ceremony of the Church.

References

1. Bertrand III:171-2
2. Marchand II:318-319
3. Bertrand III:175-76
4. Bertrand III:173
5. Bertrand III:175
6. Bertrand III:180
7. Bertrand III:182; Antommarchi 30th April 1821
8. Bertrand III:188-9
9. Antommarchi 3rd May 1821; Frémeaux (2), page 142
10. Richter-Collin I:118
11. Marchand II:322-24
12. Bertrand III:177
13. Montholon I:166

44

The Coup de Grâce

WHEN THE MEDICAL consultation had reached a decision Marchand was summoned in his role of head valet. The valets were the only persons who had the right to serve Napoleon and in command of them was Louis Marchand. Without his co-operation nothing could come of the call for calomel medication.

Marchand refused. He had received very definite orders: *Never* was he to give Napoleon any drink or other medicine without the latter's express permission.

All were fully aware, of course, that Napoleon would not knowingly take calomel; it could only be administered by stealth.

Bertrand managed to persuade Marchand, however; surely they could not leave Napoleon to die without having made some effort to help him. The doctors were now of the opinion that calomel could save his life. Could Marchand really refuse him this assistance?

Put like this, and in a way he could appreciate, the loyal Marchand reluctantly promised to co-operate.

Marchand took the doctors' dose of calomel and stirred it in sugared water. The next time Napoleon signalled for something to drink, as so often he had done these past days, Marchand offered him the calomel preparation.

Napoleon opened his mouth, took the drink and swallowed it, though with a certain amount of difficulty. His mouth and throat were raw from the tartar emetic. Then he realized that there was something different about the customary sweet-flavored water. He struggled to throw it up but could not. He turned to Marchand and said reproachfully yet with affection in his eyes: *"Tu me trompes aussi* — you also deceive me."

Bertrand, who witnessed the scene and saw how distressed

Marchand was at this reprimand, tried to console him: "*Que d'amitié dans ce reproche!* — how much friendship there was in that reproach!" And it was with this reproach Napoleon spoke his last cogent words. Soon the mercuric cyanide had overcome his consciousness, almost certainly sparing him at the end from the worst of those terrible pains corrosive sublimate, gnawing the stomachal walls, will provoke. It may be doubted that de Montholon pictured himself, at any point, in the role of anaesthetist.

Marchand's remorse at having deceived his master was hardly helped by Napoleon's words or Bertrand's kindly consolation. But after a while Napoleon asked for more to drink and willingly took the glass of wine and water that Marchand handed him, thanking him with a barely audible, *"C'est bon, c'est bien bon."* Marchand felt reassured. He had not wholly lost Napoleon's trust.[1]

To judge from Marchand's description of Napoleon's last days, it was clearly not generally realized that the Emperor's once great intellect had been destroyed. His mental functions became little more than automatic, in keeping with the declining capability of his brain to carry messages to nerves and muscles and evoke voluntary response.

It was half past five in the afternoon when Napoleon was given the dose of calomel, writes Bertrand, who was present. Arnott and Antommarchi, who were not present, place the time at 6 o'clock (May 3).

When Bertrand entered the sick-room a little later, he encountered the priest, Vignali. Someone obviously had planned that Napoleon should expire in the arms of the Church. For this reason Vignali had been summoned to the dying emperor.

Bertrand sent the priest away, telling him he was not to put in an appearance again unless Napoleon himself should call for him.

Bertrand explains his action in his diary: It was not going to be said *que l'empéreur, cet homme si fort, mourait comme un capucin* — that the Emperor, so strong a man, died like a Capucin monk.[2]

At first Napoleon lay quietly after his medication and his breathing was fairly calm, but suddenly an attack of hiccoughing overtook him and he sighed as though in pain. His eyes were those of a dying man. He would thereafter utter barely a word but his occasional "Give me my chamber-pot."

He lay thus hour after hour. At eleven o'clock the doctors still had seen nothing of the functional effect they had wished to achieve. Arnott wanted to give a further dose of calomel. Obviously he still believed in the power of his medicine to save the dying man. Antommarchi, who once more proved that he was the better doctor of the two, absolutely refused to agree to such an added measure. He was entitled to demur. Ten grains of calomel was a monstrous dose.

Once again the doctors were at cross purposes; Bertrand saw that they must call in the arbitrators, the chief doctors, who were close at hand.

At half past eleven it became obvious that Napoleon had not been given calomel in vain. The patient had a mighty evacuation, enormous, copious, black, according to Bertrand. It had the consistency of tar, wrote Antommarchi. It was more than everything else of the sort that Napoleon had produced during a whole month, wrote Bertrand. We may judge what was happening in Napoleon's system.

When prussic acid (HCN), as in bitter almonds, reacts upon calomel (HgCl), and the hydrochloric acid (HCl) contained in gastric juice, the result will be mercuric cyanide ($Hg(CN)_2$) + corrosive sublimate ($HgCl_2$) + metallic mercury in colloidal suspension. Such colloidal suspension is black as India ink. Mercuric cyanide rapidly kills the brain; corrosive sublimate acts more locally, corroding the stomach walls. In spite of this corrosion, the victim then will feel no pain thanks to the mercuric cyanide. Stools from a bleeding stomach are very dark brown. Colloidal mercury makes them more black. The witnesses found Napoleon's stool astonishingly black.

Napoleon was so utterly exhausted that for a while it was thought he would die. But, wrote Bertrand, perhaps this stool might save the Emperor's life.

At four o'clock on the morning of May 4 Arnott even thought that Napoleon had emerged from critical danger.[3]

Arnott could not imagine that his decision, so in accordance with the established art of medicine, could be other than a blessing.

Antommarchi, on the other hand, was sorely beset with worry. He wrote in reference to this massive stool that Napoleon had completely collapsed, experienced great difficulty in breathing, with cold sweats, an irregular and hardly noticeable pulse, a rumbling in his stomach, icy chill in the lower extremities, and a constant desire to urinate.[4]

On the other hand, Arnott was sanguine in his judgment of the results of the treatment. Never suspecting the truth of the situation he reported to Sir Thomas Reade: "Calomel had the desired effect. The patient does not appear to be worse but rather better. After thorough consideration I have decided that there is more hope today than yesterday and the day before. Tell the governor this."[5]

Certainly Arnott was perfectly cast to be the foil for clever Montholon in this drama. Calomel had had "the desired effect," he wrote. He had clearly not seen and understood that that copious evacuation consisted greatly of blood. It was black, it had the consistency of tar. What else could it have been? For more than a week Napoleon had scarcely eaten anything solid, and nothing at all after his last bowel movement on the first of May. Well, as a matter of fact, he had eaten two biscuits on the second and one on the third of May. Biscuits do not result in black stools.

The responsibility for the unfortunate prescription must be shared by Arnott and the two chief doctors, Shortt and Mitchell, but the driving force behind it was undoubtedly the man who, in a letter to his wife of December 20, 1820, had claimed to be Napoleon's *de facto* physician, namely Count de Montholon.[6] What is more, the Marquis de Montchenu himself bears witness of this. He speaks in his diary of the difference of opinion between Arnott and Antommarchi concerning the suitability of giving Napoleon calomel. *"The discussion was referred to Montholon, who sided with the English doctors and the medicine was consequently administered."*[7]

At midnight Napoleon sank into unconsciousness. At three in the morning his hiccoughing recurred. At half past six he had another large, black bowel movement. For a moment Bertrand was overjoyed, thinking he may have heard the words, *"Eh bien, Bertrand, mon ami."*

At midday another severe tar-like stool was passed. At a

quarter to two and again an hour later the same observations were recorded.

During the day Napoleon had also vomited once a substance which Marchand found to consist of a black mass. There can be no doubt whatsoever of its meaning. What the colomel medication had caused was, among other things, a massive gastric haemorrhage.

Antommarchi now knew for certain that Napoleon was dying.[8] Dr. Arnott on the other hand was optimistic. At 9 o'clock on the evening of May 4 he sent a report to Plantation House: "I have just left our patient fast asleep. He appears better than he was two hours ago. He has no hiccup, his respiration is easy and in the course of the day he has taken a considerable quantity of nourishment for a person in his state."[9]

From a security agent's point of view how, indeed, could Dr. Arnott have been improved upon? Not only did he confuse blood with biscuits but he also confirmed what he had not himself seen but about which he merely had been told by Montholon.

The "considerable quantity of nourishment" that Napoleon, according to Arnott, was supposed to have taken consisted of a little cold consommé that he was given to drink at a quarter past three in the afternoon. The amount, we are told, was about 8-10 tablespoonsful.[10]

Every five or ten minutes, however, Napoleon was given *eau de fleurs d'oranger* to drink. We must suppose there was more in the drink than orange flower water. Too much suggests that the drink was orgeat.

At 8 o'clock in the evening still another copious black stool was passed. Arnott was satisfied with the pulse, which was now regular. Antommarchi remained convinced it would be only a matter of hours before Napoleon died.

Napoleon lay still almost all day. When he wanted something to drink he made a slight sign with his hand. When he did not want more he turned away his head. He had now obviously lost the power of speech. It is an accepted fact that in cases of acute mercury intoxication the voluntary muscles, including those used in speech, become more or less paralyzed.

On the night of May 4 his immobility became even more

pronounced. Only a few sounds were made. It was almost as though a musical instrument were being played, the sounds being not like ordinary moans, thought Bertrand.[11]

But according to his own account in his famous *Récits*, Montholon managed to interpret these sounds — undoubtedly caused by over-pressure due to fermentation in the stomach and intestines — as: *"France, armée, tête d'armée, Joséphine."*[12] It was Montholon's literary contribution to history. Like so much else of his reporting, it was quite untrue, but it became part of the continuing legend of Napoleon, as did Montholon's forthright cancer explanation of death.

On May 5 Napoleon lay quite still.

At eleven minutes to six in the afternoon Antommarchi was able to declare that life was gone. For the legendary Eagle of France death had come in a guarded cage the secret poisoner had penetrated.

References

1. Marchand II:324-25
2. Bertrand III:191
3. Ibid III:192
4. Antommarchi 3rd May 1821
5. Frémeaux (2), page 144
6. Gonnard 7 page 65
7. Firmin-Didot 224
8. Bertrand III:192; Antommarchi 4th May 1821
9. Forsyth III:286
10. Bertrand III:193
11. Ibid III:195
12. Montholon (2) II:548

45

The Certificate of Death

NAPOLEON, WHO HAD A deep respect for the truth, had grown determined that an autopsy should be performed on his body at which special attention should be paid to the pylorus. He was of the opinion that the man whom, in his later years, he certainly believed to have been his father, had died of a scirrhous condition at the pylorus. It was this very fact of a concern with the state of the pylorus muscle that helped Montholon develop his myth of tumerous stomach cancer.

Napoleon, for all his antagonism to Antommarchi, respected him as an anatomist and pathologist qualified to conduct a critical task of research. We are fortunate in having Antommarchi's report to refer to in this generation. He had no political end to serve; only the judgment of science.

All Montholon's efforts to get rid of Antommarchi, whose professional ability he had every reason to fear, had ended in failure. We may suppose that this was in good part due to an unavoidable fact. Antommarchi may have been disliked but he was a Corsican, and therefore someone to be trusted . . . by another Corsican.

Fortunately for Montholon, however, there were several English doctors on St. Helena. However skillful they may have been as far as their own soldiers were concerned, they would not possess the quite specialized knowledge of a French security agent; knowledge with roots deep in the courts of the Medici, of Louis XIII, Louis XIV and the Regent; lore of a kind not to be found in books. The English doctors may not have heard of the Marquise de Brinvilliers. Even if they had, they still would not have believed in her methods or achievements, just as Napoleon had not — nor had simple, honest Gourgaud.

When Napoleon died it was in keeping with the custom of the time that his body should not be removed before midnight. But when midnight had passed, the body was lifted from the bed, washed and dressed. The Emperor had directed that souvenirs for various persons he named should be made from his hair. Some of the hair was to be stranded into a watch-chain for his son, then titularly the King of Rome. Another lock would be woven into a bracelet for the Empress Marie-Louise. Each of the members of his immediate family should receive a locket enclosing a wisp of the silky brown hair.[1]

The task of cutting was entrusted to Abram Noverraz, second valet. It had been instructed that since a death mask was to be made and so many souvenirs of hair were to be distributed, the hair should be shaven from Napoleon's scalp rather than be clipped by scissors. We shall see that the method of cutting made a difference which not even the far-seeing de Montholon could have remotely suspected.

As he performed his task on the night of May 6th, 1821, Noverraz was barely enough recovered from his critical bout of Longwood illness, to be able to provide this last service to his royal master. As with Napoleon himself, when stricken with this strange malady, Noverraz had found his legs had become weak and painful under the weight of his body. There, in the near silence of the room at Longwood, a man who was only by chance still amongst the living administered to the dead monarch. More than likely he did so under the personal instruction of the poisoner. By the irony of fate Noverraz's simple operation with soap and razor would do more to remove the mystery of Napoleon's illness and death than would Antommarchi's skilful scalpel.

Again, as though by providential arrangement, not only did Noverraz remove the hair in such a way that under a microscope each single strand of hair would show the characteristic cut of a straight-edged blade rather than the scissoring cut of opposed blades, but he was moved to keep a small quantity of hairs for himself. Those particular hairs he knotted and fastened into a folder of paper with a seal of wax at the knot fixing the hair securely to its mounting. On the folder, in typical Noverraz handwriting easily verifiable as to authenticity by comparing with other specimens of the valet's writing, was the legend: *"Cheveux de l'immortel Empéreur Napoléon."*

The folder with the locks would be enclosed in a larger envelope and in this there was a letter from Noverraz, in which he wrote that he himself had shaved these hairs from Napoleon's head on May 6, 1821.

When in the turn of events after Marchand's memoirs were published I decided to send hairs to Glasgow for clinical test to determine their arsenic content, it was from this remarkable souvenir that a few hairs had been received. The valet's wax seal on a firm knot made it impossible to imagine that this was other than a valid lock of Napoleon's hair and that it was exactly what the accompanying words by Noverraz declared it to be.

This souvenir, in the course of time, had come by inheritance into the hands of a Swiss industrialist named Clifford Frey. He willingly and generously agreed to allow Dr. Hamilton Smith, eminent Scottish chemist and specialist in the activation analysis of hair, to study a certain number of hairs. The only condition he made was that the original knot should not be broken. He was impressed by the poisoning thesis as he read of it and became dedicated to the project of referring the riddle to science so that truth could be established for history.

Mr. Frey personally turned over the lock to Dr. Hamilton Smith at the Forensic Laboratory of the University of Glasgow. Thus, as well as to the servant Noverraz, history is deeply indebted to the late Mr. Frey for his interest and readiness to place this much-prized family heirloom at the disposal of research. Clifford Frey died in 1970. In his mind the contribution of hairs had fully served its purpose.

The analysis of these strands confirmed what might have been suspected at least two decades ago by studying the closely described symptoms of Napoleon's failing health. That his critical illness from the late summer of 1820 until April 1821 was symptomatic of arsenical poisoning could be deduced through careful reading by a person trained in toxicology.[2]

In the Napoleonic hairs in question, as taken by Noverraz, forty different arsenic peaks were identified. *The conclusion must be that on at least forty distinctly separate occasions Napoleon had been poisoned with arsenic.*

The longest hair was 13 cm, that is to say, it could register the course of arsenic ingestions into the Emperor's system during the period of about one year.

These test results give us of this nuclear age generation a time-reversing method by which, as if in a television replay, we can bring back to an indistinct screen the events in the sickroom at Longwood. Our view, however, will offer a far clearer understanding of what went on than the actors in the dramatic events were permitted to have by a mere exposure to the visible illness and distress of a very sick man whose time had come — by orders from Paris.

The lowest arsenic content in a 1 mm section was 2.8 p.p.m; the highest value was 51.2 p.p.m. against a norm of 0.8.

Between these extremes a prickly graph depicting the accumulation of arsenic was plotted for all the hairs tested.

The appearance of this arsenic accumulation graph is crucial in deciding whether or not, as some suggested, arsenic had been applied *externally,* before or after the hair had been removed from its owner. It would likewise indicate if the person in question had been intoxicated by a continuous, even consumption of arsenic as, for instance, in drinking water containing arsenic, or whether arsenic had been received internally in a series of ingestions on clearly separated occasions. The accumulation of arsenic in the hairs examined by Dr. Hamilton Smith proved to have been biologically deposited in the hair from the circulating blood of the living owner. It could not have existed on the hair by external application as a hairdressing, as a preservative or for any other purposes.[1] The peaks in the arsenic accumulation graph were caused by the consumption of larger amounts of arsenic on specific and definite occasions.[4] The scientific conclusion jointly reached with Dr. Smith could not accept any suggestion that these extraordinarily irregular arsenic accumulation graphs should have had their origin in some form of external applications to the hair, or to any dietary or benign medication sources.

But to return to the scene of the tragedy at St. Helena:
It is 2:30 p.m. of May 6, 1821. The saddened household is

hushed. A table covered with a sheet had been placed in Longwood's billiard room for the autopsy.

Napoleon's wish that his physician-in-ordinary should conduct the autopsy proceedings is being observed without questioning by the governor or by the English doctors who participated in the examination of organs. In all there were seventeen persons present at the post-mortem. They included the English doctors Arnott, Shortt, Mitchell, Livingstone, Burton, Rutledge and Henry along with Antommarchi, who performed the dissection. Sir Thomas Reade, Major Harrisson and Captain Crockat attended for the governor. Of those resident at Longwood there were Bertrand, Montholon, Marchand, Saint-Denis, Pierron and Vignali.

The St. Helena physicians were astonished to find Napoleon's body quite smooth, like that of a newborn child, and amazingly that the normal fine body hair had disappeared.[3] Had a modern expert on forensic medicine been on that post-mortem team he would certainly have been concerned by the coincidence of two such classical symptoms of arsenical poisoning being present.

An autopsy is an unsavory affair. There is no need to record every twist and turn of Antommarchi's revealing scalpel strokes. Scrutiny of the post-mortem reports will serve our needs. In particular, we shall interpret the findings in relation to Antommarchi's observations as he worked.

Knowing the tell-tale symptoms of Napoleon's illness and with the advantage of the many hair analyses in our hands, and well knowing, too, what happens when orgeat is taken at the same time as calomel, we of this generation can know in advance what to expect from the post-mortem. His autopsists were at the double disadvantage of being without such knowledge and the tools of today for their task. Beyond that, only Antommarchi was a qualified anatomist. The team could not adequately read the significance of what it saw.

Napoleon had been poisoned with arsenic over a long period of time, as repeated illnesses before his arrival at St. Helena indicated. Thus substantial layers of fat should have tended to remain on his body, in spite of his long and severe illness. He should also have been quite free of the fine hairs natural to most of the surface of the human body.

This condition we already know to have been readily and outwardly apparent.

An intoxication by arsenic should have left considerable traces in the lungs, where a certain degeneration through swollen lymph nodes around the bronchi should be evident. The pleural sacs should have been fairly full of fluid.

The liver should have been swollen, also the spleen. It is improbable that the dissector would identify any pathological inner change in the liver on dissection. It is only recently that, in cases of intoxication by arsenic, a microscopic examination has discovered characteristic fatty degeneration of the liver cells.[5,6,7]

Grave damage to the stomach would be evident. During his last two days Napoleon had suffered severe gastric haemorrhages. Large amounts of blood had passed through the intestines, a reaction first observable six hours after the calomel medication. While the antimony of emetic wines prepared the way, we need not doubt that the cause of the haemorrhages was the calomel. What had so often occurred during the calomel-as-laxative period in the practice of medicine had thus occurred again — calomel had been converted in the stomach to corrosive and soluble mercuric salts.

The mucous membrane of the stomach, except possibly in the area around the oesophagus, therefore should have been severely corroded. This would be so because the poison had not been imbibed in a prepared state but had appeared when the calomel reached the stomach in the presence of orgeat. It is the genius of this method of poisoning that there is no tell-tale evidence in the mouth or throat of the mercuric solution that will ravage the system through the corroded stomach. The annular muscle around the pylorus should have been swollen and hard. That swelling was what became interpreted by the nineteenth century doctors present as a *scirrhus at the pylorus*.[8]

If we now examine the reports of the autopsy we shall see that all our expectations as to what clinically would be found were, indeed, reported to exist.

We can fairly safely assume that none of the British doctors present at Napoleon's post-mortem knew that the commonly used purgative calomel could be made so dangerous and could cause such frightful corrosion — *ulcérations cancéreuses* or cancer-like ulcerations. At that time, though, it was common knowledge in French medical circles. The poison-mixers had most certainly known about it for as long as calomel had been used as a medicine. In 1814 a French doctor called François Broussais had published an account of experiments on dogs. The wretched animals had been given tartar emetic and calomel, which had severely damaged their stomachs and intestines.[9]

Shortly after Antommarchi had opened Napoleon's abdomen, a lively dispute broke out amongst the English doctors present. Dr. Shortt in fact had cried out, on seeing the liver, that it was obviously enlarged. It was contrary to English military discipline on St. Helena to presume there could be anything wrong with Napoleon's liver. That could suggest an adverse climate at the carefully selected place of exile.

Shortt's colleagues tried to convince him he had not seen an enlarged liver. It was not until Sir Thomas Reade, the chief of police on the island, had intervened that Dr. Shortt realized his medical observation was virtually insubordination. But Antommarchi as dissector, who unlike Dr. Shortt had no reason for fear, noted that the liver was enlarged, though no direct damage to the tissue could be observed when the organ had been sliced open. The spleen was much enlarged.[18]

There were four reports on the post-mortem. The English doctors wrote one and requested that Antommarchi sign it. He searched in vain in the English papers for some note that the liver was enlarged. When he found none, he refused to add his signature.

Antommarchi wrote two reports. One he handed to Bertrand. Another, somewhat more explicit, he would include in his memoirs. At the request of the governor, Dr. Henry later drew up his own report.

The autopsy provided a logical explanation of the Emperor's severe abdominal symptoms around March 20 until the beginning of April. The stomach was found to be perforated, but a provisional closing of the lesion in the wall of the stomach was found to have occurred by its adhesion to the liver. It is understandable that this circumstance could easily have caused the "razor-cut" pains that Napoleon complained of at the time.

Not one of those reports mentions a tumor. Antommarchi writes that he observed a distension and a scirrhous (adj.) hardness around the pylorus, of a breadth of a few lignes (1 ligne = ½ of an inch), which formed a circular mass at the right extremity of the stomach. So the pyloric muscle was hard and swollen, just as should be expected in cases of acute mercurial intoxication.[8,10]

But what about the cancer that, according to all orthodox historians and consequently according to the school history books, supposedly caused Napoleon's death?

None of the autopsists mentioned existence of a distinct cancer either in tumor or small nodule forms. Antommarchi says of the corroded stomach wall that nearly the whole of the internal surface of the stomach was occupied by *un ulcère cancéreux.*[10] He did not call it a cancer. In that case he would have written *un ulcère de cancer.*

The English, none of whom were pathologists, found that the internal surface of the stomach over nearly its whole extent *except* — as we had thought — *the area around the upper orifice of the stomach was a mass of cancerous disease or scirrhous portions advancing to cancer.*[11] No doctor in 1821 could point to any damage that could justifiably be considered a forerunner of cancer.

In any case the English doctors did not state that Napoleon had an identifiable cancer. Still less could they then have reason to assume he had died of a cancer.

At the governor's request Doctor N. Henry, who was then very young, wrote a report of his own on the post-mortem, which is an example of naivete coupled with stupidity. He was able to state that those "cancerous ulcers" his colleagues had mentioned were *fast advancing to cancer.* He was the man who thought Napoleon must have led a very chaste life as he had no body hair and on the dissecting table his masculine appendage appeared extremely small.

In his book "Napoleon Immortal" Dr. James Kemble presents as an appendix a translation of Dr. Antommarchi's post-mortem report.[22] There we can read the forthright statement that Antommarchi found "the right extremity of the stomach at the distance of an inch from the pylorous surrounded by a tumor, or rather a scirrhous induration . . ."

Antommarchi then, after all, had found a tumor in the

stomach of the dead Napoleon? No, Kemble's translation is far from correct. Antommarchi, in the post-mortem report contained in his memoirs, states that there was by the pylorus *"un léger engorgement comme scirreux, très peu étendu et exactement circonscrit"* — a slight swelling, *almost* scirrhous, very little extended and exactly circumscribed.[21] We must note that there was no tumor, only a swollen pylorus muscle.

Clearly then, Napoleon died as a result of acute intoxication by mercuric salts, which had caused among other things a swelling of the pylorus muscle, large corrosions leading in their turn to very considerable massive gastric haemorrhage and a toxic damage of all the body tissues, including in the first place the sensitive brain cells.

Napoleon's cancer was a political diagnosis, a considered diagnosis, for it could be accepted by both the French and British governments.

The British government thought that this diagnosis would absolve them nicely in the matter of the common French accusation of intentionally transporting Napoleon to an out-of-the-way place where the dreadfully adverse climate sooner or later would cause his death.

As far as French royalty was concerned the post-mortem diagnosis was splendid. It proved Napoleon was by no means a superman. He had died comparatively young of a degenerative disease, the product of a weakness no doubt inherited from his father. He thus had been a defective human being, unqualified to found a dynasty. Bourbonist propaganda could hardly have been better served.

One wonders whence came the spark that could kindle in Europe such a conflagration as might calculably destroy the cult of Napoleonism, erected on the myth of invincibility.

When Bertrand sat down on the evening of May 6, 1821 to write to the relatives and tell them that Napoleon had died on the previous day, he believed Napoleon had died of the same disease as Carlo Buonaparte — of a *scirrhus at the pylorus* although none of the reports of the autopsy mentioned anything of the sort. Where could Bertrand have received this idea?

But on the same day Bertrand noted that Napoleon had long

had a bad heart, which was supposed to have been the cause of slow circulation, which in its turn explained why Napoleon's legs were often so icy cold. In the reports of the autopsy Napoleon's heart was pronounced apparently without fault. The tale of the slow blood circulation, however, reveals the source of Bertrand's mysterious pathological knowledge. Napoleon's sluggish circulation was a Montholon invention.[13]

It was Montholon, then, who gave Bertrand that extraordinary death verdict which was not consistent with what the reports on the autopsy had to say. It is probable that Montholon had told Bertrand privately what the autopsy reports really meant, and that they had to be read in a certain way and not be taken literally.

On that same day Montholon penned a letter to his wife. In it he said plainly and forthrightly that the autopsy had shown that "Napoleon had died of the same disease as his father, *un squirre ulcéreux à l'estomac près du pylore* — an ulcerous scirrhus in the stomach near the pylorus." Seven-eighths of the stomach wall was ulcerous. "It is probable," he continued, "that the ulcer started four or five years ago. *It was a great relief that Napoleon's illness was not due to his captivity.*"[14]

How should this letter be read and interpreted? All letters from a good security agent should be re-read carefully for special meaning. The addressee was indeed the Countess de Montholon, but before ever she received it the letter would have been read by the French security service. They had no reason for rejoicing in the fact, so comforting to the British, that captivity had not been the cause of illness. What logically must have been intended and received as a positively favorable piece of news was that *poisoning had not been discovered to be the cause of death.*

It is quite interesting to see how Montholon interpreted the English report of the autopsy, which was the official one. It said that there was something mysteriously cancerous, "advancing to cancer". This Montholon managed to read as a scirrhous condition which killed Napoleon *after having been developing for the previous four or five years.*

As early as in 1816 Montholon had told the Austrian commissioner Stürmer that Napoleon bore within himself the seed of a disease which, with the St. Helena climate, would lead to his death.[15]

Anyway, Montholon's unofficial "death certificate" in the letter to Albine was to become the explanation of death officially and popularly accepted in France. It was made known in France by official circular that Napoleon Bonaparte had died on May 5, 1821, of a wasting disease, *maladie de langueur* which had kept him to his bed for more than forty days. The post-mortem had shown that the cause of death was the same as that which had brought his father to the grave, that is to say, cancer of the stomach. "He was conscious until the last and died without pain."[16] (An extraordinary cancer of the stomach, indeed — one without pain and accompanied by no wasting of the flesh!)

We already know that this diagnosis of *maladie de langueur* was made long before the post-mortem. It had been forecast in that letter by Montholon to his wife on December 5, 1820.

None of the doctors present at the autopsy, puzzled by the evidence of unexplained stomach wall corrosion, can justly be accused of having said that Napoleon's death was due or partly due to a cancer. They noted a corrosive ulcer. But Montholon said the scirrhous (hardening) condition of the sphincter was a cancer of the kind that had killed the Emperor's father.

The vital difference for us now to note is that whereas, by Montholon's account, death had ensued from one cause, cancer, the autopsists' findings of an ulcerated condition of the stomach or a condition "leading to cancer" were consistent with what we know to be the symptoms and effects of poisoning. Napoleon's symptoms in his protracted illness were by no means the common and accepted symptoms of cancer. Antommarchi found that the Emperor was a victim of the climate of St. Helena, which had affected his liver and damaged his lungs.

Historians of the era did not concur in the theory held by the only pathologist present on St. Helena as to the cause of Napoleon's death. They relied on Montholon and paid scant attention to Doctor Antommarchi's testimony. He was not an aristocrat; but Montholon was.

The scirrhus in question was to be useful in more ways than one. Clara Tschudi, who wrote a book on Letizia Buonaparte, thought the verdict would put an end to those malicious rumors from Corsica that Napoleon's real father was Marbeuf and not Carlo Buonaparte. Now everyone would know that Napoleon had died of the same complaint as Carlo Buonaparte; therefore Napoleon must have been his son.

Cancer of the pylorus must have been a very common cause of death during the calomel-epoch of the medical profession.

When the autopsy with its ambiguous reports was over, four coffins stood ready. We may assume it was Count de Montholon who had scheduled the time of arrival and managed events thereafter with precision and dispatch. There was no unreadiness, no fumbling. Plainly the arrangements following death had been carefully contemplated and the various needs anticipated.

First there was an inner coffin of tin, padded and lined with silk. After the Emperor, dressed in his uniform, had been laid within it, it was sealed by soldering.

Antommarchi had expressed a wish to take Napoleon's stomach with him to Europe, but both the French Counts at Longwood would not hear of this. The governor was not opposed to what was a reasonable plan but the Counts wanted Napoleon's heart to take to Europe for presentation to the Empress Marie-Louise, who had already declined to accept the macabre bestowal. So the governor would not agree to this gesture. Committed to a special sealed vessel, filled with alcohol, both stomach and heart were therefore placed in the coffin. The sealed tin coffin was then placed within a wooden one and this in its turn in a lead coffin. It, too, was sealed by soldering. Lastly came the outer coffin of mahogany.

Napoleon was not left entirely destitute to await the Resurrection, however. In the manner reminiscent of burials in Egypt's Valley of the Kings, in the Emperor's coffin had been placed a silver vessel with the imperial arms, a plate and spoon and fork in silver, six double *napoléons d'or* from France and two from Italy, four single *napoléons d'or*, one double and one single *napoléon d'argent* and a coin of exchange.[19] Of course no coin would bear a Bourbon image.

It might be interesting to know for what reason Napoleon was placed in so many coffins. None who made the arrangements gave any explanation. Ironically, it was Napoleon who, in order to feed his armies with less danger of food poisoning, had caused research to be conducted and an award made to the inventor of hermetically sealed tinned foods. He was unlikely to have foreseen that his own mortal remains would be doubly soldered into metal containers.

References

1. Marchand II:311
2. Forshufvud, Smith, Wassen 214
3. Henry's post-mortem report
4. Forshufvud, Smith, Wassen 216
5. Wätjen 86-116
6. Petri
7. Beckman 739
8. Merkel 293
9. Fahraeus
10. Marchand II:343-4
11. Shortt et consortes, Lowe's Papers
12. Henry, Lowe's Papers
13. Forsyth III:267
14. Gonnard 80-81
15. Bourgoing 137
16. Aubry (1) page 589
17. Marchand II:338
18. Antommarchi (2) page 134
19. Marchand II:345
20. Aubry 1 p. 564, Antommarchi 2, p. 137
21. Antommarchi 1 p. 163
22. Kemble 1 p. 285

46

Montholon Produces Alibis

AT THE AUTOPSY the English doctors had never considered whether or not Napoleon's severe internal injuries had developed from some form of poisoning. Their attitude could easily be explained in its relation to political considerations. Nevertheless it is interesting that a medical team should have given the subject of foul play no apparent thought. After all Napoleon had expressed the suspicion that Sir Hudson Lowe had been commissioned to poison him to death "under slow fire". And there certainly existed in the case the circumstance of high political contention with a throne at stake.

In the mystery of the Emperor's fatal illness there were grounds for suspicion that the post-mortem team had been less than thorough, especially as regards developing anything that could demonstrate alertness to possible poisoning. A broader concern at the autopsy table could have helped refute Napoleon's testamentary angry accusation that Sir Hudson had murdered him.

But of course, at the time the English did not know the contents of Napoleon's accusatory Will in which he would fling to the world the charge that he had been murdered by intent of the English oligarchy. This testament was not to be opened before his followers had once more reached European waters, which they did on July 25, 1821.

So Montholon could feel safe. Moreover, as long as the house of Bourbon held power in France he had no need to fear any old claims. He need not have been afraid of anything of the sort either under the regime of Louis-Philippe, the bourgeois king. Montholon served him, too.

Montholon's contribution to French state strategies of the

second restoration surely must have been recorded in a secret recommendation filed among the documents of the security police of the time; but it has never come to light and may have been discreetly disposed of to ensure total silence on the subject.

During the 1840's, however, Montholon could not have failed to experience anxiety and a reluctance to claim credit for discharge of a disagreeable duty at St. Helena. The strong current of opinion in favor of Napoleon, which *le Retour des Cendres* — the return of Napoleon's body — had inspired in 1840 represented a potential hazard, in scale with the outstanding success of his secret mission.

It was in that year obviously only a matter of a short while before Louis Napoleon, the Bonapartist pretender to the throne, would replace King Louis-Philippe at the helm. Much seems to point to the possibility that Louis Napoleon, who made a confidant of Montholon, had discerned Montholon's double agent role in the abortive coup d'état at Boulogne. What would happen to Montholon and the secrets concerning the role he had played at the exiled court of Napoleon I when the services of the security staff with all their archives were placed at the disposal of Napoleon III? In fact, this is precisely what happened. The records were ordered burned.

There is no need to consider Montholon's conscience in the matter. He had been managing that very well for more than twenty-five years, before his accounts of Napoleon's captivity were published in Leipzig in 1846. Montholon had carried out a most delicate commission on St. Helena, no less to be obeyed than any other that might befall an agent in the service of the French king. He had accepted that law that stood above all others in the eyes of a courtier — the King's desire must be met.

In his own circle of aristocrats Montholon, after St. Helena, could feel he deserved the recognition due to a successful performer of a crucially important mission. He had done a little private business on the side — a little moonlighting as it were — and thereby had managed to gain entitlement to receive Napoleon's largest bequest to a court attendant. It was a considerable fortune. But could he really have refused to accept the generous gifts from his victim, thereby inviting suspicions as to his loyalties? He had a task to do and any legacy would not be disqualified as to its acceptability by the fact it came from the chief enemy of his royal protectors.

Whatever his motives may have been — literary, diversionary or mercenary — Montholon published in 1846 a book on the drama of St. Helena. According to this version, he could not possibly have had anything to do with Napoleon's sufferings and death. Oblique though they were, his alibis are all clearly discernible. They tell far more than he intended.

If a person is accused of having committed a grave crime — murder, for instance — and the evidence is against him, an alibi established and accepted can set him free. If however, the alibi does not hold, but in fact is found to be based on lies, suspicion then falls with crushing force upon the accused. Better no alibi than one disproven.

A fate such as that should have befallen Montholon with his publishing of the collection of alibis in 1846 under the title *Histoire de la Captivité de Sainte-Hélène,* had historians checked the narratives of Montholon upon reading his "history". Someone, in any event, must have thought the contents did not justify the pretentious title. In the following year the book was re-issued in Paris entitled: *Récits de la Captivité de Sainte-Hélène.* The title might better have read: *Mensonges sur la Captivité de Sainte-Hélène* — Falsehoods concerning the Captivity on St. Helena.

In this book Montholon builds in depth an entire set of defences around his role at St. Helena. If the first rampart of falsehoods should be breached, the next would hold. Behind that were more and still more ramparts.

For instance, should suspicions of poisoning by arsenic arise, they would be quelled by various defences: It was quite impossible for Napoleon to have been poisoned. The Emperor ate nothing that had not first been tasted by a servant, and the dessert was always partaken of by the valets as well. Montholon always had breakfast and dinner with Napoleon and the Count always tasted the drinks that were placed on Napoleon's bedside table, usually lemonade or orgeat. Here we might do well to observe that Montholon wanted it established that Napoleon customarily drank orgeat on St. Helena, and not just during his last weeks, as Marchand and Bertrand reported.[1]

Montholon could be seen to be ignorant of the nature of

poison, for if ever Napoleon, in Montholon's account, had thought a drink suspicious, it was the odor that had aroused doubts. By this, Montholon sought to show that he considered all poisons must smell vile and thus he should be deemed an illiterate on the subject of poisons.[1]

Napoleon himself had said that arsenic did not affect him nearly so much as *le poison de l'âme* — the poison of the soul, whatever that may have meant.[2] If Napoleon died of sorrow and frustration, who had destroyed him? Not Montholon.

Once, however, Bertrand's plans to leave for home had been just such a mortal "poison of the soul" for Napoleon. Actually, Bertrand never meant to leave Napoleon for good, but he did on several occasions ask permission to accompany his wife and children to England after which he would return. According to Count de Montholon, these suggestions were supposed to be more dangerous to Napoleon's life and health than arsenic. He would have us believe that this was what Napoleon himself had declared. In 1846, when all this was published, everything that Napoleon was *supposed* to have said at St. Helena was likely to be taken as gospel truth.

If nevertheless anyone should have reason to suspect poisoning, Sir Hudson Lowe was to take the brunt. This was quite safe, for when Montholon published his book poor Lowe had been dead two years, accused by the whole world of having "murdered" Napoleon by cruel harassments. So Montholon in his *Histoire* lets Napoleon say, on an occasion when the governor supposedly had come visiting, "Throw away that coffee in my cup. I don't want to drink it, for that fellow has been near it. *I think he is capable of anything, even of poisoning me.*"[3]

As to the attacks of sickness that might have made a doctor suspect acute arsenic intoxication, the explanation, according to Montholon, lay in the damp climate of St. Helena. "I saw him often, returning from his nightly strolls, succumb to those attacks of coughing that ended only when vomiting began." We must remember at this point that certain sentries, as arranged through Montholon's representations to Admiral Cockburn, prevented Napoleon from leaving his apartments at night.[4] And neither Marchand nor Bertrand reported a similar pattern of physical reaction to the night air of the island.

If anyone should happen to know that intoxication by arsenic affects the legs and that consequently a person thus intoxicated cannot ride well, Montholon accommodatingly tells that Napoleon went on long riding excursions at times when no one else had seen him on horseback. For instance, Montholon says that Napoleon went for a long ride over to the other side of the island on January 1, 1820.[5] To do so he would have ridden uphill and downhill. It must have been a very tiring expedition. No one witnessed it but Montholon. Everyone else knew that Napoleon had only ridden on St. Helena for the first three months of 1816 and for a short while in the summer of 1820. Why construct that careful falsification, if not as part of a calculated cover?

According to Montholon's account, Napoleon even went for a very long horseback ride in the period of his severe illness from September 1820 to May 1821 — on January 20, 1821, to be precise.[6] But for that day Bertrand had noted: "Bad weather. The emperor goes out *in his carriage.*"

We know that the next day Napoleon for the first time used the see-saw that Antommarchi had produced to help him get some exercise when he could not walk, much less ride.[7] It was Montholon who gave him the health to ride — twenty years later. Bertrand's account when published in our time now refutes this statement after generations had come and gone.

If we are to believe his *"Recits"* or *"l'Histoire"*, Montholon had nothing to do with the fatal calomel prescription of May 3, 1821. It was the doctors who, entirely on their own initiative, had given Napoleon that strong dose of calomel. He plainly does not deny that the dose was a very strong one but — and this we should, of course, note and remember — Napoleon was not given the dose on May 3, as all other witnesses had said, but on the fourth of May.[8] That is to say, the calomel was administered many hours *after* the severe gastric haemorrhages. Therefore calomel could not be blamed! Montholon did not tell us about Antommarchi's objections and his warnings against calomel or that calomel was given to Napoleon against orders. What Montholon did and did not say about calomel would one day testify against him.

Should someone, unfortunately, arise with proof that the dose of calomel was given on Montholon's suggestion and encouragement and in spite of Antommarchi's and Marchand's vigorous protests, and that it was given not a day after but only six hours before the first massive gastric haemorrhage had passed through the intestines, why, then, Montholon could not be blamed for relating to the doctors, as already mentioned, how, on some inexact date *calomel once saved Napoleon's life.*

If that rampart of lies did not hold and someone should indicate that it was clear that the calomel must have been tampered with so that it became extremely poisonous on reaching the stomach, then orgeat could threaten his carefully built up tissue of falsehoods.

For anyone uncertain about the part played by orgeat in the case history of Napoleon's last illness, Montholon could relate how, on the occasion of earlier attacks of sickness on St. Helena, Napoleon had actually been cured by orgeat or the milk of almonds. (Let us always remember it is the milk of almonds, provided *bitter* almonds have been used, too, that makes orgeat a dangerous substance to swallow, along with calomel.) But according to this Montholonian edifice of falsehoods, it was none other than *milk of almonds* that had cured Napoleon from his illness at the beginning of 1819.[9] By giving milk of almonds and orgeat a favorable reference Montholon sought to defend the fateful chemical reagent and so divert suspicion from him as the provider.

As for *eau de fleur d'oranger,* Seville orange-blossom water, the other ingredient of orgeat apart from milk of almonds, it was this perfume that was Napoleon's own trusted medicine, the medicine that saved him when "Antommarchi on March 22, 1821, had poisoned Napoleon with tartar emetic" — if we are to believe Montholon.

In *Recits* Montholon said that, on March 27, 1821, Napoleon had wanted to send the incompetent Antommarchi away and had declared that he would cure himself *with milk soup and orgeat.*

No reader of Montholon's *Histoire* could therefore doubt that orgeat clearly had been found to be a drink that suited the patient well whenever he had taken it. Indeed, the reader of Montholon could hardly fail to gather that the best "medicine" for Napoleon, according to His Imperial Majesty's own testimony, was none other than the orgeat Montholon had been so sedulously careful to provide.

No other witness among those at Longwood knew anything of the orgeat before about April 7, 1821. It was then that Marchand noted that the new beverage stood on Napoleon's bedside table, this in spite of the fact that the latter had forbidden all drinks but licorice water. But it was still not the true orgeat, for that would have contained not only sweet almonds but bitter almonds, too; and *no bitter almonds,* as has been mentioned, *had been seen on St. Helena until their sudden and unexplained appearance on the twenty-fifth of April.*

Should Montholon's orgeat defence hold and were it really believed that Napoleon was well acquainted with orgeat, and that it was a drink to which he owed his life on an earlier occasion, then it could still seem strange that Napoleon was not given orgeat during his last days. For Montholon writes that on those days Napoleon drank orangeade (orange juice) while everyone else thought he drank orgeat or *eau de fleur d'oranger.* Of course, it was orgeat Napoleon was given, in order to accustom him to it as a refreshant. In the absence of calomel, it would be harmless in the small sips the Emperor took, even if it contained bitter almond.

Thus in his elaborate efforts to furnish for himself a believable alibi insofar as his connection with the providing of orgeat went, Montholon attracts suspicion more and more to himself. After all the years that had passed since he was on St. Helena we see him unnaturally preoccupied with the ministration of what, in his own account, was merely something to soothe the Emperor's taste in the presence of an upset stomach.

To his dying day the Count de Montholon would never forget orgeat! His book would leave a perceptive reader of today, knowing the dreadful formula for gastric haemorrhaging, in no doubt that Montholon deliberately and not very subtly labored to offset the obvious.

But in addition to orgeat and calomel there was tartar emetic to explain.

So that everyone would realize that Montholon had nothing to do with the tartar emetic which Napoleon drank unawares on or about March 20, 1821, Montholon could relate how Napoleon had on that occasion raised a glass of lemonade to his lips and had thought it had a strange odor. He had asked Montholon if he could also smell it. It seemed rather as though someone was trying to poison Napoleon, though Montholon could not imagine that this could be so and suggested that he himself should drink the suspect lemonade. This, according to his memoir, he proceeded to do. The result was that ten minutes later he was seized with severe "seasickness" and had hurriedly to retire to his room. Consequently, Napoleon then realized that Antommarchi was the poisoner and dismissed him as his doctor, so we are told by *il bugiardo,* "the liar" in his undependable yet purposeful *Histoire.*

By 1846 it had become no longer risky for Montholon to defame the name of Antommarchi. The trusted Corsican had been dead for eight years. Bertrand, too, was dead; so Montholon could venture to include a number of lies about him that could not be checked. But impetuous Gourgaud was still alive and still quick to challenge a maligner to a duel. It would be prudent to say nothing at all of the quarrel with Gourgaud. So Montholon wrote accordingly. For safety's sake he mentioned that Gourgaud was a personal friend of the Emperors of Russia and Austria. Gourgaud certainly would not mind this.

What about Las Cases? The father was dead, but the son was a brave duellist. It would be wise to speak well of Las Cases; and so, indeed, Montholon did.[12]

"The arrest of Las Cases was a great loss to us ... The departure of Las Cases made a painful impression on us ..."

Antommarchi was dead, but his book *Les derniers moments de Napoléon* might be very dangerous for Montholon should the experts of the security service come under the command of a new Napoleon with an unsettled account with Montholon. There were people in the secret services who could read. They would soon find condemning evidence against Montholon in Antommarchi's book. Montholon constructed a rampart of lies against just such an event. He accused Antommarchi of unreliability, stupidity and — most prejudicially of all in the eyes of a devoted supporter of Napoleon — of having been ill-regarded by the Emperor.

The fact that, after the ordination of May 3, Napoleon lost all strength in his voluntary muscles, the power of speech and sight, might cause a doctor to wonder if Napoleon may not have been poisoned to death with mercuric salts. What is more, following Napoleon's death, Governor Lowe received a letter from a doctor named Gooch saying that in his opinion "Napoleon's death had more to do with mercury than with the climate and cancer."[13]

In order to forestall and allay any such possible suspicion, Montholon prepared an alibi. It clearly revealed that he himself was well acquainted with the most striking outward symptom of acute mercury intoxication, namely, paralysis of movement.

It seems that, when Montholon was on night watch in Napoleon's sick-room the night before death came on May 5, 1821, Napoleon had suddenly thrown himself out of bed at two in the morning. Montholon had tried to prevent him, but *Napoleon's strength had been greater than the Count's.*

By Montholon's wholly incredible account, Napoleon had overthrown him onto the carpet and had pinned him there so firmly that Montholon had been unable to call for help. (Unless Napoleon had him by the throat it is strange that Montholon's vocal cords did not function.) Fortunately Archambault, the groom, who was awake in the room next door, heard the noise and came rushing in to help Montholon get the raving patient back into bed. A few seconds later both Bertrand and Antommarchi entered, but by then all was again quiet, wrote Montholon to end his cock-and-bull story.[14] We must assume Montholon had a good reason for fabricating this completely unsubstantiated story. Surely it was for only one reason: to remove suspicion of Napoleon having been destroyed by mercuric poisoning. His muscles were strong and unparalyzed.

What about the then still living Louis Marchand, who watched so faithfully by Napoleon's bedside and who usually relieved Montholon at exactly two in the morning? Where was he?

Marchand? Marchand was sick all through Napoleon's last illness. He knew nothing of events of this period, according to Montholon's *Histoire*.[15] Such fiction was only made possible by the withholding of publication of Bertrand's diary notes until 1949. Had it preceded Montholon's *Histoire* there would have been no such story, since Bertrand, in fact, repeatedly mentions Marchand on duty in the sick-room throughout that entire time.

By thus describing Napoleon's last night, Montholon could

hope to kill two birds with one stone. Any possible rumor that Napoleon had been poisoned by mercuric salts hopefully was scotched and Marchand's testimony as a witness would be neutralized, should the latter ever say or write anything to compromise Montholon.

Yet a time was to come, more than a century later, when a valet's word was as valuable as a count's and when Bertrand unintentionally would show that Montholon was a prevaricator, beyond all doubt.

Bertrand gives us the names of those who were present in Napoleon's sick-room on the night of the fourth and fifth of May. He did not notice Archambault there, but he did see Vignali, Saint-Denis, Montholon, Marchand, Arnott and Antommarchi. In fact in the daily entries from April 29 to May 5, when Napoleon died and again on May 6, when the post-mortem was held with Marchand as witness, the first valet was consistently named as being in attendance duties.[17,18]

When Marchand's memoirs were first published in 1955, Montholon, to anyone with a slight knowledge of how acute mercurial intoxication works, was indirectly revealed through his story of Napoleon's last night as the self-indicted killer of Napoleon. Nevertheless, several medical reports on Napoleon's death were published after that, all passing over the fatal mercurial intoxication. Montholon's decades-long fear of discovery was proven by events to have been exaggerated. It would not occur for more than a hundred years when science came to the aid of a strengthening suspicion of foul play.

It is clear that Marchand read Montholon's *Histoire* or, at all events, the second edition, his *Récits*. He wrote notes into his own completed memoirs on what he thought of Montholon's extremest fantasies.

Thus, Marchand writes of Montholon's struggle with Napoleon that it was *un écart d'imagination,* a flight of fantasy. In other words, it never happened. Furthermore, he writes: "Montholon's memory failed him too when he put me to bed for the whole of Napoleon's illness." Another of Montholon's *écarts d'imagination,* we are assured by Marchand, was the appearance of Archambault upon the scene. Archambault was not one of the staff permitted in the ex-emperor's apartments. Archambault was only allowed to see Napoleon on the morning of May 5, when all the servants of lower order filed through to bid a last farewell to the dying Napoleon.[16]

The truth about the night of the fourth and fifth of May is that a comatose Napoleon had lain practically motionless since the evening of the third. He could signal for a drink but could not speak. The only sounds that could be heard came, as mentioned previously, from an over-pressurized stomach. *"Ce n'est plus qu'un cadavre"*, noted Bertrand on Napoleon's condition at four o'clock on the morning of May 5. "He is no more than a corpse."[17]

In two separate instances when Montholon had wanted to get rid of two doctors whose presence he considered a nuisance, he had accused them before the Governor of having caused Napoleon's illness by their medicines. He had said nothing about arsenic then. It had been better to let sleeping dogs lie. Significantly, in his *Histoire* he does not repeat his accusations against the doctors.

But there is a small coterie of Frenchmen today who have tried in every way possible to free the ancestral Montholon from these "accusations", and they have resorted to the doctors' medicines as the ultimate effort to prove Montholon innocent.

To start with, they treated the matter fairly lightly, evidently assuming that their best defence lay in the specious claim that "arsenic tends to accumulate in buried corpses". When told that in this case the *corpus delicti,* the arsenic-laden Napoleonic hairs, had been shaved from the Emperor's head *before* he was placed in his several-layered coffin, and that Napoleon's body was never interred in the earth but entombed in cement and stone, objectors to the truth resorted to a series of other similarly indefensible arguments. It was said that the arsenic content of the hair was due to the use of an arsenic hair lotion, to drinking water containing arsenic, to arsenic in cooking utensils, etc.

A French author, Alain Decaux, has published a handsomely illustrated work, dealing largely with Napoleon's illness and death. In it he mentions Montholon's accusations against Napoleon's doctors and suggests that they gave Napoleon arsenic as a "strengthening medicine". An *opinion gratuite,* as the French say.

By sectional analyses of hairs it is very simple to distinguish arsenic administration as a sustaining tonic from deliberate poisonings. On this evidence there is no doubt whatsoever the irregularly received arsenical poisoning of Napoleon's system was by deliberate intent, not by misadventure.

It was not until much later in the century that arsenic was considered by some to have "strengthening" properties, whereas earlier it had been used only as a murderous poison — mostly for rats.* Decaux, moreover, tells us nothing of how he imagined Napoleon's intoxication to have been carried out at a time when no doctor had been accepted by him to prescribe for his treatment. For instance, Napoleon had been ill for several months in 1816 with symptoms typical of "climatic sickness" before Dr. O'Meara was called in. He was also ill in 1819, when he was attended by no doctor who could have prescribed arsenical potions.

Decaux does not explain, either, the illnesses of the Emperor's attendants, recognized as typical "climatic sickness". Were they, too, supposed to have been poisoned, with the "medicine" that Napoleon's physician-in-ordinary, according to this author, had secretly prescribed for him?

In spite of the fact that Gourgaud occasionally suspected poisoning, both of his Emperor and of himself, he seems never to have connected the so-called climatic sickness with arsenic. He speaks of wine poisoned with lead.

Another member of the same French group of modern times presented quite a different argument in Montholon's favor. He said there was no arsenic on St. Helena when Napoleon was there. He does not mention the source of his information. Marchand writes that at Longwood the staff intended to put an end to the rats with arsenic. What this apologist for Montholon may have meant was that there was no arsenic left for Napoleon after the rats had been treated. But then the rats were not given arsenic, Marchand tells us — because of the fear of a stench from their dead bodies. We are well assured there was arsenic at Longwood. It was used for no recorded purpose.

Instead of building up Montholon's defence on assurances that he was a true aristocrat, and by his own lights, a courageous

*In England the arsenious *Tinctura Fowleri* was at the time used therapeutically, not as a tonic.

and meritorious servant of the lawful and existing ruler of France, his protagonists have attempted to shield his memory with a series of shallow fantasies. These show good will, it is true, but considerable ignorance of the facts.

As could be expected, the Montholonians denied that the hairs examined by the scientists were genuine, this in spite of the fact that the only hairs examined were from souvenirs whose history was certifiably established. They were hairs that had never been placed on the common souvenir market but had been preserved in absolute safekeeping or isolation. The uniformity of results from many specimens was wholly beyond the power of any miracles of coincidence to produce.

The Montholonians' serious shortage of arguments has expressed itself in one or two fairly amusing ways. It was stated that the Museum of the Royal College of Surgeons of England had in its possession two pieces of Napoleon's intestine, each containing a cancer node, "metastases from Napoleon's gastric cancer."

This might seem quite plausible. Unfortunately there has never been the slightest reason to suppose that these pieces of intestine were ever near Napoleon. On the jar in which they were preserved in alcohol was a label on which it was written that the preparation had been a gift from Dr. O'Meara, Napoleon's physician-in-ordinary. That was alright, but O'Meara left Napoleon three years before the latter's death and certainly had never performed a drastic surgical operation upon him.

These sections of intestine were examined histopathologically in 1910 by a well-known pathologist named Shattock. He found that the node in one of the pieces of intestine was quite simply a so-called solitary follicle and in the other he found only what is called Peyer's plaque. There was in it not the slightest trace of cancer.[19] A solitary follicle is a finer name for one of the lymphatic glands in the wall of the small intestine and Peyer's plaque is a collection of such follicles. Thus, apart from the fact the intestine specimens were not attributable to the Emperor, they were, in any case, not cancerous.

But the most spirited defence of Montholon can be ascribed to a Swedish Napoleon expert appearing on television. He was able to tell the public that it was quite absurd to suspect Montholon of the murder of Napoleon, since Montholon had been with

Napoleon III in the abortive landing at Boulogne in 1840. The Swedish television swallowed this and cancelled a previously arranged program on the thesis of the murder of Napoleon by poisoning!

References

1. Montholon (1), page 240
2. Montholon (1), page 222
3. Montholon (1), page 112
4. Montholon (1), page 183
5. Montholon (1), page 211
6. Montholon (1), page 239
7. Bertrand III:40
8. Montholon (1), 4th May 1821
9. Montholon (1), page 207
10. Montholon (1), page 247
11. Montholon (1), page 248-49
12. Montholon (1), page 146, 152
13. Gooch, Lowe's papers
14. Montholon 5th May 1821
15. Montholon 6th May 1821
16. Marchand II:437
17. Bertrand III:194
18. Marchand II:326
19. Keith 54 et seq.
20. Forshufvud and co-authors
21. Hamilton Smith 197

47

Napoleon's Mythical Attempts at Suicide

MONTHOLON'S DEFENCE, BUILT up of false alibis and with considerable knowledge and cunning, would not, however, have left him in peace from the consequences of his work on St. Helena if a Bonapartist régime were to return. So he prepared yet another strong defence in accounts of those "facts" concerning Napoleon's attempt at suicide which people did not know of. Montholon seems to have wanted to say that Napoleon was typically suicidally inclined. It would be absolutely ridiculous to suspect, in the event that such accusation should be made, that he had been poisoned. If he should be found to have been poisoned, then it should be remembered Napoleon had once tried to take his own life by poisoning.

It is true that on several occasions Napoleon had expressed a suspicion that the English meant to drive him to suicide and he had therefore had several discussions with Gourgaud, O'Meara and Bertrand on suicide as a way of escaping from adversity. But in these discussions he had consistently called suicide the method of cowards and fools.[1,13]

It is said — and the story is almost too good to be true — that during the Italian campaign Bonaparte had been quite concerned by the large number of suicides in his army. He was supposed to have issued a general order strictly forbidding suicide. It is also said that, proving the perfect discipline of his army, the epidemic of suicides ceased.

But Montholon knew that Napoleon, on various occasions, had tried to commit suicide. In his *Histoire* Montholon has a whole chapter entitled *Tentatives de suicide de l'Empéreur*, attempts by the Emperor at suicide.

If we are to believe Montholon, Napoleon started thinking

416

about taking his life early in his career. Soon after his great triumph at Toulon, where he was first made a General, Bonaparte, heavy at heart, had wanted to drown himself because his mother was living in straitened circumstances in Marseilles! (This was a serious and often repeated fallacy.) Just as Bonaparte was about to carry out his tragic intention, he met a man dressed in working clothes, who joyfully greeted him. It was Démasis, an old companion-at-arms. He had emigrated but had returned to France in disguise to look after his old mother.

"What's the matter? You're not listening, you're obviously not glad to see me," said the fictitious Démasis to Bonaparte.

Napoleon had then told him of his troubles.

"Was it no worse that that?" cried Démasis. "Look, take these 30,000 francs in gold and give them to your mother." He removed a money belt that he carried concealed by his worn jacket.

Napoleon was so overjoyed that he did not think of thanking the noble giver, who, in a manner worthy of a fairy tale, had suddenly disappeared. Indeed, the giver must likewise have felt relieved. A belt with 30,000 golden francs, weighing at least ten kilos, must have been uncommonly burdensome to wear.

This story tells us a lot about Montholon and his ability at fiction. Anyway, his *Histoire* was entertaining if inaccurate. The story also reveals a certain amount about the perceptivity of those many historians who allowed themselves to be duped by Montholon's lies about Napoleon's captivity on St. Helena.

Later in the same very entertaining chapter on Napoleon's attempts at suicide there is a moving story of how the latter told Montholon on St. Helena — but obviously not anyone else — how he had at last found this noble benefactor and had rejoiced to give him an imperial reward.

In the same chapter we read of Napoleon's famous attempt at suicide at Fontainebleau. It was another of the cock-and-bull stories, *de la facture du comte de Montholon,* of Count Montholon's making . . . or of someone else in the same band.

No one had heard of any Napoleonic attempts at suicide until Napoleon lay, well and safely packed, in the sealed tomb the Royal Engineers built for him on St. Helena.

But then, there came, from several quarters, definite information that Napoleon had tried to take his life at Fontainebleau on the night between the 12th and 13th of April, 1814. Perhaps it was the 11th of April. But no, it was the night of the 12th/13th April, because on the night of the 11th Caulaincourt was not at Fontainebleau. He may not have been there, but Marchand, Constant, Bourienne and Thiers all say it was the night of April 12. Montholon, however, would have it that it was the night of April third.

Who witnessed the attempt at suicide?

Marchand says that he had heard that Maret, Caulaincourt, Turenne and Bertrand were told by Napoleon himself at 11 o'clock on the evening of the 11th of April that he had tried to take poison.

But the attempt at suicide was supposed to have failed because Napoleon had vomited immediately.[2]

Napoleon's head valet, Constant, who escaped from his service with his pockets full and who was succeeded by Marchand, includes in his apocryphal mémoires a wonderful story of how Napoleon attempted suicide at Fontainbleau. In short, it proceeds as follows:

Constant was sleeping soundly near Napoleon's bedroom on the night of the 12th of April, when he was awakened at midnight by Pelard, the valet on duty, who told him that Napoleon had put something into a glass and had drunk it.

Constant rushed in and found Napoleon in a pitiful state. *"Je vais mourir,"* he murmured slowly to Constant. On the floor Constant had found a small bag made of leather and silk, which Napoleon always wore around his neck and which contained a quick-working poison, given to him by his doctor at the time of the Spanish campaign.[3]

(Marchand also mentions the famous bag of poison, but he says that Napoleon had been given it in Moscow.)

Constant entreated Napoleon to take *une potion adoucissante,* a soothing drink, whatever that could have been in such a dramatic situation.

Napoleon refused; he had decided to die. All the same, he asked Constant to call Caulaincourt and Dr. Yvan. When these gentlemen arrived the Emperor had asked Caulaincourt if he would act as father to his wife and children. One cannot help wondering whether Caulaincourt was a better choice for this task than Napoleon's father-in-law, the Emperor Franz of Austria.

In the meanwhile both Yvan and Caulaincourt humbly begged his dying majesty graciously to drink a cup of tea. Their request was granted. Constant rushed out and hastily made the cup of tea, which Napoleon drank. The vomiting stopped — so it had been a question of vomiting. And Constant had saved Napoleon's life. After a few hours' sleep Napoleon was once more back to normal.[3]

Had there been present a medically informed friend to Napoleon, he would have humbly begged His Majesty to let the vomiting continue. It would have been safer for him. Well, no doctor was on hand — but neither was Caulaincourt. He only arrived at Fontainebleau on April 12 at two in the afternoon.[4]

Constant, like Marchand, was of course innocent of this trumped-up tale of Napoleon's suicide. It is a fact that Constant's so-called mémoires have been written by a number of authors, such as Roquefort, Méliot, Auguste Luchet, Nisard and especially Villemarest.[5] One or other of these must have helped Constant to remember what happened at Fontainebleau, just before he left his post, thoughtfully taking with him a considerable amount of Napoleon's money, jewels and other valuables.[6]

Many historians have dismissed as apocryphal Constant's and other authors' reports of Napoleon's so-called attempt at suicide. Now, however, it is generally thought that an attempt at suicide really did take place, possibly a day later than the first reports recorded. Caulaincourt's memoirs, published more than a century after the alleged events, definitely declare this.

There is reason to doubt their authorship as wholly Caulaincourt's, but let us see what those memoirs have to say. It was the time of Napoleon's defeat in the East and his first abdication. At three o'clock in the morning of April 13, in the year 1814, Napoleon summoned Caulaincourt.[7] The Emperor was in bed.

"Give me your hand," he said.

"Embrace me," he continued, and drew Caulaincourt close to his heart.

"Tell the Empress I die with the impression that she has given me all the happiness that lay in her power, that she has never afforded me the least cause for dissatisfaction . . ."

Have we not heard that before? Ah yes, indeed, in Napoleon's Will, written with Montholon's kindly assistance! Para. 3 reads: *"J'ai toujours eu à me louer de ma très chère épouse Marie-Louise, je lui conserve jusqu'au dernier moment les plus tendres sentiments . . .* I have always had cause to praise my very dear spouse Marie-Louise. I shall preserve until my last moment the greatest affection for her . . ."[8]

Napoleon's voice was weak. He had hiccups and severe pain. Caulaincourt wanted to call for Bertrand and Dr. Yvan. He was not allowed to.

"Je ne veux que vous, Caulaincourt," said Napoleon. "I don't want anyone but you, Caulaincourt."[9]

But surely we recognize that too! Napoleon was to utter almost exactly the same words seven years later. That is to say, he did so, by Montholon's account. According to him, on April 30, 1821, Bertrand had sought to relieve Montholon as Napoleon's nurse. Napoleon had apparently refused this, with the assurance that Montholon was quite good enough. *"Je ne veux plus d'autres (que Montholon)",* Napoleon had said.[10] "I don't want anyone else (but Montholon.)"

Caulaincourt tried to get away to call for help, but Napoleon held him back *d'une force irrésistible,* with irresistible force. The doors were closed and the valet could not hear Caulaincourt's cries for help. (Also that, too, we have heard before.)

Icy cold followed a cold sweat, then came burning heat. It seemed as though Napoleon would give up the ghost at any time. Caulaincourt managed then to break loose to call for the valet and Dr. Yvan together with Bertrand.

However, Napoleon was not so ill that he was unable to tell Caulaincourt that he had taken a strong dose of opium. In a little water. (Trifling details are very important when writing stories.)

After a while, however, Napoleon felt ill and began to vomit. The vomit was "something greyish".

Napoleon told Caulaincourt that he had had the opium in a little silken bag that he had carried ever since the Cossack assault at Maro-Jaroslawetz (October 27, 1812). This was another bag, then, and not the one Constant had seen or that Marchand had heard about.

Finally Bertrand and Yvan arrived. The little group of three men looked one another in the eyes and the same thought passed through their minds, that "it would be a good thing for the Emperor were he to die now."[11]

Through this statement of Napoleon's great favorite Caulaincourt, then, Montholon and the group to which he belonged had it on the best of authority that it could be a blessing were Napoleon to die an early death. Even better, Napoleon himself had said in private to Caulaincourt that "his death would be a blessing for France."[9] In other words: if it came to the worst at St. Helena, Montholon had earned his country's gratitude. In a way, he had really done a kindness to Napoleon by assisting him in his earlier than normal departure from life!

Thus the account went on, unverifiable, unreasonable, untruthful and all designed to support the Montholon diversion.

In the meanwhile, Napoleon at Fontainebleau had continued to suffer in the extreme. (It was a strange sort of opinion he had taken.) Caulaincourt and the other gentlemen left anyway, but Caulaincourt was soon asked to go in to Napoleon again.

Napoleon tried to take a few steps, but Caulaincourt had to help him. Then he took him to the window, which he opened. The fresh air seemed to do the Emperor good. Caulaincourt thought that Napoleon's legs suffered from *atonie,* that is to say they were quite limp and unable to make any movement. (Just as on St. Helena!)

Obviously the Fontainebleau attempt at suicide was wholly imaginary. The description was certainly inserted later in Caulaincourt's memoirs in order — after his death — that the much-respected man should convince the world that Napoleon's attempt at suicide, a matter of such controversy among the experts, really did take place.

A great many Napoleonic experts in our time, convinced by their acceptance of the doctored "Caulaincourt" account, are quite sure that Napoleon did indeed try to commit suicide in 1814.

It may be noted that Caulaincourt's memoirs, as published in 1933, are not based on the original manuscript, which was supposed to have been destroyed in an explosion at the Chateau de Caulaincourt at the beginning of the First World War.

The memoirs we read are taken from the so-called black

copy. Frédéric Masson, who had the gravest of doubts about Montholon's character, had reason to suspect this copy of containing many accounts which could not within reason have originated with Caulaincourt.[12]

Laure Junot, the widow of Napoleon's boyhood friend and aide-de-camp, the Napoleonic Duke of Abrantès, let her imagination cover 6000 pages of *"mémoires"*. She also has a certain amount to say about "Napoleon's attempt at suicide at Fontainebleau." She had, indeed. Only this time it was Hugues-Bernard Maret, Napoleonic Duke of Bassano, Napoleon's right hand, secretary, foreign minister, Minister of War and so on, who was the only witness of the attempt apart from the valet Constant.

Maret found Napoleon in bed, as pale and cold as marble. He was suffering nevertheless from severe nausea and gastric pain.

This account also says that Napoleon kept the poison in a bag hung round his neck, only this time it was not opium but hydrocyanic acid. The fair Laure failed to mention how it was possible to keep hydrocyanic acid for years in a leather bag, and why in this case hydrocyanic acid had not, as usual, killed instantly.

The Duchess concludes her account by saying that many years after the event she had asked Maret to give her a few details. He had refused, she says.[14]

On the other hand it is not quite impossible that, unknown to himself, Napoleon was poisoned on the night of April 12/13, 1814. He had a bad night. *"J'ai été fort indisposé cette nuit,* I felt very unwell last night," he told Marshal Macdonald on the morning of the thirteenth, when the latter thought Napoleon looked tired and absent-minded and that he had a yellow-greenish complexion.[4]

Count Charles Tristan de Montholon's efforts to anticipate every possible accusation against him by publishing his *"mémoires"* have failed because of testimony and documents that he had never considered would see the light of day. Montholon's alibis shatter under examination. What is more, they reveal an insight into the killing which — at the time — only the poisoner himself could have had. He, alone, knew that calomel together with orgeat was the death potion. None of the other witnesses in the drama of St. Helena knew that. So we find Montholon at pains to say that calomel saved Napoleon's life at a critical moment and that orgeat, milk of almonds and *eau de fleur d'oranger* was Napoleon's favorite drink, though — significantly enough — in *l'Histoire* Montholon does not have Napoleon drink them on his fateful last days.

No other witness seems to have realized that it was arsenic intoxication that prevented Napoleon from riding. Montholon, the only person at Longwood who knew about arsenic intoxication, makes Napoleon ride in *l'Histoire,* though no one else saw him then on horseback. In this way Montholon is concerned to show that Napoleon could not have been poisoned with arsenic.

Other witnesses did not realize that Napoleon's immobility and utter lack of strength during his last couple of days had to do with the calomel medication whose use was decided by the three doctors following the advice of Montholon. They did not know that in cases of acute mercury intoxication the power of movement in all voluntary muscles ceases. (Naturally it ceases later, also, in the other groups of muscles, which ultimately induces death.)

No one can know the details of a murder drama as well as the killer himself. Montholon knew why Napoleon had those enormous tar-like stools (bleeding from the stomach walls) and why he lay so still on May 4 and 5, 1821. He needed an alibi, so he said that calomel was given for the first time on May 4 rather than the third of May. Napoleon possessed quite superhuman physical strength on the night before he died. This statement, it would be presumed, eliminated any possibility of the poisoning of Napoleon with mercury.

Such contrived and manifestly false alibis as Montholon used constitute in a court of law palpable incrimination. They are self-accusation by the accused. A trial judge and jury must deduce strong evidence of guilt as one alibi after another by the defendant becomes demolished by the truth. It would have been a better policy of deception, insofar as Montholon now stands before the bar of history's judgment, had he never written his *Histoire* or *Récits* of events at St. Helena.

Historians tended to believe what they chose to believe from his records and to smile indulgently about the patent fabrications of *"il bugiardo"*. But it was when one had finished reading Marchand and Bertrand and then read Montholon's lies that it was clear he was not doing violence to the truth merely for his own long-established tendency to spin fanciful stories, hopefully elevating to his own status as a person of courage, position and high regard. He lied for a reason.

A murderer is someone who is at one and the same time prosecutor, judge and executioner. If we accept Montholon's self-revealed knowledge of the way Napoleon died and of his part in the tragedy, should we describe him in the ugliest of all terms — murderer? There are reasons to withhold harshest judgment.

Montholon certainly was not responsible for the decision to liquidate Napoleon. That was decided in Paris.

When in 1829 Count Bourmont was furiously attacked by the French press for his treachery at Waterloo, King Charles X, as has already been mentioned, defended him. He said Bourmont had never taken any initiative unless on orders from the King. This "amnesty" included not only the occasion of high treason at Waterloo but also the attempt to murder Bonaparte on December 24, 1800.

No one until recently had accused Montholon of the liquidation of Napoleon. But if anyone had done so in the reign of King Charles X, the latter might have defended Montholon in the same way as he shouldered the responsibility for Bourmont's actions and heaped honors and rewards upon that trusted Napoleonic general.

One of Count de Montholon's more recent descendants wrote the author about his ancestor. The letter was quite friendly and showed that the writer had understood and agreed with the author's opinion that every historical character should be judged and criticized according to the codes of honor of his time.

Montholon's descendant concluded with the words: "You must admit, sir, that Montholon was a *grand seigneur.*" He was of the Bourbonist aristocrats and may be judged to be a loyalist. For those like him there was one compelling law: *Le Roi veut*, the King desires. Without the slightest doubt the monarchy of the Bourbon succession in France had wanted Napoleon's removal ever since that day when he refused to become a latter day General Monk and in 1800 return Louis XVIII to the throne. The house of Bourbon was only able to achieve restoration after many long and bloody battles, known as the Napoleonic wars, but which could just as well have been called the Bourbon Wars of Restoration.

References

1. O'Meara II:142, 167, 261; Gourgaud II:37
2. Marchand I:20
3. Constant 632
4. Macdonald 299, 300, 301
5. Marchand I:230
6. Ibid I:231
7. Caulaincourt III:359, 360
8. Marchand II:365
9. Caulaincourt III:361
10. Montholon (1), page 274
11. Caulaincourt III:362-64
12. Caulaincourt I:224
13. Marchand II:236, 237
14. d'Abrantès X:315
15. Montholon (1), page 223

48

Montholon after St. Helena

EVER SINCE NAPOLEON had returned dramatically from Elba in 1815 to drive the royal house of Bourbon out of the country by an unbroken and quite bloodless march of triumph, Count d'Artois, heir to the throne, was in the practice of calling him *le revenant*, the "returned", meaning the spectre or ghost.

Once Napoleon had been buried, according to all the rules of the art of royal rival removal, d'Artois should have felt safe both for himself and for the Bourbons' hold on the throne to which he would soon succeed as Charles X of France.

Messrs. Montholon and Montchenu could at last breathe a sigh of relief at the end of the difficult and delicate task. Of course they could expect no public and official recognition. It is not easy, therefore, to learn in close detail how these gentlemen fared upon their return from St. Helena.

We have no knowledge of the monetary or other awards and compensations de Montholon received in appreciation of a successful mission. Secret agents are seldom acknowledged, much less conspicuously rewarded by those they have served.

We know that Basil Jackson, the English agent, along with the mistress assigned him in the line of duty, Albine de Montholon, met Charles Tristan de Montholon in 1828. He was then broad-mindedly invited to the magnificent Montholon chateau.[1] By that time de Montholon had finally received a substantial part of his inheritance from Napoleon, after the protests of the Empress Marie-Louise had been rejected by the French government. This decision of the government, which was in the reign of Charles X, might perhaps be taken as a measure of recognition of Montholon's service to the Crown and his just claim to reward — at the expense of the old enemy's estate. But there were still many good reasons for considering Napoleon's Will as void. This the Empress quite realized when she maintained that she and her son by Napoleon were the principal legitimate beneficiaries.

In 1826, however, Montholon finally managed to get 1,351,298 francs of the 2,000,000 he had been willed.[2] He lived in affluence until the fortune had been exhausted.

Great curiosity was aroused when it became known in 1827 that Montholon had been received in secret by King Charles X, that is to say, by our old acquaintance the Count d'Artois, who had succeeded to the throne following the death of Louis in 1824. It was thought that the reason for Montholon's reception, in spite of the fact that he had been so conspicuously a member of Napoleon's court in exile, was that Montholon wanted to inform the king of a hostile Bonapartist feeling against him among the officers of the army.[3] We are not surprised, but it is interesting to think that Montholon might thus appear as *mouchard* or informer among his fellow officers.

As could have been expected, Montholon lived separated from the Countess whose favors at St. Helena had made the imprisonment of unhappy Napoleon slightly more acceptable. The uninitiated at court thought it was Montholon's mistress who had interceded for Montholon with the king. She was said to have been a charming and excellent lady. Yet Montholon certainly needed no help from the opposite sex to arrange to see d'Artois, either when the latter was heir to the throne or after he had become king. But of course at an earlier time it had been discreetly done, since Montholon's step- (and adoptive) father, Sémonville, was still a favorite with King Louis' brother. De Montholon's own ambitious brother had been valet to King Louis while Charles Tristan functioned at Napoleon's exile-court.

It has been generally believed that Montholon in 1829 had gambled away his fortune and had to go to Belgium to escape his creditors.[4] In that case it was unfortunate, for just then the house of Bourbon was hard pressed to hold the throne. In July of the following year the Bourbons were compelled for a third time to leave France as the unpopular Charles X vacated the throne in favor of Louis-Philippe, Duke of Orleans.

In 1831 we find Montholon in Switzerland. He lived there, basking in the glory of his past as Napoleon's most faithful fellow exile, but reportedly in somewhat straitened circumstances.[5]

In the middle of April of that year he tried to meet Count Bombelles, the Austrian Minister to Switzerland. When finally received, a month later, Montholon opened the conversation by complaining that the Empress Marie-Louise owed him a great deal of money. She certainly — and on good grounds — thought quite the opposite. Then the real motive for his visit became clear. Montholon wanted a passport to go to Vienna.

What business could he have had there? It turned out that a political group to which Montholon belonged intended in the near future to proclaim Napoleon's son, the Duke of Reichstadt, Emperor of France. Montholon considered it important that the Austrian government be informed, and that was why he had to have a passport to go to Vienna.

Further, Montholon wanted his papers issued in a temporarily assumed name, to hide his identity and his mission.

Was Count de Montholon leader of this political group? No, he was not: he merely belonged to it. But he was well acquainted with their plans and in order to prove this he handed Minister Bombelles a draft of the constitution for the new empire.

The minister wished very much to know the name of the real leader. It then transpired that it was a Monsieur Mauguin, a deputy who was actually one of the leaders of the opposition to King Louis-Philippe's government.

Bombelles must have known a certain amount about Mauguin. He told Montholon that this Mauguin was in fact working for the return of the Bourbons. It was even known to him that Mauguin was negotiating with the Bourbon Duchess of Berry. Her son was to be proclaimed Emperor of France under the name Henry I (sic). The new Emperor's standard was to be the tricolor with the Bourbon lily and the eagle of Napoleon.

But what about Napoleon's son, the Duke of Reichstadt? Where would he fit in the picture? Montholon could supply the answer to that easily. Mauguin was prepared to abandon the house of Bourbon and join the cause of Napoleon II, provided he immediately received five million francs.

Montholon's negotiations with Minister Bombelles did not get

very far. It is not surprising; the astute Prince Metternich of
Austria was not so easily taken in by Montholon as Napoleon had
been. Bombelles, of course, would have reported de Montholon's proposal to that shrewd manager of political affairs.

In the middle of September, however, a Prince Dietrichstein
came to Berne and the question arises as to whether it could have
been the same Dietrichstein who was the Duke of Reichstadt's
tuteur, guardian.

Montholon managed to see the Prince and presented to him a
somewhat altered text. Now Montholon held three trump cards
in the political game: the Duke of Reichstadt and the Count of
Bordeaux, also known as Henry V, together with King Louis-
Philippe's eldest son, Ferdinand. The main thing was that
Louis-Philippe himself should be overthrown.

In spite of the fact that, as a cover for his original wish to meet
the Duke of Reichstadt, Montholon had managed to mobilize
two further candidates for the throne, apparently he did not
manage to get to Vienna to talk with the prospective Napoleon
II. Dietrichstein found Montholon's exposé too fantastic to be
taken seriously.[5]

Montholon must have felt that he had been unfairly treated.
It's on the record that another traitor to Napoleon, he who knew
so much about the *ragusades*, Marshal Marmont, Duke of
Ragusa, had been able to meet the Duke of Reichstadt as long
ago as on January 25, 1831. He had held forth on Napoleon to
the eagerly receptive son. Montholon could certainly have done
so, equally well. He had been with Napoleon later than Marmont.

References

1. Rose 552
2. Aubry (1), page 598
3. Lucas-Dubreton, 252
4. Forshufvud, 48
5. Bourgoing, 312-17

49

Death of l'Aiglon

As for the question of possible loyalty to young Napoleon, both Marmont and Montholon were, of course, very trustworthy supporters of the house of Bourbon.*

It is credible that here not history but a Bourbonist secret agency in the service of Napoleon's enemies repeated itself. The cases of father and son developed so similarly as to suggest a guiding hand in common, using a now familiar method.

In July 1830 the Duke of Reichstadt's doctor was worried because the 19-year-old prince had broken out in a rash, a *dyscrasie du système cutané*. It was thought especially odd that the hands, too, were affected, though these had not been subject to frostbite.[3] This was interesting. The rash obviously suggested frostbite. So there must have been blisters on the hands. Blisters on the hands would also suggest arsenic intoxication. Quite obviously the Prince's doctors did not think of that, even if they had known of it as symptomatic, which is fairly improbable.

Some parallels in this significant symptom's sudden appearance will be found in the life of Napoleon. We know that when he was Consul, Napoleon had been troubled with skin rash which the doctors thought was the itch. Early in 1802, about a year after the attempt on his life in the rue Saint-Nicaise, Bonaparte suffered from an acute pain in his right side.

In Schönbrunn in 1809 Napoleon had suffered a strange

---

*In a letter to Mme. de Boigne of May 25, 1831, Adrien de Montmorency, Duke of Laval, wrote: "I have met travellers from Vienna, who tell me wonderful things about your friend Marm [Marmont] and his acquaintance with a man of 20 and his intimacy with one of Po:s [Polignac's] ministers (the count of Montbel). There is more diplomacy than affection there."[7] To this story can be added the fact that on November 17, 1831, Montholon signed an assurance of absolute loyalty to Henry V, "that Prince whom Providence has ordained to bring my country happiness."[2]

430

skin trouble, which induced him to summon his physician Corvisart, then in Paris. As well as this skin trouble he also suffered from an affection of his eyes (conjunctivitis) and a "cold".[4]

We should note that at her trial our practitioner of poisoning, Mme. Brinvilliers, said that the first symptoms her brothers displayed after she had begun poisoning them were confined to the skin. Both suffered from itching all over the body two days after the first dose, followed by blisters on the next day.

Reichstadt's Dr. Malfatti was able to state that this weakness of the skin was due to a hereditary constitutional defect. Napoleon I and his sister Elisa had also suffered from it.

The Prince's skin disease was cured with salt baths and milk. It was a prescription Napoleon, too, had followed. The baths were certainly useful, and milk is an old and proven antitoxin, but the real reason for the Prince's recovery was probably that he was removed and isolated for fear of the great cholera epidemic which then was raging over the whole of Europe.

In the summer of 1831 it was thought that the Prince had so far recovered that he could safely begin his military education.

He passed his physical examination, joined the Prince Vasa regiment of Hungary, took part vigorously in the exercises and spent many evenings in theoretical studies. The officer commanding the regiment, Major-General Prince Gustaf av Vasa, son of the dethroned Swedish King, Gustaf IV Adolf's son, praised the duke's zeal and his courteous and winning manner. He was a good horseman and commanded cleverly and intelligently. "His health is good and he is in a condition to withstand all trials," Prince Vasa had also stated.[5]

A few weeks later, in the autumn of 1831, Reichstadt seemed often dull and heavy with sleep.[6] It was, strangely, just such a condition as his father had been observed to be in during much of the Hundred Days. Sometimes the prince was so hoarse that he could not utter a sound.[7] Just as with his father at Borodino, for example.

Malfatti began to think that the duke suffered from a liver complaint. How similar that, too, was to the medical case of his father at St. Helena! The prince's skin became yellow, his liver swollen and tender.[7]

About January 20, 1832, an "intermittent fever" set in, that is to say, precisely as Montholon had described Napoleon's illness in his letter to his wife written December 20, 1820.

In a letter to his mother of March 17, 1832, the young Duke said that his chief trouble was a swollen liver and sensitive trachea.[8] He complained, too, of a bad appetite and of occasional stomach trouble, which made him think he had the same weakness that had brought his father to the grave.[9]

As in his father's case, the Duke of Reichstadt also had periods of recuperation.[10] During these, as we recall his father on occasion had been able to do, he could go out for rides in his carriage and even for short excursions on horseback.

One of these carriage outings ended in almost the same way as Napoleon's last and interrupted outing had done. The Prince suddenly became ill of an acute "attack of fever", precisely like the illness which his father had suffered.[11] His legs failing him, he fell to the ground as he alighted from his carriage.

History was repeating itself in the case of the son so exactly that the medical records of each might have been interchanged without a major inconsistency.

The youth's appetite became steadily worse and he lost weight. In the evenings he had black rings under his eyes. (This, too, had been observed of Napoleon when his malady possessed him.) He slept badly, troubled by a cough and by nervous muscular spasms. He suffered difficulty in breathing, and in the mornings his feet would be swollen, white and drained of blood. His attendants tried to persuade him to go for short walks in the garden, but he usually shunned the exertion of walking and refused to go out. A minor difference was that the Duke was not troubled by British sentries as his father had so angrily declared himself to be at St. Helena.

The Duke's hearing became worse, exactly as his father's had done. His left ear was quite useless.[12]

The "fever" came on every evening and did not leave him until dawn, after copious sweating.[13] His father had often suffered from the same experience, as his attendants said in their reports written as the Emperor declined toward his death.

The medicine the young Duke was given tasted bitter and sour. The mucous membrane of his mouth, his gums and his tongue became sore. Occasionally he would spit blood. All this could mean tartar emetic. And why should he not have been given tartar emetic? It then was considered to have wonder-working properties. At least it was presumed to be good medicine when given in prescribed doses by a physician.

The duke had pain in his right side, exactly as in his father's case, quite near the end. He started to spit blood as Napoleon had done.

When Napoleon had spat blood it was due to bleeding in the oesophagus, but his lungs did show sufficient damage to cause Antommarchi, as autopsist, to speculate on the possibility that the Emperor once must have suffered from tuberculosis.

When the Duke of Reichstadt spat blood, it must have come from his lungs, so far as can be judged from the accounts of his illness.

Pulmonary oedema and the spitting of blood, however, are not unusual symptoms of chronic arsenic intoxication.[14]

During the summer of 1832 the Prince's condition was slightly improved and on July 6 Marie-Louise wrote to her father: "My son is getting better".

And then suddenly and unexpectedly, without apparent cause, the Duke became worse. His cough was bad, his legs swelled and would not support him. For hours his legs would be ice-cold and had to be warmed with hot compresses. The Prince's skin was yellow as parchment; he suffered from severe heart palpitations.[15] All this, of course, was wholly in the pattern of his father's illness and of young Las Cases' occasional symptoms — the syndrome of arsenical poisoning.

On July 19, however, his doctors thought the Prince was better. A modern day German pathologist, Dr. A. Heffter, a specialist researching in the intricacies of diagnosis in cases of arsenic intoxication, writes that it is unforgivable not to suspect arsenic intoxication when gastric trouble is coupled with conjunctivitis, eczema or weakness in the legs. So we should take care then, not to make this "unforgivable" mistake in the case of the young Duke of Reichstadt.[16]

The improvement did not last long. A day later a severe relapse occurred and on July 22, 1832 the once handsome and spirited young Duke of Reichstadt lay dead.

There is much to indicate that Reichstadt's death was the result of arsenic intoxication, together with antimony poisoning. But nothing was found in his stomach that could be interpreted pathologically. This does not mean, of course, that there was nothing there. Probably not much attention was paid to his stomach, as even before the Prince's death it had been presumed to be the case that he was a victim of tuberculosis.

But let us bear in mind Antommarchi's diagnosis that Napoleon, too, appeared to have suffered from tuberculosis. In his post-mortem report he wrote: *"Je trouvai le lobe supérieur (du poumon gauche) parsemé de tubercules et quelques excavations tuberculeuses* — I found the superior lobe (of the left lung) studded with tubercles and some tuberculous caverns."[17]

It is possible to poison with arsenic without the poison passing through the stomach. Poisoning can be carried out, for instance, with arsenic hydride, which is a gas. Another method is by vesicatories containing arsenic, and still another with enemas.

The Duke of Reichstadt was treated with vesicatories as his father had been. The day before he died new vesicatories were applied.[18]

Blistering vesicatories (Spanish flies) had a very good reputation among doctors — and poisoners — at the beginning of the 19th century. A certain Count Louis de Narbonne, who was the natural son of Louis XV and therefore closely connected with the royal family, had joined Napoleon and seems to have been loyal to him. This count died in 1813 of "typhus", after a week's illness. A vesicatory had been placed over his abdomen. When immediately after death the vesicatory was removed, the entire skin and abdominal muscles, together with the abdominal lining, came away too and his intestines were exposed and found to be in a state of putrefaction. Without any doubt arsenic had been mixed with the substance of the vesicatory.

Napoleon's son uttered as his last words: *"Umschläge, vesicatoren."*

No one knows what he meant. Did he want compresses and vesicatories? He already had those. Did he sense that his sickness was due to a vesicatory?

On April 30, 1821, as earlier related, Napoleon was afflicted with a severely acute attack a few hours after vesicatories had been applied. His doctor thought he would die. Napoleon asked Marchand to remove the vesicatory. Relief came fairly soon afterwards and Napoleon seemed noticeably better.

But no one removed the Duke of Reichstadt's vesicatory.

After the Duke's death Dr. Malfatti said that it was the liver and haemorrhoids which had first and most seriously worried him. The Prince's chest trouble was late in being recognized.[19]

A young man of twenty does not normally suffer from piles, at any rate not dangerous ones calculated to cause a doctor anxiety. This information from Dr. Malfatti could mean that the Prince had been given something irritating in an enema. In which case it would, of course, have been arsenic.

The liquidation of Napoleon and then of his son followed identical patterns right up to the end. Napoleon's cause of death was identified as the same illness as had taken Carlo Buonaparte. But it was a kind of "cancer" or "cankerous flesh" that could be induced by anyone initiated in the traditions of the court poisoner on anyone subjected to medical treatment. When, by doctor's order, a plaster is applied, the poisoner has only to add arsenic to produce an intoxication.

Five months before Napoleon's death Montholon had been able to tell the Countess de Montholon that Napoleon would die within half a year of a *maladie de langueur,* which is to say, consistently with the still-to-come official French communique on the cause of Napoleon's death.

Napoleon's premature death, then, was understandable enough. It was due to his own inherited constitutional weakness — a deficiency that a "murderous" climate could aggravate and increase until death ensued — death by cancer.

But it would have looked bad, indeed, if the twenty-one year old Duke of Reichstadt had died of cancer, only a year after the head of his regiment had declared the Prince in extremely good health and well able to support all the rigors involved in military training.

But Napoleon's son, nevertheless, was to die because of a "congenitally bad constitution." He was not found to be quite without any "scirrhus", but the occurrence was found in the

lungs and not in the stomach. "Scirrhus" in this connection must
have meant swollen lymph nodes, which Napoleon's autopsy had
likewise reported. In his case they were described more fully and
today can be recognized *as a typical manifestation in lung tissue of
chronic arsenical intoxication.* The Duke of Reichstadt escaped
being treated with calomel and orgeat. He died instead at the
stage of poisoning Napoleon reached on April 30, 1821 when
Dr. Antommarchi thought he was near death, and before the
three drastic vesicatories had been removed.

Both Napoleon's and Reichstadt's doctors diagnosed their
respective patients' illness in the same way. Both were convinced
that their patients suffered from a liver complaint. In each case
the patient's skin was decidedly sallow and the liver enlarged.
After the post-mortems Napoleon's doctor and Reichstadt's each
would suffer much ignominy for his "faulty diagnosis". In both
cases the liver was discovered to be sound. At least so the
ignorant thought, as it was impossible to see without a microscope the grave changes in the liver tissue caused by arsenic
intoxication. A yellow skin was absolutely certain proof that the
liver was affected. Those who thought that the liver was healthy
because they could not see the sickly changes were guilty of that
very common basic scientific mistake in academic circles: judgment passed on the basis of the invisible instead of being
confined to what was clearly visible.

Reichstadt's announced and publicly accepted congenital
weakness produced tuberculosis. He had not inherited that
tendency from Buonaparte genes but from someone much
closer — his own mother. She was supposed to have a pulmonary
weakness. But she was a lively woman who survived two
husbands and it was only the third she left a widower. The fact
that she died of "rheumatic pleurisy" at 56, does not mean she
was constitutionally weak.[20]

There were more than medical similarities between Napoleon's illness and his son's. Bonapartist propaganda would
have it that Napoleon died as a result of his captivity and because
he was not allowed to ride horseback for exercise. Riding was
assumed to have been a vital necessity for him. *La Revue des Deux
Mondes* reported on the Duke of Reichstadt's official death
certificate, saying that the poor young man had been bound to

die, "suffocated as he was at that fusty court that had been made into his prison."[21]

As in the case of Reichstadt's father's death, someone might easily start talking about poisoning. In Napoleon's death a scapegoat existed in Sir Hudson Lowe. In the Reichstadt case it was Prince Metternich.

The French are generally realists provided — *bien entendu* — that reality does not diminish *la Gloire de France,* the honor of France. That a Frenchman could have poisoned Napoleon and his son is unacceptable as a reality to a patriotic Frenchman. The author has personally and rather unpleasantly experienced this. As long as an author could content himself with advancing proof merely that Napoleon was poisoned, he could be supported and encouraged by all the French authorities he spoke with. To go farther and say that the killer must have been one of Napoleon's trusted attendants was not acceptable. It was certain that Napoleon had been poisoned. But climate, harassment and cancer of the stomach sounded better.

The Bonapartists believed that Metternich had sent the Duke of Reichstadt poisoned melon.[22] Those Bonapartists obviously were not especially well acquainted with the technique of poisoning, a fact which stands to their credit.

In England people understood Metternich's dilemma. The *Times of London* wrote: "The [Austrian] Emperor and his shrewd advisor Metternich knew only too well what an admirable hostage they held in the person of Napoleon's son for any enterprise they wished to embark upon against France."[21]

The *Times* had seen, then, that the Austrian government was trying to protect the Duke of Reichstadt in every way for the very reason the British government had been anxious about Napoleon's security.

Yet another similarity between the two killings should be noted. Just as the French king, Louis XVIII, had an official representative in Napoleon's "prison camp", so our old friend D'Artois, deposed as King Charles X in 1830, but still a Bourbon power, had his personal representative at the court in Vienna, namely the Count of Montbel.

Here we may note the intriguing fact that many of the agents of Charles X (d'Artois) had names that included the syllable "mont". There were Montholon, Montchenu, Montmorency (a Jesuit like Artois himself)[23], Montbel, Bourmont, Marmont, Montgaillard, Montciel, Montrond, Montesquiou (the abbé), Sémonville. Could it be that the superstitious Count d'Artois once had consulted a fortune-teller who advised him only to recruit people whose names began with that syllable? Mont could relate to ultramontain, one who wants to restore the Pope's absolute power in France as did d'Artois himself.

The Count de Montbel would have realized that his presence in Vienna during Reichstadt's illness would attract attention. While there he assumed the name of Capdeville and pretended he was a Swiss.[24]

It is probable that several persons in a position to observe the Duke of Reichstadt's illness suspected that the prince had been poisoned. His quick recoveries after days of very severe illness, his many "relapses" and his sudden fatal illness were accompanied by very many symptoms that ought to have suggested poisoning. At that time it was one thing, however, to suspect poisoning, and quite another to show the courage or imprudence to say so. Poisoning can so easily spread into an epidemic fatal to those who do not know the merits of silence.

It was King Ludvig I of Bavaria who bluntly asked the Austrian envoy in Munich if the Duke of Reichstadt really had died a natural death. The envoy was most insulted. Thereupon the king had to explain that of course he had not for a moment believed that any Austrian had been involved in a possible attempt at murder.

He went on, however, to point out that there were two political groups in France interested in the removal of Reichstadt. "Had neither of these really made any attempt to take the life of Napoleon's son?" asked King Ludvig.[21]

In any case there was relief and much rejoicing among Bourbon supporters and at the exiled Bourbon court in the Edinburgh Palace of Holyrood where King Charles X was living again in exile, just as he had done as the Count d'Artois.

The philosophy of King Charles toward murder as a political instrument was clarified in a conversation at the time of the July revolution of 1830, when *Le Revenant* — that is to say the organized Napoleonic cult — struck a blow to banish the hated

Bourbon monarch. The great mass of the French people then wanted the Duke of Reichstadt on the throne of France as Napoleon II. But the leading politicians preferred the Duke of Orléans, Louis-Philippe.

In an apparently rather casual conversation Charles X observed to the Duke of Orléans that King Henry III had done a very sensible thing in arranging the murder of the Duke de Guise. The duke was threatening the royal power.

Louis-Philippe, the Duke of Orléans, had objected: "I don't think anything could make murder permissible." To this King Charles had replied: *"Vous vous trompez,* you are mistaken."[2]

It is well to remember that the Duke of Reichstadt's last illness coincided with the Duchess of Berry's most energetic efforts to get back the throne of France for her son, Henry V. At the same time Charles X was repeating his request, which earlier had been refused, to be allowed to live in Austria. That request was granted shortly after Reichstadt's death.[25] The Duchess of Berry's supporters expected help from Austria after Napoleon's heir was dead.

References

1. Boigne, IV:456; III:265
2. Garnier, 400
3. Bourgoing, 341
4. Cabanès, 166
5. Wertheimer, 310
6. Bourgoing, 350
7. Ibid 344
8. Ibid 345
9. Ibid 356
10. Ibid 347
11. Ibid 346
12. Ibid 356-7; Aubry (2), pages 395, 397
13. Aubry (2), page 396
14. Fazekas 287; Heyman 401
15. Aubry (2), pages 411; 416
16. Heffter 853
17. Antommarchi (1) II:161
18. Bourgoing 358
19. Wertheimer 334
20. Aronson 226
21. Aubry (2) 446
22. Ibid 445
23. Boigne IV:450
24. Wertheimer 330
25. Garnier 410

50

The Revenant

To PUT AN END TO Napoleon was, for the house of Bourbon, really no great problem. Although it was a time-consuming and delicate exercise it had been fairly easy to arrange. The problem was how to prevent the rival's ghost from returning as the immortal hero of his people. Even a dead rival's reputation can haunt a ruling monarch, as history so often has shown.

Napoleon now lay, safely entombed, on the other side of the world and no alarm had been raised that the house of Bourbon had had a hand in his death. It had been a slow and careful operation, successfully completed. Perhaps Napoleon might have been finished faster — like d'Enghien for instance — but though the Congress of Vienna had called him outlaw a Pope had anointed him Emperor. Heaven might count it a murder if he were to be dispatched too unceremoniously. Yet he had confessed the crime of killing the popular d'Enghien. He had been given the Last Sacrament. It had all been done correctly. Louis the Eighteenth was a man with religious principles, not an unscrupulous murderer. Doubtless d'Artois had had to bear that in mind.

But though Napoleon was well and truly sealed and cemented away, he lived still in his son Napoleon II, alias the Duke of Reichstadt and King of Rome. In July 1830, therefore, it was once more necessary for the house of Bourbon to retreat from Paris. Once more, they must plan with elaborate care how to return and remain.

The Bonapartists, too, were disappointed in 1830. Charles X (d'Artois) was replaced by the likewise Bourbonist King Louis-Philippe, the so-called bourgeois king. But as against this scion of the houses of Valvis, Orleans and Bourbon, the masses of France

440

began to call for another Bonaparte, with cries of *Vive l'Empéreur,* long live Napoleon the Second! A Bonapartist eruption might be expected at any moment. That danger, however, had been handled even more easily than the case of the Usurper.

Since July 22, 1832, Napoleon II, too, had been lying in a well-sealed leaden coffin. The third Bourbonist restoration had occurred and was being consolidated to rule as well as to reign.

In place of the Duke of Reichstadt as head of the French state *in spe,* however, there now stepped forward a nephew of Napoleon's, one of the former Queen Hortense's adulterine sons, Louis Napoleon, who had become the Bonaparte pretender to the throne after the Duke of Reichstadt's death.

Thus Louis Napoleon became the new menace to the current enjoyment of the throne by Louis-Philippe of the house of Orleans, related to the Bourbons by ancient royal relations, and "citizen king" who was son of the Duke of Orleans and of Adelaide de Bourbon.

After an abortive coup against the king in 1836 in Strasbourg and a consequent deportation to America, Louis Napoleon found himself in 1838 in London, where he established his headquarters. And there we come once more upon the tortuous and broken trail of Charles Tristan de Montholon.

Only a few weeks prior to his appearing in Berne as a supporter of the Duke of Reichstadt and in any case as the enemy of the newly-elected king, Louis-Philippe, Montholon had, according to the military lists, just rejoined the French army on March 22, 1831.

In *Archives administratives de la Guerre* we find an entry on August 15, 1839 concerning Montholon, recording that he was then placed on the reserve of the General staff. On September 26 of the same year he joined the first section of the General staff — and briefly disappeared to London.[14]

Masson tells us that at this point the government of Louis-Philippe sent off to London a "bankrupt general, whom the credulous and inexperienced Louis Napoleon received as his most valuable assistant." Valuable, that is to say, if he helped overthrow Louis-Philippe's régime.[5] De Montholon shortly would come to sight as the only general, bankrupt or otherwise, in the ill-fated attempted coup. He qualified for this description.

It would be familiar to meet him again in the role of double agent. What was the background of this new complicity?

It had become more and more difficult for King Louis-Philippe to survive and to navigate in the political low pressures which the rapidly increasing Napoleonic cult was causing in France. Thiers, President of the Council, therefore suggested a switch of course by sailing along with the enthusiasm for Napoleon's memory. As a move in this direction, it was decided to bring Napoleon's body home from St. Helena. But this, without doubt, would be a risky undertaking, unless they could put the Bonapartist pretender to the throne under lock and key — and for life!

After Louis Napoleon had been imprisoned, Louis-Philippe told Thiers that he (the king) had set a snare into which Louis Napoleon had flown like a starling.[6] As Louis Napoleon's chief of staff, General Montholon was captured with the small invading party at Boulogne on August 4, 1840 and was condemned to 20 years imprisonment at Ham in Picardie. His role has never been clarified but his early release for reasons of health suggests he was not feared by Louis-Philippe.

The snare of which Louis-Philippe was proud was already a familiar device of Bourbon family strategy. Louis-Philippe had perhaps learned it directly from his father-in-law, Ferdinand IV of both the Sicilies, who was a Bourbon. He employed it when he was going to put ex-king Joachim I Murat, Napoleon's brother-in-law, out of action.

Baron Barbara, a trusted Bourbon agent, had managed under false pretences to lure Murat on board his ship and had later put him ashore at an appointed place in his former kingdom, where a numerous and well-armed committee of reception had taken charge of him and thrown him into a pigsty. Once there the hero's halo had quickly fallen off poor Murat. He was found ready for a summary trial, the Last Sacraments and execution.[19] Louis Napoleon and Montholon fared much better than Murat.

La Belle Poule set sail for St. Helena on July 7, 1840, under the command of the personable Prince de Joinville, Louis-Philippe's third son.

On board as appropriate guests of honor were many of our

acquaintances, such as Bertrand, Gourgaud, Las Cases junior, Arthur Bertrand, Marchand, Noverraz, Saint-Denis, Pierron, Archambault.

But what about Montholon? Was he not invited? Yes, he had been sent a royal invitation, but it was for quite a different cruise. Whether it was luck or skill on the part of Montholon is open to discussion, but one thing is certain, it would have been too much to ask of him that he should go on playing the part of the loyal, affectionate and grief-stricken servant of Napoleon in the presence of the exhumed remains of his victim.

Perhaps it was less embarrassing a fate for him to be going with Louis Napoleon to prison at Ham while the body of his victim was arriving at Les Invalides amidst emotional acclaim.

When, at the opening of the tomb on St. Helena the innermost metal coffin was cut open on the afternoon of October 7, 1840, a gruesome atmosphere must have hung over those present. What would he look like, the heroic Emperor of the French, after nineteen years in the tomb? A surprise was in store. Instead of a grinning skull they were confronted with the Emperor himself, virtually unchanged — looking as though asleep.[17] Those who had experienced his exile had aged with the intervening years. He was as he had been when laid away in 1821.

A miracle, without a doubt; a Napoleonic miracle. His body had not been embalmed. It was not immersed in alcohol. It had been soldered into metal containers true, but these were without vacuum seal, so biologically the remains should have been corrupted by the natural processes to which all flesh is subject.

No one, not even Dr. Guillard, the doctor present, guessed at one natural explanation — arsenic — for the preservation of the unembalmed body.[18,20] Or did they? A strange lack of scientific interest and speculation on this phenomenon of preservation has persisted to modern times. Surely the favorite poisoning medium of the age might have been suspected by some as having doubled in the function of preservative and to have been a silent accuser of Napoleon's poisoner from 1840 on down to modern times. Biologists have long known the preservative uses of arsenic in preparing museum specimens of bird and small animal life. Was there enough arsenic to make effectual the partially efficient seal of the two containers that were soldered?

But this time the monarchy in France must have considered that the four coffins that had enclosed Napoleon's remains had not been enough. The amazingly lifelike body was now placed within six strong coffins, for subsequent enclosure in a porphyry sarcophagus. The thirty-five ton cover would be the final guarantee that Napoleon remained in his grave. Six coffins: The first was of tin, the second mahogany, the third of lead. The fourth coffin was also of lead, the fifth of ebony and the sixth and last of oak.[17]

Many Napoleonic authors have felt obliged to excuse Montholon's absence at the tomb re-opening by saying that this faithful Napoleonid was prevented by the incidence of his capture at the side of the future Napoleon III. Actually *La Belle Poule* sailed for St. Helena nearly a month before Montholon followed the future Napoleon III to their common billet in the castle of Ham.

It was on August 4 that Louis Napoleon, in his attempted coup to depose Louis-Philippe, embarked with a group of supporters on board a hired steamboat and landed at Boulogne. The prince's trump card was considered to be Montholon. A few hours later the whole company was under arrest.

The Prince was condemned to life imprisonment and, for appearance's sake, Montholon was given twenty years. Had Montholon not been condemned and arrested, his role in this drama would have become easily evident and the Bonapartists would then certainly have taken a dreadful revenge. After a time it became clear that Montholon's health was such that he could not stand the air of the prison and with a degree of solicitude on the part of his captors worthy of remark as unusual for the times he was sent to a nursing home. (Masson).[15]

After Louis Napoleon had been in prison for six years, he disguised himself as a carpenter one day, took a plank from some on-going repair work, shouldered it and walked out the gate.

When Montholon heard of the prince's escape he said: *"Comprenez-vous ce jean-foutre?* What do you think of that scoundrel? I, his friend and supporter, who have sacrificed everything for him, was not forewarned."[17]

Louis Napoleon would never meet his "trusted friend" again. When he came to power, Montholon was out of favor, say the latter's autobiographical notes for *La Grande Encyclopédie* ... because he had not taken part in the *coup d'état* of December 2, 1851, by which Louis Napoleon gained the imperial throne. At this point it has become so difficult to swallow any of Montholon's statements that we dare suspect that his disgrace with Napoleon III dated, indeed, from the time of the Boulogne coup.

References

1. Hugo 125
2. Delderfield 113
3. Aretz 93
4. Marchand II:402, 403
5. Masson (2) III:297
6. Lucas-Dubreton 369
7. Lucas-Dubreton 394
8. Lucas-Dubreton 373
9. Brett-James 207
10. Ganière 38
11. Bourrienne 146
12. Las Cases I:487, footnote
13. Gril
14. Chantemesse 220
15. Garnier 400
16. Ibid 49-51
17. Garros 499
18. Guillard 22 et seq.
19. Dupont 336 et seq.
20. Wistrand 289, 305
21. Hugo 264
22. Savant (2) 15

51

Montholon's Approach to Napoleon

IN SO MANY WAYS did Charles Tristan de Montholon, alias
Montholon-Sémonville, under study of his actions at St. Helena,
appear to be the person most likely to have destroyed Napoleon
that investigation necessarily turned to his life both before and
after his years at Longwood.

Could it be that by some slim chance he was being seen in a
false light; that the abnormalities and stresses of the exile
establishment distorted everything including the image of the
man who more than any other was responsible for what went on
in the strained routines of the captive monarch's household?

One knew there had been a reported defalcation of two
regimental funds. But he had never been tried and convicted of
theft. More than that, he had been elevated to the rank of Major
General of the Army of France *after* the time of the alleged
crime. How could he have been treated as an officer and a
gentleman if he were in disgrace and subject to court martial and
punishment?

At the outset of the investigation little was known about de
Montholon's antecedents beyond Masson's research and Montholon's own *Histoire* or *Récits*. Initially it seemed unwise to allow
the flawed character of the writer of those flagrantly faked
journals to influence dispassionate judgment. The man had the
right to be deemed innocent until evidence of guilt became too
massive for the benefit of a doubt to be given.

If, by any chance, a turn of events had occurred under which
the poisoning had been discovered in 1821 and Montholon had
been brought to trial for a crime he denied committing and no
one could testify from positive knowledge that he was guilty, how
would things then have been handled?

It seemed that this was essentially what the situation now represented, these many years later. A British court would have been troubled by the fact that this was a case that turned on that always hazardous thing: accusation founded wholly on circumstantial evidence.

To convict, such a court would have to satisfy itself beyond reasonable doubt that a guilty verdict was justifiable. In review, then, the court would require that a verdict of guilty be plainly consistent with all the evidence available and not inconsistent with the known or apparent character of the accused.

Consequently it became necessary, so far as possible, to study Montholon's career before he joined Napoleon's small retinue and in the years after he returned.

Normally, a chief source of such information might be considered to be Montholon's own biographical information contained in his memoirs and letters. These have not yet been as well assembled and analyzed as they deserve to be. But it would certainly be better for his case at law if Montholon's own statements could be kept out of court proceedings. He is found to be a veritable Baron Munchausen of deliberate disregard of truth. He lied compulsively when lying was purposeless and purposefully when he had selfish ends he believed would be served by unvarnished falsehood.

We know that persons on St. Helena who had not known Montholon until they met him there nicknamed him *il bugiardo*, the liar. This would hardly result from a very occasional lapse from truth or some polite 'inexactitude' designed to escape embarrassing himself or others. The nickname suggested that Montholon and the truth tended to be strangers one to the other by the nature of the individual.

However, because a man lies does not mean he would tend toward homicide. Indeed, it is probable that a high percentage of murderers might be found to be characteristically correct in what they said though somewhat careless as regards the rights of others to live. Nevertheless, through his own writings, Montholon would lose so many marks on the score of honesty that except in a very broad sense what he testified concerning himself would be of little use in tracing his history.

We had known and have mentioned the fact that he was raised

from the time he was a small child in the household headed by his stepfather, Huguet de Montreau Sémonville.

An adherent of the Bourbon establishment who luckily survived the Terror, Sémonville has intrigued the respect of historians less on the basis of any notable quality of character or service to his country than by the skill with which he could so readily accommodate himself acceptably to the powers in authority regardless of changes in the political situation. He was unquestionably first and foremost a Bourbonist but seemingly without giving offense to Louis and his brother, d'Artois, he could adapt to be equally at home in the circle of civil administrators around the rather tolerant Emperor Napoleon.

It is to be presumed that such a past master in genial duplicity was proud enough of his dexterous changes to lecture helpfully on the subject to Charles Tristan, whom he treated as a son.

Montholon credibly relates that his family escaped the perilous period of the Revolution by the fortunate fact that Sémonville with his wife and Charles Tristan were out of the vortex of the savage storm that swept urban France. They were in Ajaccio, Corsica, says Montholon, enroute to Turkey where Sémonville was to represent France. It was another of the comfortable and lucrative assignments that Sémonville had excelled in obtaining. The signer of the credentials which Sémonville would present to the government of Turkey was Sémonville's patron, Louis XVI.

Stopping at Ajaccio as a way point east, Sémonville had learned of the upheaval of his familiar world and the imprisonment and death of his King. Corsica would be as good a place as any to stay until things sorted themselves out. Charles Tristan was about ten at the time.

The inference is to be drawn from the Marquis de Montholon's 1847 account of events that occurred more than half a century earlier, that as a youngster at Ajaccio he was welcomed into the Bonaparte family, that Napoleon taught him arithmetic and Lucien tutored him in Latin. That there was an acquaintanceship between the Sémonvilles and Madame Bonaparte's family is not doubted but historians have discounted the Montholon claim that close ties were formed then which gave him an enduring friendly connection with the Emperor through the years until Waterloo.

His diplomatic role ultimately confirmed, Sémonville with his small family set out for Austria. They were waylaid en route and despite grievous wounds young Montholon, not yet eleven, defended his stepfather with great vigor and success. Historians have believed scarcely a word of it, partly because Count de Montholon in maturity had a body almost unmarked by scars, but mainly due to the incident, like so many others, having failed to turn up in official records. Other doughty deeds at arms and grievous wounds suffered in the heat of battle by the imaginative writer of his own history were never verifiable. If Montholon was wounded in any engagement at arms he could lay claim to distinction on the basis that his lesions mended without leaving so much as a trace by which he could support the exciting accounts of his adventures.

It is a fact, however, that he was a cadet and at sixteen was commissioned in the Army of France on May 31, 1800. He was appointed aide de camp to Gen. Augereau but was discharged for reasons that might have ended the military career of a less pertinacious man. He finessed the incident in his *Récits* and after a period that is obscure resolved to return to the Army, not under a cloud but under epaulets of a Lieutenant-colonel of the Fourth Regiment of Dragoons. His stepfather, not discouraged by the youth's marred introduction to an officer's career, prevailed upon Napoleon's Marshal Berthier to join in a petition that Charles Tristan, at 22, should be granted his wish to be gazetted a lieutenant-colonel.

Napoleon curtly rejected the proposal. In his own handwriting he made the notation: "This officer has not fulfilled sufficient length of service."

For Montholon, or perhaps the credit should go to Sémonville, there were yet other routes to preferment. His sister Félicité, following the death of her husband, General Joubert, had married General Macdonald. Disappointed as to rank but with a steady income restored by a service posting, under Macdonald, Tristan was again an officer and a gentleman of sorts. He was described in youth as "sinister" by John Theodore Tussaud, author of "The Chosen Four".* Other adjectives

---

*Jonathan Cape, London

applied out of Tussaud's research were "vain, wayward, irresponsible." He was "the victim of many failings even his most intimate friends found it difficult to forgive."

Not the least of the Montholon shortcomings was his inability to control extravagant tastes and to stay out of debt. He had been raised in a household of considerable affluence. It was his conviction that as an aristocrat he owed it to himself to live well in consequence of which he owed constantly to creditors and money lenders. It is not clear if gambling helped deplete his occasionally large acquisitions of money. His stepfather's fortune, his wife's dowry and eventually his large legacy from Napoleon each quickly wasted away leaving the Count again in an impecunious state.

On the 13th of May in 1809, with an added five years of service for which the Army's official record does not relate any ways in which the lieutenant had distinguished himself by courage or ability, we find him promoted to adjutant-commander with the rank of colonel. He was eligible to be a court chamberlain.

Before that year had finished, however, for some reason the 27-year-old officer's sudden rise was reversed by an abrupt discharge. It was the year Napoleon was campaigning against the Austrian Army under Archduke Charles in such grim encounters as at Essling and Wagram, a time when gallant young officers' stars could easily zoom into the ascendant; not a time to be leaving the army. But Montholon drifted in obscurity for two years until good fortune or good connections again revived his unstable career. In 1811 he was appointed court chamberlain in the household of the young Marie Louise of Austria, newly married to Napoleon, and sent on a mission to her uncle, the Grand Duke of Würzburg. Montholon now was nearer the core of France's Bonaparte Government than his erratic approach would seem to have forecast. He had friends, indeed.

We know from the commonly accepted account of Montholon's career that this appointment was worth 40,000 francs a year and that it was the kind of auspicious start any young man with an eye to a diplomatic service career would covet and try to protect by exemplary behavior. But within a year this great chance had collapsed. With it went the handsome salary and appointments of prestigious office to a respected court.

It is probable that the first significant attention given by Napoleon to the young Count de Montholon was early in 1812 when he received a request from him for permission to marry Mme. Albine Helene de Vassal. Born in 1780, she was three years older than Charles Tristan. What Napoleon, with his elaborate provision for receiving and dealing with detailed information from within the boundaries of his empire, no doubt objected to would be the report that Albine's husband, a member of the prominent Roger family of financiers, had divorced her for unfaithfulness. He may or may not have heard also the current gossip that the prospective bride was pregnant and that Montholon was considered to be the offending third side of the triangle and father of the expected child.

Napoleon refused to approve the wedding.

Giving Montholon the benefit of assuming he felt that in fairness to Albine Roger he should legitimize her child, he nobly resorted to subterfuge. He made a new application for official sanction, this time saying that his affianced was none other than the niece of President Seguer. He did not mention that the woman still was Mme. Albine Roger née de Vassal. Assuming too much, Montholon anticipated approval. He persuaded a very reluctant mayor of Draveil to perform a civil ceremony. Such a ceremony was necessary, considering the firm proscription of the Catholic Church against divorce and remarriage.

Busy as he was with the details of his most arduous campaign against the evasive forces of Tsar Alexander, Napoleon despatched a message to Paris — possibly from the Kremlin where he had set up his headquarters in half destroyed Moscow. Early in October of 1812 Count de Montholon was stripped of his appointment as minister plenipotentiary and envoy extraordinary to the court of the Grand Duke of Würzburg. It was made cruelly clear to the newly-married Montholon and his bride that the Emperor was angered by the act of disobedience. The attempt to gain approval by deception would aggravate that anger.

"His Majesty considers the union you have contracted incompatible with the credible office with which he has deigned to entrust you," read the message of dismissal.

It is reasonable to suppose that the effect of thus peremptorily removing Montholon from office made of the disgraced novice diplomat a man who could not look with hope to any further favors in army or government service. But he would well know that with his Bourbonist origin and connections his fortunes could rise again if Louis rather than Napoleon were the head of state.

Count d'Artois, exiled in England, but whom Napoleon later would credit with having had "sixty assassins in Paris", and whose royal family had long counted the Montholons as adherents to their various causes by long-standing close relations, would have remarked the dismissal with interest if not sympathy. He had one mission in life — to restore his easy-going and somewhat indolent brother Louis to the throne of France. Conspiracies to that end were centered in him and he was evidently both tireless and capable in behalf of the restoration.

The route back to Versailles and the Tuileries involved for the future King Charles X preparedness, intrigue and ruthlessness. The time logically must come when an increasingly ailing emperor had suffered military reverses and the country had grown tired of war. Then France would be ready for revival of the monarchy — but a monarchy behind a facade of constitutional safeguards after the pattern of those that kept the throne of Britain secure following the Cromwellian era.

But, so long as the Emperor lived, any king who replaced him would not sit securely and confidently in his place. None would know this better than ambitious d'Artois.

His brief interlude of honor and ceremony only a bitter memory, Count de Montholon went into a period of relative obscurity. It is known that his wife, who soon after their marriage presented him with a son, brought family money to the household they established impermanently. It was a time of uncertainty and unsettlement generally and the news from Russia was distressing. In due course the Emperor returned to Paris, his immense army all but totally lost. Marshal Ney with incredible strength and bravery fought to bring the remnants home. Royalist agitators made the most of the defeat.

All of France in those months would suffer extreme war weariness and unrest. The supreme military commander of his or any other age was subject to bouts of illness that left him physically drained of the sort of *braveur* and dash, the kind of mastery of minor details on a major scale that once accounted for the legend that he was of unconquerable stuff.

As late as in November Napoleon, with his customary painstaking attention to the minutiae of civil administration, had taken the time to see that the Mayor of Draveil was put out of office. His offense was that he had performed the Montholons' marriage ceremony without authority. But now in 1813 and 1814, with a newly drafted army of mere youngsters in uniform, former allies taking courage to defect from the Emperor's direction, the civilian National Assembly increasingly dismayed by debts due to the costs of continuous war, the lustre of Napoleon's career was dimming. There were flashes of his old spirit, moments of acute military perception that made him still extremely dangerous in the field, but the glory days of conquest and invincibility were strangely past. The Emperor as soldier was prematurely showing signs of infirmity, including a hampering corpulence. He was visibly changing for the worse — and so were the fortunes of France.

Until April, 1813 Montholon lived in relative seclusion, not in Paris but in the village of Changy près Nogent-sur-Vernisson. From that date forward it would be from Napoleon's reverses that he would gain advantage. Dreadfully costly in men and material, the Russian campaign faced Napoleon with the need to replenish depleted officer strength in his forces. Since the list at that time showed Montholon without appointment he was recalled to active service and ordered to report at Metz. This was the signal for evasive action by the Count. He replied:

"I am extremely sorry to be bound to state that owing to my wounds, and more particularly to a fracture in my left side, it is impossible for me to ride on horseback without having a haemorrhage."

Evidently the war office pulled the Montholon file and could not recognize him as having suffered any such distressing injury on military service. He was advised that he had been reinstated in the same command as when he had retired from service. However, it was not insisted that he report at Metz. Instead, in September he was asked to go to Toulon where he was to join the staff of Marshal Massena, who had become the Prince of Essling.

Though this was a staff job, without arduous and dangerous field duties, the reluctant Montholon managed to avoid involvement.

The Army was persistent but perhaps felt service in the Low countries, then reasonably quiet while France was engaged with the armies of Russia and Prussia, would suit their man. He was advised that on December 14 he had been placed at the disposal of General Decaën, headquartered at Gorkum. Always courteous with his disappointing responses, Charles Tristan informed the Army that he would be glad to proceed there when his illness permitted. Meanwhile he was suffering a fever.

Sterner measures being indicated, the Minister of War issued a peremptory command to General Hulin to establish contact with Count de Montholon, wherever he might be, and serve on him an order to rejoin the First Army Corps without further delay. After some added contest of wills in which there was established a signal unwillingness on the officer-candidate's part to serve his country as proposed, the Army's persistence was rewarded and Montholon reported to his former chief, Augereau, on the Loire. It was not a command in which he was likely to gain a conspicuous military recognition. Augereau was one of the least competent of Napoleon's military leaders.

Tussaud's report on Montholon's further efforts to protect and advance his career is recorded in illuminating passages in his book about the four who were chosen for St. Helena — Montholon, Bertrand, Las Cases and Marchand:

> Later, he [Montholon] was given the control of some 4000 or 5000 men, hurriedly collected from the ironmills and other industries on the Loire, ill-equipped and devoid of military training, all betraying a very poor appreciation of their change of employment.
>
> The care of these men he handed over to his subordinates, while he reposed at his ease within the village of St. Bonnet-le-Château, although the neighborhood was then overrun by Austrian troops, and Montbrison itself, with the adjacent towns, almost entirely at their mercy.
>
> On the advance of the Allies during the early days of 1814, and when Napoleon and his forces were being driven

back on Paris, Montholon is to be found in the Department of the Puy-de-Dôme, taking up new quarters at Clermont-Ferrand. At the time, being woefully short of money, he puts in a pressing claim, under date of 9th April, and obtains from the paymaster at Noirétable a sum of 2000 francs for the pay due to him for the previous month of December. This sum, however, failed to satisfy his craving for money or his pressing financial obligations at the moment, for on the 14th April, three days, let it be noted, after Napoleon abdicated at Fontainebleau, he had fallen so low as to extract from the funds of the paymaster for his division a sum of just under 6000 francs, sent for the payment of his men, but into whose pockets not a sou of it ever found its way.

The approach of the enemy; authority paralysed; the abdication of Napoleon, and the return of the Bourbons, silenced all inquiry for the time being.

When the news of the Emperor's downfall reached him, he is credited with having hurried to Fontainebleau, and there to have laid before his master a scheme by which he might overcome his enemies and maintain himself on the throne of France. But we need not take this interesting statement into very serious account, for he seems to have too readily and too earnestly been exercising his mind in making advances to those who were now more likely to render him favors in the near future.

Resigning his duties into the hands of Colonel Genty, he forwarded him the following instructions under date of the 20th April, which he evidently had written from the Hôtel de Bretagne, rue de Richelieu, Paris:

'Have Louis XVIII proclaimed King of France and Navarre. On the 18th at Fontainebleau the Emperor declared to me that he had abdicated and exhorted the French to serve the King faithfully.'

On the same date he writes to Count Dupont, Commissioner at the War Office for King Louis XVIII:

'I have the honor to expose to your excellency that having been brought into disgrace with the Government eighteen months ago at the instigation of General Savary, my military promotion has been brought to a standstill, and that I have been Adjutant-commander now for nearly six years. Allow me, My Lord, to beg from your kindness a promotion to the rank of Brigadier General.

'I will serve the King as faithfully as my ancestors served Henry II and Francis I.'

But in spite of this adroitly worded application, he does not seem to have awakened sufficient interest in this quarter to have obtained the promotion he had at heart. Nothing daunted, he next importunes the King, Louis XVIII, himself in the following terms:

'Sire, I have been the object of your Majesty's kindness even before I could appreciate it. I was not six years old yet, when your Majesty by a special favor deigned to confer upon me, at the request of Mme. la Princesse de Lamballe, to whom I had the honor to belong, the post of first-master-of-hounds previously held by my father, which title I let die away; Sire, When I came to the age of sixteen, and lost my fortune and my Prince, at least I tried to show myself worthy of the honor I had received from you. Your Majesty had just ordered the disbanding of the Royal Armies.

'I have served my country: 13 campaigns, 10 great battles, in which I took part, 3 wounds, several horses killed under me, all my promotion obtained at the army such are the claims to your kindness I have the honor to lay at the feet of your Majesty. I dare to entreat you to ask from your War Minister a full report of my services and permit me to give up all my blood for you in the rank of Major General which my younger comrades hold to-day.'

He signs: *Colonel Marquis Montholon, son-in-law of M. de Sémonville, Grand Referendary at the Chamber of Peers.*

This time his prayer is answered, and he obtains promotion as a Major-General, his commission signed by the King and countersigned by his War Minister, bearing date 24th August 1814. So it is not from Napoleon he receives his brevet as a General in the French Army, but from the hands of King Louis XVIII, while the Emperor is away ruling his little kingdom of Elba.

Had Montholon been satisfied with his good fortune, things might have lain dormant concerning that little affair of the 6000 francs he had borrowed from the paymaster's war-chest at Clermont-Ferrand. But in pleading favors and importuning for preferments of every sort, the insatiable Montholon tempted Providence too far.

Though he had been inactive for several months, he here endeavored to set up some sort of claim for receiving payment as if he had been on active service, and this application awakened awkward memories in certain high quarters concerning the disappearance of monies with which the name of Montholon had been intimately associated. This resumption of the unhappy affair ended in this authority urging the necessity of holding a court-martial. How the proceedings came to be quashed has never been clearly accounted for. It has been said, and perhaps too readily assumed, that they were overruled at the instigation of the Count d'Artois, in whose family the Montholons had long found service. Anyhow, the whole affair ended in Montholon becoming seriously disrated, and treated as beyond the pale of any further consideration.

Here we may well note the author's comment of half a century ago, drawing attention to a report that had been given credence by some and in which d'Artois was suspected of having come to his protégé's rescue over the incident of the stolen regimental funds. We may be less forebearing than Tussaud and think there could indeed have been Bourbonist influence of the highest order applied to free Montholon from the dire consequences of a court martial and establish in his mind a sense of obligation — and possibly of fear.

In any case, while Napoleon was emperor Montholon had been severely punished for disobedience. When the Bourbon regime had been resumed he had been granted a great favor. As an apt pupil of Sémonville, cultivator of those at the source of influence and patronage, this contrast between Napoleonic and Bourbonist treatment would not fail to impress the subject involved in these experiences. Could it be that out of gratitude or self-interest Montholon would become a prime candidate to receive a special agent offer he could not refuse? Could the fateful price of assistance be to repay a great favor with total loyalty to the king?

Our assessment of the Montholon instincts and interests at this point may allow us to doubt that he could within a year or two become, to Napoleon, the "most faithful of the faithful". We can, however, ask if in so doing he positioned himself to return some major responsive favor to his royal protectors. Now Tussaud's review of Montholon's approach to the post of close attendant to Napoleon, prior to St. Helena service, will take on significance far beyond any that was conveyed to readers of his book when issued in London in 1928. Indeed, we could here be in touch, for the first time, with a plausible explanation of Montholon's unwavering determination to spend years in exile at St. Helena. He would be serving a man who, though interestingly wealthy, was by the evidence of all past experience anything but friendly to him.

We continue, therefore, with Montholon uncharged with his crime but still in a degree of shadow, possessed of an eminent army rank but without an assignment. Author Tussaud proceeds with his account of Montholon's fortunes:

> Profoundly mortified, he again left Paris, as usual in debt and difficulties, and for the second time sought seclusion in private life, an event which Madame de Montholon once again signalized by bestowing upon him the responsibility of a second son.
>
> Although the circumstances attending his second withdrawal into private life offered him a very meagre prospect of amendment, yet his estrangement from public affairs was again to prove of short duration.
>
> A wholly unexpected turn of the Wheel-of-Fortune cast a gleam of hope that soon reached him in his retreat, reviving his spirits and bestirring him once more into action.
>
> The news reached him that Napoleon had left Elba and was at that very moment fast making his way back to Paris.

For Montholon as for Louis and d'Artois the turn of that wheel without warning must have been cause for swift decision-making. The Bourbons would be experienced in retreating to life away from France and in setting up a strategy of action to capitalize on some further turn of events by chance or perhaps with their assistance. Montholon, whatever were his precise thoughts, was placing his bet on more than one player. If Napoleon were to return, then he would need to establish his political credit early. After all, there had been a period as chamberlain in the court of a Napoleonic Empress. His embezzling had perhaps finished any chance of a further career as an active army officer holding the rank of major general. But field service had never been his forte. His affairs were far from prospering but recently he had communicated by letter with a king, to good effect, since he had been promoted on his own word. Now he could hope to capitalize on his talk at Fontaine-bleau with Napoleon at a time when that man's edifice of power had been tumbling around him. He might be remembered favorably as a counsel on diplomacy or on royal policy.

Such would be one possible reconstruction of events. Another, and the more dramatic yet probable development was that when it became clear another strategic retreat from the throne-room was looming as a likelihood, the debt owed by Montholon to d'Artois was called. There was need for a secret agent so close to Napoleon that he would be within the establishment. What better prospect could there be for the delicate task of performing the duties of a planted Bourbonist representative than Montholon, former chamberlain in the Empress' court, a chronic debtor, and best of all a man who had good reason to demonstrate his gratitude to the Bourbon cause? The reader may weigh and choose between the two suppositions.

In his memoirs Montholon makes it clear that when he could observe that Napoleon once more would be the master in the Tuileries he set out and was fortunate to meet him on the outskirts of the forest at Fontainebleau. Napoleon was on his way to uncontested power at the Tuileries in Paris and Louis and his court attendants were scattering in disorder. One does not, however, picture the conspiratorial d'Artois as dismayed or disorganized. He had made a career of patient plotting.

If we accept Montholon's version we find him at once at his master's side and reconfirmed in his rank of major general Without specifying in what ways he justified his claim he reports himself as having told Napoleon: "From your Majesty's return to

France till your arrival in Paris, I sought for opportunities of serving you, and on March the 20th led the way to your escort."

Corroboration of that statement as being factual is made difficult for historians since the de Montholon name is missing from the carefully recorded list of officers who rejoined Napoleon after his landing and of those who were first present with him at the Tuileries.

Not until late in the Hundred Days is Montholon discovered to be Court Chamberlain at the Elysée.

Tussaud's account in "The Chosen Four" pursues the tenuous Montholon trail:

> We first hear of him officially [again] on the 2nd June through a letter he addressed to the Prince d'Eckmuhl (Davout), Minister of War, in which he asks to be confirmed in his rank of Major-General and to be put on active service. This letter does not seem to have called forth any immediate response, for, on 5th June, he is moved to write direct to the Emperor, reminding him of the advice he had offered him at Fontainebleau the previous year, and the information he had recently afforded him on his approach to Paris. So we see Montholon busy again, still extolling his merits, dwelling on his past services, and pleading for preferment.
>
> The following strong and eloquent communication surely ought to have brought him some little favor:
>
> 'Your Majesty will judge if of all your faithful servants left in France, there was one who more than me made himself worthy of your kindness by his constant devotion, and if I am entitled to lay down at your feet the pain I must have felt at seeing the preference given to several of my comrades who took just the opposite line of conduct.
>
> 'Sire, by my devotion, of which I have given you such proofs, I could hope to be appointed to some military office near your Majesty. My name is now best known in the French Magistracy, my estate and the condition of my family were such as to give me a right to belong to the Chamber of Peers. I don't claim from your Majesty that I would have felt doubly honored to receive from your kindness, but I entreat you to accept me on active service, and grant me a post of honor.'

This letter Napoleon handed to his aide-de-camp Flahaut, without comment. Montholon expressly informs us that he was immediately confirmed in the rank of major-general, which he had received at the hands of Louis XVIII.

Of the four who volunteered their services to the deposed Emperor Napoleon only Bertrand had demonstrated complete loyalty. When his predecessor as grand marshal of the palace, Duroc, had been killed in the Polish campaign he had served faithfully as his chief aide from the start — by some regarded as having been the closest of all his personal friends. So great was the honor shown to Bertrand in being appointed to fill the role in which Duroc had displayed for so long a complete dedication to his leader that a powerful tradition existed. Not even Bertrand's wife would understand such an absolute commitment by Gratien Bertrand to Napoleon that he would twice follow him into exile and never once leave him until, tragically, his master's career ended in the long anticlimax at St. Helena.

Montholon, Gourgaud and Las Cases all had compromised any right to claim complete and unwavering loyalty. They had considered that the first abdication had ended the Bonaparte era and had sought or received recognition in the brief Bourbon restoration.

Las Cases, an historian, could plead the essential privileges of a theoretically neutral observer and recorder of events that plainly must be entered into the history of France. It behooved any major figure of then current history to cultivate rather than condemn him.

Gourgaud was forgiven by Napoleon, along with numerous other generals, for having temporarily forsaken the emblem of the eagle and the golden bees in favor of the Bourbonist fleur-de-lis. When a commander as great as Marshal Ney, who had promised Louis he would meet the returned Napoleon and bring him back in an iron cage to Paris, could so reverse his position as to embrace and join him at first meeting, who could say Gourgaud had forfeited his right to return to favor? He had never denounced his Emperor.

Gourgaud pleaded, protested and even wept as he struggled to overcome an early indecision by Napoleon on his right to be part of the expedition into exile. For Ney the rededication to Napoleon cost him his life as he stood bravely before a firing squad and barked the order to fire. Gourgaud would nearly lose his life from poisoning at St. Helena but his place in history would be honorable.

Montholon's gradual inclusion into the little cadre of attendants gathered at Malmaison was not marked by histrionics. He with his countess had stayed so closely in touch with the Napoleon entourage when the Council at Paris forbade Napoleon to linger there that he was from the moment of Napoleon's return to Malmaison at his side, visible, available and eager to serve. He would never again be separated from Napoleon by a greater distance than would be involved in taking a separate coach and route to Rochefort and, later, the length of the dusty road from Longwood House to the Governor's office in Plantation House at St. Helena.

There is no doubt that at Malmaison, where he had once spent happy times with his well-loved Josephine, and which represented the only roof under which he could shelter temporarily in a country where his execution was frankly contemplated, Napoleon was excessively distraught. He had always faced coolly the chance that he might lose his life in battle. But to lose his life as the executed enemy of his country and of the people of all Europe would be an unthinkable end. There were not many volunteers to accompany him. The roles of right to attend him would tend to go to those who, of any remaining faithful, most earnestly sought them. The Count de Montholon was not the least forward of the four who offered their services and were accepted.

Epilogue

MONTHOLON WAS TO LIVE to see that all his subtle work in the service of the two French monarchies had been in one respect in vain. The Napoleon he had disfigured, tormented and killed had become more alive in the memory of the French than anyone of flesh and blood could ever be; even more invincible, infallible, just, merciful and righteous than in life.

"*Les cendres ont tourné toutes les têtes* — his mortal remains have turned the heads of all," Montholon was to write in a letter confiscated and used at his trial following the Boulogne coup.

Montholon was not spared the experience of a new Napoleon, albeit not a direct descendant, occupying the throne of Napoleon I. More than ever realized, he had contributed toward the persistence of the Napoleonic legend and the popularity of anyone bearing the name who conceivably could be the King of the French.

Murky, unsavory and perhaps not altogether necessary deeds had been fulfilled by the blandly inscrutable Montholon. But these same deeds nevertheless would have been carried out without his help. Montholon's descendants should recognize that their star-crossed ancestor would have had little if any choice but to perform at Napoleon's exiled court the task laid on his young shoulders by the representative of the anti-Bonaparte royalists in France then in control of the machinery of state. Were he to have refused he must immediately have been liquidated, since in that case he would have possessed a state secret that must never be exposed. He would then, to the detriment of his progeny, have sacrificed his own life, and incidentally theirs, without having saved Napoleon's. There were certainly many young aristocrats who willingly would have

463

taken over the noble task of bringing about Napoleon's discreetly arranged disappearance from the world scene to avert a severe threat to the country's peace and the maintenance of the older monarchy.

Montholon killed his friend and benefactor; but so did Brutus, who similarly felt he had no other choice than to stab his ambitious Caesar, the rising tyrant of Rome.

Circumstances compelled Montholon to use lies and dissimulation as his instruments, and he dissimulated amazingly well. During the height of the Napoleonic cult and to a great extent ever since, Montholon has been dubbed "the most faithful of the faithful." Even now we have no absolute right to deprive him of this title, though it may apply in another connection. He was not faithful to the man identified as the enemy of his aristocracy. Undoubtedly, however, he qualified as faithful to the interests of his king and his caste. He served those who dreamed of restoring to the monarchy all the power and brilliance it had once had under the legendary Sun King, Louis XIV.

Montholon, then, deserves our understanding in the dilemma of choosing between great personal danger and rewarded duty. Montholon obviously being trusted to serve France's "legitimate" ruling clique, it was not he who took the initiative, and it would not have been his idea that so popular a hero as Napoleon should be destroyed in the chosen manner. The Bourbons had others skilled in secret poisoning and quite willing to accept the responsibility Montholon's assignment entailed.

At the time when Montholon was French minister to Würzburg and was engaged in his diplomatic duties without thereby neglecting his pleasures, Napoleon was poisoned at Borodino. There is little doubt that he was poisoned, too, at other battles — Dresden, Leipzig and Waterloo — when Montholon was not on the scene.

The Count died in August, 1853 a minor figure in the recorded history of France. Unfathomable, kindly and yet pitilessly cruel in his relation to his victim, he was, by virtue of his role at St. Helena, unquestionably the most history-changing man of all the intimates who appear in the drama of Napoleon's life. He becomes, thus, a man for history, in his own way almost as baffling to read as the great Napoleon Bonaparte who was his enemy, his prey — and most trusting benefactor.

As has been stated, Napoleon in his Will accused the British oligarchy and their "hired assassin" of having shortened his life. He was obviously not aware of all the terms of his Will. He thought for instance that he had left Bertrand as much as he gave Montholon, but he testified to the accusation against the British in a conversation with Bertrand on April 22, 1821. It was a misunderstanding that would inhibit the fullest empathy between France and Britain for generations to come.

The charge of murder did not incite an official reaction. The French government had publicly proclaimed that Napoleon had died a natural death. Where no victim exists there can be no assassin. The British, however, do not seem to have trusted the official verdict of the cause of death, for they took up Napoleon's challenge to avenge him.

When he returned to England, Hudson Lowe went as usual to pay his respects to his sovereign King George IV, but was discourteously received by the official who was to forward his request for an audience. He was, however, very graciously received in 1825 by the French king Charles X, who obviously could not be expected to see that Sir Hudson had defaulted.

Wherever else he went, Lowe met with abuse and was called a murderer. He managed to be appointed a regimental commander in Ceylon, a sorry come-down from the rank of lieutenant-general, but not even there did he escape the vengeance of his countrymen. He returned to Britain and asked the Duke of Wellington for a pension. Wellington answered that the Home Secretary, Robert Peel, would certainly not be likely to bring the matter before the House of Commons, but that even if he did the request would most certainly be turned down.

Sir Hudson retired subsequently to a small provincial town, where he lived unknown under another name, to escape obloquy. He never received a pension and died in 1844.

Nine years later a thick volume was published on Hudson Lowe's administration of St. Helena during the period of Napoleon's imprisonment, a collection by Forsyth of letters and reports. These gave the plain facts of the affair as far as these could be recounted in the entries of a conscientious British military governor.

According to Rosebery, this collection of documents made

dull reading. He obviously found them too much for him, or he would never have passed such hard judgment on Sir Hudson, a judgment based entirely on accusations by Montholon and on their influence upon other witnesses.

It is certainly to the credit of the British and their love of fair play that they sided against one of their own generals and sympathized with the man who had caused them to shed so much blood and so many tears. But now at last the plot has been disclosed, thanks to the clues supplied by two attendants at Longwood. We can perhaps hope that the British and French peoples, who have waged wars as enemies and allies and have done so much in their time for humanity's higher ideals, will be able and ready to take a more understanding view of the tragedy at St. Helena. So much in the future, as in the two great wars of this century, depends on the existence of a comfortable spirit of trust between them.

Rebuttal and Response

THE FORSHUFVUD THESIS respecting Napoleon's illness and death at St. Helena supposes that arsenical poisoning, as indicated by hair sample analyses, persisted throughout his exile. It declares that death resulted from an induced internal reaction of calomel and milk of bitter almonds that produced mercuric cyanide in the stomach in lethal strength.

By deduction involving the self-evident fact that if a murder is assumed then a murderer is implied, Forshufvud pursued his research by eliminating those who could not have been deemed able or disposed to commit the assassination of Napoleon. Having concluded that only one person in Napoleon's establishment at Longwood had motive, opportunity, method and skill to poison the Emperor to death, Forshufvud in this work has named him.

In what could be the normal situation applying in a defence of Count de Montholon, the accused would have counsel whose mimimum object would be to raise reasonable doubts and thereby counter the claim that overwhelming circumstantial evidence pointed to guilt. Thus it was felt that, without wholly simulating the proceedings of a court trial, some basic elements of an orthodox legal resistance to a guilty verdict against Count de Montholon should be offered, with opportunity for the "prosecution to respond. — H.T. M.

DEFENCE: This is a case for which no witness lives and for which the evidence offered turns chiefly on the analyses of certain hairs. But how sure are we that these hairs have the significance claimed for them?

Even if it be conceded that the hairs analyzed were taken

from the head of Napoleon on the day following his death and that they showed high reading of arsenic content, it is not claimed that de Montholon or any other person killed Napoleon by feeding him arsenic. If, as seems to be admitted by the prosecution, arsenic was not the cause of death but merely of illness, then we may dismiss the evidence of arsenic ingestion as contained in the reports of Dr. Hamilton Smith as being relevant to the charge of assassination. Surely it is neither here nor there that a substance that did *not* cause death was to a degree present in the deceased's physical system.

The only actual medical evidence that exists as to the cause of Napoleon's death is that of the doctors who conducted the post-mortem. They saw no evidence of poisoning nor did they suggest it as even a remote possibility. They found that a cancerous condition and deterioration of the liver through chronic hepatitis were the cause of death.

PROSECUTION: The autopsists at the dissection conducted by Dr. Antommarchi saw and described clearly enough the evidence of poisoning by chemicals ingested into the digestive system of the subject. Not suspecting poisoning they did not recognize the symptoms for what they were. This was exactly the situation the poisoner, who knew there would be a post-mortem, planned and hoped would be the case. That is one reason — we may assume it was the main reason — Napoleon was given arsenic in less than lethal doses but quite regularly over a long period of time. Indeed, the accused, Montholon, merely continued what had been happening periodically ever since Napoleon ceased to be merely a military officer and rose to the rank of Consul of France and then of Emperor.

DEFENCE: Surely the prosecution is not going to blame Napoleon's every illness on arsenic.

PROSECUTION: The records show that Napoleon Bonaparte was a slim, wiry, strong and energetic man until he aspired to occupy a throne. Then he suffered illnesses similar to those he manifested at St. Helena. His physique changed to corpulence, with all the accepted outward symptoms of his being gradually made an arsenophagist by stealthy ministrations of a person or persons he trusted. If the investigating doctors had had Dr. Hamilton Smith's report on arsenic in Napoleon's hair, they would have been intensely concerned with the evidence that a poisoner was included amongst the personnel at Longwood. The mystery of Napoleon's chronic illnesses would have been no longer a mystery. But these men had no irradiation technique at their disposal.

DEFENCE: We remain concerned with a substance that did not kill Napoleon. The issue is being prejudicially confused.

PROSECUTION: If there had been no poisoning with arsenic, to simulate hepatitis and a variety of other complaints that defied treatment or identification, there would have been far greater risk for the poisoner when it came time to administer the final blow — the *coup de grâce*. The authorities would have been compelled to recognize violent death by poisoning and in that very limited company of persons who could have done the deed there would have been little doubt of discovery.

So it is vitally important to know that Napoleon was intoxicated again and again with carefully calculated doses of arsenic, enough to make him violently ill at times; enough to rob him of strength and of the image of a man who could ever again be considered qualified to be a contender for the leadership of France.

It is vital that now we can be sure a clever poisoner was at work in Napoleon's retinue. It had to be a person whose presence aroused no fear in the Emperor. That he used for so long a poison that did not kill but accustomed those around Napoleon to see him only a fat, helpless, unhealthy-looking, vomiting person from whom all accustomed power had been stripped is testimony to his skill. Such a man would know exactly what potion to kill with when the time came — and for Napoleon that time came *on the very night he signed a legacy that made his poisoner a wealthy man.*

DEFENCE: I must object. The defendant Montholon was described by Napoleon himself as the most faithful of the faithful. It was entirely to be expected that he would, as he

often said, leave Montholon a generous legacy in appreciation of his service. The citing of this coincidence of time is
wholly unfair and prejudicial in the extreme against an
honest and faithful man.

PROSECUTION: The Montholon record shows beyond doubt he
had misappropriated two minor military funds. He was in a
position where anyone might have blackmailed him to
actions he would be reluctant to perform. He was never
prosecuted. Why? In France of that time such a breach of
trust in military circles should have brought down dire
punishment on the guilty — probably years in jail. Montholon's vulnerability to being pressed into a dangerous service
by someone close to the Bourbon king to ensure the
incapacitation then the liquidation of Napoleon is a fact we
must recognize to appreciate his motives.

DEFENCE: The prosecution seems committed wholly to the
theory that Napoleon was poisoned. Without prejudice to
my position in this phase of the evidence-giving and
argument concerning Montholon, I should like to prove the
weakness of the case against him by presuming for the time
being that Napoleon was the victim of a deliberate poisoning
and that this was the cause of his death. There were many in
the world who could wish him to die. And at Longwood
there would have to be other suspects as well as the man who
nursed Napoleon so attentively in his final weeks and hours.
We know from the wording of the same will as brought
reward to de Montholon, that Napoleon hated and feared
Governor Lowe and accused him of killing him. Why does
the prosecution not look in the direction of Napoleon's own
suspicion?

PROSECUTION: Because Sir Hudson Lowe had no opportunity to
affect the quality of the food and drink going to Napoleon.
Napoleon was suspicious enough to order that nothing
whatsoever should be given him to eat or drink except by his
valets, or in his extreme illness, de Montholon, acting as his
night nurse. Napoleon's attacks of vomiting and extreme
sickness often came at night just after de Montholon had
finished his tour of duty, according to Marchand's memoirs.
Certainly Lowe was not there. The Governor appeared to

have neither motivation nor opportunity. The fact that Napoleon was being subjected to arsenic poisoning on repeated occasions before he went to St. Helena is disclosed by hair analysis. This would seem to require that we search for the poisoner in a direction consistent with the previous administrations of poison.

DEFENCE: You say Lowe was not there when Napoleon became ill at night. Could not he or someone else in control of a plan have been represented at Longwood by Dr. Arnott? He had many opportunities to reach Napoleon but particularly so on the night it is contended the Emperor suffered what you describe as the *coup de grâce*. If it was a combination of *orgeat* and calomel that produced the presence of mercurous cyanide in the Emperor's stomach, we must recognize the fact that it was Arnott who prescribed 10 grains of calomel — a drastically large dose. Surely that casts a shadow of doubt over the case that Montholon was the culprit. Why could it not have been the English doctor who is known to have prescribed the abnormal dose of calomel ready to be activated by the *orgeat*, functioning as a reagent?

PROSECUTION: It is extremely doubtful if Arnott knew the potentialities of the presumably harmless calomel to be changeable from a mere purgative to a violently effectual agent for death. Napoleon forbade Marchand to permit any prescribed medicines to be given to him. Marchand objected but yielded to persuasion by General Bertrand, who prevailed upon him through his most vulnerable point of defense. Bertrand said the Emperor was dying and the doctors were agreed it might be the calomel remedy that would save his life. But mark well, again, the influence of de Montholon. He was ready with the advice that once before calomel had saved the sick man's life. He became chairman of a conference of reconciliation of views when Drs. Arnott and Antommarchi sharply disagreed in the sick room.

We have evidence that de Montholon's view was in the affirmative for the use of the calomel. Think of the helplessness of the British doctors to prevail had Montholon staunchly supported Antommarchi and Marchand in their very determined opposition. Thus we have to assume it was de Montholon who made possible the administration of the *coup de grâce* under the cover of medical approval by a majority of the doctors present. He had been told of Bonaparte's express instructions to give him no nostrums. In this respect obviously he was not "the most faithful of the faithful". It was the most crucial moment in the long preparation to achieve a mission, the dramatic climax for which all the previous poisonings at St. Helena were a prologue. It must be admitted that the plan would have failed had Montholon not intervened. Perhaps for the only time in his life, Marchand disobeyed his revered monarch in exile. Since in that act of breach of a solemn promise to obey, Napoleon's death sentence was being enforced, it follows that Montholon was at that time and place directly responsible for making possible its execution.

DEFENCE: The list of others who had motive and opportunity is not exhausted. General Bertrand has been mentioned and well he might be. Like Marchand and like Montholon he was with Napoleon from the beginning of the expedition into exile and continuously until Napoleon died. He, as the prosecution alleges, persuaded Marchand to trick the Emperor into accepting the prepared drink that, it is alleged, resulted in his death. On the basis of the defence's own hypothesis as to the means of death, with only a change in the name of the suspect, we must say that Bertrand qualifies as a man who exercised an opportunity to have the calomel consumed.

The prosecution is so sure that in linking alleged opportunity and motivation in the case of the accused de Montholon the argued evidence of guilt surely must be accepted as fact.

How weak this case is can be demonstrated by a similarly malign assumption of guilt directed at General Bertrand. True, he was long and closely associated with Napoleon but never so closely as at St. Helena. There the strong personality of his royal superior permeated almost every hour and certainly every aspect of his life. In almost claustrophobic closeness, he was confined with Napoleon on that hated island. What an appalling situation for a man still young and whose whole life had been one of exciting military action. Napoleon suffered from a climatic illness. Bertrand, we might declare, had his mental health destroyed by the maddening realization that there was no escape except by this man's death. Is that explanation not equally as believable as the supposition of guilt in the case of faithful Montholon?

PROSECUTION: The defence's proposition loses validity in the fact that of those who were with Napoleon at Longwood only Bertrand did not reside at Longwood. The Bertrands were a happily married couple. He had a wife, a quite normal home life and family to occupy him. In strictest terms, though he was grand marshal, he had no regular duties to perform. He was a court attendant to the former monarch — a man who read to him occasionally, took some messages, discussed the affairs of the lack-lustre court and then escaped the intensely strained atmosphere of Longwood House to enjoy the felicities of quiet, orderly domestic relations. He was, true, a general out of a military job, but he was a soldier in a role he fitted well.

DEFENCE: This depiction of a scene of domestic tranquillity and of even tempered relations of a warrior at rest does not ring true, by the testimony already presented.

It is on the record, in fact, that while relations between Count and Countess Bertrand may have been exemplary, those between Napoleon and the Bertrands were not similarly so. Indeed, it has been testified not once but by several witnesses that Napoleon coveted the affection Madame Bertrand gave her husband. He attempted to have his doctor, Antommarchi, virtually order Madame Bertrand to be his mistress. He was disappointed that the Bertrands did not reside at Longwood or attend court far more assiduously. When none of these invitations or proposals that his senior attendant's wife should place herself at his disposal was accepted, as the testimony conveys, Napoleon resorted to calumnious attacks on the virtue of his general's wife. At one point he declared to Antommarchi that she was a whore. We have heard, too, that Napoleon accused his doctor of having an affair with the woman.

Beyond that, the evidence goes on, he flatly declared to General Bertrand that Madame Bertrand was prostituting herself to Antommarchi and others in a most open and scandalous way.

Could the prosecution now maintain, and could any reasonable person believe in the face of the evidence presented, that relations between Bertrand and the man whom he had served so well were unstrained and cordial? Is it not much more likely that instead of trust and friendship there was burning resentment — perhaps even hatred and a secret, deep-down determination to have revenge and to terminate what could have seemed like endless misery?

PROSECUTION: At this point the evidence is familiar to us all, from being much reviewed in search of a just conclusion. The examination of all possible suspects to sustain acceptance of their innocence naturally had to concern itself with the case of General Bertrand and his wife. Superficially, the aggravation any honorable man would feel under the circumstances described would arouse suspicions in a careful investigation. This indeed has been the case respecting the relations of the Bertrands with Napoleon.

One must remember the mores of those times in France, the disciplines of the army, the laxity of the moral code in the upper echelons of any European court of the era. In so doing one must wonder that the Emperor did not have his way. There is not the slightest suggestion that outside the agitated mind of the seriously ailing Emperor there was any substance to the accusations against Madame Bertrand.

We may wonder that General Bertrand did not resign his post and ask to be returned to France with his wife and family. But we must remember the man's literal dedication of his life to Napoleon. When such a mutual trust has existed as between Napoleon the Great and Bertrand the faithful it is the product of many tests each proving its durability. A general places his own life and those of all for whom he is responsible at absolute hazard. A grand marshal presumes obedience to his orders. He will give unquestioning obedience to his monarch, life itself being not a withheld price if events should require it to be sacrificed in service.

General Bertrand was plainly an officer of that kind. He might remonstrate with Napoleon in behalf of his wife's peace of mind and her good name, but he would not quit the service at St. Helena. The kind of general who will follow his chief voluntarily into the cul-de-sac of exile will long since have qualified to be one who meets life's crises with composure. As for Countess Bertrand, she had certain of her own standards to which she was adamantly true. One does not know the mental turmoil, the embarrassments that Napoleon's demands made upon her but she emerges as a person of character and kindness, dutiful to her husband and young family under the stresses of the exile existence. She is pictured as showing plainly in physical appearance the pressures in the last days of knowing Napoleon was dying, that he had never publicly retracted his scandalous statements about her and that to the end he persisted in showing his displeasure that *Madame la grande maréchale* did not match the accommodating Countess Albine de Montholon in honoring her Emperor with her more frequent attendance and a more responsive attention. Mme. Bertrand was a disappointment to Napoleon, we may be sure, but a comfort and an assurance to her husband. In this fact lies the illogic of harboring any serious suspicion that General Bertrand could have been the plotter or had been knowingly involved in a plot against Napoleon's life.

Beyond these considerations, however, lay the questions turning on skill and opportunity. Bertrand was an improbable person to have competence in the forming and placing of potions upon which the effectiveness of poisoning depends. Further, he lived off the premises of Longwood. He was not a regular bedside attendant of Napoleon at any time, having no ministrations to perform unless Napoleon should send for him. Marchand's account makes it very clear that Bertrand himself felt excluded by Napoleon in the final days. Napoleon rejected his requests that he be allowed to relieve Montholon in night nursing duties. Instead the Emperor preferred de Montholon, the faithful and sympathetic. Time and again the record shows that onsets of violent illness occurred while Bertrand was not at

Longwood. Significantly, these illnesses did not come except when Montholon had been previously present. Finally, we should not forget that Bertrand and his wife very often were attacked by the *maladie de climat;* Madame had many miscarriages during the exile, not before, not after. Arsenic provokes miscarriage.

DEFENCE: If we are to complete the list of those theoretically in a position to have poisoned Napoleon, of course the man who prepared his food throughout his entire time at St. Helena should not be overlooked. The chef, Pierron, prepared what was served to Napoleon to eat and drink. There is no cause to suspect him and yet in theory he could have tampered with the Emperor's food.

PROSECUTION: There is, indeed, no reason to suspect the chef. He may have had opportunity of a kind. But whereas at least two major motives can easily be identified in the case of de Montholon, none existed so far as the chef was concerned.

As to opportunity we must recognize that in the case of the chef it was of the wrong kind. Any opportunity he had to poison Napoleon was at the same time an opportunity to poison all at the court. How could a chef poison so selectively and at night when no food was being prepared, or so coincidentally that it would be at just the right times to be of assistance to de Montholon's scheduled needs? The chef served no food except the dessert to Napoleon. Only the valets had that privilege. How could he decide which portion, which glass Louis Marchand was to place before Napoleon? In the constant presence of assistants in the kitchen, was he in any position to inject carefully calculated poison doses into what the valet would serve the Emperor? Obviously, he could not.

DEFENCE: Nevertheless, the accuser must admit that alone or in conspiracy the chef was better placed than most to poison Napoleon.

PROSECUTION: On the contrary, through centuries chefs could so obviously be suspected of poisoning unsuspecting victims in high positions that for precisely that reason they consequently were given less opportunity. Those who served kings were always at risk since royalty had the right to fear the arts of the poisoner. The king's portion could be switched at will to see what effect it might have on some selected taster, which might include the chef or the head waiter, to ensure their innocent intent.

In Pierron's case, however, we must ask ourselves a significant question: "If he or any other man had it on his conscience that he had poisoned another to death nineteen years before, and if he were to receive, along with others, an invitation to be present at the opening of the tomb and see the body of his victim exposed to view, is it likely that he would attend?" Pierron, of his own volition, returned to St. Helena and participated in the ceremony.

DEFENCE: The name Marchand has been mentioned. Again one mentions it not to accuse but to emphasize how many there were who had opportunity to give arsenic to Napoleon. Marchand is on the record as having the Emperor's complete confidence to the point where he alone was to hand food, beverages and refreshments to the Emperor. That being the case, must he not be seen as a more likely person than de Montholon to have done the alleged deed?

PROSECUTION: There could indeed have been opportunity in the case of Louis Marchand but, as with the chef, the situation would be wholly without motivation. The alleged role and crime of a suspect must not be inconsistent with all that is known about him. A poisoner to accomplish his end must have not only opportunity but motivation, knowledge or skill, the substances with which to work and the qualities of character or mind that must go with such sinister purposes.

We must remember that Marchand was very dangerously poisoned. Would he have administered it to himself?

Perhaps least of all people on St. Helena, because of his background, his nature and his faithful dedication to the opening of the tomb and the removal of Napoleon's body to Paris, should we suspect Marchand. Of all the principal members of Napoleon's household who, 19 years after his death, were available to be there when Napoleon's tomb was opened, only de Montholon was absent.

DEFENCE: That is a slight basis on which to erect a theory of guilt.

PROSECUTION: Any single circumstance mentioned concerning

de Montholon's position may be judged too slight of itself to warrant the accusation of guilt.

When the memoirs of Bertrand and Marchand became available for study in the 1950's, the detailed descriptions of Napoleon's illnesses, strikingly symptomatic of arsenical poisoning, should have aroused almost immediate suspicion. One can only assume that no professionals in medicine or crime investigation with toxicological knowledge and particularly with knowledge about the physical reactions to intoxication with arsenic were sufficiently interested in history to read these books. Had they done so the reaction should have been predictable that the post-mortem at St. Helena had failed to recognize symptoms inconsistent with a verdict of death from natural causes such as cancer or a disease of the liver.

No cancer tumor had been discovered. The liver was dissected and though enlarged — as should be expected in the presence of arsenical poisoning — was not pronounced cancerous, cirrhotic or incapable of functioning.

Given those facts a diagnostician today, referring to his medical school course in toxicology, could readily equate these and other symptoms with poisoning.

When, in confirmation, the hair analyses on many samples of Napoleon's hair, gathered from many sources, all certifiable as genuine, all having the quality and distinctive coloring of Napoleon's hair, all yielding similar results of arsenic concentration far in excess of normal, an amendment to the autopsy verdict would be compelled. The post-mortem verdict would then become "death by administrations of poisons by a person or persons unknown."

Then, germane to the whole subject of how and by whose hand Napoleon had died in his fifty-second year, would be the scrutinizing and weighing of every written word of evidence as to the behavior of those conceivably capable of the act of poisoning.

Finally, Montholon condemned himself in his own memoirs by his discernible attempts to divert attention from himself by clumsy alibis that must increase not abate suspicion about his role at St. Helena.

An unprejudiced and judicial examiner would be confronted with the fact that only in the case of one court attendant, Count de Montholon, would the act of poisoning be consistent with what was known about the man. The circumstances in the case, remarkably available and documented, thanks particularly to the Bertrand and Marchand memoirs, taken all together, point to de Montholon and to him alone. In his lifetime Napoleon trusted de Montholon. Dying from an illness mystifying to him, he laid upon his own and other doctors who would conduct a post-mortem the responsibility to solve this mystery of a fatal malady. Posterity in general — for Napoleon was a man for the ages — but the people of France, in particular, owe it to him to see that, in every possible respect, what he asked should be granted. He asked a judgment that is within the capability of this generation, this court of public opinion, aided by scientific and professional skill, to give justly and without equivocation.

Part Five

Exhibits in the Case

Why is that man still alive;
and in English hands, too?

— THE DUKE OF RICHELIEU,
Minister of Foreign Affairs
to Louis XVIII.

Exhibit No. 1

Discovery at Glasgow and Harwell — 1960

Having obtained his first authenticated specimens of Napoleon's hair, one taken previously to death and the other shaved from his head May 6, 1821, the day following death, Dr. Forshufvud wrote the following letter to a forensic laboratician reputed to be the best in his field:

Göteborg, Sweden
June 22, 1960

Dr. Hamilton Smith,
Department of Forensic Medicine,
University of Glasgow,
Glasgow, Scotland

Dear Dr. Hamilton,

With thanks for your promise to help me I send you now in a separate registered envelope the following samples of hair:
    H.S. about 2 mg, and I.13, about 4 mg.
The samples are supposed to come from the same person at different ages. My principal question is: Is arsenic to be found?
If you don't need whole the samples for your arsenic-analysis, the rest could possibly be used to answer the following subordinated questions:
    1) Do the samples of hair belong to the same person?
    2) Do the samples contain also antimony and mercury?
It is just a wonder that I found these samples, which are invaluable.

483

After your analyses it should be a real pleasure to tell you the whole story.
Would you, please, let me know in a simple card, that you have received the samples.

Sincerely yours
Sten Forshufvud

He awaited impatiently the results of the investigation.

If Dr. Hamilton Smith could, indeed, by neutron irradiation, determine in detail the arsenic content in single hair specimens from the body of the long-dead Emperor, then it would not be necessary for science to have access to the body to establish the answers to Forshufvud's deductions. The tests might alone prove the existence of arsenic in Napoleon's system from the chronic intoxication the St. Helena diaries had led the doctor strongly to suspect.

Exhibit No. 2

An Historic Letter

Opposite is the now historic letter that first confirmed the belief foul play had produced Napoleon's illnesses before and after his captivity at St. Helena. The reply was fully corroborative, as Forshufvud had expected.

UNIVERSITY OF GLASGOW

DEPARTMENT OF FORENSIC
MEDICINE

TELEPHONE : KELVIN 2231

THE UNIVERSITY,
GLASGOW, W.2

Tuesday, July, 11d, 1960.

Dear Dr Forshufved,

Here are the results of the analysis.

Ref	As. (micrograms As / gm of hair)
H.S.	10·38
I. 13.	10·53

The subject has had exposure to large amounts of arsenic. I am surprised that the value obtained should be so high if taken at different times. If this is the case exposure must have been continuous, even so it is surprising that the value is so constant.

I am trying to have the hairs physically compared, and will send the results if and when I get them.

I would be most interested to hear the story of this case.

There will be no charge for analysis.

Yours faithfully,
Hamilton Smith.

The tests had shown 10.38 and 10.58 parts per million in each of two samples. A normal reading in that period should not have exceeded today's norm of 0.86 p.p.m. and more likely should not have read higher than 0.65.

Dr. Smith was stunned and disturbed when he was informed by Dr. Forshufvud that the subject of the hair he had analyzed was Napoleon Bonaparte. He was reassured that the test did not lead to any embarrassing discovery that the famous prisoner of St. Helena had been done to death on British orders. On the contrary, it could at last free French and British relations from the handicap of Napoleon's anguished testimony in his will that he had died prematurely a victim of the Governor, Sir Hudson Lowe, and the British oligarchy whose policies the Governor had administered.

Exhibit No. 3

Methodology Employed in Analyses of Napoleon's Hair

SUMMARY: Having arrived at the conclusion that on the unconsciously-furnished evidence contained in notes by Napoleon's St. Helena attendants the symptoms pointed very strongly to his having died by poisonings, Dr. Forshufvud concluded that the only physical evidence available to him would be in specimen hairs preserved as souvenirs. He therefore chose to follow that course of research. The first test would be made using two hairs slightly more than five inches long, certifiably those of the subject.

Through the voluntary collaboration of senior laboratician Dr. Hamilton Smith at Glasgow University's School of Forensic Medicine and with access to the facilities of an atomic pile at the Harwell Atomic Research Station west of London, a practical approach to the testing of his theory was at the service of the Swedish researcher.

The procedure would be to bombard each hair with neutrons in the nuclear reactor. This would convert the hair sample to a radioactive isotype by irradiating its arsenic content. While the hair would be destroyed, the residue, under a delicate Geiger counter, would give a reading to measure with exactness from so small a specimen its number of parts of arsenic per million of the sample's weight.

It is estimated that in Napoleon's era of relatively low pollution of man's environment by chemicals, the arsenic reading for the average individual's hair or bone structure would be of the order of 0.5 to 0.65 ppm. (Today's norm is accepted to be about 0.86.) The first hair analysis by Dr. Smith gave measurements of 10.38 ppm. and 10.53.

The finding was significant but would be open to challenge as having experienced external contamination by arsenic. Much knowledge in technology of testing was added to the science of forensic medicine by the motivation to discover how Napoleon died. Dr. Smith continued with repeated tests of specimens from many sources in subsequent years.

By encapsulating the hairs in consecutive sections measurable in millimetres rather than centimetres as before, it was possible to read the highly irregular variations in arsenic deposit that not only proved absence of external contamination but disclosed poisonings at measurable intervals and of identifiable severity. From that point forward the validity of the declaration of undependability by opponents of the Forshufvud thesis in Paris had been scientifically collapsed. Napoleon obviously had been poisoned.

Dating back from the time when the specimen hairs were shaven from his scalp on the day after death, the laboratory readings could be matched with the dated notes of the first valet, Louis Marchand. Forty poisonings were indicated, mainly in the final four months of the victim's life and these could be related to the severe illnesses described by notes of his doctors and attendants.

For the benefit of readers professionally interested in the procedures employed the following reports and excerpts from papers to learned society journals are supplied.

EDITOR

Refinement of testing methods to identify timing
of arsenic ingestion

The more than 140 separate tests made on authentic specimens of Napoleon's hair between 1960 and 1964 helped give Dr.
Hamilton Smith an extensive body of knowledge on activation
tests for arsenic poisoning.

In October, 1964 the Journal of the Forensic Science Society in
Great Britain (Vol. 4, No. 4) published a paper by Dr. Smith
titled The Interpretation of the Arsenic Content of Human
Hair.

Excerpts from it throw further light on the methods used to
analyze Napoleon's hairs and the significance of his more
advanced methods after first test of whole hairs had indicated
poisoning. Sectional analyses permitted timing of intakes to be
compared with diary entries on Napoleon's condition at known
times.

Hair is a useful source of investigation and study in arsenic poisoning
or alleged poisoning. Normal hair always contains arsenic in small
amounts. Often this arsenic cannot be detected by chemical
means, due to the low concentration present, the small amount
of hair available and the masking effect of the arsenic introduced
by the reagents. This last is a very serious cause of many faulty
reports of significant arsenic levels. Neutron activation analysis
eliminates these difficulties and allows accurate determination of
the normal arsenic content of hair. It is possible to analyze
samples . . . of about 2 mm in length with accuracy.

Using this method, (Smith, 1959) on over 1000 samples (1-2
mg), chosen at random from living subjects, gave results as
follows:

ARSENIC DISTRIBUTION VALUES

description	arsenic (ppm)
Mean	0.81
Median	0.51
Range	0.03—74
95% samples	Less than 2
99% samples	Less than 4.5
99.9%	Less than 10

(Abnormal arsenic readings are measured against these standards.)

Contaminated hair

Internal contamination is caused by the deposition of arsenic in the growing hair from the blood stream, which in turn reflects the arsenic content of the diet and possibly of the respired air. In this way the hair is a continuous record of the absorption of arsenic. Any rise in arsenic intake causes a rapid rise in concentration. No value has been found to be above 100 ppm and it is much less when a whole hair or large section of one is analyzed.

(Whole hair analysis was employed in the first discovery tests made on specimens of Napoleon's hair. Later, when it became possible to analyze by millimetre sections accuracy rose and timing of the poisonings became calculable. Dr. Smith's paper compared the relative efficiency of the two methods.)

THE EFFECT OF WHOLE HAIR AND SECTIONAL ANALYSIS

Sample	Arsenic content (ppm)
Whole hair (30cm)	0.86
Whole hair excluding 1st cm and root	0.55
Root and 1st cm	9.40
1st mm including root	90

This possibility of error makes it necessary to perform some type of sectional analysis, so that a clearer basis of interpretation is obtained. In general, a hair of about 10 cm length can be examined in four sections with a very good chance of detecting any undue contamination. Doubtful samples should be examined in centimetre lengths or smaller. In these small sections many of the trivial as well as the major variations become apparent. There is always some variation from section to section due to environment, but not so great as that caused by even a therapeutic dose of arsenic. The following table shows a few examples of analysis of quarters of normal hair and one contaminated hair.

SECTIONAL ANALYSIS OF HAIR ARSENIC
(parts per million)

Sample	Proximal quarter	2nd quarter	3rd quarter	Distal quarter
Normal	0.05	0.10	0.12	0.08
Normal	0.15	0.19	0.21	0.03
Normal	0.068	0.076	0.036	0.051
Normal	0.14	0.14	0.17	0.23
Contaminated	0.91	0.72	0.82	8.00

Figure 4 shows an example of millimetre length analysis of hair from a subject with chronic exposure and compares it with centimetre analysis (calculated).

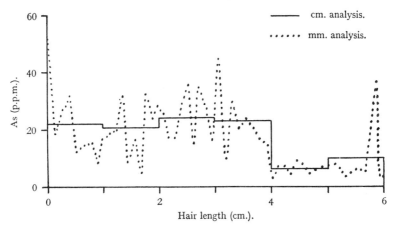

Fig. 4.   The sectional analysis of a single hair from a subject suffering from chronic arsenical poisoning

Sectional analysis is . . . useful in showing the difference between internally and externally contaminated hair. With the latter all the sections tend to show similar or high results, but with the former there are usually large variations from section to section, some being normal and some quite high. In acute poisoning a definite peak is found. In chronic poisoning there is a rise and fall all along the hair, but the values are low unless a superimposed acute stage is present. Arsenic administered (as a tonic) regularly is very difficult to distinguish from external contamination, unless of course the values found are high.

Experiments were made in which subjects ingested 3 mg arsenic trioxide in a cup of tea about an hour after breakfast. Hair was taken from the head, complete with roots, before the experiment and at 30-minute intervals after ingestion. The arsenic content of a 5 mm section including the root was found and gave results as shown below.

EXCRETION OF ARSENIC INTO HAIR

Time after ingestion (hours)	Arsenic content of roots	
	Subject 1	Subject 2
before	0.36	0.22
½	0.48	0.42
1	0.45	0.45
1½	1.13	0.78
2	—	1.20
3	1.00	1.45
4	2.05	4.94

This indicates that root values are in relatively close equilibrium with the trace elements of the blood stream . . .

As hair complete with roots is not generally available, the experiment was extended to find the time taken for the arsenic to appear in the hair at the surface of the skin. The subjects shaved daily with electric razors, taking care to avoid contamination from sample to sample. These samples showed no change until the third day, when the value was found to have risen significantly. In one subject this rise was as great as five times.

By the twelfth day the band of arsenic contamination had reached and begun to grow out of the 5 mm length of hair which was being used in the analysis, but arsenic was still being excreted, as demonstrated by the abnormal amounts still present in the beard shavings. The level in these shavings returned to normal after three weeks, and this is about the time range normally given to a single dose exposure.

Note: Tests showed that a high level of exactness existed in conclusions drawn from peaks and troughs of sectional analysis of hairs in the case of a subject whose actual times of arsenic ingestion were positively known.

In this way the Marchand and Bertrand journals, when read in relation to estimated growth periods of hairs shaved from Napoleon's head on the day following his death, gave a revealing corroboration of Dr. Forshufvud's suspicions concerning the last three or four months before the victim's death.

EDITOR

Exhibit No. 3A
(1962)

DISTRIBUTION OF ARSENIC IN NAPOLEON'S HAIR

By Dr. HAMILTON SMITH, Dr. STEN
FORSHUFVUD and Dr. ANDERS WASSÉN

Department of Forensic Medicine, University of Glasgow,
and Vasagaten 33, Göteborg C, Sweden

THE illness Napoleon suffered during most of his captivity on St. Helena was actually the syndrome of chronic arsenic intoxication with intercurrent attacks of acute arsenic poisoning, as reported briefly in Nature[1] and discussed at length in a reassessment of the disease history by one of us (S. F.)[2]. Among the facts adduced in support of this theory was the finding that a few rather short hairs known to have been taken from Napoleon's head, presumably the day after death, showed a total arsenic content of 10·38 p.p.m., a value approximately thirteen times higher than the normal mean arsenic content of about 0·8 p.p.m. It would have been interesting to examine the distribution of the arsenic, but the sample was too small (1·72 mgm.) and we were then unable to obtain further hairs from the same source.

However, on November 6, 1961, not long after the news of Napoleon's deliberate poisoning and tragic mode of death had become public property, M. Clifford Frey, a textile manufacturer of Münchwilen, Switzerland, called at the Department of Forensic Medicine, Glasgow. He brought with him a family

(Reprinted from Nature, Vol. 194, No. 4830, pp. 725-726,
May 26, 1962)

heirloom in the form of a small bundle of Napoleonic
hairs. It was attached to a piece of paper with intricately knotted twine. We were permitted to take
as many hairs as required within reason, provided
the knot was not undone. Thus, although some of
the brittle hairs broke when being pulled free of the
knot, we were able to acquire a supply of hairs which
were appreciably longer than those we had previously
analysed, the longest measuring 13 cm. It could
be distinctly observed that most of these hairs had
been shorn off with a razor and not cut off with
scissors.

The paper to which the hairs were attached was
folded into a small envelope inscribed "Cheveux de
l'immortel Empereur Napoléon" It was inserted in
a larger envelope which, in the same characteristic
handwriting, bears the names of the addressee and
sender, respectively, "Monsieur Mons-Riss, St. Gall,
Suisse", and "Abram Noverraz, La Violette près
Lausanne, le 8e, 7bre 1838"; it is post-marked
Lausanne, September 9, 1838. The larger envelope
includes a covering letter written in the same characteristic hand and signed by J. Abram Noverraz. It
states, among other things: ". . . Je me fait un plaisir
aujourd'hui Monsieur Mons de vous envoyez quelques
cheveux de l'Empereur Napoléon que j'ai pris sur sa
tête après sa mort, c'etait le six Mai 1821".

The hairs remained in the possession of the Mons
family until, according to documentary proof, it was
procured by M. Clifford Frey, sen., an officer of the
Swiss Army, from Mme Mons-Im-Hoff, the widow of
the aforementioned Monsieur Mons's grandson.

A Swiss, M. J. Abram Noverraz, born in the
neighbourhood of Vaud, was appointed to Napoleon's
domestic staff in 1809 and became his valet throughout the captivity on St. Helena. After Napoleon's
death he returned to Switzerland. Noverraz has the
reputation of being completely reliable and absolutely
faithful to his master and his memory. Napoleon
died on May 5, 1821, and during the following night
his entire head was shaved, with the alleged two-fold
aim of providing as much hair as possible for distribution as souvenirs and of facilitating the making of a
death mask. The barber on this occasion was none
other than Noverraz[3].

Accordingly, it seems beyond doubt that the hairs
put at the disposal of the laboratory by M. Clifford
Frey came from an authentic souvenir of Napoleon.

The average daily growth of hair on the scalp is
about 0·35 mm. (ref. 4). On this basis a 13-cm. hair

should register a record of the exposures to appreciable amounts of arsenic for a period of a little less than a year. Hence. the longest hairs in Clifford Frey's sample should tell us whether Napoleon was exposed to significant doses of arsenic over the last year.

The hair was irradiated for 24 hr. by a flux of 10^{12} thermal neutrons/cm.²/sec. in a nuclear reactor at the Atomic Energy Research Establishment, Harwell. On return from the pile the hair was fixed by means of self-adhesive tape to a piece of graph paper and then cut into 5-mm. lengths, suitable for counting by an end-window Geiger counter. The results were plotted in a graph against distance from an end of the hair.

The graph in Fig. 1 shows the distribution of activity along a hair, the distal end of which is at A. This was a hair that had never been cut before and the very fine end (responsible for the sudden fall in

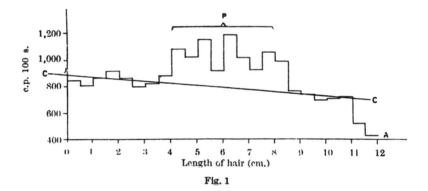

Fig. 1

activity) was easily seen. We have estimated that the line C is the usual average for the hair. It is certain that the peak marked P is due to some trace element being present in larger amounts than normal, because its height lies more than 50 per cent above the average. Accordingly, it is evident that for a period of about 4 months Napoleon was exposed to abnormally large amounts of a substance which was transformed into a radioactive isotope by the irradiation. Other hairs gave similar graphs.

In order to ascertain whether the isotope really was arsenic-16, the arsenic content was estimated[5] in consecutive 1-cm. lengths of a 9-cm. hair, the respective values being 11·0, 7·70, 4·20, 3·79, 1·06, 4·46, 5·80, 2·79 and 3·44 p.p.m. (average 4·91). Since this hair was 3 cm. shorter than that yielding the graph in Fig. 1, it lacked the older portion which was relatively free from arsenic.

The arsenic content was estimated in two pooled samples of broken hairs, the respective values being 3·75 and 3·27 p.p.m.

Estimation of arsenic by activation analysis is an extremely sensitive method. Nevertheless, the method has its limitations. When it is used on less than about 1 mgm. of ordinary hair, it yields values which tend to be obscured by the background. Accordingly, it is rather risky to apply this method to 1-cm. lengths of Napoleonic hair which weigh about one-thirtieth of a mgm. We have done so merely to provide a general picture of the distribution of arsenic in Napoleon's hair, knowing that any quantitative error will be well on the conservative side.

These distribution studies show that Napoleon was exposed to arsenic intermittently. Indeed, judging by the only hair with the distal end uncut, the periodicity of the exposures agrees remarkably well with what can be deduced about the course of Napoleon's disease from the accounts of the eye-witnesses.

The arsenic cannot have been added afterwards, by spraying, dusting or dipping, as suggested by some critics[6]. No estimate of the size of the arsenic dosage given Napoleon can be made on the basis of our results; such very desirable information could probably be obtained after exhumation of the corpse.

In a forthcoming paper it is hoped to publish the results of similar distribution studies on hairs from other sources and other periods of Napoleon's life.

The work of one of us (H. S.) was supported by the Medical Research Council (Great Britain).

[1] Forshufvud, S., Smith, H., and Wassén, A., *Nature*, **192**, 103 (1961).
[2] Forshufvud, S., *Who Killed Napoleon ?* (Hutchinson, London, 1962).
[3] Marchand, L., *Memoires de Marchand*, **2** (Plon, Paris, 1955).
[4] Myers, R., and Hamilton, J., *Ann. N.Y. Acad. Sci.*, **53**, 526 (1951).
[5] Smith, H., *Anal. Chem.*, **31**, 1361 (1959).
[6] Smith, H., *J. Forensic Med.*, **8**, 165 (1961).

Exhibit No. 3B
(1961)

ARSENIC CONTENT OF NAPOLEON I's HAIR PROBABLY TAKEN IMMEDIATELY AFTER HIS DEATH

By Dr. STEN FORSHUFVUD, Dr. HAMILTON SMITH and Dr. ANDERS WASSÉN

Vasagatan 33, Göteborg C, Sweden, and Department of Forensic Medicine, The University, Glasgow, W.2

IT has generally been deduced from the report of the post-mortem dissection dated St. Helena, May 6, 1821, and signed by the British medical officers, Thomas Shortt, Archibald Arnott, Charles Mitchell, Francis Burton and Matthew Livingstone, that Napoleon I's death the preceding day was due to extensive cancerous lesions of the stomach.

The view that Napoleon died of 'cancer' was not accepted by Francesco Antommarchi, the man who actually performed the autopsy, who had been Napoleon's household physician for the last twenty months, and was the only physician on St. Helena with a pathologist's training. He maintained that the hepatitis the Emperor had suffered from for a long time was the cause of death. Furthermore, the Emperor's enlarged, tender liver, jaundiced complexion and yellow conjunctivæ had also been diagnosed as signs of severe hepatitis by Barry O'Meara, Napoleon's household physician during his first three years in exile, and John Stokoe, who had attended Napoleon for a week in January 1819.

Consequently, apart from Dr. Arnott, who assisted Antommarchi during the last few weeks when the morbid picture was especially baffling, those medical men who personally had attended Napoleon during his illness refused to admit that he had died from cancer.

Many medical writers with doubts about the cancer diagnosis have attempted to identify Napoleon's disease on St. Helena by analysing compilations of his signs and symptoms. This has produced surprisingly disparate results. Thus, when exiled on St. Helena, Napoleon is alleged to have had, or suffered from the sequels of, the following diseases: peptic

(Reprinted from Nature, Vol. 192, No. 4798, pp. 103-105, October 14, 1961)

ulcer, intestinal ulceration, various liver inflammations, undulant fever, malaria, dysentery, rheumatoid
arthritis, heart failure, congenital extremely slow
blood circulation, epilepsy, tuberculosis, pleurisy,
severe hormonal imbalance leading to obesity and
impotence (dystrophia adiposogenitalis), syphilis,
gonorrhœa, intoxication from defective teeth (so-
called focal infection), gout, piles, and a constitutional
predisposition to severe constipation which, it is said,
was fatal owing to auto-intoxication and poisoning
by laxatives.

If a suitable selection is made from the variety of
signs and symptoms manifested by Napoleon on St.
Helena, it is a simple matter to make out a convincing case for every one of these diagnoses in turn.
But if what, after all, was a fairly unchanging disease
pattern on St. Helena is taken as an entity, and
allowance is made for all the signs and symptoms and
their interrelations, then one cannot escape the
impression that all the pieces form an orderly picture
of two highly characteristic syndromes, namely, the
chronic and acute types of arsenic poisoning.

Napoleon's condition was rather poor during the
Hundred Days. However, his health improved while
he was being taken into exile on board H.M.S.
Northumberland; and Napoleon's general health
remained good during the initial period on St. Helena
when, with his sole companions and collaborators,
the Chamberlain Las Cases and his son, he lived in a
simple cottage on the estate, 'The Briars'.

Soon after moving to 'Longwood', which became
his permanent residence, Napoleon's ailments again
became manifest. He turned moody, had various
aches and pains, the lower legs swelled up and would
not carry him, exanthemata broke out, particularly
on the legs, his sleep was abnormal with either
insomnia or somnolence, diarrhœa and constipation
alternated, headaches occurred with increasing
frequency and severity.

His indispositions at first lasted only a few days
at a time, his mental powers returning undiminished
in the intervals. Nevertheless, members of his staff
noticed marked changes in his expression and increasing difficulties in locomotion. Napoleon's legs
were swollen and often collapsed under him.

On May 1, 1816, Napoleon had an attack lasting
for a whole week. Las Cases mentions that he complained of weak legs, headache, hypersensitivity to
light, and felt cold and shivery; his facial expression
had changed markedly, he spoke sluggishly, and was

morose and taciturn. Napoleon believed himself to
have gout, suggesting that his feet were swollen and
painful. Though Napoleon's teeth were perfectly
sound, O'Meara recorded on June 16, 1816, that his
patient had toothache. Later it turned out that the
toothache was due to 'scurvy', that is, stomatitis.
On July 26, 1816, Napoleon experienced the first stab
of that pain in the hypochondrium which was a
constant source of distress through the rest of his
life. After a number of brief attacks of malaise,
Napoleon fell ill for six weeks in succession on October
1, 1816. A troublesome cough was now added to the
list of symptoms; he had pustules on the lips as well
as in the oral cavity and throat. Napoleon was
tormented by an insatiable thirst and had become
perceptibly hard of hearing. Lassitude alternating
with restlessness was a characteristic feature. He
always felt cold and liked to sit near the fireplace.
He could scarcely walk, because the swollen and
weak legs would not carry him. The gums swelled
up and the teeth became loose. Diffuse nausea with
a predisposition for spasmodic vomiting without
actual regurgitation of food were also noted. Napoleon
had a relapse with the same manifestations as before
on December 3 and 4, 1816, and his companions now
became aware of his very jaundiced complexion. On
December 14, 18 and 28 there were further attacks
the symptoms of which included spastic involuntary
movements and unconsciousness on several occasions.
According to the head valet, Marchand, one of these
bouts was combined with dysentery (that is, severe
diarrhœa). For the first time in two months Napoleon
went out of doors on January 26, 1817. Apart from
brief indispositions in May, June and July, Napoleon's
health seemed to remain comparatively good until
September 25, 1817, when a period of illness set in
which lasted approximately a whole year. The signs
and symptoms were on the whole the same as before,
but now features had been added. For example, in
Dr. O'Meara's case notes for October 1817, we read:
on the third a swelling was palpable on the right side
near the liver, on the ninth the pains in the legs and
neighbourhood of the liver had increased and pains
in the shoulder supervened, on the eleventh the
patient was seriously distressed by tachycardia.
Afterwards severe constipation developed, the skin
and conjunctivæ were yellow and the appetite was
poor. The vomiting tendency was now accompanied
by stomach-ache. The stomatitis was very distressing
and on several occasions caused the cheeks to swell.
Constant phenomena were 'febrile attacks' at

nightfall and profuse sweating at daybreak. The tongue was coated, the pulse often very rapid and irregular.

Although Napoleon now had no physician in attendance—the British authorities had ordered O'Meara away from 'Longwood' on July 25, 1818— his health underwent a gradual improvement in the latter half of that year. Some symptoms nevertheless persisted for another few months, such as lancinating hypochondrial pains and painful and weak legs. Often the feet were ice cold and had to be warmed with hot towels, and the ex-Emperor frequently sat before the fire with his feet in a flannel bag.

In the final months of 1818 it seemed as though Napoleon was well on the way towards full recovery. Once more he began to take interest in his literary work and in his garden. He started taking regular exercise, a sign that his legs would support him again. In the beginning of November 1818 Bertrand, le Grand-Marechal du Palais, wrote in his diary: ". . . le malheur a passé sur son caractère, comme sur un roc, sans l'abattre et sans y laisser de traces".

But Napoleon again became seriously ill towards the end of December 1818. The manifestations included tachycardia, chills, fever, and the old trouble from the legs. In the night between January 16 and 17, 1819, his life was threatened, he lost consciousness several times, and Dr. Stokoe was summoned. (He had been asked to become the Emperor's household physician the week before.) In his bulletins, Stokoe stated that he had found the patient in a state of extreme exhaustion, his complexion was yellow and he had pains in the region of the liver and in the shoulder. There was excruciating headache, vertigo and fainting fits. Some improvement took place when the patient began to sweat profusely. Similar attacks recurred the next night and the next night but one. Stokoe issued three bulletins about Napoleon's health, and these so displeased the Governor, Sir Hudson Lowe, that Stokoe was constrained to leave St. Helena. So on January 22, 1819, Napoleon again found himself without a physician. His health nevertheless improved, and in the latter half of 1819 he was busily at work every morning from 4 a.m. to 10 a.m. supervising the extensive landscaping projects he was undertaking in his garden. He could now walk with a stick, had recovered his former good temper, and conversed pleasantly and cheerfully with his companions. Apart from a few brief indispositions, this state of good health lasted for fifteen months.

However, a new long period of uninterrupted ill-health commenced on September 18, 1820. This period was marked by at least six intercurrent attacks of violent illness with severe and acute symptoms, but during the intervals of remission Napoleon's health improved day by day even though some of the symptoms persisted. During these periods of convalescence he could be up and about and also, albeit with tottering steps, go for short strolls in the garden.

According to Dr. Antommarchi's case notes, the acute attacks were accompanied by the following symptoms: headache; dyspnœa; weak, rapid and irregular pulse; ice-cold feet and legs; gastric pains; loss of appetite; somnolence that seemed refractory to treatment; yellow conjunctivæ; yellow complexion; excessive paleness; dark rings under the eyes; coated tongue; burning thirst; tachycardia; tremor; nervous dry cough; vertigo; vomiting; sensation of heat in the viscera; pain in the legs and from the liver, sternum and shoulder regions; constipation and diarrhœa; spasmodic contractions of triceps; remarkably weak legs; restlessness; nightmares; exanthemata; loose teeth; bleeding gums; insomnia; hardness of hearing; extreme hypersensitivity to light; impaired vision; very severe general exhaustion.

On March 22, 1821, Napoleon's disease changed character, with constant severe vomiting supervening. This was doubtless because he had been prescribed and—without knowing it—taken tartar emetic. Accordingly, antimony poisoning was now an added complication. A remission lasting for two and a half weeks occurred in the beginning of April 1821, and Napoleon took this opportunity to write his last will and testament.

Late at night on April 24, 1821, there was a severe relapse with typical manifestations of acute antimony poisoning. Additional relapses occurred over the next few days. However, a moderate improvement seems to have taken place on May 3. In the afternoon of that day Napoleon unknowingly took a large dose of calomel. Thirty minutes before midnight he had copious stools with the appearance of tar. Additional evacuations of blood occurred on May 4. He died on May 5, 1821, after lying absolutely motionless for approximately 24 hr.

At the post-mortem examination the stomach was full of black blood and the gastric mucosa was very badly corroded. These findings were probably sequels of the calomel given on May 3 rather than of arsenic. On the other hand, the following signs of arsenic poisoning were encountered: enlarged and hardened liver, enlarged spleen, fluid effusions in the pleuræ, bronchial and mediastinal lymph nodes degenerated and in suppuration, loss of all body hair, large fat deposits under the skin and in the abdomen.

Napoleon was not embalmed. Yet, when his coffin was opened in 1840, those present were astonished at finding him extremely well preserved.

In the light of the foregoing, it seems that on St. Helena Napoleon suffered from chronic arsenic poisoning with intervening periods of acute arsenic poisoning. In such circumstances, we deemed it interesting to apply the activation technique in a study of Napoleon's hairs from the period on St. Helena. Through the courtesy of M. le Commandant Henry Lachouque, the great French expert on Napoleon's life and the organizer of the permanent Napoleonic exhibitions on St. Helena and in the French Army Museum, hair taken from Emperor Napoleon I's head, probably on the day after his death, has been made available to us.

The hair sample thus obtained was sent to the Department of Forensic Medicine at the University of Glasgow, where it was examined using an activation analysis technique (Smith, 1959) as follows.

The hair sample was weighed (1·72 mgm.) and sealed in a polythene container. It and a standard arsenic solution sealed in a silica ampoule were irradiated by thermal neutrons for one day at 10^{12} neutrons/cm.^{2}/sec. in a nuclear reactor at the Atomic Energy Research Establishment, Harwell. Thereafter the sample was returned and the arsenic extracted with added carrier arsenic by a modified Gutzeit technique. The activity from the hair sample was compared with that from the standard arsenic sample and the arsenic content of the hair was calculated.

The value found for the sample of hair was 10·38 parts per million. This is high by comparison with the normal mean arsenic content of about 0·8 p.p.m. Unfortunately, it was not possible to make any distribution studies as no further hair samples were available. It is impossible to tell from the value alone whether the arsenic was evenly distributed (as expected in continuous exposure) or located in one point (as would be the case in a single large exposure).

This investigation shows the great advantage of

activation analysis when only very small quantities of sämple are available.

BIBLIOGRAPHY

Antommarchi, F., *Les derniers momens de Napoléon* (Paris, 1825).

Arnott, A., *An Account of the Last Illness*, etc. (London, 1822).

Beckmann, K., "Krankheiten der Leber", in *Handbuch der inneren Medizin*, **3**, 2 (1953).

Bertrand, H.-G., *Cahiers de Sainte-Hélène* (Paris, 1949, 1951, 1959).

Boutron *et al.*, *Annales d'Hyg. pub. et Méd. leg.*, **25**, 11 (1841).

Cabanès, *Au chevet de l'Empereur* (Paris, 1924).

Cabanès and Nass, *Poisons et Sortilèges* (Paris, 1903).

Douris, R., *Toxicologie moderne* (Paris, 1951).

Forshufvud, S., *Le drame de Poison à Sainte-Hélène* (Plon, Paris, 1961; in the press).

Forsyth, W., *History of the Captivity*, etc. (London, 1853).

Funck-Brentano, F., *Le drame des poisons* (Paris, 1920).

Gigon, A., "Krankheiten der Mundschleimhaut", in *Handbuch der inneren Medizin*, **3**, 1 (1953).

Gonnard, Ph., *Lettres du Comte et la Comtesse de Montholon*, 1819–1821 (Paris, 1906).

Gourgaud, G., *Journal de Sainte-Héléne* (Paris, 1947).

Gril, E., *La Marquise de Brinvilliers Empoisonneuse* (Paris, 1933).

Hansen, F., and Møller, K., *Acta pharm.*, **5**, 135 (1949).

Heffter, A., *Deutsch. med. Wschr.*, **47**, 853 (1921).

Kalima, T., *Acta chir. scand.*, **72**, 1 (1932).

Kemble, J., *Napoleon Immortal* (London, 1959).

Kratter, J., *Lehrbuch der gerichtlichen Medizin* (Stuttgart, 1912).

Las Cases, E., *Mémorial de Sainte-Hélène* (Paris, 1823).

Liebegott, G., *Deutsch. med. Wschr.*, **74**, 855 (1949).

McNally, W., *J. Amer. Chem. Assoc.*, **39**, 826 (1917).

Marchand, L., *Mémoires de Marchand*, **2** (Lachouque, Paris, 1955).

Mayers, M., *Arch. Indust. Hyg.*, **9**, 388 (1954).

Merkel, H., "Die Magenverätzungen", in *Handbuch der spez. path. Anatomie u. Histologie* (Henke and Lubarsch, Berlin, 1926).

Montholon, Ch., *Histoire de la Captivité*, etc. (Leipzig, 1846).

Munch-Pedersen, C. J., "Polyneuritis", in *Nord. lärobok i internaed*, **5** (1958).

Nass, L., *Les empoisonnements sous Louis XIV* (Paris, 1898).

O'Meara, B., *Napoleon in Exile* (London, 1822).

Petri, E., "Path. Anatomie und Histologie der Vergiftungen", in *Handbuch der spez. path. Anat. u. Hist.* (Henke and Lubarsch, Berlin, 1930).

Saint-Denis, L., *Souvenirs du Mameluck Ali sur l'Empereur Napoleon* (Paris, 1926).

Smith, H., *Anal. Chem.*, **31**, 1361 (1959).

Wätjen, J., *Virchows Arch. path. Anat. u. Phys.*, **256**, 85 (1925).

Exhibit No. 4

Common Symptoms of Poisoning by Chemical Substances

compiled from works of standard authorities on toxicology

(a) *Symptoms of chronic arsenic intoxication*

The dosages may be small enough that none will produce immediate distress though a general sense of discomfort and sickness will be apparent and may baffle diagnosis. Individual symptoms:

1. Frequent headaches.
2. A marked general fatigue.
3. A noticeable change in disposition, disinclination for work, depression, which can nevertheless occasionally change to an exaggerated optimism.
4. Disturbance in sleep rhythm (somnolence alternating with insomnia).
5. Polyneuritis in both motory and sensory nerves most pronounced in the sensory nerves. (In cases of intoxication with mercury salts, the contrary is the case; the motory nerves are those most affected.) A chronic case of arsenic intoxication, therefore, will feel pain in different places, mostly in the lower legs, the shoulders and in the region of the liver ("les douleurs hypochondriaques de l'Empéreur").
6. The feet and lower legs become swollen.
7. The muscles of the calf are subject to fatty degeneration, and become consequently very weak. The victim can walk only with difficulty and can hardly ride except at walking pace.
8. Increase in weight, the body finally becoming corpulent or bloated.
9. Increase in the size of the liver, which is subject to fatty degeneration in the actual liver cells.
10. The skin tends to turn bronze in color.
11. The entire body itches.

12. Pimples develop, often around the mouth.
13. The fine hairs of the body diminish or disappear.
14. Hair of the head grows thin.
15. The victim manifests a general lack of appetite, followed by considerable gain in appetite after the body had adapted to the continuing intake of arsenic or when it is no longer administered.
16. Impairment of hearing eventually amounting to pronounced deafness.
17. Sensitivity of the eyes to sunlight or bright artificial light. The victim may prefer a nearly darkened room.
18. Tendency to periods of emotionalism as expressed by tearfulness.
19. Difficulty in urination. Scanty urine, discharged slowly and painfully.
20. A persistent dry cough.
21. A tendency to pleurisy.
22. Sensation of fever without rise in body temperature.
23. Sweats, often heavy.
24. Icy cold legs (when dosage increased).
25. Severe hoarseness by affection of the pharynx and larynx.
26. Tachycardia.
27. Quick and irregular pulse, or very slow pulse, according to the degree of intoxication.
28. Frequent painful cramps, especially in the muscles of the lower leg.
29. Spasms in various parts of the body.
30. Loose teeth and bleeding, swollen gums. The latter may appear mordantly pale, depending on the dosage and the body's degree of adaptability to assimilation of the poison. The symptom of whiteness of the gums has often been wrongly attributed to scurvy.
31. A post-mortem will reveal as especially typical an enlarged but microscopically unchanged liver, together with swollen lymph glands in purulent decomposition, especially around the bronchii and in the mediastinum. Considerable quantities of liquid in the pleural sacs. In an earlier stage of medical knowledge the latter condition might be diagnosed as due to tuberculosis. (In the death of Napoleon's son, the

Duke of Reichstadt, supposedly due to tuberculosis but soon after passing physical examination to enter an officer's training course, other symptoms existed consistent with arsenical poisoning, along with liquid in the pleural sacs. Doubt exists as to the correctness of the medical verdict.)

32. Exhumation may disclose the body in a chronic arsenic intoxication case to be surprisingly well preserved.

(b) *Symptoms of acute arsenic intoxication*

Reactions produced by a lethal dose (>0.2 grams As) Individual symptoms:

1. Extreme thirst.
2. Violent vomiting.
3. Very severe diarrhoea (could be mistaken for cholera).
4. Severe pain over the entire body.
5. Weak pulse.
6. Cramps and spasms resembling an epileptic attack.
7. Unconsciousness followed by death.

NOTE: The symptoms appear about half an hour after ingestion of the poison. Death usually occurs within twenty-four hours. The severe vomiting in some cases will save the victim's life.

(c) *Arsenic dosage capable of causing death within two to ten days*

The symptoms: Symptoms 3, 4 and 7 have often suggested influenza as in the case of the Empress Josephine. Yet, the same symptoms were attributed to tuberculosis as was the case with Napoleon's son, the Duke of Reichstadt.

Most historians agreed that Cipriani was poisoned on St. Helena. He suffered from symptoms 1, 2, 5, 6 and 7. Doctors suggested peritonitis.

1. Burning pain in all the digestive organs, especially in the abdomen.
2. Vomiting.
3. Difficulty in breathing, irritating cough.
4. Severe hoarseness.

5. Fall of blood pressure.
6. Fainting spells.
7. Fits of shivering and severe sweats.
8. Painful cramps.
9. Spasms.
10. Icy chill in the legs.
11. Impaired sight.
12. Impaired hearing.
13. Sensitivity to light.
14. Jaundice.

The symptoms arise 1-3 hours after ingestion of the poison. Death occurs after 2-4 days, but the patient may survive and recover after a long convalescence, during which he will show symptoms of chronic intoxication. (Such were the reactions in the cases of Marchand and Noverraz. This probably applies as well to at least two of Gourgaud's severe illnesses, which were diagnosed as dysentery.)

The symptoms are the same whether the poison is administered orally, by means of an enema or through the application to the skin of vesicatories impregnated with arsenic. In the latter case, an added symptom is noticed — the skin under the vesicatory becomes "cadavereux". (Napoleon's vesicatory of the 30th April, 1821. Napoleon's vesicatory was removed and an improvement took place. The Duke of Reichstadt's last words were *"Vesicatoren, Umschläge"*. No one realized that he wished them to be removed. In a short time he was dead.)

(d) *Symptoms of acute intoxication with hydrocyanic acid*
(calomel and *orgeat*)

Harmless to the system in ordinary use as a cathartic, calomel releases mercurial salts or mercurous cyanide in the presence of *orgeat*. The latter is a beverage whose recipe frequently included milk of bitter almond to add tang to the taste. The hydrocyanic (Prussic) acid of the bitter almond functions as a reagent on the calomel to release the otherwise inert mercury to be dangerously poisonous and corrosive to mucous membrane.

Severe vomiting is the most usual reaction following ingestion of mercurial salts or mercurous cyanide. Emptying of the stomach content by vomiting may save the life of the poisoned person.

To ensure against such natural defense of the body, poisoners using this medium frequently arranged that there be a foregoing series of treatments with emetic wines. This reduced the capability of the stomach with the aid of healthy pyloric muscle reaction, to close the sphincter to the upper intestine or to expel the contents of the stomach in a normal reaction to mercuric poisoning.

Forshufvud proves from the accounts of attendants in Napoleon's sickroom that all of the classic steps to an unsuspected fatal poisoning were taken in the emperor's case. Tartar emetic or emetic wine was administered followed by an abnormally heavy dosage of calomel at a time when the emperor had become habituated to welcoming as a refreshing bedside drink the beverage *orgeat*, a mixture which included the milk of almond needed to activate the mercury in calomel. All of the poisoner's requirements for an unsuspected killing thereby existed, since the corrosive mercuric cyanide would have been chemically retorted in a stomach unable to expel it naturally yet no substance ingested having been corrosive when it entered the mouth, throat or the tract to the stomach, there would be no evidence of poisoning in mouth or throat or oesophagus.

Very shortly after drinking such a lethal mixture, the victim loses consciousness. All the voluntary muscles become paralyzed and both sight and hearing functions cease. This is attributable to the fact that the poison is achieving not instant but progressive death of the brain. The autonomous sympathetic nerve system will function for a time. When this ceases death supervenes.

While the corrosion of the stomach proceeds under such conditions massive haemorrhaging occurs which, a few hours later, produces large stools, black and describable as of the consistency of tar.

It might be expected that, except for factors of variance in the size of the poison dosage or the capability of the victim's constitution to resist, the heart will cease to beat about 24 hours after taking calomel and *orgeat*.

In an autopsy, examiners will discover, in addition to the

corrosion of the stomach walls, that an annular swelling will be observed at the pylorus. This is merely the swollen and immobilized sphincter at the outlet to the stomach. As in the case of the autopsy at St. Helena, doctors not suspecting poisoning, may be misled by this swollen tissue in the midst of puzzling circumstances and work back from effect believing it to be a cause, due to organic disease, such as a cancerous condition. In Napoleon's case, this occurred but the chief autopsist would not sign the report with its use of the term *cancereuse*.

(e) *Symptoms of antimony intoxication*
(intoxication by means of tartar emetic)

Chemically, antimony is closely related to arsenic. The symptoms of antimony intoxication are therefore on the whole much the same as for arsenic intoxication. There are certain differences, however, which make it possible to say whether, in a chronic case of arsenic intoxication, antimony intoxication has begun or has enforced the intoxication with arsenic.

Tartar emetic, a remedy that had been used by doctors for several centuries, is a double salt, being a mixture of tartrate of antimony and potassium. Doctors prescribed it in doses of a few hundredths of a gram, but for an evilly-disposed nurse, as was Madame Brinvilliers, it was of course possible to increase the dose without the patient becoming suspicious through the taste. Antimony has an unpleasant metallic taste, even when strongly diluted. Thus it is impossible to poison with tartar emetic without a doctor having first prescribed it. The unpleasant taste could cause the victim to be suspicious. (Arsenic has neither taste nor odor.)

A lethal dose of antimony is ½ to 1 gram. Dangerous symptoms can arise, however, with only 0.2 gram. (Antommarchi says that the dose of tartar emetic that he had persuaded Napoleon to take was 0.0125 gram. However, Napoleon suffered very severe and acute symptoms after taking the drink that was supposed to contain so small an amount of antimony, and he forbade his attendants to give him this "medicine" again. Nevertheless he did receive it for a few more days, unknowingly.

Marchand's memoirs say that Dr. Antommarchi was not responsible.)

Symptoms of antimony intoxication, differing from those of arsenic intoxication are:

1. Constant vomiting that cannot be stopped. Small volume arsenic intoxication does not produce this reaction. Vomiting occurs when a dangerous dose has been administered.
2. Haemorrhage in throat, oesophagus and stomach, the vomit containing what resembles coffee grounds as well as small amounts of red blood.
3. Pain in the mouth and throat, due to the corrosive effect of the tartar emetic. Blisters in mouth and throat.
4. Unlike arsenic trioxide which does not corrode the stomach walls unless swallowed as such, antimony salt solutions corrode the mucous lining of the stomach and, in the case of a large dose, will actually perforate the stomach wall.
5. Polyuria and no difficulty in urinating, unlike the penuria and painful urination characteristic of arsenic intoxication.
6. After a few weeks of intoxication, the corroding effect on the mucous lining of the stomach inhibits the vomit reflexes of the stomach. Thus an intended victim was rendered no longer capable of vomiting preventively by natural response to danger in preparation for the second "wonder-working" remedy of those days.

Calomel can be converted into soluble mercurial salts, which corrode the stomach walls if a drink like *orgeat* is given at the same time as the colomel. *Orgeat* is especially suitable, for it is sweet and it also releases hydrocyanic acid from the bitter almonds in the recipe. The corrosive damage to the tissues of the stomach walls, in Napoleon's case, was noted by English autopsists as having a "cancerous" or in other words a canker ridden appearance. Having no visual evidence of a corrosive substance having passed through the throat, poisoning was not suspected.

In earlier times it was often difficult to distinguish between antimony intoxication and tuberculosis. The effect on the breathing apparatus was similar to arsenic intoxication, but more pronounced — as in the case of the Duke of Reichstadt. (Antommarchi thought that Napoleon had once suffered from tuberculosis of the lungs.)

(f) *Calomel and milk of almonds*

The poisonous effect of calomel in association with milk of almonds is detailed in *Larousse Médical Illustré* (741-2).

Substances there mentioned as incompatible with and therefore dangerous to mix with calomel are *looch* and *lait d'amandes.* The former denotes almond milk from sweet and bitter almonds, together with both orange blossom water and gum arabic. If from that combination gum arabic is dropped the result is the recipe for the drink known as *orgeat.* At St. Helena Napoleon was encouraged to sip it as a mouth freshener or cooling beverage in the period of his final illness.

Exhibit No. 5

Authentication and Analyses of Hair Specimens

EDITOR'S NOTE: Inasmuch as authenticity of the specimens of hair analyzed by the irradiation process to determine the degree and approximate times of arsenical intoxication of Napoleon Bonaparte necessarily must be established, the following report by author Forshufvud on samples referred to in his text is vital to the Forshufvud thesis.

The nature, origin, ownership and history of each specimen analyzed is here detailed along with the range of arsenic content in parts per million as reported by Dr. Hamilton Smith, University of Glasgow.

Unless it is maintained that all the hair specimens used by Dr. Hamilton Smith at Glasgow University School of Forensic Medicine were invalidated by legitimate doubt as to their origins and genuineness, or that for some reason the arsenicizing of the hair was external or came from some innocent and accountable source, it must be conceded that someone or several persons had cleverly and successfully administered unsuspected doses of arsenic trioxide to Napoleon.

It is conceivable that not all instances of Napoleon's illness occurred from that cause. But it is inconceivable that sudden very sharp rises in arsenic in his system from time to time, as registered in his hair under irradiation tests, would *not* be accompanied by adverse physical reactions of quite a pronounced kind.

In the case of the Napoleon hair tests the tendency of toxicologists, without exception, is to enquire whether the tests showed a general level of approximately equal arsenic readings segment by segment along the length of the hairs, or instead, an irregular peaks-and-valleys incidence in graphic depiction of reading results. If the hairs received from different sources, convincingly certified to have been Napoleon's, appeared under magnification to come from the same individual, and if all showed abnormal arsenic deposition irregularly as the various hairs were similarly tested, the results would be conclusive. They would indicate that the arsenic was internally contained in the hair, that it had been deposited there through the bloodstream and positively was not an accidental phenomenon due to the hair coming in contact with arsenic from an external source. At the same time the irregularity of deposition would rule out the possibility that the owner of the hair had been receiving measured small quantities of arsenic regularly by prescription of an attending physician.

Only in instances where the validity of the hair specimen analyzed could be confidently assumed by research into origins have laboratory results been used as a basis for judgments in the author's work. — *H. T. M.*

(a) *Hairs, cut and collected by the painter Jean B. Isabey*

Documentation: The hairs were enclosed in an envelope, upon which Isabey, portraitist to Napoleon, had written in his own identifiable hand: *"Cheveux de l'Empéreur, Troyes en Champagne, Isabey, le 14 germinal an 13* (4th April, 1805)." Napoleon left

Troyes the 5th April, 1805 in order to proceed to his coronation as King of Italy at Milan. (Garros 236)

Sender of the hairs to Department of Forensic Medicine at Glasgow: Sten Forshufvud, who had received from Commandant Lachouque of Paris some hairs of this parcel. The late Commandant Henry Lachouque was a foremost collector of Napoleonic relics. He had been director of *Musée de l'Armée* at Paris and was famous as an author of Napoleonic subjects.

Arsenic content: 10:53 p.p.m. Only one hair was analyzed by the activation analyzing method of Dr. Hamilton Smith, and it was examined in one single procedure.

This high arsenic content — about 20 times more than the normal value — suggests that the poisoning of Napoleon had already begun in 1805. It would have been desirable to have at least one hair of this parcel analyzed in sections. Unfortunately, Commandant Lachouque did not make available any more hairs from the Isabey envelope. He had been dissuaded by certain French historians, antagonistic to the poisoning thesis, and did not favor more hair-analyses, either by Dr. Hamilton Smith or, as suggested, by Professor Henri Griffon, eminent head of the Toxicological Laboratory of the Police of Paris.

(b) *Hairs collected by First Valet Louis Marchand*

Documentation: The hairs were given to Commandant Lachouque, who had published the second volume of Marchand's Memoirs, by arrangement with Marchand's family. The hairs had been kept in a small box together with Marchand's relics from Napoleon's last days. In his memoirs Marchand mentions this box, which he named his "reliquaire" (Marchand II: 336). In the box were a small twig from the weeping willows at the St. Helena tomb, the famous playing card on which Marchand had written Napoleon's last testamentary dictation, the notes of the Funeral March, Marchand's own sketches of the Burial Service and a small envelope, on which Marchand had written in his typical handwriting: *"Cheveux de l'Empéreur"* (hairs of the Emperor). In his memoirs Marchand mentions that these hairs were shaved by the valet Abram Noverraz the 6th of May,

1821 and deposited by Marchand in his "reliquaire". Micros-copic examination shows that these hairs had been shaved, not cut with scissors.

Sender of the hairs to Department of Forensic Medicine at Glasgow: Sten Forshufvud, who had received some hairs from this parcel personally from Commandant Lachouque.

Arsenic content: 10:38 p.p.m. Only one hair was analyzed, using Hamilton Smith's earlier activation method. It was examined in one single procedure.

These hairs had grown during a period when Napoleon had been ill many times with the now familiar syndrome of arsenical poisoning. Thus the high arsenic content of the examined hair was not unexpected. It was desired to have more hairs from this parcel in order to have them analyzed in consecutive sections. For reasons previously mentioned Commandant Lachouque would release no more hairs for analysis.

(c) ***Hairs collected by Abram Noverraz, Napoleon's valet, who shaved all hairs from Napoleon's head on the day following his death***

Documentation: The hairs were attached to a piece of paper with an intricately knotted twine. The knot was sealed with a small clot of wax. The paper was folded into a small envelope inscribed *"Cheveux de l'immortal Empéreur Napoléon"* (hairs from the immortal Emperor Napoleon). It was inserted in a larger envelope, which bears the names of the addressee and sender respectively, Monsieur Mons-Riss, St. Gall, Suisse and Abram Noverraz, La Violette près Lausanne, le 8e, 7bre 1838; it is post-marked Lausanne, September 9, 1838.

The larger envelope includes a covering letter written in the same characteristic hand signed J. Abram Noverraz. It states, amongst other things: "It is a pleasure to send you, Monsieur Mons, some hairs of the Emperor Napoleon which I have taken from his head after his death, it was the sixth May 1821."

The widow of this Mr. Mons' grandson sold the souvenir to Clifford Frey, Sr., an officer of the Swiss Army. His son, Clifford Frey, Jr., a manufacturer, called at the Department of Forensic

Medicine in Glasgow and invited Dr. Hamilton Smith to take as many hairs as he needed in order to make a complete arsenic test, provided only that the knot should not be undone. It could be observed under magnification that these hairs had been shaved off, not cut with scissors.

Arsenic content: 120 analyses were completed of these hairs in one millimeter sections. The values of the arsenic content swayed from 2.8 to 51.2 p.p.m.

These analyses indicate that Napoleon was exposed to arsenic on at least 40 separate occasions between the summer of 1820 and April 1821.

(d) *Hairs given to Betsy Balcombe*

Documentation: The hairs were fixed with two knots to a piece of paper on which was written: "Napoleon's lock of hair presented by him to Betsy Balcombe, on the eve of her family's departure from St. Helena in the year 1818."

In her memoirs published in 1844, Betsy Abell, née Balcombe, mentions that Napoleon on March, 16, 1818 gave her a lock of his hair, cut the same day by Marchand. (Aretz 255)

Betsy Abell had no children and the lock was inherited in the family of one of her brothers, the grandfather of Dame Mabel Balcombe-Brooks, D.B.E.

Sender: Dame Mabel, who sent the lock to the Department of Forensic Medicine, Glasgow, for arsenic determination. Two hairs, about 3 cm. long, were analyzed in one centimeter sections.

Arsenic content: 6.7 — 26 p.p.m.

The analyses of these hairs reveal that Napoleon was exposed to arsenic in the year 1817 during a period of at least three months.

(e) *Hairs given to commander John Theed, R.N.*

Documentation: A letter from Dame Mabel Balcombe-Brookes mentioning that she had bought the locket with the hairs from a member of Commander Theed's family.

Commander Theed, Master of H.M.S. *Leveret,* was received by Napoleon January 14, 1816. (Las Cases I: 347; Gourgaud I: 101) He was given some hairs from Napoleon, enclosed in a locket.

Sender: Dame Mabel Balcombe-Brookes conveyed these to Dr. Hamilton Smith at his laboratory, University of Glasgow.

Four hairs of 2-4 cm. length were analyzed in one centimeter sections.

These analyses disclose the fact that *Napoleon was exposed to arsenic before being exiled;* during the period of the Hundred Days or earlier.

(f) *Hairs given by Napoleon to Admiral Sir Pulteney Malcolm*

Arsenic content: 3, 5-76, 6 p.p.m.

Documentation: According to a family tradition, Admiral Sir Pulteney Malcolm was given a lock of Napoleon's hair on July 3, 1817 when he paid a farewell visit to Napoleon before returning to England. This visit is mentioned by both Bertrand and Gourgaud. The lock is now owned by one of the Admiral's descendants, Lieut.-Col. Duncan Macauley, O.B.E., who sent Dr. Hamilton Smith one hair from this lock of 4 cm. length. It was analyzed in one centimeter sections.

Sender: Lieut.-Col. Duncan Macauley

Arsenic content: 4.94 — 1.75 p.p.m.

The arsenic values are rather low in comparison with the other analyzed hairs from Napoleon. They may register a period of Napoleon's exile, when he was comparatively well, probably in 1816.

Betsy Balcombe noted in her memoirs (Aretz 152), that the hairs of the lock she had got from Napoleon's head were so thin that one could think they belonged to a young child. A member of the Bonaparte family, who inherited a lock of Napoleon's hair, had long believed that her relic must have been taken from Napoleon as a baby, since the hairs were so extremely fine.

All the hairs mentioned above were very fine, resembling hair from a child. All had the reddish-brown color characteristic of Napoleon's hair, according to many witnesses. The hairs, which according to the documents were shaved off, were, under magnification, found truly to have been cut with a blade and not with scissors, so that they identify credibly with May 6, 1821.

NOTE: All analyzed hairs yielding the results here reported had been kept separate and in different countries — France, Switzerland, England, Russia and Austria — by entirely different persons. In the cases of three of them each still was held by the family of the original receiver, therefore had come under only one ownership and care. In no single instance were the analyzed hairs sold and handled on the open souvenir market. With one exception the hairs have a very high arsenic content, *irregularly localized.* In the exceptional case the arsenic value was nevertheless twice to five times normal.

The testimony or origins together with the characteristic resemblances between *all* of the hair samples leave no doubt that the analyzed hairs were from a single source. The origin of all is attributed to Napoleon. The fact that all specimens contain irregularly spaced depositions of arsenic appears positively to testify that these specimens can legitimately be read in direct relationship to the known illnesses of Napoleon from the syndrome of arsenical poisoning, as described by then currently diarized observations.

Exhibit No. 6

Poisoning Symptoms in the Saxony Campaign — 1813

(a) *Illness after the Battle of Dresden*

In the war in Saxony in 1813 Napoleon fought with brilliant success the series of engagements near Dresden, culminating in the victory of August 27th. J. G. Lockhart in his History of

Napoleon Bonaparte, 2 Vol., J. & J. Harper, New York 1830, Vol. 2, p. 187 wrote:

"But fortune had only revisited the banners of her ancient favorite with a momentary gleam of sunshine. The fatigues he had undergone between the 15th and 18th of August would have broken any other frame, and they, for the time, weakened his. It is said that a mess of mutton and garlic, the only food he tasted on the 26th, had besides deranged his stomach. Unable to remain with the columns in the rear of Schwartzenberg, he returned to Dresden, weary and sick; and thenceforth evil tidings awaited him."

(b) *Warm baths symptomatic of sensation of chills from arsenic intoxication*

In the autumn action before the Battle of Leipzig and the October retreat following the defeat at Leipzig, evidence of the effects of poisonings existed. It is noted in some accounts that the night of the seventh of October was spent in unusual indecision as to the choice between several alternatives for the next day's action.

During the night, *the Emperor took two warm baths.* One historian noted: "The habit of drinking strong coffee to prevent drowsiness had induced attacks of nervousness, and these were not diminished by his load of care. To allay these and other ailments, he had recourse for some time to *frequent tepid baths.*" (Life of Napoleon, William Milligan Sloane, New York, 1906 Vol. IV p. 68.) This behavior was remarked by the historian as if of only incidental account.

The Forshufvud thesis, however, identifies the compulsive desire of Napoleon to indulge in hot baths as being strongly suggestive of his reaction to the sense of extreme cold — especially in the legs — a symptom of arsenical poisoning. He bathed so frequently in hot water at Elba in 1814-15 as to promote comment on the practice as being in the nature of an eccentricity. During periods of aggravated illness at St. Helena he very frequently ordered hot tubs or hot footbaths, regardless of how warm the room temperature might be.

Exhibit No. 7

Comment on Napoleon's health at the Battle of Waterloo

From the World-Wide Encyclopedia, New York 1899 Vol. VI P 4390

Military writers point out several errors, some of them considerable, committed by Wellington, but their criticism of Napoleon, which begins by sweeping away a mass of falsehood devised by himself and his admirers in order to throw the blame upon others, is so crushing that it seems to show us Napoleon after his brilliant commencement acting as an indolent and inefficient general. He first, through mere want of energy, allows the Prussians to escape him after Ligny, and then sends Marshal Grouchy with 33,000 men in the wrong direction in pursuit of them. Owing to this mismanagement Grouchy is at Wavre on the day of the battle of Waterloo, fighting a useless battle against the Prussian corps of Thielemann, while Blücher is enabled to keep his engagement to Wellington. Everywhere during these days Napoleon appears negligent, inactive, inaccessible, and rather a Darius than an Alexander, so that it has been plausibly maintained that he was physically incapacitated by illness. The battle itself was one of the most remarkable and terrible ever fought . . .

NOTE: The foregoing is representative of the comments of many histories and encyclopedias on Napoleon's uncharacteristic lassitude and indecision before and on the day of the Battle of Waterloo. That his illness included the symptoms of arsenical intoxication was never remarked by any contemporary observer or historian of his century. Neutron activation analyses of many Napoleonic hairs at Glasgow University's School of Forensic Medicine in the 1960's included one specimen that came from a lock of authenticated hair indicated to have been growing at the time of Waterloo and possibly even at Elba. It had been impregnated through the bloodstream with internally deposited arsenic. The earliest positive reading of arsenic in a hair test in the Forshufvud-Hamilton series involved a hair specimen recorded as cut at the time Napoleon left for Milan in 1805 to be crowned King of Italy. He had mounted the throne of France the previous year.

Exhibit No. 8

Napoleon's Enemies

A DETECTIVE IN search of an unknown killer will first inform himself of any peculiarly significant circumstances surrounding the crime, then search for the most obvious enemies of the victim.

In such a case as Napoleon's the hunt should logically turn to thoughtful consideration of those whom his successes had most disturbed.

From an obscure origin Napoleon, by bold enterprise and undoubted genius in military strategies, had become Emperor in command of thrones considered to belong to Bourbon, Hapsburg and other dynasts. Feudal kings in consternation watched his amazing career, saw his popularity with the masses, and feared their own futures were being permanently injured.

Britain was a constitutional monarchy, her merchant princes already more in command of the country's policies than was the Prince Regent. In London, Napoleon's challenge to Britain was seen to be economic as well as military. Napoleon's France was attempting to limit British trade on the continent.

Britain was a Protestant kingdom whose friendships with the ruling royal families of continental Europe were definitely tenuous and pragmatic. At any given time, the enemies of her enemy were her friends.

In Europe of that period it was the Bourbons who most of all had suffered from Napoleon's presence and prestige.

At the Congress of Vienna Bourbonists and feudal monarchies friendly to the Bourbons were implacably hostile to Napoleon. The enmity of ancient monarchies gleamed through the Declaration of Vienna. In its terms the Declaration gave Napoleon the evil name of outlaw — a man living beyond the right of appeal for protection. No one killing him could be called a murderer or be tried as such. That stigma of outlawry was never formally lifted. Insofar as the crowned heads of Europe were concerned, they heartily hoped that this disturbing soldier would never again claim a place of regality amongst them.

The relevant statement of condemnation of Napoleon to a position placing him beyond the pale of any European court of law must be read today in relation to his death by poisoning.

In Napoleon's time, without doubt, there were some in high position in England who, having counted costs to the nation in lives, armament and added debt, charged it all to Napoleon. They could favor death for the emperor. Some actually demanded it. Saner views prevailed, however, based on the rationale that there was very dubiously any willingness of the British nation to endorse execution of a head of state as the standard price paid for defeat at arms. Desperate enemies do not make for peaceful solutions to war; and Napoleon was a man all too easily heroized.

The British had good cause down through history to regret having made a martyr of the Maid of Orleans. Should Napoleon become martyred how predictably great would be the temptation to the French, given the opportunity, to enthrone his son and perpetuate his succession.

Upon it being expressed to the Duke of Wellington that Lord Liverpool desired that the conquered Napoleon should be shot, as an appropriate aftermath of his post-Elban coup, the Duke to his credit replied: "For shame, does it become such men as us, to act as executioners; if the Kings of Europe want to put Napoleon to death let them find another executioner for I shall not do it."

Indirectly the duke was lending credence to the assumption that the feudal kings of Europe, with the Bourbons in the forefront, were the mortal enemies of Napoleon.

Exhibit No. 9

Paris, 24 juillet I960.

4, RUE DE L'ABREUVOIR. XVIIIe

MONTMARTRE 35-37

Je certifie que les cheveux de l'Empereur
Napoléon Ier, remis par moi à

Monsieur le Docteur Sten FORSHUFVUD

Vasagatan 33

<u>Suède</u>   <u>Göteborg</u>

ont été prélevés dans un paquet provenant de la
succession de <u>Louis MARCHAND</u>, valet de chambre
de l'Empereur à Sainte Hélène, dont j'ai publié
les Mémoires.

Paris, 24 juillet 1960.

4, RUE DE L'ABREUVOIR. XVIII.
MONTMARTRE 35-37

    Je certifie que les cheveux de l'Empereur
Napoléon Ier, remis par moi à

       Monsieur le Docteur Sten FORSHUFVUD

      <u>Suède</u>   Vasagatan 33<u>Göteborg</u>

proviennent d'un paquet constitué par le <u>peintre
ISABEY</u>. Il porte sur l'enveloppe sa signature et
l'inscription suivante, écrite de sa main :

     Cheveux de l'Empereur.

                Troyes en Champagne
   Le 14 germinal an 13.   Isabey.

    Ce jour là 4 avril 1805, l'Empereur, après
une visite à Brienne, est rentré à 2 heures
après midi à Troyes, où il était arrivé la
veille.

Principal Characters

l'AIGLON, the Eaglet, Napoleon's son, see REICHSTADT

ALEXANDER I, Tsar of Russia (1777-1825)

AMHERST, Earl of Arakan, William Pitt (1773-1857), diplomat, Governor-general of British India

d'ANGOULÈME, Louis (1775-1851), Duke, heir to the French throne 1824

d'ANGOULÈME, Marie-Thérèse (1788-1851), wife of Louis, daughter of Louis XVI

ANTOMMARCHI, Francesco (1779-1838), surgeon 1812, Napoleon's physician-in-ordinary September 1819-May 1821

ARCHAMBAULT, Achille Thomas, stablemaster and groom at Longwood

ARNOTT, Archibald (1771-1855), British army doctor, Napoleon's assistant physician-in-ordinary 1st April-5th May, 1821

d'ARTOIS, Charles, duke, heir to the French throne 1814, see CHARLES X

d'AUBRAY, Antoine, Dreux (1600-1666), trusted high-ranking official, father of the Marquise de Brinvilliers

AUGEREAU, Pierre (1757-1816), Marshal of France

BALCOMBE, Alexander Beatson, William's youngest son, great grandfather of Dame Mabel Balcombe-Brookes

BALCOMBE, Betsy, William's youngest daughter, friend of Napoleon

BALCOMBE, Jane, William's eldest daughter

BALCOMBE, William (1779-1829), merchant, Napoleon's host at "The Briars"

BALMAIN, Alexander (1779-1848), count, Russian commissary

BARRAS, Paul (1755-1829), viscount, director, Josephine de Beauharnais' friend and consequently Bonaparte's protector

BATHURST, Henry (1762-1834), earl, British Minister for War and the Colonies 1812-1827

BAXTER, Alexander (1777-1841), head doctor of the garrison on St. Helena

BEAUHARNAIS, Eugène (1781-1824), Napoleon's stepson

BERNADOTTE, Jean (1763-1844), Marshal of France, Prince of Ponte Corvo, King of Sweden 1818-1844

BERTHIER, Louis-Alexandre (1753-1815), Prince of Wagram and Neuchâtel, Napoleon's Chief of General Staff

BERTRAND, Henri Gratien, count, lieutenant-general, grand marshal of the palace at St. Helena.

BERTRAND, Fanny, wife of Lieutenant-General Bertrand

BINGHAM, Sir George (1776-1833), Major-General commanding the garrison on St. Helena October 1815-24th May, 1820

BUONAPARTE, Carlo (1746-1785), Letizia's husband

BONAPARTE, Hortense, née Beauharnais (1783-1837), Napoleon's stepdaughter, mother of Napoleon III

BONAPARTE, Joseph (1768-1844), Napoleon's elder brother, King of Naples 1806-1808, King of Spain 1808-1813

BUONAPARTE, Letizia (1750-1836), Napoleon's mother

BONAPARTE, Louis (1778-1846), Napoleon's younger brother, King of Holland 1806-1810

BONAPARTE, Louis Napoleon (1808-1873), son of Hortense Bonaparte

BONAPARTE, Napoléon, see NAPOLEON I

BOMBELLES, count, Austrian envoy to Berne

BOURMONT, Louis-Auguste-Victor (1773-1846), count

BOUTON DE ROSE, see NYMPHE

BRINVILLIERS, Marie-Madeleine (1630-1676), Marquise and poisoner

BROOKES, Dame Mabel, great-granddaughter of William Balcombe, provisioner to Napoleon's court at Longwood.

BRUNE, Guillaume (1763-1815), Marshal of France, famous for his chivalry towards the civil population. Met Gustav IV Adolf in 1807, after which he fell out of favour with Napoleon. In service again during the Hundred Days.

BURTON, Francis (1784-1828), doctor with the 66th Regiment at St. Helena

CAPDEVILLE, see MONTBEL

CASTELLANE, Victor (1788-1862), Napoleon's adjutant, later Marshal of France.

CHANDELIER, Jacques, cook at Longwood September 1819-May 1821

CHARLES X (1757-1830), King of France 1824-1830, formerly Count of Artois as heir to the throne

CIPRIANI (1757-1818), security police, Napoleon's butler

COCKBURN, Sir George (1772-1853), Rear-Admiral, officer commanding the St. Helena squadron July 1815-July 1816

CONSTANT, real name Constant Véry (1778-1845), Napoleon's first valet. Deserted Napoleon at the beginning of April 1814

COOK, lieutenant on the staff of Lord Amherst

CORVISART, Jean-Nicolas (1755-1821), Napoleon's first physician-in-ordinary

COURSOT, Jacques (1786-1856), butler at Longwood September 1819-May 1821

DECAZES, Elie (1780-1860), French duke and Duke of Glücksbjerg, statesman, President of the Council, former secretary of Mme. Letizia

DE LA TOUR DU PIN, Henrietta-Lucy, née Dillon 1770-1853. Author of interesting mémoires

DIETRICHSTEIN, Moritz, b. 1775, guardian of the Duke of Reichstadt

DILLON, Arthur, General, father of Mme Bertrand, guillotined in 1794.

DILLON, Madame, née de Rothe, General Dillon's first wife

DILLON, Madame, widow of Monsieur La Touche and Arthur Dillon's second wife, mother of Mme. Bertrand

DOVETON, Sir William (1753-1843), estate owner at Mount Pleasant, St. Helena

EGGIDI, poisoning expert in the service of Queen Christina of Sweden

ELLIS, Henry, ambassadorial secretary in Lord Amherst's suite

ENGHIEN, Louis-Antoine (1772-1804), duke, great-grandson of the famous General Prince Louis II of Condé, a branch of the house of Bourbon. Shot by Napoleon in 1804

ESTHER, see VESEY

EXILI, see EGGIDI

FEHRZEN, Oliver (1786-1820), major of the 53rd Regiment

FINLAYSON, John, registrar at the Admiralty

FLAHAUT DE LA BILLARDERIE, Auguste-Charles-Joseph (1785-1870), Napoleon's aide-de-camp, Queen Hortense's lover. Rumoured to be the son of Talleyrand and father of the Count of Morny, Hortense's son, later Minister of the Interior and duke

FRANZ II, Emperor of Germany and Rome, Emperor of Austria after 1806, father or the Empress Marie-Louise

FREDRIK WILHELM (1770-1840), King of Prussia
FREY, Clifford, d. 1970, collector of napoleoniana and generous donor of Napoleonic hair

GENTILINI, footman at Longwood
GLASER, apothecary, chemist, Mme. Brinvilliers' advisor on poisoning
GLOVER, John, Admiral Cockburn's secretary
GORREQUER, Gideon (1781-1841), Major, adjutant to the governor
GORS, Jean-Claude, b. 1782, captain of the French King's Guard. Montchenu's adjutant or superintendent
GOULBURN, Henry, under-secretary of State at the British Colonial Office
GOURGAUD, Gaspard (1783-1852), Napoleon's first ordnance officer, major-general, imperial baron
GRIFFON, Henry, professor, head of the Forensic Laboratory of the Paris police
GRIFFITH, chaplain in Lord Amherst's suite
GROUCHY, Emmanuel (1766-1847), marquis, Marshal of France during the Hundred Days, later demoted to lieutenant-general but again Marshal of France under Louis-Philippe

HARRISON, Charles, major of the 53rd Regiment
HENRY, Walter, assistant surgeon of the 66th Regiment

JACKSON, Basil (1795-1889), officer of the Engineers, security agent, Mme. Montholon's last lover on St. Helena
JÉROME, see BONAPARTE, Jérome
JOSÉPHINE, née Tascher de la Pagerie (1763-1814), Napoleon's first wife, widow of General Beauharnais and grandmother of the Swedish Queen Josefia

KEITH, Sir George Elphinstone (1746-1823), viscount, admiral, Commander-in-Chief of the naval station at Plymouth
KING OF PRUSSIA, see FREDRIK WILHELM

LABOUILLERIE, baron, administrator of Napoleon's estate
LAFITTE, Jacques, Napoleon's banker
LAMBERT, Robert (1772-1836), admiral commanding the St. Helena squadron July 1820-September 1821
LAS CASES, Emmanuel Dieudonné (1766-1842), count, Napoleon's chamberlain on St. Helena, author of *Mémorial de Sainte-Hélène*, "the Koran of the Napoleonic cult"

LAS CASES, Emmanuel (1800-1854), son of the foregoing. Page at Longwood

LEBRUN, Charles François (1739-1824), Duke of Piacenza, third Consul (1799-1804)

LOUISE, Queen of Prussia (1776-1810)

LOWE, Sir Hudson (1769-1844), lieutenant-general, governor of St. Helena

LOWE, Lady Suzanne, née Howe

MAINGAUD, Louis-Pierre, Napoleon's doctor on board H.M.S. *Bellerophon*

MAITLAND, Frederick Lewis, Commander H.M.S. *Bellerophon*

MALCOLM, Pulteney (1768-1838), Rear-admiral commanding the St. Helena squadron July 1816-July 1817

MALFATTI, the Duke of Reichstadt's doctor

MARBEUF, Louis-Charles-René, (1712-1786), count

MARCHAND, Louis (1791-1876), Napoleon's head valet

MARIE-THÉRÈSE, see d'ANGOULÈME

MARLBOROUGH, John Churchill (1650-1722), duke, general

MARMONT, Auguste (1774-1852), Duke of Ragusa, Marshal of France

MAUGUIN, French politician

MAXWELL, captain in the suite of Lord Amherst

MESTIVIER, Napoleon's physician-in-ordinary

MITCHELL, Charles (1783-1856), doctor on board H.M.S. Vigo, Admiral Lambert's head doctor

MONGE, Gaspard (1746-1818), Count of Peluse, mathematician

MONK, George (1608-1669), Duke of Albemarle. Supported Charles II of England in restoration of Monarchy.

MONTBEL, Count, Charles X's commissary at the Austrian court

MONTCHENU, Claude Marin Henri, b. 1757, brigadier-general, the French King's commissary on St. Helena

MONTHOLON, de, Albine, b. 1780 (?), wife of Charles Tristan

MONTHOLON, de, Charles Tristan (1783-1853), major-general, Napoleon's adjutant at Longwood. His true name was Montholon-Sémonville; Count and protégé of d'Artois.

MONTHOLON, Napoléone (1816-1907), born to Albine de Montholon on St. Helena

MONTHOLON, Tristan de (1810-1831), son of Tristan and Albine de Montholon

MURAT, Joachim (1767-1815), Marshal of France, King of Naples (1808-1815), married to Caroline Bonaparte

NAPOLEON I (1769-1821), Emperor of France, King of Italy

NAPOLEON II, see REICHSTADT

NAPOLEON III, see BONAPARTE, Louis Napoléon

NARBONNE, Count Louis de (1755-1813), natural son of Louis XV, general, diplomat

NEY, Michel (1769-1815), Prince of Moscow, Marshal of France

NICHOLLS, George, captain, escort officer September 1818-February 1820

NOVERRAZ, Abram, Napoleon's valet

NYMPHE, Miss Mary-Anne Robinson, b. 1800, married Captain Edwards of merchant navy. Favored by Napoleon at St. Helena

O'MEARA, Barry (1786-1836), Napoleon's physician-in-ordinary July 1815 - July 1818

PAOLI, Pasquale (1725-1807), champion of freedom in Corsica

PIERRON, chef at Longwood

PLAMPIN, Robert, (1762-1834), Rear-admiral commanding the St. Helena squadron July 1817 - July 1820

POLIGNAC, Jules (1780-1847), count and papal prince, ultra-royalist leader. Probably son of the Duke of Artois

POPPLETON, Thomas-William (1775-1827), captain, escort officer at Longwood December 1815 - July 1817

PORTEOUS, innkeeper at Jamestown

PRINCE REGENT, (1762-1880), regent during his father's (George III's) madness 1811-1820. Later King of Great Britain, Ireland and Hanover, under the name of George IV

QUEEN OF PRUSSIA, see LOUISE

READE, Sir Thomas (1785-1849), lieutenant-colonel, diplomat, chief-of-police on St. Helena during the exile

REICHSTADT, François-Charles-Joseph Bonaparte, Napoleon's son, in favour of whom Napoleon abdicated in 1815. When born received the title King of Rome, that of Prince of Parma after the first abdication, but forfeited the inheritance of Parma on being created Duke of Reichstadt in 1818. Often known as *l'Aiglon*, the Eaglet, among the French. (1811-1832)

RÉMUSAT, Augustin (1762-1823), prefect in Toulouse for a few weeks in 1815

RICHELIEU, Armand, Duke (1766-1822), President of the Council

ROSEBERY, Archibald, Earl of (1847-1929), British statesman, Foreign Minister 1892-1894

ROSS, Charles (1778-1849), Captain of H.M.S. *Northumberland*

ROUSTAM, Mameluke, gift from Sheik El Becri to Napoleon Bonaparte. Overwhelmed with gifts from Napoleon, whom he betrayed in 1814

RUTLEDGE, George (1789-1833), doctor with the 66th Regiment

SAINT-DENIS, Étienne, Napoleon's valet, usually called Aly

SAINTE-CROIX, real name Godin, cavalry officer, Mme. Brinvilliers' lover and collaborator in poisoning

SEMONVILLE, Charles-Louis (1759-1839), marquis, Montholon's stepfather

SIXTUS (1521-1590), forceful Pope of the counter reformation. Elected because he was supposed to be ailing and weak.

SKELTON, John (1763-1841), Lieutenant-Colonel, vice-governor of St. Helena when the island belonged to the East India Company

SMITH, Hamilton, chemist, senior lecturer at the University of Glasgow in forensic medicine.

SOMERSET, Charles (1767-1831), Lord, governor of Cape Colony

STAËL, Germaine, née Necker (1766-1817), author, married to Eric Magnus Staël von Holstein, Swedish ambassador to Paris

STENDHAL, Henri Beyle's pseudonym (1783-1872), author

STOKOE, John (1775-1852), doctor on board H.M.S. *Conqueror*

STRANGER, Amy, female passenger on board H.M.S. *Northumberland*

STÜRMER, Barthelemy (1787-1853), Austrian commissary

TALLEYRAND, Charles Maurice (1754-1838), Prince of Benevento, Duke of Talleyrand-Périgord, former bishop, foremost instigator of the *Brumaire coup*, the imperial coronation and the July revolution

THEED, John, captain of H.M.S. *Leveret*

THIERS, Louis Adolphe (1797-1877), President of the Council 1836 and 1840. First President of the Third Republic

VERLING, James (1787-1858), army doctor with the Artillery

VESEY, Esther, Mme. Montholon's extra chambermaid, officially Marchand's fiancée, probably Napoleon's mistress

WARDEN, William (1777-1849), doctor on board H.M.S. *Northumberland*

WYNYAR, Edward Buckley (1780-1865), colonel. Officially on St. Helena as Hudson Lowe's secretary.

Bibliography/Parts 1 and 2

BROOKES, Dame Mabel: *The St. Helena Story,* London 1960.

BUSSEY, George Moir: *History of Napoleon,* London 1840 (2 volumes).

CHANDLER, David G.: *The Campaigns of Napoleon,* London 1966. New York 1973.

DE L'ARDECHE, Laurent: *Histoire de l'Empéreur Napoléon,* Paris 1840 (2 volumes).

FORSHUFVUD, Sten: *Who Killed Napoleon?* London 1961.

FORSYTH, William: *History of the Captivity of Napoleon at St. Helena,* 1853 London (3 volumes).

FREMEAUX, Paul: *The Drama of St. Helena,* New York City, N.Y. 1910.

GANIERE, Dr. Paul: *Napoléon à Sainte Hélène, La Lutte Contre Hudson Lowe,* Paris 1960.

KEMBLE, James: *Gorrequer's Diary,* London 1969.

LAS CASES, The Count de: *Journal of the Private Life and Conversations of the Emperor Napoleon at St. Helena,* London, England 1823 (8 volumes).

LOCKHART, J. G.: *Napoleon Bonaparte* (2 volumes) New York 1830.

MARTINEAU, Gilbert: *Napoleon's St. Helena,* London 1968.

MONTHOLON, Gen. Count de: *History of the Captivity of Napoleon at St. Helena,* London 1847 (4 volumes).

O'MEARA, Barry E.: *Napoleon in Exile,* London 1823 (3 volumes).

PADDINGTON PRESS LTD.: *Napoleon's Last Will and Testament,* New York and London 1977.

SLOANE, William Milligan: *Life of Napoleon Bonaparte,* New York City, N.Y. 1906 (3 volumes).

YOUNG, Norwood: *Napoleon in Exile, St. Helena, 1815-1821,* Philadelphia 1915 (2 volumes).

WORLD-WIDE ENCYCLOPEDIA, New York 1869 (12 volumes).

Bibliography/Part 3

ABRANTÈS, L.: *Mémoires*. Paris.
ALMANACH ROYAL, Paris 1821.
ANTOMMARCHI, F. (1): *Les derniers moments de Napoléon*, Paris 1825.
          (2): *Derniers moments de Napoléon*. Soc. publ. litt.,
          Paris.
ARONSON, Th.: *The Golden Bees*, London 1964.
ARETZ, K.: *Napoleons letzte Freundin*, Munich 1919.
AUBRY, O. (1): *Sainte Hélène*, Paris 1935.
        (2): *Konungen av Rom*, transl., Stockholm 1933.
BALCOMBE, Betsy, see Aretz.
BECKMANN, K.: *Krankheiten der Leber, Handbuch der inneren Medizin*,
    III:2, Heidelberg 1953.
BERTRAND, H.:   I, *Cahiers de Sainte-Hélène 1816-17*, Paris 1951.
               II, *Cahiers de Sainte-Hélène 1818-19*, Paris 1959.
               III, *Cahiers de Sainte-Hélène 1821*, Paris 1949.
BOIGNE, Adèle: *Récits d'une Tante*, 4 vols. Paris 1907, 1908.
BOURIENNE, L,: *Mémoires*, Fayard, Paris.
BOURGOING, J.: *Le fils de Napoléon*, Paris 1950.
BRETT-JAMES, A.: *The Hundred Days*, London 1964.
BROOKES, Mabel: *St. Helena Story*, London 1960.
CABANÈS Dr.: *Au chevet de l'Empéreur*, Paris 1924.
CAULAINCOURT, A.: *Mémoires*, 3 vol. Paris 1933.
CHANTEMESSE, R.: *Hertiginnan d'Abrantès okända roman*, transl.
    Stockholm 1929.
COCKBURN, G.: *Napoleon's Last Voyage*, London 1888.
CONSTANT, see Dernelles.
DARD, E.: *Napoléon et Talleyrand*, Paris 1935.
DARESTE, M.: *Historie de France*, Paris 1880.
DECAUX, A.: *Grands secrets, etc.* Paris 1966.
DELDERFIELD, R.: *The Golden Millstones*, London 1964.
DERNELLES, E.: *Constant, Mémoires intimes de Napoléon I*, Mainz 1967.

531

DOURIS, R.: *Toxicologie moderne,* Paris 1951.

DUPONT, M.: *Murat,* Paris 1934.

FAZEKAS, A. et cons.: New Engl. Journ. Med. 1956: 254: 401 et seq.

FIRMIN-DIDOT, G.: *La Captivité de Sainte-Hélène d'après les rapports inédits du Marquis de Montchénu,* Paris 1894.

FORSHUFVUD, S.: *Who Killed Napoleon?* London 1961.

FORSHUFVUD, SMITH H. & WASSÉN A.: Archiv. f. Toxikologie 1964: 20: 219.

FORSYTH, W.: *History of the Captivity of Napoleon,* 3 vol. London 1853.

FRÉMEAUX, P. (1): *Napoléon prisonnier,* Paris.

             (2): *Der sterbende Napoleon,* Berlin 1911.

FUNCH-BRENTANO, F.: *Le drame des poisons,* Paris 1903.

FÄHRAEUS, R.: *Läkekonstens Historia,* Stockholm 1944.

GANIÈRE, P.: *Corvisart, Médecin de Napoléon,* Paris 1951.

GARNIER, J-P.: *Charles X,* Paris 1967.

GARROS, L.: *Quel roman, que ma vie,* Paris 1947.

GLOVER, E.: see Rose.

GONNARD, Ph. (1): *Lettres du Comte et de la comtesse de Montholon, 1819-1821,* Paris 1906.

             (2): *Les origines de la Légende Napoléonienne,* Paris 1907.

GOOCH: Letters from Dr. Gooch, Lowe's Papers, Brit. Mus.

GOURGAUD, G.: *Journal de Sainte-Hélène 1815-1818,* 2 vols. Paris 1947.

GRIL, E.: *La Marquise de Brinvilliers Empoisonneuse,* Paris 1933.

GRUNWALD, C.: *La Campagne de Russie,* Paris 1963.

GUILLARD, R-J.: *Annales de l'hygiène publique,* 1841: 25: 22.

HEFFTER, A.: Deutsche Med. Monatschr. 1921: 47: 853-4.

HENRY, N.: Appearances on the examination of the body of Napoleon Bonaparte, Lowe's Papers, Brit. Mus.

HEYMAN, A. et cons., New Engl. Journ. Med. 1956: 254: 401.

HUGO, V.: *Histoire d'un crime,* Paris 1877.

KEITH, A.: Brit. Med. J. 1913, pp. 54-58.

KEMBLE, J. (1): *Napoleon Immortal,* London 1959.

             (2): *St. Helena, Gorrequer's Diary,* London 1969.

LACHOUQUE, H.: *Connaissez-vous Napoléon?* Paris.

LAROUSSE MED. ILL., Paris 1924.

LAS CASES, E.: *Mémorial de Sainte-Hélène,* 2 vols. Paris 1951.

LUCAS-DUBRETON, J.: *Le Culte de Napoléon 1815-48,* Paris 1960.

MACDONALD, A.: *Souvenirs,* Paris 1892.

MARCHAND, L.: *Mémoires de Marchand,* 2 vols. Paris 1952, 1955.

MASSON, F.: (1): *Napoléon à Sainte-Hélène*, Paris 1912.
    (2): *Autour de Sainte-Hélène*, 3 vols. Paris 1909.
MERKEL, H.: *Die Magenverätzungen, Handbuch von Henke und Lubarsch*
    IV:I, Berlin 1930.
MONTESQUIOU, A.: *Souvenirs*, Paris 1961.
MONTHOLON, Ch. (1): *Histoire de la Captivité de Sainte-Hélène*,
        Leipzig 1846.
    (2): *Récits de la Captivité de Sainte-Hélène*,
        2 vols. Paris 1847.
O'MEARA, B.: *Napoleon in Exile*, London 1922, 2 vols.
PETRI, E.: *Path. Anatomie und Histologie der Vergiftungen, Handbuch von
    Henke und Lubarsch*, Berlin 1930.
RICHTER-COLLIN: *Speciel Therapi*, 8 vols., Norrköping 1824-34.
ROSE, J.: *Napoléon I*, London 1924.
        : *Napoleon's Last Voyage*, London.
ROSEBERY, A.: *Napoleon, The Last Phase*, London 1900.
SAVANT, J.: (1): *Les amours de Napoléon*, Paris 1956.
    (2): *Cahiers de l'Académie d'Histoire* 1970:1.
SAINT-DENIS, E.: *Souvenir du Mameluck Ali sur L'Empéreur Napoléon*,
    Paris 1926.
SHORTT, ARNOTT et cons.: Report on appearances on dissection of
    the body of Napoleon Bonaparte, Lowe's Papers, Brit. Mus.
SMITH, Hamilton & cons.: *Distribution of Arsenic in Napoleon's hair*,
    Nature 1962: 194: 725.
STIRLING, M.: *Letizia*, Stockholm 1962.
TSCHUDI, Clara: *Napoleons moder*, transl., Stockholm 1899.
WARDEN, W.: *Letters from Saint Helena*, London 1816.
WERTHEIMER, E.: *Napoleon's Son*, transl., Stockholm 1915.
WISTRAND, A.: *Handbok i Forensiska Medicinen*, Stockholm 1838.
WÄTJEN, J.: *Virchows* Archiv 1925: 256: 86-116.

Index